The Many Worlds of Anglophone Literature

New Horizons in Contemporary Writing

In the wake of unprecedented technological and social change, contemporary literature has evolved a dazzling array of new forms that traditional modes and terms of literary criticism have struggled to keep up with. *New Horizons in Contemporary Writing* presents cutting-edge research scholarship that provides new insights into this unique period of creative and critical transformation.

Series Editors:
Martin Eve and Bryan Cheyette

Editorial Board:
Siân Adiseshiah (University of Lincoln, UK), Sara Blair (University of Michigan, USA), Peter Boxall (University of Sussex, UK), Robert Eaglestone (Royal Holloway, University of London, UK), Rita Felski (University of Virginia, USA), Rachael Gilmour (Queen Mary University of London, UK), Caroline Levine (University of Wisconsin–Madison, USA), Roger Luckhurst (Birkbeck, University of London, UK), Adam Kelly (York University, UK), Antony Rowland (Manchester Metropolitan University, UK), John Schad (Lancaster University, UK), Pamela Thurschwell (University of Sussex, UK), Ted Underwood (University of Illinois at Urbana-Champaign, USA).

Volumes in the series:
Creaturely Forms in Contemporary Literature, Dominic O'Key
Thomas Pynchon and the Digital Humanities, Erik Ketzan
Northern Irish Writing After the Troubles, Caroline Magennis
Jeanette Winterson's Narratives of Desire, Shareena Z. Hamzah-Osbourne
Transatlantic Fictions of 9/11 and the War on Terror, Susana Araújo
Life Lines: Writing Transcultural Adoption, John McLeod
South African Literature's Russian Soul, Jeanne-Marie Jackson
The Politics of Jewishness in Contemporary World Literature, Isabelle Hesse
Writing After Postcolonialism: Francophone North African Literature in Transition, Jane Hiddleston
David Mitchell's Post-Secular World, Rose Harris-Birtill

New Media and the Transformation of Postmodern American Literature,
Casey Michael Henry
Postcolonialism After World Literature, Lorna Burns
Jonathan Lethem and the Galaxy of Writing, Joseph Brooker
The Contemporary Post-Apocalyptic Novel, Diletta De Cristofaro
David Foster Wallace's Toxic Sexuality, Edward Jackson
Wanderwords: Language Migration in American Literature, Maria Lauret
Contemporary Fiction, Celebrity Culture, and the Market for Modernism,
Carey Mickalites
Utopia Beyond Capitalism, Raphael Kabo

Forthcoming volumes:
Encyclopaedism and Totality in Contemporary Fiction, Kiron Ward

The Many Worlds of Anglophone Literature

Transcultural Engagements, Global Frictions

Edited by
Silvia Anastasijevic, Magdalena Pfalzgraf
and Hanna Teichler

BLOOMSBURY ACADEMIC
LONDON • NEW YORK • OXFORD • NEW DELHI • SYDNEY

BLOOMSBURY ACADEMIC
Bloomsbury Publishing Plc, 50 Bedford Square, London, WC1B 3DP, UK
Bloomsbury Publishing Inc, 1385 Broadway, New York, NY 10018, USA
Bloomsbury Publishing Ireland, 29 Earlsfort Terrace, Dublin 2, D02 AY28, Ireland

BLOOMSBURY, BLOOMSBURY ACADEMIC and the Diana logo are trademarks of
Bloomsbury Publishing Plc

First published in Great Britain 2024
This paperback edition published 2025

Copyright © Silvia Anastasijevic, Magdalena Pfalzgraf, Hanna Teichler and contributors 2024

The editors and contributors have asserted their right under the Copyright, Designs and
Patents Act, 1988, to be identified as Authors of this work.

For legal purposes the Acknowledgements on pp. xi–xii constitute an extension of this
copyright page.

Cover design by Namkwan Cho
Cover image © Shutterstock

All rights reserved. No part of this publication may be: i) reproduced or transmitted in any form,
electronic or mechanical, including photocopying, recording or by means of any information storage or
retrieval system without prior permission in writing from the publishers; or ii) used or reproduced in
any way for the training, development or operation of artificial intelligence (AI) technologies, including
generative AI technologies. The rights holders expressly reserve this publication from the text and data
mining exception as per Article 4(3) of the Digital Single Market Directive (EU) 2019/790.

Bloomsbury Publishing Plc does not have any control over, or responsibility for, any
third-party websites referred to or in this book. All internet addresses given in this
book were correct at the time of going to press. The author and publisher regret any
inconvenience caused if addresses have changed or sites have ceased to exist,
but can accept no responsibility for any such changes.

A catalogue record for this book is available from the British Library.

Library of Congress Cataloging-in-Publication Data
Names: Anastasijevic, Silvia, editor. | Pfalzgraf, Magdalena, editor. | Teichler, Hanna, editor.
Title: The many worlds of Anglophone literature : transcultural engagements, global frictions
/ edited by Silvia Anastasijevic, Magdalena Pfalzgraf and Hanna Teichler.
Description: London ; New York : Bloomsbury Academic, 2024. |
Series: New horizons in contemporary writing ; vol 19 | Includes bibliographical references.
Identifiers: LCCN 2023030501 (print) | LCCN 2023030502 (ebook) |
ISBN 9781350374072 (hardback) | ISBN 9781350374119 (paperback) |
ISBN 9781350374089 (pdf) | ISBN 9781350374096 (ebook)
Subjects: LCSH: English fiction–History and criticism. |
Literature and transnationalism. | English-speaking countries.
Classification: LCC PR821 .M15 2024 (print) | LCC PR821 (ebook) |
DDC 823.009–dc23/eng/20231016
LC record available at https://lccn.loc.gov/2023030501
LC ebook record available at https://lccn.loc.gov/2023030502

ISBN: HB: 978-1-3503-7407-2
PB: 978-1-3503-7411-9
ePDF: 978-1-3503-7408-9
eBook: 978-1-3503-7409-6

Series: New Horizons in Contemporary Writing

Typeset by Newgen KnowledgeWorks Pvt. Ltd., Chennai, India

For product safety related questions contact productsafety@bloomsbury.com.

To find out more about our authors and books visit www.bloomsbury.com
and sign up for our newsletters.

Essays in Honour of Frank Schulze-Engler

Contents

Acknowledgements — xi
List of Contributors — xiii

Introduction: The Many Worlds of Anglophone Literature – the mobilizing potential of transcultural World Literature — 1
Magdalena Pfalzgraf and Hanna Teichler

Foreword: On excentric proximity – some thoughts for Frank — 31
Homi K. Bhabha

Part One Theories and concepts

1. 'World Literature'? A perspective from the centre, a perspective from the edge — 41
   Michael Chapman

2. Traversal, transversal: A poetics of migrancy — 61
   Robert J. C. Young

3. On transcultural globalectics: Ngũgĩ meets Schulze-Engler — 87
   Tanaka Chidora

Part Two Transgressive kinships

4. Not-so-happy families: Durrell, Goodall and the myth of Africa — 107
   Graham Huggan

5. The 'makings of a diasporic self': Transcultural life writing, diaspora and modernity in Stuart Hall's *Familiar Stranger* (2017) — 121
   Katja Sarkowsky

6. Toward re-centring the senescent: Pedagogical possibilities of Anglophone short fiction — 141
   Mala Pandurang and Jinal Baxi

7 Notes from a classroom: Teaching Anglophone transculturality amidst environmental devastations 155
   Kathrin Bartha-Mitchell and Michelle Stork

Part Three Transversal readings

8 Transculturality and the law: Witi Ihimaera's *The Whale Rider* and a river with personhood 187
   Mita Banerjee

9 'Mobility at large': Anglophone travel writing as a medium of transcultural communication in a global context 209
   Nadia Butt

10 The transcultural imaginary: South Asian writing from Aotearoa New Zealand 233
    Janet M. Wilson

11 Passages to India: Jewish exiles between privilege and persecution 255
    Flora Veit-Wild

Afterword: 'Objects in the rear-view mirror' 283
   Yvonne Adhiambo Owuor

Index 289

Acknowledgements

In April 2022, our guest of honour, Frank Schulze-Engler, turned sixty-five. German academic mores would have called for a *Festschrift* to mark this occasion. However, as Frank broke the protocol and did not retire at the appropriate age, we also decided not to celebrate his intellectual legacy while he was still working as full professor of New English Literatures and Cultures (NELK) and dean of the Faculty of Modern Languages at Goethe University Frankfurt. Instead, we prepared the publication of this volume to coincide with his official retirement.

This volume is the result of our endeavour to present contributions in honour of our (former) mentor – our *Doktorvater* – and now our colleague and friend, to summon his intellectual partners, kin and detractors and examine the value of some of his key interests for our field today: transculturality and World Literature. And of course, it cannot be denied that the idea for this project emerged out of our – the doctor siblings' – wish to honour the German tradition of the *Festschrift*.

This volume's theme – The Many Worlds of Anglophone Literature – begs the question of this genre's place in today's world of global Anglophone scholarship and publishing. With its 'Teutonic' history, and because it necessarily centres on one person's intellectual position, what can it possibly add to the discussion of the transcultural and the Many Worlds of Anglophone writing today? The *Festschrift*'s demise has been oftentimes predicted and it has, for instance, been denounced as collective flattery, as stuffy, outdated and lacking unity and coherence, and, most important, as failing to achieve its tricky purpose: To look back on a lifetime of intellectual achievement and carry it into the future.

This is why our greatest note of thanks goes to our contributors. They took this task seriously, they examined, grappled with, turned upside down Frank's key concepts and ideas, they pointed out flaws, frictions and limitations of earlier discussions, staged new conversations, probed the pedagogical and didactic value of transculturality, unearthed uneasy kinships between literature and, for instance, law, and explored the place of non-English histories in the Many Worlds of Anglophone Literature. They also stayed patient, reliable and supportive during the volume's genesis, and we thank them for that, too.

Our friend and colleague Karsten Levihn-Kutzler – our doctor sibling with the encyclopaedic knowledge of the Anglophone sphere – played an important role in this project's conceptual birth and remained a valuable discussion partner and supportive companion throughout. A further note of thanks goes to Astrid Erll, who alerted us to the fact that Frank's birthday was around the corner, which kicked off the commencement of this volume. We are further grateful to Ben Doyle and Laura Cope, who supported this volume's inclusion in Bloomsbury's series *New Horizons in Contemporary Writing* and saw our project through to completion.

Contributors

Silvia Anastasijevic, Goethe University Frankfurt/University of Bonn

Mita Banerjee, Johannes Gutenberg University Mainz

Kathrin Bartha-Mitchell, Goethe University Frankfurt

Jinal Baxi, Dr. BMN College Mumbai

Homi K. Bhabha, Harvard University

Nadia Butt, Goethe University Frankfurt

Michael Chapman, Durban University of Technology

Tanaka Chidora, Goethe University Frankfurt/University of the Free State

Graham Huggan, University of Leeds

Yvonne Adhiambo Owuor

Mala Pandurang, Dr. BMN College Mumbai

Magdalena Pfalzgraf, University of Bonn

Katja Sarkowsky, Augsburg University

Michelle Stork, Goethe University Frankfurt

Hanna Teichler, Goethe University Frankfurt

Flora Veit-Wild, Humboldt University Berlin

Janet M. Wilson, University of Northampton

Robert J. C. Young, New York University

Introduction:
The Many Worlds of Anglophone Literature – the mobilizing potential of transcultural World Literature

Magdalena Pfalzgraf
University of Bonn
and
Hanna Teichler
Goethe University Frankfurt

In 2005, the news website *China Daily* covered the remarkable story of Mwamaka Sharifu, a then nineteen-year-old inhabitant of Lamu Island just off the East African coast.[1] Sharifu had recently been awarded a scholarship to pursue her university education in China, for her parents were unable to sustain her education at home. As is reported in the news clipping, Sharifu had contacted the Chinese Embassy in Kenya the previous year, claiming that she was of Chinese descent and had hoped to receive support for her studies of traditional Chinese medicine. This request more or less coincided with the 600th anniversary of the Chinese Treasure Voyages to the East African coast, famously undertaken by Admiral Zheng He (1371–1435).

Zheng He embarked on as many as seven such Ming Treasure Voyages across the Indian Ocean until he perished at sea. These voyages were diplomatic in nature and intended to foster and sustain the vibrant exchange between the Swahili coast and the Chinese Empire. Gold, silver, porcelain and silk were gifted to and traded with East African dignitaries, and, in return, China received valuables such as ostriches, zebras, camels or ivory. Zheng He is regarded to be the first explorer to use a direct sea route westward. Legend has it that his fleet was shipwrecked, and the surviving sailors sought refuge on the islands

---

[1] *China Daily*, n.a., 'Is This Young Kenyan Chinese Descendant [sic]?', http://www.chinadaily.com.cn/english/doc/2005-07/11/content_459090.htm, published 11 July 2005, last accessed 14 July 2022.

surrounding the Swahili coast. These sailors went on to marry local women and converted to Islam. *China Daily* further reports that nowadays, only six people on the island of Lamu are considered to be Kenyans of Chinese descent; their genetic linkage to China was confirmed by a group of experts in 2002. Today, Mwamaka Sharifu is a medical doctor and, as the news website *Nation* reported in 2012, 'returns home' to Kenya to run for senator.[2]

In 2019, Kenyan author Yvonne Adhiambo Owuor published her second novel, *The Dragonfly Sea*, in which she fictionalizes Mwamaka Sharifu's story. Set on Paté Island, just off the Kenyan coast, this complex, intriguing and highly unusual coming-of-age novel tells the story of young Ayaana, who is discovered to be of Chinese descent. Ayaana's heritage earns her the moniker 'the Descendant' and, in a similar manner to the real Mwamaka Sharifu, she receives a stipend to study in China. This trip, as the reader quickly learns, is both free and costly for the protagonist. She is a guest of the Chinese government, whose interests do not seem to extend further than 'excavating, proving, and entrenching Chinese rootedness in Africa' (Owuor 2019: 396). It is a dense narrative, rich in lyrical prose and magic-realist elements, with shifting time frames, and as such poses a challenge to the reader.

This novel is representative of an increasing interest of writers and artists to highlight 'South–South solidarities' (Achenbach et al. 2020) and 'lateral networks' (Hofmeyr 2012: 585), as it engages with a specific historical legacy – the Treasure Voyages – and explores its nature, tensions and (in)consistencies. What we can see at play here is identity politics in the sense that Sharifu's story provides the narrative backbone to frame these Afrasian relations as mutually beneficial and positive. Owuor's fictionalization, however, paints a much more ambivalent picture of these connections and shows that they are by no means unproblematic. Moreover, *The Dragonfly Sea* opens the mnemonic legacy of Zheng He's Treasure Voyages up to other histories and shows how, through their aestheticization, they intertwine the extremely local and the inescapably global. Notwithstanding its focus on Chinese–African relations, *The Dragonfly Sea* evokes the impression that, through a specific connection to the Indian Ocean, this tiny place is where the world comes to meet, and where the grand and not-so-grand narratives of Islamic terrorism and 9/11, human trafficking from the East to the West and the 2004 Indian Ocean Tsunami all come to bear – on Paté Island in general, and on Ayaana in particular.

---

[2] *Nation*, n.a., 'Girl's Journey to Ancestral Land in China', https://nation.africa/kenya/life-and-style/lifestyle/girl-s-journey-to-ancestral-land-in-china-820958, published 21 July 2012, last accessed 14 July 2022.

We open our introduction with recourse to *The Dragonfly Sea* because this novel gestures into directions central to our volume and the questions it sets out to explore. As an English-language novel by a Kenyan author who creates linguistic and cultural contact zones which span the Swahili coast, the Kenyan mainland and China, it bears witness to the globality of Anglophone fiction and to the mobility inherent to English as a globally shared medium of literary expression and transcultural imagination.

Yet, Owuor's novel is also remarkable for the power constellations it envisions – and for the absences it explores. While postcolonialism's political tenets have broken into the mainstream through worldwide activist movements such as Black Lives Matter and *Rhodes Must Fall*, Kenya's colonial past plays a very minor role in Owuor's novel, and this text's Englishness does not appear as a legacy of imperial rule or as a testimony of neocolonial power dynamics. Indeed, if postcolonialism's paradigmatic 'writing back' takes place, it is directed not towards the West but to the 'self' (to borrow the title of Evan Maina Mwangi's groundbreaking study) and to geopolitical power constellations which exist outside of the common North–South polarity. As noted by our guest of honour, Frank Schulze-Engler, *The Dragonfly Sea* 'manages its exploration of historical and contemporary Sino-Kenyan relations entirely without recourse to the postcolonial triangulation with the West' (2023: 3). Instead, it 'explores Africa's role in a multipolar world where the centrality of Europe and North America has already given way to complex new realignments between countries, cultures, memories and people' (2023: 10).

This collection of essays takes examples such as Owuor's novel as an occasion to shed light on literary expressions from diverse contexts around the world today – including New Zealand, India, the Caribbean, West Africa – which are aesthetically and politically highly divergent but share one feature: They are written in English. In light of the multicentred, multipolar realities from which literature in English emerges today, we are interested in exploring questions of relationality. On what terms and concepts can we ground the comparative study of Anglophone literatures and cultures today? What connects contemporary English-language literature around the globe? What, if anything, unites Stuart Hall's *Familiar Stranger* (2017), Witi Ihimaera's *The Whale Rider* (1987), the travelogue-cum-reportage *Afropean: Notes from Black Europe* (2019) by the Black British writer Johny Pitts, Leila Ahmed's *A Border Passage: From Cairo to America – A Woman's Journey* (1999) and other examples of Arab literature in English, to name but a few examples of Anglophone writing discussed in this volume? If the colonial past no longer provides a shared frame of reference (if it ever did), then how do we as scholars adjust our perspectives?

Guided by questions such as these, we explore the globality of Anglophone fiction both as a conceptual framing and as a literary imaginary. In the spirit of Schulze-Engler, we seek to understand how Anglophone literary texts, which stem from and create diverse life worlds, nonetheless relate to each other through the shared medium of the English language. This also requires us to move away from the suspicion and unease which is, paradoxically perhaps, so prevalent in global English studies, and which sees the wide catchment area of Anglophone literature predominantly as a legacy of imperial rule. Instead, we argue *with* Schulze-Engler that English is an inherently transcultural literary medium that facilitates the mobility of stories within, across and beyond nations and societies. Drawing on Pheng Cheah's notion of worlding as 'an ongoing, dynamic process of becoming' (2016: 30–1), we use the term Worlds in our title to highlight the plurality and diversity of life worlds represented and storyworlds constructed in Anglophone writing. This includes the diverse imaginations of transnational connections articulated – from tricontinentalism and pan-Africanism to the Black Atlantic and other Oceanic imaginaries, and the global futurities of the Anthropocene.

From postcolonialism to transculturality as a philological perspective

Transculturality entered English literary studies out of the need to account for the globality of Anglophone literatures and understand their multipolarities and relationality beyond the idea that the West constitutes a centre to which the literature 'of the rest' would invariably look towards or write back. Davis et al. (2004–5) are credited with transporting this term from its origins in the social sciences (Ortiz [1940] 2002) and philosophy (Welsch 1992, 1999) into English studies, but the key figure who developed it into a productive and dynamic philological paradigm is Frank Schulze-Engler, who proposed thinking of the 'New Literatures in English in terms of a transcultural World Literature' (2007: 28).

Central to Schulze-Engler's development of transculturality is his critique of the postcolonial as a conceptual frame for Anglophone literatures and cultures. His critique focuses on three recurring arguments characterizing postcolonial criticism which render this framework's relevance for decentred reading practices questionable. These are (1) the use of a too-wide umbrella term which subsumes highly divergent geopolitical and social contexts – Africa, India, Australia, New Zealand, Canada, the Caribbean – under one label hinged on a 'problematic privileging of the colonial past' (2007: 25), (2) a nostalgic idealization of anticolonialism and Third World liberation – which brushes over the particularities of these histories and over the atrocities committed in the name and spirit of anticolonialism – and (3) the endurance of centre-periphery models. This leads to a central paradox: Postcolonialism's political agenda aims at a decentred view of literature, politics, art; however, these cornerstones of postcolonial criticism are built on the belief that the West still constitutes the centre against which the postcolonial periphery defines itself. It is worth quoting Schulze-Engler at length:

> [L]iteratures from Africa, Asia, the Caribbean and various other parts of the English-speaking world such as Canada, Australia and New Zealand have generally become identified with 'postcolonialism'. ...[I]t has indeed become so pervasive in literary studies that many participants in postcolonial debates seem to have forgotten that the history of the New Literatures in English in fact began long before postcolonialism entered the theoretical scene with such aplomb. ... [I]t seems more highly questionable to suggest that the New Literatures in English are inevitably characterised by a postcolonial 'rewriting' of Western 'master texts'. ... The construct of 'postcolonial' cultures and literatures, which all find themselves in intellectual opposition to 'Western culture', thus represents a simplifying mode of wishful thinking that can hardly do justice to the cultural and social complexity of contemporary societies around the world. (2007: 20, 25)

The origins of contemporary academic use of transculturality go back to Fernando Ortiz's seminal study *Contrapunteo Cubano del Tabaco y el Azúcar* ([1940] 2002), translated as *Cuban Counterpoint: Tobacco and Sugar* ([1947] 1995). In a rather humble gesture – '[f]ully aware of the fact that it is a neologism' (1995: 97) – Ortiz proposes 'transculturation' as an alternative to 'acculturation' (1995: 97), a term 'used to describe the process of transition from one culture to another, and its manifold social repercussions' (1995: 98). Acculturation is (like 'intercultural' and 'multicultural' criticized by Welsch fifty years later) based on the idea of cultural discreteness that cannot account for the 'highly varied phenomena as a result of the extremely complex transmutations of culture that have taken place' (1995: 98) in Cuba.

Ortiz's case study is, of course, the very specific context of Cuba (and its products tobacco and sugar), which he describes as one of 'intermeshed transculturation' (1995: 98) as the result of voluntary and forced migrations, settlements, uprooting, re-routing, transplantations and encounters since the arrival of Palaeolithic hunters on its shore: 'First came the transculturation of the Palaeolithic Indians to the Neolithic .... Then the transculturation of an unbroken stream of white immigrants. ... At the same time there was going on the transmutation of a steady human stream of African negroes coming from all the coastal regions of Africa ... as far away as Mozambique' (1995: 98).

As Welsch points out in his work on transculturality (1992, 1999), this is true for Europe and its art history as well, whose styles 'developed across the countries and nations' (1999: 6). What is specific in the case of Cuba (and other former colonies, too) – and allows us to link the idea of the transcultural to the Many Worlds of Anglophonia – is the condensed trajectory of this development. As Ortiz writes: '[T]he whole gamut of culture run by Europe in a span of more than four millennia took place in Cuba in less than four centuries' (1995: 99).

Among the major contributions of Welsch's work is the radical break with traditional 'container culture' approaches. Welsch is highly critical of the 'traditional concept of single cultures' (1999: 194), in particular of its three mainstays: 'social homogenization, ethnic consolidation and intercultural delimitation' (1999: 194). Welsch argues that multiculturalism and the intercultural remain essentially tied to traditional notions of the single culture. These well-intended and pluralistic ideas of different cultures meeting, coming together, coexisting convivially still carry the idea of a self-contained cultural identity, characterized by 'inner homogenization and outer separation at the same time' (1999: 194).

Against this, Welsch proposes transculturality as a concept which not only takes into account cultures' external networking but also the 'inner differentiation and complexity of modern cultures' (1999: 197). When there is no singularity and discreteness, cultures appear mobile, porous and in constant flux. According to Welsch, this also means that no one really 'owns' a culture, that sensibilities and practices are shared across national, linguistic, geographic borders, and that we all maintain multiple memberships and connections. Hence, 'there is no longer anything absolutely foreign. Everything is within reach. Accordingly, there is no longer anything exclusively 'own' either. ... Today in a culture's internal relations – among its different ways of life – there exists as much foreignness as in its external relations with other cultures' (1999: 198).

Which begs the question: Who 'owns' English, who defines its proper use, and can there be such a thing as foreignness – or autochthony – in today's many worlds of English? Transculturality is no easy way out, and no vague, unpolitical, happy-clappy conviviality. As Caryl Phillips notes, in the absence of clear questions of ownership and belonging, we all participate in a 'new conversational babble' in which belonging 'is a contested state' (2001: 6). In fact, we all share an uneasy residence and precarious citizenship in the many republics of English letters.

What Schulze-Engler transports from Welsch into the realm of literary studies is this radical break with the idea of the 'container culture' and of canon defined along national or cultural lines. Rather than seeing authors and their works as representatives of national literatures, cultures and traditions – and therefore as carriers of cultures, hemmed in by their outer boundaries – authors are seen as active practitioners of literary cultures and as creators of complex fictional life worlds: 'Transcultural authors are not simply representatives of "their" cultures; their texts challenge readers and critics to come to terms with processes of negotiation and change between and within cultures' (Schulze-Engler 2007: 30).

From transculturality to literature as worlding

It seems to have become a habit and a pervasive gesture to start a mapping of the vast field of World Literature with recourse to Johann Wolfgang von Goethe, who is credited with the earliest use of the term (see Cheah 2016; Damrosch 2014; David 2013; Gremels et al. 2022; Ngũgĩ 2012; Seigneurie et al. 2020). We certainly do not wish to repeat this for protocol's sake. However, a look at Goethe's term serves to show that some of our central concerns – the mobilizing and enabling potential of the World Literature notion as well as an emphasis on process rather than on a fixed entity or canon – are already present in this early conceptualization. This is, no doubt, a reason why Ngũgĩ, in his call to break down the barriers of 'national one-sidedness and narrow-mindedness' (2012: 48) and to embrace World Literature, returns to Goethe's original formulation: '[N]ational literature is now a rather unmeaning term; the epoch of World Literature is at hand, and everyone must strive to hasten its approach' (Goethe 1835, qtd in Ngũgĩ: 44). So, despite the fact that Goethe's idea of World Literature is often seen as elitist, Eurocentric and exclusionary (probably due to his insistence on the special status of Greek poetry and his staunch promotion of classicism), his idea entails thoughts which prefigure our concerns of transcultural World Literature: Goethe's disavowal of national boundaries as well as nationalist chauvinism and his insistence on the free circulation of literature resonate with our concept of the Many Worlds of Anglophone Literature.

The earliest mention of *Weltliteratur* dates back to 1801. In his journal *Propyläen*, Goethe expresses criticism of the rise of ethnic and cultural nationalism under German Romanticism and its promotion of patriotic–national values and *Volkskunst*. A staunch proponent of humanist universalism, Goethe writes:

> The universally human is being ousted by the patriotic. It is to be hoped that people will soon be convinced that there is no such thing as patriotic art or patriotic science. Both belong, like all good things, to the whole world, and can be fostered only by untrammelled intercourse among all contemporaries, continually bearing in mind what we have inherited from the past. (Qtd in Strich 1949: 35)[3]

More than a hundred years later, we can hear these thoughts echo in Dambudzo Marechera's disavowal of nationalism: 'Either you are a writer or you are not. If you are a writer for a specific nation or a specific race, then fuck you. In other words, the direct international experience of every single entity is, for me, the inspiration to write' (qtd in Veit-Wild 1992: 121).

As Strich writes, Goethe's idea of *Weltliteratur* had 'negative origins', as it was defined in 'opposition to the European chaos, to national separatism and to Romantic nationalism' (1949: 36). In contrast to this, it is our interest to approach World Literature in affirmative terms. Rather than envisioning the Many Worlds of Anglophone Literature in demarcation to other ideas, we emphasize the enabling potential of our critical notion.

This is not to suggest, of course, that this vision was lacking in Goethe's. Indeed, the mobilizing potential of his pronounced disavowal of ethnic and cultural nationalism was crucial. In numerous iterations on the term in the first half of the nineteenth century, Goethe therefore muses about what it is that enables national literature to maintain its 'vitality', and he subsequently identifies the constant interest in and exchange with other literatures as fiction's driving force (qtd in Strich 1949: 350). To be sure, Goethe's idea of World Literature, for all its mobilizing potential, remained tied to the national frame and to the corresponding national languages as the natural habitat of literatures. Translation is both the skill required and the connective thread woven among these literatures; the translator becomes the relay station between discrete national literatures. Goethe was fully cognizant of the heterogeneous nature of texts and writers subsumed under this rubric. Yet, in his terms, an emerging field of

---

[3] Das Menschliche wird durchs Vaterländische verdrängt. Vielleicht überzeugt man sich bald, daß es keine patriotische Kunst und patriotische Wissenschaft gebe. Beide gehören wie alles Gute der ganzen Welt an, und können nur durch allgemeine, freie Wechselwirkung aller zugleich Lebenden, in steter Rücksicht auf das, was uns vom Vergangenen übrig und bekannt ist, gefordert werden (qtd in Strich 1949: 49).

intersecting literary consciousness – World Literature – would eventually enable mankind to engage in the 'untrammelled intercourse among all contemporaries' (qtd in Strich 1949: 35) mentioned later by Ngũgĩ (2012: 44). As one can gather, 'all contemporaries' functions as a reverse metonymy, for notwithstanding the spread of European languages due to imperialism and colonialism, these languages and access to education and its institutions remained unattainable for the vast majority of this world's inhabitants.

The field has since come a long way to loosen the grip that the national frame exerts on World Literature. As a consequence, the idea of World Literature has become much more accommodating of frameworks beyond national containers and linguistic discreteness – arguments that we will return to below. What remains groundbreaking about Goethe's notion, however, is his emphasis on relationality, which both cuts across and is brought about by literary texts and their aesthetic protocols. In what follows, we therefore draw, in broad strokes, an outline of the key figures and approaches to World Literature in order to integrate some of the recent debates with our idea of the Many Worlds of Anglophone Literature.

One of the formative figures in the field of World Literature, David Damrosch, frames it in a manner that resonates with Goethe's general idea: World Literature, for Damrosch, is first and foremost a comparative frame to productively juxtapose and cross-read texts from an 'increasingly multipolar literary landscape' (2014: 2). As Damrosch further argues, this comparative frame is not without its inherent problems such as the persistence of a few dominating languages and literary marketplaces, to name but a few. One of the most surprising aspects of outlining the field of World Literature is to discover that some of these problematic aspects are, in a sense, homemade.[4]

Consider, for example, how Pascale Casanova's seminal *World Republic of Letters* (2004), first published in 1999, introduced one of World Literature's most enduring conceptual legacies: that of an unequal access to a (pre)supposed

---

[4] In fact, some conceptualizations fall behind Goethe's World Literature, which he described in radically democratic, non-normative terms, of which he did not think as an additive project (e.g. as a canon of selected texts) but as an abstract, ephemeral quality which is present throughout the world, and throughout the ages, and which both subsumes and belongs to everyone who creates art. Two passages from Goethe's *Dichtung und Wahrheit* serve to illustrate this point:

> eigentlich gibt es nur Eine Dichtung, die ächte, sie gehört weder dem Volke noch dem Adel, weder dem König noch dem Bauer; wer sich als wahrer Mensch fühlt wird sie ausüben; sie tritt unter einem einfachen, ja rohen Volke unwiderstehlich hervor, ist aber auch gebildeten, ja hochgebildeten Nationen nicht versagt. (qtd in Birus 2004: 3)
>
> Dichtkunst überhaupt eine Welt- und Völkergabe sei, nicht ein Privaterbteil einiger feinen gebildeten Männer. (Qtd in Birus 2004: 2)

global literary field, and a very normative understanding of literature. World Literature, in Casanova's terms, amounts to a global structure of symbolic and aesthetic domination, defined by a seemingly universal literary quality (see also David 2013). Jérome David quips that, for Casanova, '[i]t is not the meaning of the work that matters ... but the strategic positioning the works give rise to, on behalf of the writer. Here, philology dissolves into sociology' (2013: 21). Casanova's identity-political and highly reductive idea of World Literature somewhat carried over to subsequent contributions to the field. In Franco Moretti's terms, World Literature is not an 'object' of analysis, but a 'problem' (2000: 55). Although he is highly critical of Casanova and calls for a return to the roots of the professional study of literature, namely narratology, he never quite abandons his critique of Western capitalism as the root cause of many of World Literature's tribulations. Thus, he subscribes to the same Western-centric stance Casanova holds – albeit from an opposing ideological outlook. Moretti holds that

> international capitalism is a system that is simultaneously *one*, and *unequal*: with a core, and a periphery (and a semiperiphery) that are bound together in a relationship of growing inequality. One, and unequal: one literature (*Weltliteratur*, singular, as in Goethe and Marx), or perhaps, better, one world literary system (with inter-related literatures); but a system that is different from what Goethe and Marx had hoped for, because it is profoundly unequal. (2000: 55–6; emphases in the original)

Participating in World Literature, or to be called a writer of the World Literature canon, is thus seen as perpetuating imbalance. This centre–periphery representation and organization of the world is part and parcel of much of postcolonial critique and its theoretical foundations. It preforms and presupposes a world that is inescapably polar, or tilted to one side, as Russell West-Pavlov so aptly remarks in relation to the equally problematic term 'Global South' (2018).

To us, it remains obscure to what extent Marxist ideas of literature and of the societies in which these artworks resonate are still valid paradigms to foster a deeper understanding of the issues at hand, or how, in fact, a society built on the principles of a socialist counter-modernity would lead to a more just World Literature system and a more equal access to texts. Schulze-Engler hits the nail on its head when he writes that

> the idea that socialist internationalism has been able to retain the transformative and utopian potential it may once have had in pre-Stalinist days seems hard to reconcile with the realities of a world that has witnessed the anti-communist

revolutions of 1989–90, and it is hard to imagine who in the twenty-first century should actually be the carrier of the socialist 'counter-modernity' that was championed by the so-called socialist world. (2015: 21–2)

He urges us not to

forget that we not only live in a postcolonial but also in a postcommunist world, and that the original grand ideas and projects of both socialist internationalism and anti-colonial nationalism ... have often become aligned with oppression rather than freedom. Some of the most dictatorial and murderous regimes in the second half of the twentieth century ... have, in fact, been erected on the ideological foundations of a combination of socialist internationalism and Third World Liberation. (2015: 22–3)

To be sure, it is not our aim to debunk postcolonial criticism with a sweeping gesture, nor to offhandedly dismiss its emancipatory interventions. Neither do we use the transcultural as postcolonialism's Other. Important for us to highlight is, however, that World Literature is not imperialism's new robes. On the contrary, World Literature is deprived of its emancipatory and, indeed, critically subversive potential if it is understood as a force in singular that eradicates positionality, multipolarity and hybridity – of form, content and context.

Pheng Cheah poses the right question, then, when he asks: 'What is a world?' (2008, 2016). Cheah writes against an idea of World Literature that '[e]quates the world with circular movements that cut across national-territorial borders' (2016: 3). With that, Cheah touches upon a sore point in World Literature debates: The prevalence of World in its singular grammatical form – a rhetorical gesture which emphasizes the monolithic nature of the world as a spatial totality whose borders and shape seem to be collectively agreed upon. There is a North and a South, both clearly definable, and there is a centre ('the West') and many peripheries ('the rest'). The world becomes a singular perceptual, experiential and representational realm that is governed by socioeconomic forces which operate outside of the reach of human agency, or at least human agency that stems from the 'Global South'. As already noted above, the world here becomes a reverse metonymy; instead of pars pro toto, toto comes to stand for pars. Cheah distinguishes himself and his 'normative idea of world literature' (2016: 5) from the aforementioned figureheads of this debate:

The theory of world literature I propose suggests that the world is a normative temporal category and not the spatial whole made by globalization. Because world literature has the normative vocation of opening new worlds, its study cannot merely consist of historiographical or sociological analyses of how literary texts circulate globally and the effects of that circulation at the level of form and style. (2016: 16)

Here Cheah emphasizes the importance of rethinking World Literature beyond the systems and routes of circulation, commodification, market value and reception. The world, thus conceived, is not an accumulation of national entities that can be traversed, consolidated or contested in one or the other manner. Nor does the corresponding literature merely pursue the 'paths' that were envisaged for it *qua* its author or theme (e.g. postcolonial literature, Indian or Atlantic Ocean writer, Global South author, etc.), its aesthetic value – or *qua* travelling literary genres (see Bartlett [1932] 1995; Fludernik 1996; Herman 2004; Iser 1987). The normative force of World Literature, according to Cheah, is its *worlding power* – a term that harks back to Heidegger's idea of being in the world (1962). Recently, this term has also been reframed as a concept of ecocritical narratology (James 2015, 2022) – an aspect we shall return to below. Important for our notion of the Many Worlds of Anglophone Literature is that for Cheah, the World in World Literature is not a presupposed structure or self-contained entity that is somewhat pre-literary, but much rather one that is born, created, *worlded* in literary texts and through literary imagination. Put differently, literary texts are not reduced to pinballs in the machine that is globalization, but actively intervene in its formation. Cheah joins the chorus of voices (see also Ngũgĩ 2012: 49) who shift the attention towards the processual nature of World Literature and hence emphasize the productive, unfinished nature of worlding.

It comes as no surprise that the primary material upon which Cheah bases his analysis forms the corpus of what he calls 'postcolonial world literature' – texts which stem from and deal with (post)colonialism and imperialism and their contemporary forms (see Cheah 2016: 17–18). Thus conceived, Cheah's World Literature is inextricably tied to the experience of colonialism, its legacies in the present and its ability to speak to a potentially global audience. Clearly harking back to Moretti, Cheah realigns the political project that is postcolonial literature with questions of form and aesthetics. For Cheah, any conceptualization of World Literature falls short if it does not pay attention to the historical specificity of the comparative frames that World Literature is constructed around. He highlights the impetus to think World Literature not only in terms of spatial categories but much rather as temporo-spatial formations. We subscribe to this critical stance, as any thorough discussion of a literary text, its forms and functions, requires a grounding in specific historical and sociopolitical contexts, especially when it comes to the many and diverse experiences of the (post)colonial. Moreover, our (and Cheah's) notion of World Literature is not far removed from Damrosch's, who argues: 'It can be said that world literature and national literature display a kind of figure-ground reversal: while in the one sense world literature is the broad framework within which individual literatures are formed, it is equally true that for any given reader, world literature exists first and foremost within a national or local context' (2014: 9).

It is the shifting scales in which the local and the global, the regional and the transnational, the cultural and the transcultural are encoded, circulated and received that are of central importance to a more dynamic notion of World Literature. World Literature, we like to emphasize, is unfinished business, always in the making and constantly shifting – between nation, region, globe, between the past, present and future. In that sense, we subscribe to a processual quality of World Literature emphasized by Cheah, Damrosch and by Ngũgĩ wa Thiong'o, and we are less concerned with static, spatial notions of World Literature.

Interestingly, there is a gap in Cheah's consideration of World Literature: He does not suggest reconsidering the stakeholders and power hierarchies embedded in the notion of World Literature. Cheah's world in its temporo-spatial configuration remains structured along the axes of centre and periphery and is built on an understanding of a postcolonial literature that 'writes back' to the powerful centre – a notion which has been identified as highly problematic (if not obsolete) by Schulze-Engler and other proponents of the transcultural. Thus conceived, Cheah's account remains locked in the well-known centre–periphery models in which theorists of World Literature 'see[k] stability' against the backdrop of an ever-increasing 'multipolar web of literary entanglements' (Gremels et al. 2022: 9–10). Yet, in the world and in the process of worlding, it seems to become ever more difficult to identify clear-cut binary oppositions. This is not to say that there is no inequality in the world, but that the axes alongside which such issues are aesthetically remediated and commented upon seem to be less linear, and more complexly intertwined. Andrea Gremels et al. thus propose to (re)think World Literature as emerging in 'a multipolar world of globalised modernity' and suggest 'that we rethink the idea of World Literature along the notion of "entanglements": as a field of variously criss-crossing relations of literary activity beyond the confines of literary canons, cultural containers and national borders' (2022: 8). Gremels et al. write against an emphasis on corpus and national and cultural space in their singular form (2022: 9, 15). They argue against a European and North American centre that seems to persist as reference points for World Literature (albeit with all the good intentions on the part of postcolonial scholars to think beyond them), but also point out that 'paradoxically, in such "breaking away", Europe remains the necessary centre, in the very critical gesture of departing from it' (10).

This paradox could be described as World Literature's intentional fallacy, or inherent double-bind: In its attempts to highlight and mobilize the activist, identity-political agency of World Literature – an aspect that is particularly prominent in the idea of 'World Literature from below' (Wenzel 2019) – it recasts Europe, the West, the Global North, North America and the like as nodal points against which to negotiate identities and histories. This is also visible in Cheah's approach to World Literature. In order to carve out his particular concept, Cheah lines up virtually all leading figures, most of whom are of European descent and belong to a particular tradition of thought: from Kant to Marx, from Goethe to Heidegger, from Hegel to Arendt, Derrida, to Benjamin. The texts discussed and analysed, however, are written by writers from the Global South and are labelled as postcolonial. Cheah comments on this rather surprising aspect of his book:

> The organization of this book can give the wrong impression of a division of labor between European philosophy and literature from the postcolonial South, where postcolonial literary texts have the subordinate function of illustrating the ontological and normative problems concerning wordliness that European philosophy elaborates. In fact, no such division exists. … The philosophical and literary texts are concerned with the same issues of the world's reality, literature's worldly force, and the corrosive impact of (colonial and neocolonial) global modernity on the temporalities of human worlds, especially the exclusionary characters of communities of globalization. (2016: 14)

We have to admit that we are not entirely convinced by this assertion that there is no ontological and epistemological dividing line between European high theory and non-European postcolonial writing that runs through Cheah's text. Rather, one seems to be used to explain the other. Usually, we try our utmost to refrain from such identity-political arguments, as we fear that they significantly narrow the theoretical frameworks and languages available. Yet, since Cheah puts forth a normative and ultimately political conceptualization of World Literature, one that argues along the lines of Europe versus the Global South, globalization versus subalternity, capitalism versus Marxism, it appears very problematic that he approaches the interesting idea of 'worlding' from an abundance of European thinkers.

There are several interesting contributions to move beyond the centre-periphery model that is (possibly inadvertently) reiterated. The idea of 'provincializing' the Western superpowers relates back to Dipesh Chakrabarty's seminal contribution (2000) and has been recently framed in thought-provoking ways: Consider, for example, how Evan Maina Mwangi (2009) calls for a reorientation of African literary criticism towards how Africa 'writes back to self' as opposed to the former (and new) imperial powers. It resonates with Mukoma wa Ngũgĩ's call to 'rethink the Global South':

> Writers and scholars from the Global South often engage with one another through their own relationship to the West. But triangulating ideas, whether political or literary, through the West ends up masking historical South–South relationships while feeding and giving cover to cultural nationalism and protectionist scholarly practices. We need to fracture this dialectical linkage to the West and allow South–South cultural, historical and political conversations to take place. (2012: n.p.)

These South–South relations, or lateral connections, is what Isabel Hofmeyr is primarily interested in when she calls for rendering the Indian Ocean 'method' (2012). Building on Glissant ([1990] 1997), Gremels et al. advocate for a newly configured 'poetics of relations' in their 'vision of a globalised world determined by transversal movements, transcultural encounters and heterogeneous realities' (2022: 18).

Towards the Many Worlds of Anglophone Literature

One important question has been neglected in our tour d'horizon of World Literature and related debates: What is the status of English in all this? How do we treat the vexed question of linguistic dominance? Granted, the spread of English across the world is one of the most audible – and visible – remainders of colonial dominance. Generations of postcolonial scholars have rightfully argued against the monolithic predominance of the colonizing powers' languages in general, and English in particular (e.g. Mufti 2016; Ngũgĩ [1986] 2004; Pennycook 2007). As students, we were introduced to the effects and legacies of linguistic colonialism by way of, for example, learning about the role of William Wordsworth's famous poem 'Daffodils' (1807) in English language education in India, by the story of Ngũgĩ's son having to memorize a poem about finches, thinking they were little fish, or by reading how English became 'the most important vehicle' of colonial power and led to the 'systematic suppression' of native languages (Ngũgĩ 2004: 9, 12–13). But we also heard the story of how Chinua Achebe's groundbreaking novel *Things Fall Apart* (1958) went global before it became local; how it was first published by Heinemann in London and went on to become one of the foundational texts of modern African literature, globally marketed and available. Postcolonial language politics can also be messy and multidirectional. It was none other than Ngũgĩ wa Thiong'o who, in *Decolonising the Mind*, famously disavowed English as his means of thinking and expression, pledging to solely publish in Gĩkũyũ henceforth, only to return to English in his critical practice 'without explanation' and to his 'familiar role as a critic of imperial European languages writing in English' (Gikandi 2000: 194).

Of course, the role of English as a lingua franca of global capitalism (see Mufti 2016) and its pre-eminence as a literary language (see Mufti 2016, Walkowitz 2015) often render it a hegemon towards other languages. However, it seems also quite limiting to remain satisfied with the contention that English cripples other languages and thus homogenizes literary expression and aesthetics. This argument goes hand in glove with questioning the status that originally European/Western literary forms such as the novel take up too much space in the global literary economy. We hope to have already successfully troubled the notion of a global literary market in its singular form and seek to continue to do so with regard to the English language.

Jerome David takes us back to Erich Auerbach ([1957] 2018) and Edward Said (1993) when making a point about the English language and its role in World Literature. Auerbach, as David shows, states very early on that our 'philological home is the earth, [it] can no longer be the nation' (qtd in David 2013: 16). David explains: 'This conception of philology leads to a dual consequence for "world literature": the "world philologists", by underscoring the diversity of languages and literatures, would strive not to determine the genius of different languages and different nations, but to index the "forms of life" ("Lebensformen") humanity has used to conceive of itself' (David 2013: 16). Rebecca L. Walkowitz poignantly argues that '[s]ince the early twentieth century, migrant and postcolonial writers have been laying claim to dominant languages by occupying, renovating, and transforming them' (2020: 323). She identifies a shift in the role that the English language plays to the 'children of globalization' (2020: 323) and 'first-generation migrants producing fiction in second or third languages' (324):

> Instead of transforming dominant languages, contemporary novelists Jhumpa Lahiri, Yoko Tawada, and Kazuo Ishiguro have been choosing not to know them. Not knowing, by which they often mean not knowing well (Lahiri) or

not knowing intrinsically (Tawada, Ishiguro), brings visibility to the history of conflict and collaboration within languages and focuses on linguistic hospitality rather than linguistic ownership. ... They are not clearing the space for the right to use a colonial language, as Joyce and Rushdie were .... Instead, they are incorporating histories of literacy, language access, and multilingualism while tactically stripping linguistic confidence from even the most fluent reader of their works. (324)

This understanding of the role of English is fundamental to our concept of the Many Worlds of Anglophone Literature: The English language does indeed create an 'Anglophone marketplace' (Walkowitz 2020: 324) and enables literary communication across national and cultural barriers, but it has ceased to uniformly function as a tool of Western domination. The texts we subsume under Anglophone literature do indeed exert pressure on the *Englishness* of Anglophone literature, to paraphrase Walkowitz (2020, 2015). It is worth quoting Walkowitz here again as she elaborates on Lahiri's 'two ideas of language':

The first [idea] imagines that there is a national language to know and that there can be a perfect understanding of that language, which some people possess. The second treats language as a custom of the tribe, for which the appearance of perception depends on social, political, and corporeal assumptions about who possesses language and how. In theories of world literature, ... the first idea of language – monolingual, coherent, synchronic – dominates. (2020: 327–8)

This monolithic understanding of the English language renders a conceptualization of World Literature as dependent on languages and canons in such languages limiting rather than enabling. Writing in English is immersion in and expression of the different 'life worlds' that David was referring to above. He succinctly comments on both the reductive as well as the productive potential of World Literature:

In all of these cases, 'world literature' is not so much an object, but a challenge – a challenge that demands a radical, epistemological litmus test of literary studies. In this sense, 'world literature' designates everything our interpretive habits do not incorporate: neglected languages, forgotten works, and silent cultures. It invites us to imagine the type of theory that could save what our present is in the process of losing or has not retained: the diversity of cultures, for Auerbach; the thousands of novels that no one reads anymore, for Moretti; the multitude of 'subalterns', for Spivak. 'World literature' is merged with an attempt to symbolically restore or repair – an attempt that knows it is condemned from the start, by the vastness of its task, but that demands, by its very intention, a certain form of aesthetic or cultural justice. (David 2013: 23)

Anglophone World Literature is (among other things) a literary market, as we have already stated, but it is also a professional field – the study and teaching of Anglophone literature – that we scholars need to navigate. This aspect seems to be sorely missing in the recent interventions in the debates on World Literature. Literary scholars by training, we have all learned and read about how the question of language in art and criticism contributed to the emergence of postcolonial criticism. From the traditional study of English literature as a form of national literature towards Anglophone literatures and cultures as more dynamic ways to conceptualize literature in English, the question of the role of English seems to have always been a vexed one. However, job descriptions and positions offered oftentimes still employ container logic in their framing, to which we have to adhere as we apply for positions in departments of English and American literatures and cultures (another example of odd distinctions between literary fields) or to departments of Comparative Literature, whose structure is very often tied to discrete linguistic entities. It is quite a recent and still rare phenomenon that positions are offered with more flexibility. Our focus on Anglophone literatures is hence also motivated and to a degree dictated by the logic of the academic job market.

In our understanding of Anglophone World Literatures, we take into account the entangled nature of languages in plural, aesthetics and form on the level of text and alongside its routes of circulation. We are also very aware of the politics of publishing, marketing, translation and circulation, which are more often than not dictated by a capitalist logic. We are fully cognizant of the dominance of the English language as a medium of expression and as a selling point. Yet, if these factors are regarded as given, unalterable and inevitable, the idea of World Literature indeed does not hold a lot of conceptual currency vis-à-vis the texts that our contributors analyse in this collection.

The history of the spread of English across the world is naturally tied to migration, (involuntary) movement and mobility – oftentimes the driving forces behind the literatures and cultures we study. The entangled nature of history (colonialism, independence, etc.) and memory as the sociocultural processes of framing the past for *present* purposes also creates a tension that is creatively explored by many of the designated Anglophone writers. The negotiations of what counts as a 'usable past' (see Olick 2007) or pressing concerns in the here and now produce enchanted as well as 'disenchanted solidarities' (see Schulze-Engler 2015) among various communities. It is quite evident that many of these communities cannot be contained by notions such as the Global South, or postcolonial, or subaltern.

To us, it is centrally important to continue to pluralize the idea of 'World' in World Literature. There is no such thing as one coherent Anglophone world, or one Anglophone literature or one Anglophone literary marketplace. The globe is comprised of many worlds: There are the countless diegetic worlds that engage with political and historical contexts (or they do not, as Walkowitz would have it). There are numerous life worlds that are given expression to in literary texts. The recognition of several worlds as opposed to one world puts into focus a shift in agency, or, more precisely, a shift in an understanding of what space and place means in relation to literary texts (see James 2015, 2022; Ryfield et al. 2019). This shift allows for the introduction of post-human agents and frameworks into the discussion of what Anglophone worlds consist of. It enables a comparative reading of, for example, cli-fi novels and oceanic poems against the backdrop of multiple epistemologies that are drawn upon to represent transcultural life worlds.

Our idea of the Many Worlds of Anglophone Literature seeks to describe the mechanisms in which the local and the global, the regional and the national, the cultural and the transcultural are brought to bear on each other. In a sense, there is no global without the local, and vice versa. Local knowledges come to intersect with global frames, and these encounters more often than not produce and live off frictions, tensions, untranslatability, but also off mutual relationality which runs against the grain of received dichotomies, or geopolitical formations. In this manner, we regard literary texts as 'analytical units' (David 2013: 21) that act in and react to various contexts, both with regard to production, circulation and reception. We thus take into account a certain uncontrollability of these texts and their authors, as they refuse to adhere to the pigeonholes that the professional study of literature but also market rules allocate to them. We are aware that it is possible that encounters may fail, that the emphasis remains on the local, consequently refusing to engage with the heuristically global, the transnational and, eventually, the cosmopolitan. Our approach is hence also Post-Anglophone, to borrow a term from Rebecca Walkowitz (2021: 95). The post here takes on an ambivalent role similar to the notion of post in postcolonial: It seeks to encompass the more-than-Anglophone in order to be able to theorize and work with the Anglophone framework in a productive manner.

The contributions to this collection

The chapters in this collection seek to triangulate the relationship between the transcultural as a philological paradigm, World Literature as the field in which the transcultural fully unfolds its productive and enabling potential, and the postcolonial as an expression of subject positions and historicized identities. What we hope to show is the critical potential that such a triangulation holds, as this volume brings together scholarly voices probing many aspects, strands of and thoughts on how these concepts – when set in relation – mobilize received categories and analytical frameworks.

This collection starts with a foreword by Homi K. Bhabha, which honours Schulze-Engler's influence and intellectual hospitability and proposes the idea of excentric proximity as a further dimension of transculturality. Developing this perspective, Bhabha maps out the relationship between postcolonial thought as represented by Frantz Fanon and the emergence of a transcultural World Literature paradigm as a close one. Reading Fanon against the grain, Bhabha transculturalizes this 'classic' postcolonial thinker and concludes on a note of transcultural hospitability in which the 'birth of the One is inseparably, if uncomfortably, linked to the birth of the Other' (37).

The chapters following this foreword are organized into three sections. The first three chapters engage in a theoretical mapping of the relationship between the transcultural as a reading, writing and analytical paradigm and the field of World Literature. In this manner, the questions raised and the positions outlined in this chapter (Introduction) resonate with this first theoretical session.

Michael Chapman's tour d'horizon '"World Literature"? A Perspective from the Centre, a Perspective from the Edge' considers World Literature as 'object and/or concept' (41) and asks important questions in regard to Schulze-Engler's idea of transcultural World Literature: What is the status of 'world' in the 'transcultural', and can 'world' and 'transcultural' be conflated when speaking of World Literature? How do we handle the division between texts that are 'from somewhere' and those untethered, which come from and potentially travel anywhere? What follows is a careful interrogation of different approaches to World Literature with particular attention to Damrosch, Moretti and – chiming with our insistence that World Literature is a process – the multi-volume anthology *World Literature and Thought*. Chapman makes a case for the often-discredited approach of World Literature as object, that is, as an array of significant texts. Attempts at compiling World Literature canons or anthologies have an important function, as they make texts available to readers 'circumscribed by their own "localities"' (54). At the same time, Chapman does not make an argument for these text's universality: World Literature, he argues, is mobilizing, it comes from and offers us a perspective from *somewhere,* and a perspective on World Literature is thus necessarily a perspective from *somewhere.* A real gem of his contribution concerns the aspect of teachability. If World Literature, as object and concept, is to fulfil the hopes and expectations scholars place in it – such as the mobilization of both text and reader – then academic discussions need to consider that World Literature must be manageable, for 'without teachability, World Literature remains so abstract, so arbitrary, as to fail to percolate down from academic journal debate to peers and students' (54–5). True to his own advice, Chapman ends in a gesture that teachers will appreciate: a practical toolbox on how to build a feasible schedule and reading list for a course on World Literature.

In his chapter 'Traversal, Transversal: A Poetics of Migrancy', Robert Young grapples with the vexed question of cultural difference, in particular, whether difference is effectively erased by the transcultural. Young argues that due to the pervasive decline of binary oppositions in theory and artistic practice (which Schulze-Engler would probably dispute), the critical edge of the prefix 'trans' is lost if attached to culture (see 74 of this volume). The 'trans' remains steeped in an 'aura of trespass' and 'transgressivity' because it is bound to find 'evidence' of the 'disruption and decline of monocultures (if they ever really existed)' (74). For Young, the transcultural remains stuck in the process of creating an Other in order to subsequently be able to identify commonalities and processes of mutual exchange. Instead of being confined to this conceptual impasse, Young suggests thinking of transformation, transgression and transcultural processes as oblique, queer, as unfolding at an angle to something and someone. In this sense, Young's claims tie in with our contention that not knowing, uncertainty and 'queerness' (*sensu literalis*) are part and parcel of the Many Worlds of Anglophone Literature.

Tanaka Chidora's chapter 'On Transcultural Globalectics: Ngũgĩ Meets Schulze-Engler' is a tour de force through Ngũgĩ wa Thiong'o's theoretical oeuvre, whereby Chidora particularly traces the remarkable development from the earlier nationalist, Afrocentrist manifestos to the theoretical outlook formulated in *Globalectics*. Chidora argues that while Ngũgĩ's earlier writings, steeped in a clear anti- and decolonial agenda, were marked by a reductive view on literature, culture and class which reduced Kenyans 'to a simplified dichotomy that can be captured thus: English/written literature = petty bourgeoisie; Gĩkũyũ and other Kenyan languages/orature = peasant' (92), his more recent work betrays a more complex, nuanced understanding of literature in the world and of World Literature. Detecting a kinship between Schulze-Engler's work on transculturality and World Literature and what can be termed Ngũgĩ's *Spätwerk*, Chidora's innovative approach places Schulze-Engler's and Ngũgĩ's work into conversation. The result of this endeavour is an intriguing insight into the differences and common grounds of Ngũgĩ's *Globalectics* and Schulze-Engler's conception of transcultural World Literatures, leading to a deeper understanding of both as well as revealing the productivity of their shared concerns, which Chidora calls globalectical transculturality.

In the second section, titled 'Transgressive Kinships', the contributors explore different forms of kinship as a basis for the way we relate to people but also to texts. These kinships are framed in terms of familial ties and (blood) relations, or are understood in broader terms, for example, as (arguably colonial) constructs such as the Family of Man (Huggan) or the idea of a 'host society' in the context of migration (Sarkowsky). The ties we forge with others are fundamental to the idea of transcultural Anglophone literature as we develop it in this volume. It is because of the encounter between the familiar and the foreign, the old and the new, the human and the non-human, the material and the representative that a transcultural literary space emerges. By the same token, it is because of the manifold entanglements of the *Zoon politikon* that a transcultural space is required in the first place.

Graham Huggan's contribution, 'Not-so-Happy Families: Durrell, Goodall and the Myth of Africa', calls for a productive inclusion of post-human, transspecies perspectives to the transcultural. Here, the Many Worlds of Anglophone Literature extend towards the multiple environments that surround and condition us, and that we make use of for self-fashioning and representation. Huggan evaluates the legacies of two twentieth-century celebrity conservationists, Gerald Durrell (1925–1975) and Jane Goodall (1934–), who made it their lives' mission to save wildlife from extinction and raise awareness of their cause. Although, as Huggan outlines, their approaches to conservationism and animal activism (as we would probably frame it today, with a proper social media account to go with) could not be more different, both Durrell and Goodall find common ground in their attempt to broaden the notion of who or what belongs to the Family of Man. Huggan uses the analysis of these two examples of 'modern animal writing' (118) to argue for a revised transcultural perspective. In his terms, the transcultural paradigm works best when it allows for the 'recognition of shared properties and characteristics that work *beyond* prescriptive classificatory systems, but also *across* them' (118, emphases in the original). Huggan declares himself a 'postcolonialist first' (119) and a sceptic of the transcultural paradigm. He maintains a tongue-in-cheek tone throughout the chapter but also shows a particular warmth regarding our honoree, Frank Schulze-Engler, and their lifelong commitment to oppositional views on the postcolonial and the transcultural, which render them, in Huggan's words, 'kin' (119).

Katja Sarkowky's contribution 'The "Makings of a Diasporic Self": Transcultural Life Writing, Diaspora and Modernity in Stuart Hall's *Familiar Stranger* (2017)' explores the idea of self-fashioning in relation to kinship and environment. Through her analysis of Stuart Hall's posthumously published memoir, Sarkowsky troubles the notion underlying all forms of life writing. Her chapter reflects upon 'the ways in which life – or rather: a specific life, the writer's life – can be told, and how this life and its possibilities of narrativization are conditioned (not: determined!) by social, cultural and historical structures and dynamics' (124). Life writing, in Sarkowsky's terms, unfolds at the intersection of individual and collective dynamics. The title of Hall's memoir seems to be just the right choice of oxymoron to describe not only the position of the diasporic subject (Hall), but also, it seems, the transcultural paradigm. *Familiar Stranger* is a deeply 'relational text' (122) in the way in which it intertwines sociohistorical frameworks with a 'self-reflexive constitution of subjectivity' (137). Diaspora and cultural identity are not only the key concepts that are associated with Hall as a vanguard of postcolonial criticism, but they function also, as Sarkowsky poignantly works out, as parameters to form the (literary) persona 'Stuart Hall'. Sarkowsky thus links her approach to life writing to fictional texts: Fiction engages in 'worlding' by employing and deploying the conditional 'by way of the "what if"' (138). Transcultural life writing, in Sarkowsky's terms, thus offers an opportunity to explore the 'link between self-representation, self-construction, and theoretical reflection' and to consider how transcultural life writing offers a way of 'theorizing both transculturality and the possibilities of life writing' (124).

Mala Pandurang's and Jinal Baxi's chapter 'Toward Re-centring the Senescent: Pedagogical Possibilities of Anglophone Short Fiction' emerged from a proposed project aimed at strengthening and promoting intergenerational interactions through literature. This project was partly born out of the need to deal with the local consequences of a global crisis, namely the restrictions to the sphere of the home due to the COVID pandemic, which led to increasing intergenerational conflicts due to the joint family structures common in India. Apart from the clash between modern and traditional attitudes which can ensue when senior members of the family and the young are forced into close proximity, the authors of this chapter draw attention to the problem of ageism. Reading, but also writing literature, becomes an important tool of intervention and fostering understanding: For students, 'postcolonial creative writing' can serve 'as an entry point to explore subjective aspects of ageing' (142). Moving the focus beyond the Indian context, Pandurang and Baxi propose the idea of a 'literary gerontology' (78) from a transcultural vantage point. Through a juxtapositional reading of selected Anglophone texts from the Global South, the authors show how a re-centring, a re-introduction of the aged into the focus of mainstream society and cultural productions mirrors the counter-hegemonic tendencies in what they perceive as postcolonial literature. The process of excluding the elderly is identified as similar to strategies of 'othering' of the postcolonial subject. This contribution maps out conceptualizations and understandings of age and ageism across the cultural board and points to literature's potential of fostering inclusion and mutual understanding.

Michelle Stork and Kathrin Bartha-Mitchell's contribution 'Notes from a Classroom: Teaching Anglophone Transculturality amidst Environmental Devastations' is focused on the question of how to teach transculturality in higher education. Reflecting on transculturality in relation to university teaching and didactics and on Schulze-Engler's teaching legacy, they draw on their own experiences of teaching a seminar course at Goethe University. Connecting theoretical considerations with practical experiences, they particularly engage with student responses and conclude that for students, transculturality is relevant mostly as it relates to pressing issues of our time, in particular, migration, the climate crisis and the extinction of species. Hence, they argue that the life worlds and existential concerns of students should take a more central place in the seminar room and advocate a stronger engagement of transcultural theory with concerns relating to the environment and to global migration: 'debates around terminology, such as 'transculturality vs. postcoloniality' – while highly relevant for experts in the field – seem to engage students at BA level far less than pressing concerns related to climate change, sustainable mobility and various forms of migration' (156). Seeing the classroom as a contact zone, they detect a need to rethink teaching methodologies and conditions and propose transcultural ecocriticism as a way to mobilize the concept of transculturality beyond its roots in the humanities.

The final section assembles contributions focused on issues of mobility, migration, passage and translation. Taking a cue from Robert Young's theorization of traversal and transversal as a 'poetics of migrancy', which always entails intersections and 'going beyond the limits of the parallel lines of established' (78) paths – literally, in terms of traversal, but also metaphorically – we gave this section the heading 'Transversal Readings'.

Mita Banerjee's chapter 'Transculturality and the Law: Witi Ihimaera's *The Whale Rider* and a River with Personhood' approaches transculturality from the angle of translation: of Maori epistemology into New Zealand law and of literary thought into legal text. Her case study is the court ruling *Whanganui River Claims Settlement Act/Te Awa Tupua Act* (2017), which grants the River Whanganui the status of a legal person. According to Banerjee, New Zealand law 'thus acknowledges and honours a Maori concept it does not understand' (192). For Banerjee, transculturality lies, unexpectedly perhaps, in the Indigenous notion's resistance to translation; she even considers the impossibility of translating Maori epistemology into Western thought. That a 'concept that is both untranslated and, to an extent, untranslatable' (193) is nonetheless transported into modern New Zealand law reveals the dynamism of both Maori epistemology and contemporary legal practice. In this context of reconciliation and redress, Banerjee tests the idea of transculturality, arguing for its merits despite the fact that in scenarios where the boundaries between victim and perpetrator need to be clear and upheld – such as a politics of redress – transculturality can at first seem counterintuitive. These aspects lead Banerjee to explore transculturality, kinship and overlaps between legal and literary thought and text.

In '"Mobility at Large": Anglophone Travel Writing as a Medium of Transcultural Communication in a Global Context', Nadia Butt approaches transculturality from a mobility studies perspective, with particular focus on different traditions of travel writing. Butt defines transcultural communication as central to the twenty-first century, which she describes as an age of travel and mobility in which the previously dominant notions of territorial and national borders and fixity are replaced by cross-border realities and communities in flux. For Butt, this calls for new configurations of communication which go beyond the established paradigms of intercultural communication or attempts at understanding the Other. In this respect, transcultural communication 'not only deviates from treating cultures as singular entities but offers a perspective on culture that goes beyond the traditional vision of culture as authentic or fixed. For Butt, this has ethical, artistic as well as practical implications. Butt puts her thesis to the test by focusing on Anglophone Travel Writing as a tool of transcultural communication which, due to its history of several centuries, prefigures concerns relevant for the contemporary age of global mobility. By drawing attention to examples of Asian, African and Arab Anglophone Travel Writing and by presenting a detailed close reading of Johny Pitts's *Afropean: Notes from Black Europe* (2019), she defines the genre of Anglophone Travel Writing as a medium particularly suited to capture contemporary realities and as a particularly potent tool of transcultural communication itself.

Janet Wilson's contribution 'The Transcultural Imaginary: South Asian Writing from Aotearoa New Zealand' draws attention to a unique case in point to this collection's overarching theme of literary worlding: Due to an increase of (South) Asian migration to Aotearoa New Zealand, especially since the late 1980s and as a result of New Zealand's accommodating immigration policies, the 'bicultural framework' (Māori and 'white settlers') that seems to govern Aotearoa's postcolonial identity is fervently shaken up by South Asian writers as they claim and imagine the immigrant experience. Wilson holds that the 'Kiwi Indian' and their cultural productions increasingly gain visibility in Aotearoa New Zealand and beyond, thus putting forth a transcultural imaginary as a means to explore the 'migrant condition' as well as notions of national belonging. These texts are, according to Wilson, both 'globally inflected' (235) as well as grounded in the local and the national. Narrative modes range from reflection to refraction, from self-reflexivity to self-doubt and trauma, to boastful affirmation, affiliation and negotiation. Wilson shows how the novels analysed in her chapter play with the literary registers of intercultural contact (as the process to strategically emphasize a particular cultural identity) and transcultural entanglement.

This section is concluded by Flora Veit-Wild's chapter 'Passages to India: Jewish Exiles between Privilege and Persecution'. Veit-Wild's chapter is a work of memory and in itself the product of travel, of a passage during which she retraces the history of her Prussian family by locating, sifting through and analysing documents such as letters and diaries. Veit-Wild's focus is on two journeys to India undertaken by her grandparents under very different circumstances: In 1909, as a young married couple looking towards a bright future in the Prussian administration, they embarked on a tour around the world. In 1939, they were forced to leave their native country, Germany, because of their Jewish roots and to seek refuge in India. Veit-Wild's ancestors hold a peculiar position which, in line with our conception of the Many Worlds of Anglophone Literature, complicates and even runs counter to the conventional reading practices of postcolonialism. As part of the Prussian administration and as an admirer of the British colonial project, Veit-Wild's grandfather was involved in national and imperial endeavours. In their first journey, he and his wife enjoyed the privileges of affluence and worldliness, but 'in their own country they were segregated and persecuted' (255). This history lends complexity to contemporary notions of migrancy and literature: While today's migrant or refugee story takes place mostly in the context of the journey from South to North, and sees the migrant placed in a 'subaltern' position, this cannot be said of these biographies. Here, cosmopolitan German Jews find refuge in the East, in India under British rule, partly recreating a journey conducted earlier. Flora Veit-Wild's chapter is a poetic and deeply personal journey, a story of travelling texts and material traces of much-overlooked entanglements between outposts of the British Empire and Jewish Germans in need of shelter.

Yvonne Adhiambo Owuor's 'Afterword: "Objects in the Rear-view Mirror"' marks the end point to our collection. Crucially, it is her artist's voice which adds another dimension, another World, to our Many Worlds of Anglophone Literature by pointing to the kinship that exists between the Worlds of Literature and Academia. Echoing the famous words by Nobel laureate Rabindranath Tagore, she shows that neither is a world fragmented by narrow domestic walls. Owuor's afterword serves as a reminder to us English studies scholars that, contrary to how our professional practice is often seen, and how we often enough see ourselves, our work is not *weltfremd*, not removed from 'real life' or cordoned off, but a World in relation to Many Worlds of Anglophone Literature. As she recounts her personal story of coming to perceive scholarship and its seemingly tedious mores 'not as handcuffs, but instead playmates' (284), she turns to our honoree's legacy: 'Through Frank Schulze-Engler, I learn what others probably take for granted, that there is room in academia for a wild and imaginative experimentation with ideas, that one can play with others' thoughts and experiences to re imagine worlds' (285).

Yvonne Adhiambo Owuor's afterword also allows us to transition to another element of triangulation at play in our volume. The conceptual framing as well as the contributions in this book explore individual relations to Frank Schulze-Engler's intellectual legacy. All contributors relate, in one way or another, to his lifelong commitment to shedding light on the in-between, on entanglements, cross-fertilizations as well as frictions that the postcolonial world is so replete with, and which pose so many analytical challenges. Schulze-Engler's continuous promotion of the transcultural throughout his illustrious career has prompted us – students, former PhD candidates and colleagues alike – to think about what cultural contact actually means and how we can productively theorize it. In this sense, and although one might not always agree with Schulze-Engler, we are indebted to this legacy. With this collection, in which we showcase the many aspects and also problems of 'all things transcultural', to borrow a turn of phrase from one of this volume's distinguished peer reviewers, we want to say: Thank you, Frank!

References

Achebe, C. (1958), *Things Fall Apart*, London: Heinemann.

Achenbach, R., J. Beek, J. N. Karugia, R. Mageza-Barthel and F. Schulze-Engler (eds) (2020), *Afrasian Transformations: Transregional Perspectives on Development Corporation, Social Mobility and Cultural Change*, Leiden: Brill. doi: https://doi.org/10.1163/9789004425262_002.

Auerbach, E. ([1957] 2018), 'Philologie der Weltliteratur', *Zeitschrift für interkulturelle Germanistik* 9 (2): 177–86.

Bartlett, F. C. ([1932] 1995), *Remembering: A Study in Experimental and Social Psychology*, Cambridge: Cambridge University Press.

Birus, H. (2004), 'Goethes Idee der Weltliteratur. Eine historische Vergegenwärtigung', *Goethezeitportal*, 1–27.

Casanova, P. ([1999] 2004), *The World Republic of Letters*, Cambridge, MA: Harvard University Press.

Chakrabarty, D. (2000), *Provincializing Europe: Postcolonial Thought and Historical Difference*, Princeton, NJ: Princeton University Press.

Cheah, P. (2008), 'What Is a World? On World Literature as World-Making Activity', *Daedalus* 137 (3): 26–38.

Cheah, P. (2016), *What Is a World? On Postcolonial Literature as World Literature*, Durham, NC: Duke University Press.

China Daily, n.a., 'Is This Young Kenyan Chinese Descendant [sic]?'. Available online: http://www.chinadaily.com.cn/english/doc/2005-07/11/content_459090.htm, published 11 July 2005 (accessed 14 July 2022).

Damrosch, D. (2014), *World Literature in Theory*, Chichester: Wiley & Blackfield.

David, J. (2013), 'The Four Genealogies of "World Literature"', in J. Küpper (ed.), *Approaches to World Literature*, Munich: Akademie Verlag, 13–26. https://doi.org/10.1524/9783050064956.13

Davis, G. V., P. H. Marsden, B. Ledent and M. Delrez (eds) (2004–5), *Towards a Transcultural Future: Literature and Society in a 'Post'-Colonial World*, 2 vols, Leiden: Brill.

Fludernik, M. (1996), *Towards a 'Natural' Narratology*, London: Routledge.

Gikandi, S. (2000), 'Review of Traveling Theory: Ngũgĩ's Return to English, by Ngũgĩ wa Thiong'o', *Research in African Literatures* 31 (2): 194–209.

Glissant, E. ([1990] 1997), *Poetics of Relation*, Ann Arbor: University of Michigan Press.

Gremels, A., M. Scheurer, F. Schulze-Engler and J. M. I. Wegner (eds) (2022), *Entanglements: Envisioning World Literature from the Global South*, Stuttgart: Ibidem.

Heidegger, M. ([1927] 1962), *Being and Time*, London: HarperPerennial.

Herman, D. (2004), *Story Logic: Problems and Possibilities of Narrative*, Lincoln: University of Nebraska Press.

Hofmeyr, I. (2012), 'The Complicating Sea: The Indian Ocean as Method', *Comparative Studies of South Asia, Africa and the Middle East* 32 (3): 584–90. https://doi.org/10.1215/1089201X-1891579

Iser, W. (1987), *The Act of Reading: A Theory of Aesthetic Response*, Baltimore, MD: Johns Hopkins University Press.

James, E. (2015), *The Storyworld Accord: Econarratology and Postcolonial Narratives*, Lincoln: University of Nebraska Press.

James, E. (2022), *Narrative in the Anthropocene*, Columbus: Ohio State University Press.

Moretti, F. (2000), 'Conjectures on World Literature', *New Left Review* 1: n.p. Available online: https://newleftreview.org/issues/ii1/articles/franco-moretti-conjectures-on-world-literature (accessed 2 March 2023).

Mufti, A. (2016), *Forget English! Orientalisms and World Literature*, Cambridge, MA: Harvard University Press.

Mwangi, E. M. (2009), *Africa Writes Back to Self: Metafiction, Gender, Sexuality*, Albany: State University of New York Press.

Nation, n.a., 'Girl's Journey to Ancestral Land in China'. Available online: https://nation.africa/kenya/life-and-style/lifestyle/girl-s-journey-to-ancestral-land-in-china-820958, published 21 July 2012 (accessed 14 July 2022).

Ngũgĩ wa Thiong'o ([1986] 2004), *Decolonizing the Mind: The Politics of Language in African Literature*, London: James Currey.

Ngũgĩ wa Thiong'o (2012), *Globalectics: Theory and the Politics of Knowing*, New York: Columbia University Press.

Olick, J. K. (2007), 'From Usable Pasts to the Return of the Repressed', *Hedgehog Review* 9 (2): 19–29.

Ortiz, F. ([1947] 1995), *Cuban Counterpoint: Tobacco and Sugar*, Durham, NC: Duke University Press.

Ortiz, F. ([1940] 2002). *Contrapunteo Cubano del Tabaco y el Azúcar*, Madrid: Catedra.

Owuor, Y. Adhiambo (2019), *The Dragonfly Sea*, London: Penguin Random House.

Pennycook, A. (2007), *Global Englishes and Transcultural Flows*, London: Routledge.

Phillips, C. (2001), *A New World Order: Selected Essays*, London: Secker & Warburg.

Ryfield, F., D. Cabana, J. Brannigan and T. Crowe (2019), 'Conceptualizing "Sense of Place" in Cultural Ecosystem Services: A Framework for Interdisciplinary Research', *Ecosystem Services* 36: 1–13. https://doi.org/10.1016/j.ecoser.2019.100907

Said, E. (1993), *Culture and Imperialism*, London: Chatto & Windus.

Schulze-Engler, F. (2007), 'Theoretical Perspectives: From Postcolonialism to Transcultural World Literature', in L. Eckstein (ed.), *English Literatures across the Globe: A Companion*, 20–32, Paderborn: Fink.

Schulze-Engler, F. (2012), 'The Commonwealth Legacy: Towards a Decentered Reading of World Literature', in B. Ashcroft, R. Mendes, J. McGonegal and A. Mukherjee (eds), *Literature for Our Times*, 1–14, Leiden: Brill.

Schulze-Engler, F. (2015), 'Once Were Internationalists? Postcolonialism, Disenchanted Solidarity and the Right to Belong in a World of Globalized Modernity', in

B. Heidemann, P. K. Malreddy, O. B. Laursen and J. Wilson (eds), *Reworking Postcolonialism*, 19–35, London: Palgrave Macmillan.

Schulze-Engler, F. (Forthcoming 2023), 'From British Lakes to Afrasian Sea: Recalibrations of the Indian Ocean in Yvonne Adhiambo Owuor's *The Dragonfly Sea*', in S. Sukla Chatterjee, J. Chojnicka, A. Hornidge and K. Knopf (eds), *Postcolonial Oceans: Contradictions and Heterogeneities in the Episteme of Salt Water*, Heidelberg: Heidelberg University Press.

Seigneurie, K. et al. (eds) (2020), *A Companion to World Literature*, Toronto: Wiley.

Strich, F. (1949), *Goethe and World Literature*, London: Routledge.

Veit-Wild, F. (1992), *Dambudzo Marechera: A Source Book on His Life and Work*, London: Hans Zell.

Wa Ngũgĩ, M. (2012), 'Rethinking the Global South', *Journal of Contemporary Thought*, reprinted in globalsouthproject.cornell.edu, n.p.

Walkowitz, R. L. (2015), *Born Translated: The Contemporary Novel in the Age of World Literature*, New York: Columbia University Press.

Walkowitz, R. L. (2020), 'On Not Knowing: Lahiri, Tawada, Ishiguro', *New Literary History* 51 (2): 323–46. https://doi.org/10.1353/nlh.2020.0021

Walkowitz, R. L. (2021), 'Less than One Language: Typographic Multilingualism and Post-Anglophone Fiction', *SubStance* 50 (1): 95–115.

Welsch, W. (1992), 'Transkulturalität – Lebensformen nach der Auflösung der Kulturen', *Information Philosophie* 20 (2): 5–20.

Welsch, W. (1999), 'Transculturality: The Puzzling Form of Cultures Today', in M. Featherstone and S. Lash (eds), *Spaces of Culture: City, Nation, World*, 194–213, London: Sage.

Wenzel, J. (2019), 'World-Imagining from Below', in S. Ferdinand, I. Villaescusa-Illán and E. Peeren (eds), *Other Globes*, London: Palgrave Macmillan. https://doi.org/10.1007/978-3-030-14980-2_8

West-Pavlov, R. (ed.) (2018), *The Global South and Literature*, Cambridge: Cambridge University Press.

Foreword: On excentric proximity – some thoughts for Frank

Homi K. Bhabha
Harvard University

As soon as you and your fellow men are cut down like dogs there is no other solution but to use every means available to reestablish your weight as a human being. You must therefore weigh as heavily as possible on your torturer's body so that his wits, which have wandered off somewhere, can at last be restored to their human dimension.

Frantz Fanon, *The Wretched of the Earth* (1961: 221)

Age will not wither Frank, nor will custom stale his infinite variety. Like Shakespeare's Greco-Egyptian Cleopatra, disporting herself on her gilded barge, I now see the Admiral of AFRASO[1] Studies at the mast of his barque, undertaking yet another scholarly voyage. Retired scholars rest awhile, in their idyllic Styrian cottage perhaps, before setting out on yet another transcultural turn around the Afrasian world. Of this, I am as convinced as are the searching and spirited contributors to this *Festschrift*.

My brief foreword has a limited itinerary. What I share with these fine chapters by several hands is a sense of gratitude to Frank for his hospitable critical concepts that provide an open house for diverse perspectives. Frank is an impeccable intellectual host to friends, students and colleagues who occupy his broad tent, speaking in many tongues, writing in many languages, free from the constraints of cultural authenticity or disciplinary territoriality. Transcultural pedagogy, as elaborated by Frank and his followers, is an inquiry that travels

---

[1] Africa's Asian Options was an interdisciplinary research project at Goethe University Frankfurt which studied African–Asian relations. https://www.afraso.org/en/content/home [accessed 3 August 2023].

across multiple tropes of ceaseless movement – distance, transition, delay and relay – embedded in the true spirit of the prefix 'trans': 'across, through, over, to or on the other side of, beyond, outside of, from one place, person, thing, or state to another' (*Oxford English Dictionary* [*OED*]).

Transculturality, as a form of inter-textual analysis, is an inter-discursive mode of *écriture* that scans a wide literary and political landscape while bringing into focus the *zone* where cultural negotiation takes place: 'Transcultural authors are not simply representatives of "their" cultures; their texts challenge readers and critics to come to terms with processes of *negotiation* and change between and within cultures, and to move beyond a rigid understanding of cultures as self-contained normative frameworks' (Schulze-Engler 2007: 30).

Cultural translation, a term of art grafted on Walter Benjamin's renowned essay 'The Task of the Translator', has produced a rich yield of writings on transcultural negotiations. Trans-agency, whether it is creative or critical, poetic or political, charts a new curricular pedagogy of *excentric proximity*. Excentric proximity stands in opposition to canonical sovereignty, which is frequently authorized and authenticated by its close cultural relation to territorial sovereignty. The extended metaphor Benjamin develops to describe the enunciative position that translation takes in relation to the work of literature and the world of language resonates well with my sense of the excentric proximity to which the transcultural relational is predisposed. Translation occupies an excentric enunciative site: It is not at the centre of the language-forest but outside, facing the wooded ridge. It is the projection of the 'call' of the language of translation from a distance, 'without entering', that finds the 'one spot' in the work capable of emitting an echo 'of the work in the alien one' (Benjamin 1923: 80).

Excentric proximity has to mark its distance from the centre of the sovereign rule of textual wholism or cultural hegemony in order to succeed in the arduous task – *Aufgabe* – of proximity. From a distance, generally outside the canon and often beyond the curriculum, it must hit 'that single spot' that raises a translational echo (Benjamin 1923: 79). Excentric proximity initiates a dialogue of reverberating references and representations that place diverse cultures 'in' proximity, but outside the centre; the process of interpretation and exegesis is caught up in the temporality of the *trans*: 'across, through, over to, or on the other side of, beyond' (*OED*). Excentricity is an engagement with those peoples, policies and principles that have fallen into the fault lines of freedom – off-centre. However, let me be clear, that although what is excentric is 'out of the center' (*OED*), the force of its being, and the power of its meaning, cannot be relegated to the marginal or the peripheral, as is so often assumed to be the fate of those who are 'out' of sight/site. The language of marginality barely touches the terror of the '[person] who is forced each day to snatch [her personhood], his identity, out of the fire of human cruelty that rages to destroy it' – if I might freely adapt James Baldwin – nor can the prose of peripherality describe the agency of survivance that survives the fire this time: '[I]f he survives his effort, and even if he does not survive it … he achieves his own authority, and that is unshakeable' (Baldwin 1963: 98–9). This is because, in order to save his life, he is forced to look beneath appearances, to take nothing for granted.

What, then, are the terms of transcultural negotiation in relation to the concept of excentric proximity?

Frank suggests that transcultural authors resist the responsibility of carrying the burden of autochthonous authenticity; they renounce the sovereignty of nationalist patrimony and patriarchy; their aim, as I understand it, is to give voice and shape to what may be called the excentric proximity of poetics and politics. In Frank's words, as cited in the introduction to this volume, Yvonne Adhiambo Owuor's novel *The Dragonfly Sea* 'manages its exploration of historical and contemporary Sino-Kenyan relations entirely without recourse to the postcolonial triangulation with the West' (Gremels et al. 2022: 3). Instead, it 'explores Africa's role in a multipolar world where the centrality of Europe and North America has already given way to complex new realignments between countries, cultures, memories and people' (Gremels et al. 2022: 10).

Displacing the centrality of the history of European colonialism to avoid a 'triangulation with the West' in transcultural relations has a long postcolonial history. It is a form of child's play to place two equilateral triangles upon each other, facing in opposite directions, to derive a star: A multipolar figure pointing in different directions, opening up new lines of intersection and diverse angles of relationality, while maintaining a geometry of joints and joists. Fanon's conclusion to *The Wretched of the Earth* has always struck me as a brief and beautiful attempt to flip the triangles around, and establish a foundational direction for the primacy of South–South dialogues while steering the ship of state towards what used to be called the Third World. I am entirely persuaded by his grave indictment of Europe – 'its crimes, the most heinous of which have been committed at the very heart of man, the pathological dismembering of his functions and the erosion of his unity … racial hatred, slavery, exploitation, and above all, the bloodless genocide whereby one and a half billion men have been written off' (1961: 238). At the same time, I am awed by the ecumenical endurance that informs his call for a new humanism that accommodates, even affiliates, those who have been antagonists:

Come brothers, we have far too much work on our hands to revel in outmoded games. Europe has done what it had to do and all things considered, it has done a good job; let us stop accusing it, but let us say to it firmly it must stop putting on such a show. We no longer have reason to fear it, let us stop then envying it.

The Third World is today facing Europe as one colossal mass whose project must be to try and solve the problems this Europe was incapable of finding the answers to. (1961: 238)

Fanon's severe judgment against Europe neither begins with accusations nor ends in excluding Europe from a new humanism. The reparative process of forging a decolonized agency of political independence and psychic re-constitution – after the colonial trial by fire – is the project of a new humanism which demands a revolution in *ontological consciousness* that provides a form of embodiment for revolutionary consciousness. A collective agency of national independence (not *nationalist* sovereignty) and regional solidarity has to actively engage with the agony and alterity of colonial alienation: While *remembering* Europe's colonial genocide, and in order to avoid *repeating* the banal evil of institutional state-forms, an emancipatory consciousness has to *work through* traumatic moments in the transition to freedom.

Working through, as developed in psychoanalytic theory, is a temporal process of repetition that overcomes resistances to traumatic memories through a practice of interpretation, both intellectual and affective. As Laplanche and Pontalis point out, 'working-through permits the subject to pass from rejection or merely intellectual acceptance [of the trauma] to a conviction based on lived experience (*Erleben*) of the repressed instincts which "are feeding the resistance"' (1988: 488). Fanon's genius and wisdom combine in refusing to smooth out the resistant traumas and political contradictions that cause 'the trials and tribulations of national consciousness', to snag his chapter title. The most enduring tribulation of the *colonial past-in-the-national-present* may be the *trial of time itself*. The historical record can be set right; political consciousness can, with difficulty, be reorientated; but the revaluation of the phenomenological matrix of time in the re-measuring of progress, or in re-visioning subjectivity – all these aspects of working through the conscious record as re-inscribed in the unconscious register – are formidable challenges to 'making a new start … and endeavor[ing] to create a new man [sic]' (Fanon 1961: 239).

The core elements of Fanon's new charter of rights, representation and recognition of 'the new man [sic]' are as follows:

> To nationalize does not mean organizing the state on the basis of a new program of social relations. For the bourgeoisie, nationalization signifies very precisely the transfer into indigenous hands of privileges inherited from the colonial period. (1961: 100)
>
> But what matters now, is not a question of profitability, not a question of increased productivity, not a question of production rates. No, it is not a question of back to nature. It is the very basic question of not dragging man in directions which mutilate him, of not imposing on his brain tempos that rapidly obliterate and unhinge it. The notion of *catching up* must not be used as a pretext to brutalize man, to tear him from himself and his inner consciousness, to break him, to kill him. (1961: 238)
>
> So comrades, let us not pay tribute to Europe by creating states, institutions, and societies that draw their inspiration from it. Humanity expects other things from us than this grotesque and generally obscene emulation. (1961: 239)

Fanon's Manichean map of colonial power has been acknowledged for its stark spatial divisions between the sovereign territory of colonial power abutting the colonized territory of indigenous and subaltern peoples. The political regime of Time as the great divider of peoples ranked on an ontological timescale of historical progress versus archaism, or civilizational supremacy versus cultural belatedness, raises racial temporal issues of lasting importance. What is to be done to avoid the exigency of emulation in times of postcolonial transition? How can 'triangulation' be transformed to provide a post-Imperial Europe with a chance to start *again* as part of a postcolonial *ecumene* of shared suffering and shared success? In the conclusion to *Wretched*, Fanon provides an answer that places the burden of ethical responsibility for transforming the Euro-American axis of power on the shoulders of the subaltern agency of the decolonized. Sharing James Baldwin's insistence that the American Black is 'the key figure in his country, and the American future is precisely as bright or as dark as his' (1963: 94), Fanon believes that the transformation of colonial power relations between Europe and the Third World is the political fate of the decolonized who are privileged to 'reexamine the question of man' because they know from bitter lived experience – better than anything the colonialists know about themselves – the extent to which Europe has defaced and degraded the human ideal.

Let us re-examine the question of cerebral reality, the brain mass *of humanity in its entirety* whose affinities must be increased, whose connections must be diversified and whose communications must be humanized again (1961: 237–8).

The Third World must stop playing the imitation game so that Europe's narcissism may lose its power of spectacle, and its theatre of exemplarity: *'Let us say to it firmly it must stop putting on such a show'* (Fanon 1961: 238; emphasis added). Without a mimetic hold on the audience, the show can't go on because the audience refuses the mimetic contract to emulate colonial authority. To shatter Europe's mimetic narcissism, visible in its political sovereignty and racial supremacy, requires more than a transfer of power; it requires a radical shift in the practice of being-in-time. When the decolonized subject refuses to play catch-up in Empire's imitation game, there is no belated native subject – yet to be 'developed' or waiting to be made civil and productive – gazing keenly into the mirror of exploitative emulation while being placed in a carceral enclosure outside the frame of reference and reflection. To re-examine the question of man requires, as Fanon argues, the affirmation of 'cerebral reality' or 'brain tempos' – affective drives, *Nachträglichkeit* (deferred action), the vulnerability of the bodily schema; or, as in this telling narrative that follows, the victory of life over death as seen in the cultivation of a date palm:

> In a context of oppression like that of Algeria, for the colonized, living does not mean embodying a set of values, does not mean integrating oneself into the coherent, constructive development of a world. To live simply means not to die. To exist means staying alive. Every date grown is a victory. Not the result of hard work, but a victory celebrating a triumph over life. (Fanon 1961: 232)

Until the coherent, constructive development of the world makes room for the parable of the victory of the 'date', and until questions of productivity and profitability – European signifiers of market-driven capitalist progress – are capable of integrating the dark truth that for the colonial native 'to live simply means not to die' – until that time, the fruits of our labour will wither on the tree of time, and 'the question of man' will blow restlessly in the wind.

So much has happened since Fanon's passionate mustering – *'Come brothers … try and solve the problems this Europe was incapable of finding the answers to'* – that his call for 'a new humanism' as the driving spirit of a Third World built on convergent, non-competitive developmental goals now seems hopelessly far-fetched. After 9/11, in particular, global security has divided the world between 'healthy societies' and 'failed states'. And many of the world's 'successful' states have adopted the exclusionary politics of ethnic nationalism and exclusionary patriotism to vacate their responsibilities to the rights of minorities and migrants on the racialized grounds of national security. Where do we now look for answers that, in Fanon's words, Europe was incapable of finding answers to?

In much of what used to be referred to as the once-and-future Third World, as in much of Europe too, the politics of emulation has rapidly followed the playbook of xenophobic ethnonationalism. Fanon's theory and therapy of revolutionary time, with its emphasis on ontological emancipation in the making of a new revolutionary humanism, might be a step in the right direction. The search for a decolonizing 'ontological' phenomenology of the brain mass of *humanity in its entirety* – with its ethical emphasis on relationality rather than 'identity' or individualism – might lead to a revolutionary collective consciousness. In contrast, a 'politics of identity' that holds fixedly to the exceptionalism of its historic injury may well experience a future shaped by identitarian self-emulation. Fanon's ontological perspective enables him to extend an invitation of 'conditional' hospitality to Europe to participate in the process of excising and exceeding Eurocentrism – '*[f]or Europe, for ourselves and for humanity, comrades, we must make a new start, develop a new way of thinking*' (1961: 239; emphasis added). A new way of postcolonial thinking subscribes to an ontological project of natality in which the birth of the One is inseparably, if uncomfortably, linked to the birth of the Other.

References

Baldwin, J. ([1963] 1993), *The Fire Next Time*, New York: Vintage Books.

Benjamin, W. ([1923] 2004), 'The Task of the Translator: An Introduction to the Translation of Baudelaire's *Tableaux parisiens*', trans. Harry Zohn, in L. Venuti (ed.), *The Translation Studies Reader*, 2nd edn, 75–85, New York: Routledge.

Fanon, F. ([1961] 2004), *The Wretched of the Earth*, trans. R. Philcox, New York: Grove Press.

Gremels, A., F. Schulze-Engler and J. M. I. Wegner (2022), *Entanglements: Envisioning World Literature from the Global South*, Stuttgart: Ibidem.

Laplanche, J. and J.-B. Pontalis (1988), *The Language of Psychoanalysis*, trans. D. Nicholson-Smith, London: Karnac Books.

Schulze-Engler, F. (2007), 'Theoretical Perspectives: From Postcolonialism to Transcultural World Literature', in L. Eckstein (ed.), *English Literatures across the Globe: A Companion*, 20–32, Paderborn: Fink.

Part One

Theories and concepts

1

'World Literature'? A perspective from the centre, a perspective from the edge

Michael Chapman
Durban University of Technology

The last forty years or so have seen renewed interest in the object and/or concept, World Literature. I say renewed interest for, as Damrosch's book *What Is World Literature?* (2003) reminds us, the term has a history dating back to Goethe's coinage (*Weltliteratur*) in his interviews, in 1827, with his young disciple, Johan Peter Eckermann.[1] *Weltliteratur* offered Goethe a new literary perspective and cultural awareness; a sense of a rising global modernity. Renewed interest in World Literature, from the 1990s onwards, has coincided with the end of Cold War politics and a global diffusion of both economic and cultural products, as well as a time–space compression in information flows and human mobility. It is not surprising that renewed interest should have been most evident in the academies and publishing houses of the United States. The new millennium is synonymous with US digital expansion. Indeed, Julien discerns a connection between Wallerstein's 'world systems theory' (1997) – global, neoliberal and political/business realignments of major funders of human and social science research. The United States Social Science Research Council, she observes, has favoured transnational, multiregional studies that many see as portending the end of the deep knowledge of language and culture in specific locations: What, in the era of Cold War division, was known as Area Studies (Julien 2006: 116). Or, to quote Moretti – like Damrosch, a prominent voice in World Literature debate, or controversy – the world critic, or global comparatist, studies 'wave patterns of transformations sweeping around the world'; local specialists study the individual works, 'the trees in the [local, or even national], plantations' (2000: 57). But,

---

[1] See Goethe (1984) and Strich (1949), the latter on Goethe and World Literature.

to pursue Moretti's metaphor, the plantation (or sportswear sweatshop) in the poor South and consumerism in the rich North are not unconnected to each other. We witness conflict between the capitalist erasure of local or regional difference and 'fight backs' by specific religious and social movements. As the US military discovered to its cost, there is no undifferentiated 'Iraqi people', but Sunnis, Shi'ites and Kurds. World systems theory is not monolithic; it is entangled in multiple modernities in which, as Wilk phrases it, 'global structures may be utilized for the expression of our common differences' (1995: 22). By the same token, the object and/or concept, World Literature, involves both waves and trees.

My formulation, object and/or concept, is intended to emphasize that the category of World Literature remains elusive. It was unstable, even arbitrary, from the moment of its initial articulation. Damrosch summarizes the difficulty: 'What does it really mean to speak of a "World Literature"?' (2003: 1). Which literature, whose world? What relation to national literatures, the production of which continued unabated even after Goethe had announced their obsolescence? What might be the new relations between Western Europe and the rest of the globe; between antiquity and modernity; and between a nascent mass culture and elite productions?

Such questions arose in Stockholm at a symposium I attended, late in 2004, together with some thirty academics from around the world, including Damrosch. The purpose was to contribute to a project on 'Literature and Literary History in Global Contexts', funded by the Swedish Research Council, the aim being to find suitable methods and valid approaches for studying and analysing literature globally or, to use the title of the symposium, 'Studying Transcultural Literary History'. To continue to pose questions, several of which would gain traction in the years after the symposium but which at the time arose in discussion: Is there a significant distinction between the term World Literature and the term Transcultural Literature? Schulze-Engler has argued that transcultural literature or, by extension, transcultural literary history signals a turn from intercultural dialogue between nation-states to transnational connections; to a multipolar, decentred system of literary communication. Yet, Schulze-Engler is willing to conflate the terms 'transcultural' and 'world' as he seeks a 'transcultural world literature' (2007: 28–30).

The point, at least in the late 1990s and early 2000s, was how to attach a transcultural World Literature paradigm to globalizing expansiveness; expansiveness which, in retrospect, has proved to be not as independent of localities, regions or, indeed, national chauvinism as many at the time had hoped. Since then, Trumpism, Brexit and a raising of drawbridges around Fortress Europe have imposed new borders. The project of transcultural or World Literature requires ongoing work as Damrosch indicated in his keynote lecture, in 2017 in Copenhagen, to the Institute for World Literature, 'What Is(n't) World Literature? Problems of Language, Culture and Politics'. Has the field – he asked rhetorically – been sufficiently 'de-Westernized'? Does the field still find a kind of comfort in its preoccupation with the novel – the 'middle-class' Western form – rather than tackling the 'untranslatability' of poetry or the challenges of orature from the peripheries of the world? Then there are the issues of time and location. Should Goethe still be the starting point for discussion of the field? Is the drive still too predictably that of the West versus the Rest? Or, as Apter would respond in her study, *Against World Literature* (2013), has the concept not led students to underestimate the true extent of 'difference' in a linguistic and cultural outlook? The postcolonial Self and Other thus intrude upon Apter's argument, a point that is pursued by the Multilingual, Locals and Significant Geographies Project – the MULOSIGE Project – at the School of Oriental and African Studies in London.

Schulze-Engler's transcultural metaphor focuses on the 'New Literatures in English' while Damrosch talks of all literary works that circulate beyond their cultures of origin either in translation or in their original language. Both critics are alert, nonetheless, to a common problem of manageability. How do we construct a frame of reference for the teaching and research of the field, whether it be called Transcultural Literature or World Literature? As Schulze-Engler phrases the provisionality, we – commentators on a vast field – must reflect on the fact that we cannot, we should not want to, invoke an imaginary assembly of all national literatures; rather, we must operate within a transcultural network of significations that permit any single perspective only partial access to the full complexity of the social, linguistic and cultural articulations to be encountered in the individual literary work (2012: 12). Manageability of the field is as much an interpretative enterprise as it is a selection of texts. That such questions and issues remained provisional at the Stockholm symposium did not detract from the value of the discussion.

Let us return to Goethe, at least as a convenient starting point. He thought of World Literature less as a set of works – that is, less as an object – more as a field of relations. The propensity of manageability, however, is to cast World Literature as an object, as a set of works. It is a propensity which, at the outset of the Stockholm symposium, provoked a certain 'national' defensiveness and rivalry: Chinese literature is older and, therefore, more venerable than European literature; who is greater, Shakespeare or Goethe? World Literature as an object has provoked Guillén's retort: 'The sum total of national literatures? A wild idea, unattainable by practice' (1993: 38). Goethe was rescued from national or imperial self-projection because he lacked a secure cultural base: He had an uneasy sense of mid-nineteenth-century Germany as provincial, or what today we might call a periphery.

World Literature as object constitutes one direction in the revival of interest. The multi-volume anthology *World Literature and Thought* (see Gochberg et al. 1997) is illustrative. As general editor Gochberg explains: '[The volumes offer] a rich treasury of selections from many of the world's major civilizations' (1997: ix). From philosophical treatises and love lyrics and from ancient Akkadian to modern English, the selections have been chosen for their 'lasting historical or intellectual significance, as well as for their readability' (1997: ix). The purpose of the project is summed up, quaintly, in an allusion to Dr Johnson: 'He who tires of the wealth of humanity and its works revealed in these volumes must surely be tired of life; for there is represented in *World Literature and Thought* all that life can offer' (Gochberg et al. 1997: xi).

We are transported to an equanimous view of literature and culture. There is none of the rancour that has characterized struggles for political/textual authority in neo-Marxism, feminism, Africanism or postcolonialism, as signposts of the literary-cultural scene of the last forty years. Yet, to limit the project to Arnoldian 'touchstones' would be unfair. The selections in *World Literature and Thought* are generous and wide ranging. Antiquity is not confined to Greece and Rome, as in most Classics departments in Western, and indeed in African, academies. Concise introductions to the sections and to individual works, or extracts, provide illuminations across time and cultures. Of interest to Africa – I am based in South Africa – there is an inclusion of Egyptian, Ethiopian and Swahili texts; there is a Nyangan epic; there is oral poetry from the Fulani, Igbo, Yoruba, Ijaw and Hausa traditions; and, closer to the south of the continent, we have examples of San/Bushman, Khoi and Zulu expression.

The method is comparative, but not curtailed to what, in comparative study, is identified as 'pre-Treaty of Versailles': Two great artworks in two great languages from two homogeneous European nation-states. Rather, the project is 'post-Treaty of Versailles' in its non-hierarchical mapping of multiple civilizations and multiple nations. A shortcoming is that, although translation is implicit in the design, there is no attempt to incorporate a theory or an approach to crossing languages and cultures. The requirement of readability in target English-speaking cultures favours 'domestication' (making familiar) rather than 'foreignization' (retaining the strangeness of the source culture/text). As a result, all texts are reproduced as though originally conceived, expressed or written in smooth-flowing English. Another shortcoming is inevitable: The limits of space guarantee limits to the reproduction of longer works. Thus, Shakespeare appears not as a playwright but as a sonneteer, and the novel – arguably, the most widely travelled genre of the last 150 years – is reduced in its representation to token fragments.

Aimed primarily at a North American college audience, the volumes subscribe partly to Bernheimer's 1993 Report to the American Comparative Literature Association on the state of the discipline. Comparatists were prompted to reconceive and expand the canon to include marginal and subaltern perspectives. In this respect, one can argue whether the volumes are sufficiently bold; but the project, at least, counters the conservatism of Bloom (1987), D'Souza (1991) and others, who have had reservations about dilution and diffusion of the curriculum by book lists being opened to too many windows on disparate areas of the world.

What I term the 'great civilizations' approach to World Literature did not unduly engage the energies of the Stockholm symposium. There is limited value in prolonging the argument as to whether Shakespeare is, or is not, greater than Goethe. Instead, debate quickly identified an agreed first principle to answer the question: What is World Literature? In fact, Gochberg – despite his flourish about 'all that life can offer' – identifies the issue: 'We have chosen works because they exerted a significant influence on their own or later times, frequently even well outside their original cultures' (Gochberg et al. 1997: ix). Or, to reiterate Damrosch's point: 'I take World Literature to encompass all literary works that circulate beyond their culture of origin, either in translation or in their own original language' (2003: 4).

Such a circulation model, of course, has its own difficulties. Who or what ensures that a work circulates? Clearly, the 'quality' of the text alone is not enough guarantee; rather, we enter a network of power, whether religious, cultural, political or economic. We enter a world in which regimes of truth-imposition, or routes of travel or dissemination, are unequal in influence or cash. Circuits involving the rich North (the North Atlantic conglomerate) and the poor South (constellations that might include China, India, Brazil and South Africa) remain caught up in the binaries of metropole and periphery. Alert to the fact that texts which circulate must find willing publishing outlets and willing readers (a market), Damrosch elaborates on his definition of World Literature: Circulation beyond the original culture, which is dependent not only on what is *in* the text, but also on reader-reception. His own book, accordingly, is intended to clarify ways in which works of literature can best be read or received because 'just as there never has been a single set canon of World Literature, so too no single way of reading can be appropriate to all texts, or even to any one text at all times' (2003: 5). A work may be classified as Literature (upper-case 'L') in one period and not in another; or a work may be adjudged greater than another in one period and not in another. (We recollect T. S. Eliot's resurrection, in 1921, of the seventeenth-century metaphysical poets as precursors of a modernist sensibility.) World Literature may be conceived, accordingly, less as an object, more as a concept. Indeed, Damrosch's approach – in contrast to that of the 'World Literature and Thought' project – is conceptual: 'The variability of a work of World Literature is one of its constitutive features' (2003: 5).

The greater part of the discussion in Stockholm considered matters of concept, circulation and reception: Whose literature, whose world, what design, what methodology, who values what? Such questions are germane to several pertinent articles in the field. To make random reference, Aldridge talks of the 'difficulties of pointing to remarkably successful examples of the pragmatic application of critical systems in a comparative context' (1986: 33). To which Prempati adds: 'I do not know whether the innumerable Western critical models which, like multinationals, have taken over the Indian critical scene would meaningfully serve any critical purpose at this juncture' (1987: 63).

The last point touches on the problem of the work from a marginal culture which, to secure a 'North Atlantic' readership, may have to emulate recognizably international models. Miyoshi (1991) and Venuti (1998) both make the point: A post–Second World War reception in the United States probably has less to do with genuine openness to other cultures, more to do with American interests and needs. As Ali tartly puts it: 'Same junk food, same junk novels' (1993: 140). Instead of new preoccupations and styles arriving at the North Atlantic market from the margins – for example, magical realism from Latin America or folk hyper-realism from Africa – we have 'market realism' (1993: 140): A modernist/postmodernist internationalism adopted by the Latin American or African writer who, very often, has long left or long been exiled from home, and who plies the North Atlantic literary or academic circuit.

Despite concerns that World Literature can subjugate different local, regional or national traditions to what, in the title of her article, Abu-Lughad calls 'global babble' (2001: 131), there are compelling counterarguments, many summarized in Damrosch's introduction to his book (2003: 1–36). While the marginal, or provincial, writer may feel pressure to emulate the centre, inherited traditions can exert a crushing weight on the metropolitan work. Free of inherited tradition (as Proust or Woolf were not), writers like Joyce and Walcott had greater opportunity to be cosmopolitan. Yet, to be cosmopolitan (itself a problematic concept, as Appiah has shown)[2] is not to belong nowhere: Joyce's Ireland and Walcott's Caribbean give local strength to their author's respective sensibilities and styles.

Damrosch draws a distinction, accordingly, between World Literature (literature that comes from somewhere) and a notionally global literature which, unaffected by specific context, may be read at airport terminals, anywhere (2003: 25). Avoiding either/or in the global/local equation, Cooppan believes that a world work may at once be 'locally inflected and translocally mobile' (2001: 33). Or, as Dharwadker phrases it, 'a montage of overlapping maps in motion' (2001: 3), a concept that invokes Ortiz's idea of *transculturación*, cited by Perez-Firmat as a 'liminal zone or impassioned margin, where diverse cultures converge without merging' (1989: 25).

Thus, a 'World Literature' from an Indian perspective will not be identical to a 'World Literature' from a Brazilian perspective, to illustrate the point. As Dev has it, in India, in its multilingualism, in its class and cultural diversity, there cannot be a true appreciation of 'a single literature in absolute isolation' (1984: 14). In Brazil, a different set of forces prevails. To summarize Carvalhal, the forces in Brazil that shape any concept of 'world' must involve the complex relations among people of indigenous, European and mixed descent; inter-American relations within Latin America *vis-à-vis* the United States; and lasting ties to Portugal, Spain and France (2001: 147–54). Whereas European scholars usually see World Literature radiating outwards from metropolitan centres to relatively passive provincial recipients – Carvalhal's argument continues – Brazilian scholars are moving beyond the paradigm of 'Paris, cultural capital of Latin America' to emphasize a two-way process that is attuned as much to Brazil's dynamic heterogeneity as to the cultural authority if not of Portugal, then of France. To reiterate, a perspective on World Literature is a perspective from somewhere.

Here, the argument identifies a key difference between the approaches of Damrosch and Moretti. The latter has been extensively quoted in debates on the topic of World Literature in response to Moretti's book, *Atlas on the European Novel 1800–1900* (1998), and to his article, 'Conjectures on World Literature' (2000: 54–68). Moretti, whose views I have already introduced, uses Wallerstein's

---

[2] Cosmopolitanism is 'not the name of any solution, but the challenge (of the next, more global epoch)' (Appiah 2006: 11).

world systems theory as an index of literary circulation. If a consequence of globalization has been a centre-culture travelling to 'postcolony' margins, we may identify a parallel with the novel as the major 'travelling' form of literary modernity. Rising to prominence in Europe, its story/plot expectation has generic stability (from romance to realism, from folk types to psychological interiority); nonetheless, its transfer from the centre is not straightforward.

As I interpret Moretti, the further the novel travels from its stable centre, the more it displays discordance between plot (story-purpose travels reasonably well) and style (language, less easily transferable). The critic at the margin may wish to find value in a 'local' style (say, in an oral residue). Moretti concludes, however, that a local style or voice, even if illuminating of the indigenous culture – I return to an earlier point – is unlikely to be 'closely read' on the North Atlantic circuit: the power circuit of novelistic innovation and dissemination (2000: 66).

Moretti's argument – a hiatus between story and voice, or plot and style – is not endorsed by Damrosch, who believes that a neglect of close reading diminishes the experiential value of literature's variability, whether the work has a distinctly 'local' flavour or not (2003: 25). We are reminded that Wallerstein distinguishes between the history of the world as cultural homogenization and cultural differentiation; between globalization as a paradigm of modernity and a paradigm of multiple modernities. Following Wallerstein, Damrosch avers that a solution to the World Literature problematic 'is to recognize that we don't face an either/or choice between global systematicity and infinite textual multiplicity, for World Literature itself is constituted very differently in different cultures [...]. A culture's norms and needs profoundly shape the selection of works that enter into it as World Literature, influencing the ways they are translated, marketed and read' (2003: 26).

What, then, distinguishes the study of World Literature as object (a list, a syllabus of touchstones) from World Literature as concept, in which the circulation of texts beyond the original culture is determined not simply by textual immanence, but also by reader reception and reader demand? The distinction is not unlike a literary-critical shift from Arnoldian/Leavisian/New Critical considerations to context-based considerations. Indeed, the discussion in Stockholm invoked formulations that are identifiable within 'Post-'debates (both postmodern and postcolonial): metropole/periphery, centre/margin, all implicated in asymmetrical power; multiple perspectives (World Literature not as a single window, but as windows on the world); World Literature as literature from somewhere; readers (those who interpret the significance, the value) as readers of specific ideological, cultural, educational and class persuasions. And the question not only, what is World Literature, but also what is literature?

'Like-but-unlike'

The question 'What is literature?' forces one to complicate, to qualify, any circulation model. If measured in sales alone, World Literature would replicate what Damrosch designates as a 'global literature' of no specific context. A few examples: the contemporary, or near-contemporary novel of outdoor adventure or indoor intrigue; of crime, mystery or sexual proclivity (more commonly called 'genre fiction'); the biography of the world figure (Michelle Obama, Ronaldo, Lady Gaga); the self-help or motivational or pop-psycho book (*Men Are from Mars, Women Are from Venus*). The cultural critic, of course, will identify in such books both a context and an ideology: the North Atlantic reading group – white, college educated; sexually tolerant and politically correct, albeit both cautiously; flirtatious of relativism, but foundational in the upbringing of their children. The language will be English or French, but predominantly English, with French – notwithstanding its cultural and diplomatic pretensions – relying for its world reach on English translation. Recognizing the sales power of mass literature while wishing to safeguard World Literature from the mass, D'haen (2006: 144–51) introduced the following sub-categorizations as refinements to the argument:

- the circuit of mass literature,
- the circuit of educational literature and
- the circuit of prestige literature.

Such sub-categorizations permit flexibility of selection, perspective and purpose in any project-pursuit designated as World Literature. Shakespeare, for example, may inhabit both educational and prestige circuits or, granted his popularization in film adaptations and heritage promotion, he might even touch a mass market. Nonetheless, asymmetries of power persist. Shakespeare circulates in African education; but, to return to a previous point, the praise poem (a staple form of African expression) is unlikely to circulate in metropolitan education. As a Nobel laureate, J. M. Coetzee circulates in the prestige domain at both centres and edges but, in sales, reviews and acclaim, more on the North Atlantic circuit than in his home country, South Africa, where the prestige circuit is uneven in sales and acknowledgement. As a result of his Nobel achievement, Coetzee's circulation has increased in direct sales, university prescriptions, translations of his work and even on the screen with a film version of his novel, *Disgrace*. Coetzee is a World Literature figure; nonetheless, his *transcultural* circulation is relatively insignificant in comparison with that of Dan Brown. Again, should we wish to avoid equating World Literature with mass North Atlantic literature, further refinements are necessary to considerations of what circulates. Here, Goethe provides Damrosch with a useful guide. In his complex response to the foreign text, the German writer partly projected his national recognition outwards, partly responded in fascination to cultural difference. At one end, the foreign text may be enjoyed for its novelty; at the other, for a gratifying similarity that we find in, or project onto, the work. There is also – Damrosch continues – the middle-range response to what is 'like-but-unlike', and it is this like-but-unlike quality 'that is most likely to make a productive change in our perceptions and practices' (2003: 11–12).

A response to a text may involve, almost simultaneously, all three dimensions. It is useful for the sake of sharpening the focus on World Literature, nonetheless, to examine the dimensions separately. The work of novelty – for example, the San/Bushman story – is probably least likely to circulate; the work of gratifying similarity – a Wilbur Smith adventure novel – is most likely to circulate, widely. What, though, of the serious writer whose eye is not primarily on the preoccupations of the North Atlantic circuit: Nadine Gordimer, André Brink, Milan Kundera, Gabriel García Márquez, indeed J. M. Coetzee? Such writers – I have already alluded – owe success beyond their own culture to the 'like-but-unlike' quality of their stories. They are usually novelists since narrative plots travel with greater ease than 'non-narrative' poetry. Their 'foreign' content – apartheid South Africa, communist East European kitsch, Latin American cultural hybridism – must find consonance with North Atlantic novelistic recognition in character portrayal, concerns and style. Behind the 'national question', Nadine Gordimer's characters (usually white English-speaking South Africans) occupy private lives which, although influenced by local political demands, are not entirely alien in their aspirations, disappointments, desires and conversation to educated, middle-class readers in London, New York or (in translation) Paris. The advantages of such bifurcated vision – a trait of the circulating writer from the margin – can also have its disadvantages. I return to Moretti's issue of originality and derivation. Is Wole Soyinka's style 'original' in its incorporation of Yoruba myth, or is it imitative in its Euro-American modernist 'defamiliarization'? Does Soyinka occupy the category of 'like-but-unlike'?

That more questions than answers arise in discussion of World Literature is not peculiar to the literary domain. Commenting on the rise of world music,

Bakan asks, 'What exactly is world music?' (2004: xi–xv). Having conceded that all the world's musics – past and present, traditional and familiar, Western and non-Western, classical, popular, folk and tribal – exist in the world, why then should not all, or none, logically be categorized as world music? Fundamentally, the term 'world music' (like World Literature) is either meaningless or, at best, arbitrary. This notwithstanding, world music has come to designate a category-extension beyond existing Western categories of classical, rock and 'mainstream' jazz. What occupies the field, world music, are the traditional musics of African, Asian and Native American provenance; certain musical traditions of North America and Western Europe (Irish traditional, Cajun); and Western-influenced popular styles that are built on the foundations of traditional musics of non-Western origins. (For example, Ladysmith Black Mambaso's *isicathamiya*, especially when 'co-opted' by Paul Simon.) Whatever the value, however, the metropolitan centre classifies margins in contrast to its own perceptions of who is 'Self', who is 'Other'.

To return to World Literature, Damrosch's book avoids the 'great civilizations' approach of *World Literature and Thought*. Rather than confining his purview to the Classic (the work of transcendental or foundational value) and the Masterpiece (the evolving Canon, whether ancient or modern), he permits us 'multiple windows' onto the world. He takes comparative study beyond the pre- and post-Treaty of Versailles stages, referred to earlier, to engage with both post-Second World War decolonization and a fourth stage, a world in anticipation of the fall of the Berlin Wall. Not in sympathy with Bloom's return to Western masterpieces, but more in sympathy with Bernheimer's recognition of an increasingly multicultural world, Damrosch replaces Homer's *Odyssey* and *Iliad* as foundational texts (the Western academic choice) with *The Epic of Gilgamesh* (1960). Instead of confining his focus to the cuneiform inscriptions on the stone tablets (the 'text'), he permits questions of context to intervene: Who recovered the tablets from the lost city of Nineveh and to what purpose was the recovery put? A chapter on Kafka returns this master of the universal (read, Western) 'Kafka-esque' to his ethnic origins as the Jew of Prague. From a 'window' opening onto the Third World, the Guatemalan activist and Nobel Peace laureate Rigoberta Menchú is studied not only in relation to an ethics of witness: When, in revolutionary politics, is truth verifiable as an individual experience? When, as the reportage of an exemplary tale? She is also studied in relation to an ethics of authority and ownership. Who is the 'author' who gets the royalties when the marginal foreign text (*Me Llamo Rigoberta Menchú...*) is 'improved' in translation for Western consumption? In the case of Menchú's story, by the Paris-based anthropologist Elizabeth Burgos, a collaboration that led to acrimony (see Burgos 1985; Menchú 1984).

In Damrosch's discussion of *I, Rigoberta Menchú* (the title of the English translation), we recognize not only a pragmatics of descriptive analysis but also a reading against the grain of authorial intent: In short, we recognize the ploys of Derridean deconstruction, Foucauldian asymmetries of power and – possibly influenced by his late colleague at Columbia – Said-like ideologies of representation. When so framed, is commentary on World Literature all that different from postcolonial critique? Schulze-Engler (2007) might say no, in that an anti-Western predominance has blunted postcolonialism not only to internal divisions within the metropole, but also to a world in transformation by rapid processes of globalism. A reminder of Schulze-Engler's use of the term, Transcultural Literature.

A postcolonial intrusion, nonetheless, need not necessarily be confined to a negative critique. In this respect, it is instructive to turn to Damrosch's case study of Milorad Pavić's Serbian novel, translated in English as *Dictionary of the Khazars* (1990). In his chapter on Pavić, 'The Poisoned Book' (2003: 260–76), Damrosch observes that Western European critical reception appreciated the textual play of a postmodernist (the subtitle, 'A Lexicon Novel in 100,000 Words', signals a language game), but that in the travels of his novel – in its translation, in its relocation to new literary circuits – Pavić's primary purpose got somewhat lost. His purpose was a re-assertion of Serbian nationalism, a consequence of which would be the break-up of Yugoslavia in the vicious ethnic-identity politics of the Balkan Wars.

Despite such a 'poisoned' book, Damrosch's conclusion to his chapter contradicts its own argument:

> In *Dictionary of the Khazars,* the nightmare of history becomes the dream of World Literature: a space of freedom from the limited viewpoints that enmesh nations and individuals alike, not excluding the book's own author. The reader's meal on the mailbox, and its hinted romantic aftermath, can form an antidote to the poison with which the book itself was written. (2003: 76)

Here, postcolonial critique could have checked the facile optimism of these closing words. Julien's 'postcolonial' stance would provide such a check on Moretti.

In a satellite link-up, Julien – then professor of Comparative Literature at Indiana University – took issue with Moretti's assumption that the novel is a mature European form, the transfer of which to the margins is inevitably fraught with difficulties of adjustment. In counterclaim, she invoked Said: that there could have been no heyday of the European novel without Empire; that the European novel was enabled by contact with spaces beyond Europe; and that, consequently, the novel form in its 'rise', or history, has always been more 'creole' than has been identified by metropolitan critics such as Watt (1957) and, by implication, Moretti (1998). In the African context, we are reminded of Hofmeyr's observation (2002) that *The Pilgrim's Progress* circulated initially in the colonies – in its missionary travels of Christian conversion – to be reined in only later by Leavis as a national text of vernacular English strength. Sympathetic to invention at the margins (that Achebe's voice is not 'disjunctive', but captures an easy commerce of tradition in modernity), Julien concludes, sceptically and angrily, that in Moretti 'we have not gone far from home at all: his new World Literature amounts to an old-world order'.[3]

Despite the less prescriptive, more descriptive character of the Stockholm symposium, the postcolonial – in Julien's response to Moretti – made its point, powerfully. We were reminded that the West and the Rest, or centres and peripheries, are not distinct entities, but can be interacting sites of both contestation and enrichment. Moretti's 'distant reading' of the peripheral voice had him residing a little too magisterially in the world, a Western European world. If the ideology critique of the Posts- can be too rigidly political, then Damrosch's failure to follow up on his own best insights on Pavić's poisoned book suggests that, in turn, a non-politicized descriptive analysis can be too laissez-faire.

Centre and edge

How to marshal my observations to focus on literature at my own edge, South Africa?[4] I was reminded at the symposium that, whether we like it or not, margins without centres do not make entire sense, ethically or aesthetically. The poet, political agitator and 1820 British settler, Thomas Pringle, for example, cannot be understood or appreciated outside the traffic to the eastern Cape frontier of both Augustan Reason and Scottish (Romantic) border ballads. Roy Campbell's poetry of the 1920s – in its attachment of southern landscapes to Nietzschean energy – requires European modernist reference. William Plomer's

---

[3] Julien's response to Moretti was published, subsequently. See Julien (2006).
[4] See Chapman (1996) on the literature from South Africa, to which I refer here.

novel, *Turbott Wolfe* (1926), owes a debt to both a 'heart of darkness' and Bloomsbury aesthetics. Thomas Mofolo's romance-novel *Chaka* (1925) subjects the Zulu kingdom to a Greek or Shakespearean dramatic inheritance. Despite its Black Consciousness affiliation, Soweto poetry of the 1970s invites a wider 'transcultural' reference: the Harlem Renaissance, Brechtian anti-poetry and US Beat poetry including Charles Olson's Black Mountain 'projective verse'. The township material – in its poverty, its desire for justice and its climate of revolt – lent to the Soweto voice a projection onto the anti-apartheid conscience of the world. World Literature, we are reminded, offers a perspective from somewhere.

If such a perspective is more evident in a conceptual frame, this is not to dismiss the value of World Literature as object: that is, as a list of significant works. If my focus on Damrosch's approach has seemed to sideline the 'object' frame of the multi-volume anthology *World Literature and Thought*, such has not been my intention. I have acknowledged appreciation of the array of texts that the project makes available to readers, most of whom (like me) are circumscribed by their own 'localities'; circumscribed in knowledge and reference, linguistically, culturally and philosophically. As a critic in the field of southern African literature, I was reminded by the chosen extract from Camões's *Os Lusíadas* (1572; *The Lusiads*) that this Portuguese Renaissance epic is less concerned with Vasco da Gama's rounding of the Cape, more with his arrival – a mercantile rather than a cultural arrival – at the Indian spice-port capital of Calicut, where serious 'transnational' business deals had to be negotiated.

It was instructive, also, to encounter the several entries on Chinese literature and thought of minds and sensibilities outside the Western or African purview, but indicative of the importance of a civilization that will play a key role in the twenty-first century. I did not know that Ts'ao Hsueh-ch'in's novel, *Hung-lou-meng*, first published in 1791 and translated as *The Dream of the Red Chamber* (1958), had attracted so much commentary, initially in China and later in the West, as to have created a scholarly focus of its own, 'Red Studies': A focus which, in its aims and scope, is comparable to 'Shakespeare Studies'. One is tempted to add to one's reading list this Confucian or Taoist morality tale, which has been interpreted as both a tragic story of star-crossed lovers and a veiled depiction of degeneracy among the wealthy class of a collapsing feudal society. A comparative essay on *The Dream of the Red Chamber* and *Romeo and Juliet*?

I introduce the academic, or student, exercise. My purpose, to return to my earlier point, is to lend to the category of World Literature a design that might negate charges of unmanageability and encourage teachability within the discipline of a literary education. For without teachability, World Literature remains so abstract, so arbitrary, as to fail to percolate down from academic journal debate to peers and students, where paradigm shifts can be explored, tested in seminar discussion, illustrated in the analysis of specific works and returned with substance and clarity to ongoing knowledge production.

How might World Literature impinge on South Africa? The mass circuit – the shelves of Exclusive Books bear this out – favours the latest genre fiction from the London or New York publishing industry; the latest motivational or pop psychology book on intimate suburban relationships. Is this internationalism or colonial dependency? Or white privilege? The educational and prestige circuits, taken together, may value several importations: the Bible; Bunyan's *The Pilgrim's Progress*; Shakespeare; English Romantic poetry; Dickens; Conrad; modernist influences, whether from Britain or the United States; the 'Harry Potter' books; and books adapted to film, such as *The Lord of the Rings* or the British period novel.

What, in contrast, has the world wanted from South Africa? Paton's *Cry, the Beloved Country*; Van der Post on the Bushmen; Nobel laureates Gordimer and Coetzee; Brink, Fugard, Wilbur Smith, Mandela's autobiography *Long Walk to Freedom* and, released simultaneously in nineteen countries in 2006, *Mandela, The Authorised Portrait*, a 365-page book that includes 60 original interviews with international and local personages, including Archbishop Desmond Tutu, Nadine Gordimer, Tony Blair, Bill Clinton and U2's Bono. (World Literature, indeed!) To extend South Africa to Africa: Nobel laureates Mahfouz and Soyinka; Achebe's interchanges of the traditional and the modern, as in *Things Fall Apart* (1958); and Ngũgĩ wa Thiong'o's commentary on 'decolonising the mind' (1986).

My list is eclectic, even cavalier. The exercise, nonetheless, provokes a repurposing of the category, World Literature. Imagine that, in South Africa, one were to construct a syllabus not under the rubric, 'South African Literature', but under the rubric, 'Literature in South Africa'. The mass circuit, according to sales, would need to include, among other bestsellers, Brown's *The Da Vinci Code*, which has been read by more South Africans than Coetzee's *Disgrace* or *Slow Man*. The educational circuit, alongside Shakespeare, would include the 'Harry Potter' novels; more promisingly from the local perspective, a recent interest in attractively produced children's versions of African folk tales. The prestige circuit, alongside Gordimer, Brink, Coetzee, Krog and Fugard, would include an international dimension: Atwood, Philip Roth, Kundera, Rushdie and Marquez. Books of poetry would require subsidy, as would most local literature that is not written originally in English. While Afrikaans still commands a small but loyal market, the position of African-language literatures – reliant on school prescriptions – is dire. Whatever its global expansion, World Literature contains within its category the death of 'marginal' languages. Yet, as my inclusion of Kundera and Marquez under the rubric 'Literature in South Africa' suggests, translation gains stature alongside comparison as a necessary methodological component of the field. Such a repurposing presents a further challenge, at least to the literary critic: How to ensure that the 'sociology' of literature subserves, rather than subverts, the literary pursuit? Not only, why does *The Da Vinci Code* sell well in South Africa, but also what qualities in, say, Marquez appeal to the South African reader?

Despite the exploratory value of the exercise, I return to my point: That as a field of study, World Literature requires a systematic mapping, a curriculum design which is more manageable than that offered by arbitrary book lists. Instead of starting with texts, therefore, we might follow Damrosch and start with categories of concept, in which texts provide illustrations of thematic clusters and genre-preponderance that have world reach. (World Literature as a literature from somewhere.)

Whose world? The example that follows neither endorses any asymmetrical relationship of the West projecting its centre power onto the margins nor wishes to reverse the binary by having 'the Empire writing back'. Rather, the design permits difference within nodes of coherence across regions or nations. Whether the 'home perspective' is the West, the East or Africa, or the North or the South, interaction is 'located' in the metaphor of multiple modernities:

- *Ancient pasts/magical enlightenment.* Whether one selects *The Epic of Gilgamesh*, the *Iliad*, the *Mahabharata* or any folk tradition, similar literary-critical challenges are encountered: recovery, translation, mediation, the bridge between past and present significance (hence, the text in relation to context and reception), novelty or commonality of generic classification.
- *The 'Classic'.* Timeless or time-bound, the universal or the particular; adaptation? (Should Classics syllabuses in South Africa be confined to Greece and Rome, or is the San/Bushman tradition our 'Classical' inheritance?)
- *Old world, new world.* The Renaissance, individualism, voyaging, colonialism, migrations.
- *'Masterpieces'.* National and/or postcolonial perspectives, mass/educational/prestige circuits, the 'male' gaze.
- *Modernisms (including postmodernisms).* Centre/edges, realism/fictionalization, high art, democratic purpose. (We are reminded that in both content and style, modernism arrived at the metropole from various 'edges',

whether the United States, Sweden, Ireland or Romania, to mention but a few.)
- *Politics and art*. Limits, strengths of localities, individual truth/exemplary truth, testimony as genre, the 'popular'.
- *The rise of the novel*. Romance/realism (we are transported back not only before Defoe, but before *Don Quixote*), the woman's voice, consumerism from the railway bookstall to the airport terminal.

While my course raises issues for discussion, it need not be 'issue-driven': That is, it need not pursue a politics of blame or a politics of redress, in which a younger generation of students is expected to atone for their parents' sins of either omission or commission. Should Joseph Conrad's *Heart of Darkness* feature under the sub-section 'Modernisms', for example, one cannot ignore a Derridean or Foucauldian interpretation of suspicion (there is no return to an apolitical New Criticism): Conrad was not free of several presuppositions and prejudices of his time. However, his manner of making the reader 'see', his shifts of register, of voice, between author and narrator, and his style of montage all complicate Achebe's conclusion that Conrad was a 'thorough-going racist' ([1975] 1988: 8). There is a qualitative difference – in the perspective art of what and how you see – between *Heart of Darkness* and its precursors in the Victorian adventure library.

I have not answered Damrosch's question, 'What is World Literature?'. I have suggested, nonetheless, that despite Moretti a pursuit of the question need not erase locatedness within global consideration, or vice versa. To stay with 'Modernisms', we could fruitfully compare T. S. Eliot's 'The Waste Land' ([1922] 1954) and Aimé Césaire's *Cahier d'un Retour au Pays Natal* (1938; trans. *Return to My Native Land*, 1969). What is gained, what is lost in Eliot's adaptation of US energy to European ennui? What is gained, what is lost in Césaire's adaptation of Parisian surrealism to French Caribbean aspiration? Where is the centre, where is the edge? We are invited to circulate beyond cultures of origin and apply comparative methods, either in translation or in the original language. To quote Schulze-Engler, '[i]t is this multipolar, decentred system of literary communication that lies at the heart of the idea of transcultural world literature' (2007: 29).

References

Abu-Lughad, J. (2001), 'Going beyond Global Babble', in A. King (ed.), *Culture, Globalisation, and the World System: Contemporary Conditions for the Representation of Identity*, 131–7, Minneapolis: University of Minnesota Press.

Achebe, C. (1958), *Things Fall Apart*, London: Heinemann African Writers Series.

Achebe, C. ([1975] 1988), 'An Image of Africa: Racism in Conrad's *Heart of Darkness*', *Hopes and Impediments: Selected Essays, 1965-1987*, 1-13, Oxford: Heinemann International.

Aldridge, A. (1986), *The Re-emergence of World Literature: A Study of Asia and the West*, London: Associated University Presses.

Ali, T. (1993), 'Literature and Market Realism', *New Left Review* 199: 140-5.

Appiah, K. (2006), *Cosmopolitanism: Ethics in a World of Strangers*, New York: W. W. Norton.

Apter, E. (2013), *Against World Literature: On the Politics of Untranslatability*, London: Verso.

Bakan, M. (2004), 'Foreword', in C. Muller (ed.), *South African Music: A Century of Traditions in Transformation*, xi-xv, Santa Barbara, CA: ABC-CLIO.

Bernheimer, C., ed. (1995), *Comparative Literature in the Age of Multiculturalism*, Baltimore, MD: Johns Hopkins University Press.

Bloom, A. (1987), *The Closing of the American Mind*, New York: Simon & Schuster.

Burgos, E. (1985), *Me llamo Rigoberta Menchú y así me nació la conscience*, Mexico City: Siglo Veintiuno.

Camões, L. ([1572] 1952), [*Os Lusíadas*] *The Lusiads*, trans. W. Atkinson, Harmondsworth: Penguin.

Carvalhal, T. (2001), 'Cultura e contextos', in E. Coutinho (ed.), *Fronteiras imaginadas: Cultura nacional /teoria internacional*, 147-54, Rio de Janeiro: Aeroplano.

Cèsaire, A. ([1938] 1969), *Return to My Native Land*, trans. J. Berger and A. Bostock, Harmondsworth: Penguin.

Chapman, M. (1996), *Southern African Literatures*, London: Longman.

Cooppan, V. (2001), 'World Literature and Global Theory: Comparative Literature for the New Millennium', *Symplōke* 9 (1/2): 15-43.

D'haen, T. (2006), 'Glocalizing the Novel', in G. Lindberg-Wada (ed.), *Studying Transcultural Literary History*, 144-51, Berlin: Walter de Gruyter.

D'Souza, D. (1991), 'Travels with Rigoberta', in [ed. anon.], *Illiberal Education: The Politics of Race and Sex on Campus*, 59-63, New York: Random House.

Damrosch, D. (2003), *What Is World Literature?* Princeton, NJ: Princeton University Press.

Dev, A. (1984), *The Idea of Comparative Literature in India*, Calcutta: Papyrus.

Dharwadker, V. (2001), *Cosmopolitan Geographies: New Locations in Literature and Culture*, New York: Routledge.

Eliot, T. S. ([1922] 1954), 'The Waste Land', *Selected Poems*, 51-74, London: Faber & Faber.

Eliot, T. S. ([1921] 1962), 'The Metaphysical Poets', in D. Enright and E. de Chickera (eds), *English Critical Texts*, 302-11, Oxford: Oxford University Press.

Gochberg, D. (1997), 'Introduction', in D. Gochberg, S. S. Dulai, E. D. Graham and K. W. Harrow (eds), *World Literature and Thought, Vol.1*, x–xi, Orlando, FL: Harcourt College.

Goethe, J. (1984), *Conversations with Eckermann (1823–1832)*, trans. J. Oxenford, San Francisco: North Point.

Guillén, C. (1993), *The Challenge of Comparative Literature*, trans. C. Franzen, Cambridge, MA: Harvard University Press.

Hofmeyr, I. (2002), 'How Bunyan Became English: Missionaries, Translation, and the Discipline of English Literature', *Journal of British Literary Studies* 41 (1): 84–119.

Julien, E. (2006), 'Arguments and Further Conjectures on World Literature', in G. Lindberg-Wada (ed.), *Studying Transcultural Literary History*, 13–29, Berlin: Walter de Gruyter.

Mandela, N. (2006), *Mandela: The Authorised Portrait*, in M. Maharaj and A. Kathrada (eds), Johannesburg: Wild Dog Press.

Menchú, R. (1984), *I, Rigoberta Menchú: An Indian Woman in Guatemala*, ed. E. Burgos-Debray, trans. A. Wright, London: Verso.

Miyoshi, M. (1991), *Off Center: Power and Culture Relations between Japan and the United States*, Cambridge, MA: Harvard University Press.

Mofolo, T. ([1925] 1981), *Chaka*, trans. D. Kunene, London: Heinemann African Writers Series.

Moretti, F. (1998), *Atlas of the European Novel, 1800–1900*, London: Verso.

Moretti, F. (2000), 'Conjectures on World Literature', *New Left Review* 1: 54–68.

Ngũgĩ wa Thiong'o (1986), *Decolonizing the Mind: The Politics of Language in African Literature*, London: James Currey.

Pavić, M. (1990), *Dictionary of the Khazars: A Lexicon Novel in 100,000 Words*, trans. C. Pribićević-Zorić, New York: Knopf.

Pérez-Firmat, G. (1989), *The Cuban Condition: Translation and Identity in Modern Cuban Literature*, Cambridge: Cambridge University Press.

Plomer, W. ([1926] 1980), *Turbott Wolfe*, Johannesburg: Ad. Donker.

Prempati, D. (1987), 'Why Comparative Literature in India?', in R. Dhawan (ed.), *Comparative Literature*, 53–65, New Delhi: Bahri.

Sandars, N. (ed. and trans.) (1960), *The Epic of Gilgamesh*, Harmondsworth: Penguin.

Schulze-Engler, F. (2007), 'Theoretical Perspectives: From Postcolonialism to Transcultural World Literature', in L. Eckstein (ed.), *English Literatures across the Globe: A Companion*, 20–32, Paderborn: Wilhelm Fink Verlag.

Schulze-Engler, F. (2012), 'The Commonwealth Legacy: Towards a Decentred Reading of World Literature', in B. Ashcroft et al. (eds), *Literature for Our Times: Postcolonial Studies in the Twenty-First Century*, 3–14, Amsterdam: Rodopi.

Strich, E. (1949), *Goethe and World Literature*, London: Routledge & Kegan Paul.

Ts'ao Hsueh-ch'in. ([1791] 1958), *The Dream of the Red Chamber*, trans. Chi-chen, New York: Twayne.

Venuti, L. (1998), *The Scandals of Translation: Towards an Ethics of Difference*, London: Routledge.

Wallerstein, I. (1997), 'The National and the Universal: Can There Be Such a Thing as World Culture?', in A. King (ed.), *Culture, Globalization, and the World-system: Contemporary Conditions for the Representation of Identity*, 97–105, Minneapolis: University of Minnesota Press.

Watt, I. (1957), *The Rise of the Novel: Studies in Defoe, Richardson, and Fielding*, London: Chatto & Windus.

Wilk, R. (1995), 'Learning to Be Local in Belize: Global Systems of Common Difference', in D. Miller (ed.), *Worlds Apart: Modernity through the Prism of the Local*, 20–31, London: Routledge.

2

Traversal, transversal: A poetics of migrancy

Robert J. C. Young
New York University

Um ihretwillen bricht er morsche Schranken der eigenen Sprache: Luther, Voß, Hölderlin, George haben die Grenzen des Deutsch erweitert. – Was hiernach für das Verhältnis von Übersetzung und Original an Bedeutung dem Sinn verbleibt, läßt sich in einem Vergleich fassen. Wie die Tangente den Kreis flüchtig und nur in einem Punkte berührt und wie ihr wohl diese Berührung, nicht aber der Punkt, das Gesetz vorschreibt, nach dem sie weiter ins Unendliche ihre gerade Bahn zieht, so berührt die Obersetzung flüchtig und nur in dem unendlich kleinen Punkte des Sinnes das Original, um nach dem Gesetze der Treue in der Freiheit der Sprachbewegung ihre eigenste Bahn zu verfolgen. (Benjamin 1972: 19–20)

For the sake of the pure language, he breaks through decayed barriers of his own language. Luther, Voss, Hölderlin, and George have extended the boundaries of the German language. What remains for sense, in its importance for the relationship between translation and original, may be expressed in the following simile. Just as a tangent touches a circle lightly and at but one point establishing, with this touch rather than with the point, the law according to which it is to continue on its straight path to infinity – a translation touches the original lightly and only at the infinitely small point of the sense, thereupon pursuing its own course according to the laws of fidelity in the freedom of linguistic flux. (Benjamin 1996: 261)

I

Walter Benjamin's enigmatic, surrealist description of the relational movements of language and sense in the act of translation works so well because it catches some of the unresolvable tensions at play between the concepts and the practice of translation: distinguishing as he does between the simultaneous operations of the language breaking through its own boundaries, frontiers (surpassing them, though only to extend and expand them, not to go beyond them) as it travels outwards towards other languages, a gesture towards the redemption of the totality of the lost universal language, and the fleeting effect of that moment when the sense collides and spins off obliquely in its own direction, turning the performance of translation into a set of processes at odds with each other, as if language and signification operated individually in the distinct realms of classical and quantum physics. Any gesture of translation, whether linguistic or 'cultural', will potentially always involve these two aspects as it comes to grip with the tense interplay between material medium and the elusive semantic values which it expresses, evokes and recreates. The traditional fundamental question asks whether it can transition to a different body while preserving its sense or scripted identity, to which the answer could be summed up by that conversational responsive phrase so beloved of the British, 'yes, no!', or alternatively 'no no!', meaning, of course, as a double negative, yes, but still somehow with a lingering resonance of the negative, because the speaker, though in agreement, is about to add some additional, supplementary point of her own – which in the case of translation, would always involve an enhancement that would add to that which has been lost. But as the signification abruptly veers off in its own, divergent direction, where does what is lost in translation go? Where does what is gained come from? Benjamin's tangent metaphor suggests that translation involves illimitable collisions, in which the sense does not intersect directly with the other language but rebounds abruptly on its own course as it lurches away from the original, as 'off it goes on' (Beckett 1959: 293), bouncing diagonally from one implication to another, now as wave, now as particle, setting off on its infinite trajectory into the beyond. And logically, as on a billiard table, according to classical physics, with the 'touch' of the tangent, the original will also absorb its impact, potentially moving off in a different direction as well, ineluctably if almost invisibly transformed. Above all, the binarism of 'source' and 'target' language breaks down. Signifier and signified get separated, connotation and denotation get deflected and refracted. If speaking, according to Émile Benveniste and Julia Kristeva splits the subject, translation splits the sign. The imagined smooth flow of one language into another is revealed rather as a passageway pockmarked from the impact of unpredictable transverse trajectories.

Much more could be and has been said about this passage. I have cited it here as a way of beginning to think about a topic that forms a constant theme in Frank Schulze-Engler's lucid and always illuminating essays on issues of difference and the transcultural, questions that necessarily form a constant theoretical backdrop to his remarkable work on transnational Anglophone, particularly African, literatures. In the preparation of my chapter for this volume, re-reading Schulze-Engler's *œuvre* as a whole, rather than article by article as they have appeared over the years, has been a fascinating experience that inevitably provoked me to return to those very theoretical issues which he raises and discusses so lucidly and proactively. This chapter therefore is intended as an act of homage in which I want to think through again some of the concerns that he confronts in his work, most of which remain operative today.

Many of the key questions are encapsulated in Schulze-Engler's insightful article 'What's the Difference? Notes towards a Dialogue between Transdifference and Transculturality' (Schulze-Engler 2006), in which as a self-confessed 'sympathizing sceptic', he charges the concept of 'transdifference', developed by Erlangen professors Helmbrecht Breinig and Klaus Lösch, with 'a peculiar conservatism in its conceptualization of culture in the contemporary world, particularly in its failure to acknowledge the importance of globalized modernity on the one hand and in its persistent misunderstanding of transculturality on the other' (123). With the benefit of hindsight fifteen years later, what seems curious about the concept of 'transdifference' is that, despite all the talk in that period of a newly globalized world becoming merged through irresistible flows from one culture to another, for the most part it remains a largely German conversation that did not get picked up elsewhere. The global discussions of 'difference' that circulated from the 1980s to the 2000s were themselves an example of what Edward Said called 'traveling theory', an early version of what Barbara Cassin would later characterize as the 'untranslatable', by which she meant not that things were altogether untranslatable but that the cross-over between languages, incompatibilities between words and meanings, results in the new translated denotations and connotations setting off in a different direction, as in Benjamin's metaphor (Cassin 2004; Said 1983: 226–47). As it travels across the continents, Said suggested, theory too gets transformed by the particular situations in which it finds itself so that the significance and implications vault off on different routes. So over the decades 'difference' moved, with intervals and time lags, from Saussure in Switzerland to the linguistics of the early Soviet Union and the Prague school, to the structuralist Claude Lévi-Strauss and the fundamentally revisionist versions of Hélène Cixous, Gilles Deleuze and Jacques Derrida in France, to the UK and to the United States where it took over the French gendered inflection and added the postcolonial, after which, almost unrecognizable, it moved back to France eventually to be conflated with Black Lives Matter into what is now demonized as 'Islamo-Gauchisme', emerging in its own time in Germany where it was rewritten yet again for the optimistic era of German reunification and the early benignly viewed promises of globalization. This suggests that despite the unification of the world economy after the fall of the Second World, at the institutional level, some of the theoretical debates in universities in different national states retain their own local preoccupations and idioms, above all in the humanities and social sciences. Descriptions of different, formerly discrete cultures now all flowing ineluctably one into the other on the model of global just-in-time supply-line trajectories of commodities or of the ravaging currents of world tourism disregard the unevenness of globalization, its fractures and divisions. Any experience of separate university systems shows that, despite the fashion for 'global rankings', they at least can remain relatively separate, autonomous islands in terms of intellectual considerations that seem relevant to their specific situations. Not only do they have their own political, social and economic contexts, conditions and hierarchies, but the institutional form of universities also differs quite widely. They operate as distinct intellectual spaces or economies with their own local debates and particular forms of understanding.

Having said that, it may well have been Schulze-Engler's incisive critique of 'transdifference', in which he points to the disconcerting instability and mobility of meanings ascribed to the concept across a number of articles of the early 2000s, that accounts for why 'transdifference' seems in retrospect to have operated as an end point rather than a new beginning for perceptions of difference. As he delicately suggests, in their formulations, Breinig and Lösch seem to miss the basic point that all recent accounts of difference had shifted its conceptualization from binary to non-binary models which disallow any possibility that the one can 'transcend' the other (2006: 105). The latter think about difference in a different way: They are examples of what Edouard Glissant calls a 'poetics of relation' – where identity is relational, not substantive (Glissant 1990). While it is asserted that 'transdifference' can be differentiated from earlier terms such as transculturation, hybridity and borderland by 'not pointing in the direction of an overcoming of difference, the blending and merging of properties' (Breinig and Lösch 2006: 106), those very terms – transculturation, hybridity and borderland – were developed precisely as models that do not involve a merging of differences but rather name difference's disruptive force. While distinguished in this way from other terms denoting non-binary thinking of difference, including Derrida's *différance*, such earlier non-binary modes of thought are nevertheless included within transdifference, which is defined as 'all that which resists or escapes the construction of meaning based on an exclusionary and conclusionary binary model' (108). As it happens, this statement would work rather well to describe exactly the technique of bringing to light the hidden supplementary structures of remnants that subvert normative differential oppositions that Derrida employs, suggesting that 'transdifference' may really be no more than a reworking of *différance*, except that since the latter constitutes neither a word nor a concept it marks a dynamic effect unassimilable to the idioms of theory. Whether or not transdifference is really conceptually distinguishable in these terms, it certainly is distinctive in its claim to offer a meta theory of difference that incorporates or collects together all others, a claim already realized in the publication of the impressive collection *Differenzen anders denken: Bausteine zu einer Kulturtheorie der Transdifferenz* (Allolio-Näcke et al. 2005), in which transculturation, hybridity, interculturalism and multiculturalism are all presented as 'building blocks' that enable a master *Kulturtheorie* of 'transdifference', even while Breinig and Lösch in the same volume themselves retreat from the idea that transdifference functions as an umbrella concept (Breinig and Lösch 2004: 454). In 2006, however, we are informed that the collective term has the effect of removing the very force of all the earlier concepts which it is claimed to subsume: '[P]henomena of transdifference have no intrinsically subversive effect on the *practice* of hierarchical boundary maintenance. Transdifference is ... quickly subdued by the discourses of identity and power' (2006: 113–14). The difference of transdifference, therefore, lies in its powerlessness. If transdifference has no practical effects, we need only cite two practical examples to think of how far earlier non-binary differential relational theories of identity have transformed the contemporary world. Judith Butler's stress on gender as performativity in *Gender Trouble* (1990) suggested that even 'factual' designations of binary difference such as gender in its biological sense were, in social terms, actually a matter of an acting out of prescribed roles, which allowed sex and gender to be separated from each other. Butler's hugely influential intervention meant that 'identities' were no longer anchored to the realm of binary oppositions founded on the biological binary of sex. Freud's 'anatomy is destiny' no longer applied, so much so that today gender itself has been redefined in terms of non-binary differences, which we shall discuss shortly. Two years before Butler, Stuart Hall had made a comparable argument with respect to ethnicity (Hall 1988): In Hall's description of 'new ethnicities', the colour of your skin meant that you were no longer defined from the outside by ancestry, your ancestors' history, or the culture of your so-called 'ethnic group', for the 'new ethnicities' that Hall described demonstrated that you could create your own identity from moment to moment, defined by no one in advance, performed as you wished to make it. In other words, you can characterize your own ethnic identity yourself – unlike race, which is defined by others and put upon you by others as if you were an object, even if its 'factual' status as race was actually a mythic creation invented by a strategic alliance of Euro-American science, medicine and culture. As Edward W. Said put it (though without the element of performativity), identity becomes a matter of affiliation rather than filiation (1983: 16–20).

Breinig and Lösch's project in effect seeks to manage difference, removing any potential disruptive elements, totalizing all forms of difference into one assimilable 'transdifference'. However, if difference is being employed not just as oppositional binaries or what escapes them but also as in Saussurian differences without positive terms (Saussure 1971: 162; 2002: 64–75), then there cannot be a general theory of difference as a collective concept subsuming all distinct forms of difference by gathering them into itself. Non-binary differences will always be particular instances that cannot be raised to the level of the general because they refuse the universal and remain excessive to it. Every 'theory' of difference amounts to an account of a particular dynamic unique to its own situation: Difference is what challenges the concept as such (Derrida and Ferraris 2018). It cannot be then 'applied' to or assimilated to a second apparatus or location. Difference in its poststructuralist forms requires in other words a teleological suspension of the universal because the traces of its singularity can never be raised to the level of, or assimilated to, the general. The dialectics of its difference can never be subsumed into any more general concept, that is, cannot be abolished, affirmed, assimilated, collected up, eliminated and preserved, reconciled or transcended. They remain strangely queer, at odds, quantum to classical, putting the universal out of joint.

To the extent that discussions of cultural difference in the later-twentieth and early twenty-first centuries emerged in Europe largely in response to global immigration into the continent, then the whole invocation of 'difference', even if intended to stake out a liberal perspective, was a well-meant faux pas. Historically, the fundamental strategy of racialism in the academy and of racism in practice was designed to objectify certain other people and characterize them as different. To endorse difference in any theory of human or social difference is already to find oneself travelling on the same tracks whether one intended to or not: To emphasize difference in others, to characterize others as 'other', or even worse, 'the Other', is to make and mark out a signifying, foreignizing differentiation whose designation can be extended further, and not always in a benign direction (Young 2012: 36-9). The whole obsession with difference in terms of people involves the continuation of the Enlightenment drive for knowledge by means of classification through differentiation which, in the social and human sphere, cannot avoid becoming hierarchical. Since Blumenbach, Kant, Cuvier and de Gobineau, accounts of human differences have typically also involved rankings, especially when those theorizing them have belonged to a white majority (Young 1995: 62-117). In general, those categorized as different have always been people of colour or minorities. To characterize another person as different from yourself as a speaking subject may not be an issue, though of course this is something that psychoanalysis has much to say about. However, to label some others in terms of a 'difference' that distinguishes them from other others who are not given that label, is divisive. 'Equivalence in difference' is not just a problem for language and linguistics (Jakobson 1962-71: 2.262). To identify with difference as an individual subject is not the same as identifying others in the plural as 'other' and therefore defining them purely by an absence of sameness. Any theory of difference or differences, even if it is concerned with coexistence or fusion or trying to reach out to or come to know 'the Other', is trying to solve a problem that the characterization of difference, of other people as different, other, othered, created in the first place (Young 2012: 36-9). As a concept, in other words, difference in this context is a problem that has been self-created: The Other exists solely in you who has produced it. There is no 'Other' out there in the real, there are only real living people, though individuals or groups can be othered by society and their subjectivity reified into a stereotyped object which identifies them as different. As Frantz Fanon pointed out, it all depends on subject positions. Being characterized as different, being raced, turns you into an object that is not yourself, an alienated self that is incommensurate with your own subjective reality (Fanon 1952). The invocation of difference therefore, in that context, has passed, or should have done. Given that so much of the preoccupation with 'cultural' difference has developed in the context of migration and immigration in Western societies, one wonders why the exorbitant and ultimately hostile focus on differences was ever initiated at all, instead of likenesses, correspondences, forms of interaction? Why did we not follow from the outset the example of Aristotle in Book IX of *The Nicomachean Ethics*, where the ethical gesture is to transform apparent unlikeness into likeness and friendship?

Energy has now moved on to the more practical projects of diversifying institutions, to decolonizing the curriculum and the protocols and projects of academic research. The transience of 'transdifference' no doubt also stemmed from the fact that the terms of the debate were already changing elsewhere as the focus of difference shifted from 'culture' to gender. It's impossible today to think the term 'transdifference' without primarily associating it with 'trans' and trans people, with the epochal shift in the late twentieth century away from defining sex and gender roles in binary terms. 'Transgender' (as opposed to 'transsexual') is used to designate a 'non-binary' identification: that is, someone who does not identify with the sex that they were assigned at birth nor with any other specific, restrictive gender characterization, binary or otherwise, either – rather with agender, 'they/them'.[1] Within the contemporary context of gender fluidity, today's students can react to 1980s feminist texts that critique oppressive gender power structures but still operate on a fundamental male/female binary, such as Hélène Cixous's 1975 essay 'The Laugh of the Medusa' (2010: 37–68), almost as negatively as 1970s students reacted to the misogynist masculist literary texts analysed by Kate Millett, mirroring the fierce, at times acrimonious, contemporary debates between certain feminists and groups which affirm non-binary gender identities. Gender is made of multiplicities that relativize each other, not two antithetical points of identification. Already, in his 2008 discussion of the 'transcultural', Mark Stein opened up this transformative connection with gender. 'Trans' as a non-defining, non-binary gender term raises in turn the question of what is involved when it is put together with 'culture'.

When Breinig and Lösch develop their 2002 discussion of the term 'culture' by returning to Tylor's definition from 1870 (Breinig and Lösch 2002), we know immediately that their own conceptualizations, as Schulze-Engler points out, are going to remain inherently conservative, as the culture concept is resuscitated out of its anthropological grave as 'still valid' (Schulze-Engler 2006: 18). Schulze-Engler points to the fact that many anthropologists today would not use the term culture at all because its original conceptualization to denote the everyday 'culture' of primitive people, rather than the high culture of civilization, has remained deeply problematic, beginning with the model and methodology whereby the 'culture' is constructed by an outside (Western anthropologist) observer who claims to be entirely detached from it even as he or she creates its representation and institutes the limits that enable it to be constructed as a distinct 'culture'. Creating a culture by defining its boundaries may seem to be conceptually necessary but remains incoherent, as Etienne Balibar, Ulf Hannerz and Wolfgang Welsch have suggested (Balibar 2002; Hannerz 1996; Welsch 1992, 1999). Does 'culture' in the sense of the totality of practices of a particular society

---

[1] For some recent theoretical discussions, see Marty (2021) and Nancy and Goh (2021).

really exist? Where? Where are its boundaries and who gets to identify them, especially as 'culture'? In a recent survey of anthropological theories of culture and their demise by the end of the twentieth century, Carola Lentz does argue that anthropologists should continue to think about culture – but only so that they can observe the workings of its adapted, translated use in other disciplines (2017), where, as Schulze-Engler points out (2006: 123), it is generally used in a 'fuzzy' undefined way, skirting the problem of how meaningful it is to talk about a 'culture' or 'cultures' at all. Even if we set aside the question of whether we should still be using the concept of culture, other problems remain: As Gloria Anzaldúa put it bluntly, 'Culture is made by those in power – men' (1987: 16). A more insidious way that 'culture' is still being perpetuated comes in the concept of 'multiculturalism' which is sometimes erroneously identified with postcolonial perspectives. In fact, postcolonial writers were from the beginning critiquing the idea of a society being made up of distinct sets of populations with their own 'culture', that is, 'multiculturalism', a theory that was still being endorsed by Angela Merkel until October 2010. Had she read Zadie Smith's *White Teeth* (2000) she might have been made aware ten years earlier of how problematic, divisive and dysfunctional the concept of multiculturalism really is.

Although 'traveling theory' does allow for transformation, it has been also surprising to see earlier anthropological accounts, particularly that of Fernando Ortiz in *Contrapunteo cubano del tabaco y azúcar* (*Cuban Counterpoint: Tobacco and Sugar*, 1940), conjured up as if Ortiz's concept of 'transculturation' can be easily put side by side with, or assimilated to, later poststructuralist non-binary forms of difference as relational not substantive. This misunderstanding is noted by Schulze-Engler (2006: 128). The figure of Ortiz is invoked, of course, as a result of Welsch's 1990s elaboration of the concept of 'transculturality', even though Welsch himself does not mention him in his original essays (Welsch 1994, 1996, 1999).[2] In the 'transdifference' debates, some summaries of Ortiz rarely seem to get beyond the terms of Bronislaw Malinowski's highly problematic introduction, which deliberately misleads the reader by mis-characterizing the work of the Chicago School in terms of its use of the term 'acculturation', a claim duly repeated without challenge by generations of commentators.[3] Ortiz's own writing style, at once anthropological, historical and poetic, does not fit easily

---

[2] Reichardt (2020: 74) suggests that Ortiz 'might have inspired' Welsch. Welsch, on the other hand, says that it was Wittgenstein who provided him with 'the greatest help for a transcultural concept of culture' (1996: 25).
[3] On Malinowski's relations with the Chicago School, and Herskovits' reaction to his preface to Ortiz's book, see Santí (2005: 204–9).

into the objectivist discourse of sociology, philosophy or cultural theory, even in the reduced version of its English translation. When considered in the Cuban context, Ortiz's transculturation, as Santí points out, takes more the form of a sung dialogic contestation, *controversia*, a musical dispute rather than the production of harmony as in European musical counterpoint (Santí 2005: 174–5).[4] For this reason, it should not be simply identified with Said's theory of the contrapuntal as if they were the same thing: Indeed, despite the references that are sometimes made to Said in discussions of Ortiz, following Fernando Coronil's introduction to the English edition (1995: xxxix–xl), Said himself, surprisingly, seems to have been altogether unaware of Ortiz's book and never refers to him (Santí 2005: 171–2).[5] In musical terms, Said's contrapuntal forms of critical thinking will always in the end add up to a harmonious totality – an aspect which became stronger as the late dialogue with Daniel Barenboim developed. Music became a vision for ways in which Palestinians and Israelis might live together harmoniously. In Ortiz's version, *contrapunteo* takes the form of a staged dialectical tournament between a personified tobacco and sugar, Don Tabaco and Doña Azúcar, whose competitive interactions during the colonial history of Cuba produced the distinctive forms of Cuban culture, in which Don Tabaco claims final victory. This *contrapunteo*, the dialectical play of relations between sugar and tobacco in their contrasting qualities as commodities, reflect and embody the differences of the people of Cuba – light and dark, sweet and bitter, white and black, woman and man – together with the labour relations of their production, the forms of their consumption, the effects on the environment, that allow Ortiz to trace the specific history of the country while finally suggesting through the *controversia* between tobacco and sugar that, despite the exorbitant wealth produced by sugar for foreign plantation owners, Cuban culture is primarily that of tobacco, that is black, that is African. It was sugar that 'prefirió los brazos esclavos, el tabaco los hombres libres' ('preferred slave labor; tobacco, free men'; Ortiz 1995: 81; [1940] 2002: 234): Tobacco is identified with freedom. The political edge of the book is primarily directed against the white settler colonial Hispanic culture of Doña Azúcar which, though employing slaves for the sugar plantations, customarily ignored the importance of the African slave and indigenous populations – who made up around a third of the Cuban population – to the history and identity

---

[4] See also Santí (2005: 262 n 74) for a comparison with Bakhtin.
[5] Reichardt (2020: 79) claims that Said 'picks up Ortiz' idea' in his late works on music, despite Ortiz's name never being mentioned. See Santí (2005: 171–4) for an account of their differences.

of Cuba. For the same reasons, in his other work Ortiz was also concerned to emphasize the importance of African music and jazz for Cuban music (Ortiz 1950). The particular, distinct 'culture' of Cuba that Ortiz is elaborating has been produced by the dialectical interaction of people and commodities in a colonial slave society in which tobacco won out over sugar, not simply by different immigrants importing their own cultures and mixing together to produce a heterogeneous harmonious landscape. If transposed to Europe, then, Ortiz's model can never correspond with any exactitude to a situation of immigrants, many of them people of colour, being incorporated into a dominant historically white European culture, without any reference to their specific relation to a commodity production which dominates the national economy. To invoke Ortiz, moreover, would be to suggest that in any dialogic contestation between immigrant and European culture, then tobacco will win over sugar, that is black over white, revolutionary freedom over oppression.

Given its dialectical force, Ortiz's account can never be characterized as simply a nationalist representation of the culture of Cuba, since he is writing against settler colonial claims for Cuba as an outpost of Castilian Spain and upending them by portraying the baroque forms of Cuban culture as the product of its Black population. He does not even stop there, for unacknowledged by many commentators, much of the book is concerned with the transculturation that the export of these two commodities back into Europe brought about in the cultures of Europe itself, radically transforming them too. For unexpectedly, given how the book is customarily described, a major part of Cuban transculturation is taken up with the way that the gift of tobacco, which the friendly indigenous natives of Guanahaní offered Columbus in the very first moment of intercultural relations between 'Europe' and 'America' as he stepped onto American soil, went on to affect and transform Europe too. Tobacco created not just a new local social milieu of the Spanish conquistadors and the slaves who would be imported from Africa to grow the tobacco along with sugar on the plantations, but also very rapidly revolutionized the whole social world of Europe, and as quickly, the Middle East and Africa:

> La historia del tabaco ofrece uno de los más extraordinarios procesos de transculturación. Por la rapidez y extensión con que se propagaron los usos de aquella planta apenas fue conocida por los descubridores de América, por las grandes oposiciones que se presentaron y vencieron, y por el radicalísimo cambio que el tabaco experimentó en toda su significación social al pasar de las culturas del Nuevo Mundo a las del Mundo Viejo. (Ortiz 1940: 414)

> The history of tobacco affords an example of one of the most extraordinary processes of transculturation, by reason of the rapidity and extent to which the use of this plant spread as soon as it became known to the discoverers of America, the great opposition it met and overcame, and the very profound change operated in its social significance as it passed from the cultures of the New World to those of the Old. (Ortiz 1995: 183)

Tobacco quickly became a global cultural phenomenon: Through the gift of cigars the indigenous Caribs altered the social practices of the majority of the world's population more radically than perhaps any people have done before the invention of the iPhone, and so too with sugar, until the discovery of the chemical process of how to extract sugar from beet in 1747 by the German chemist Andreas Marggraf (Marggraf 1747). Transculturation was never, therefore, just about cultural interactions between different people in the same country: It was always about their dialogic interaction with dominant commodities, and the transformative effects of travelling commodities through a globalized commerce. Transculturation, as Ortiz conceptualized it, was never concerned with the introduction of difference or heterogeneity into a monoculture as in the case of hybridity. It's about the production of a new culture from scratch starting from the *tabula rasa* produced by colonial occupation after the new colonizers had killed off most of the indigenous population and imported African slaves to labour on the plantations. The charged interplay, contested crossings and transformations that Ortiz describes, as the power structures of master and slaves that underlie the infrastructural part of the counterpoint might already suggest, means that there was a hidden radical element lurking in the doubled nature of that gift of tobacco, disrupting dominant European culture and colonialism and looking towards a postcolonial future: 'En el torcido, el fuego y las humosas volutas del tabaco hubo siempre algo de revolucionario, algo de retorcimiento bajo la opresión, de ardimiento destructor y de elevación liberadora en el azul de las ilusiones' (Ortiz 1940: 150). ['In the fabrication, the fire and spiralling smoke of a cigar there was always something revolutionary, a kind of protest against oppression, the consuming flame and the liberating flight into the blue of dreams' (Ortiz 1995: 14).]

In the German context, with the exception of Dagmar Reichardt's recent essay (2020), Ortiz has tended to be abstracted from his own context, as if he were just another contemporary theorist of difference and transculturation, with comparatively little interest evident in transculturation's own important and long intellectual lineage in South America. As Coronil mentions in a brief paragraph, transculturation was developed in further modalities by the Uruguayan literary critic Ángel Rama in the context of his discussion of the Peruvian novelist and ethnographer José María Arguedas, and in doing so placing an additional and more emphatic emphasis on the further contrapuntal tensions produced by layerings of Amerindian cultural traces within South American Trans-Modernities (Coronil 1995: xxxvi; Rama 1982; Santí 2005: 170, 210). It is in South America too where we can also find a very different account of globalization than that of seamless flows. Rama invokes Ortiz to claim the survival of an indigenous culture that remains differentiated from Western global culture, even if it has been inevitably affected by European invasion and settler colonialism. A related argument has been proposed more recently by the Argentinian philosopher Enrique Dussel, who suggests that, from a South American perspective, the technical and economic globality of Modernity

> está lejos de ser una *globalización cultural de la vida cotidiana valorativa* de la mayoría de la humanidad. Es desde esa potencialidad no-incluida de donde surge, desde la «exterioridad» alterativa (en cuanto nunca asumida; en cuanto despreciada y valorada como «nada»), un proyecto de «trans»-Modernidad, un «más allá» que trasciende la Modernidad occidental...
>
> Hablar en cambio de «trans»-Modernidad, como lo haremos a lo largo de todo este libro, exigirá una nueva interpretación de todo el fenómeno de la Modernidad, para poder contar con momentos que *nunca estuvieron incorporados a la Modernidad europea*, y que subsumiendo lo mejor de la Modernidad europea y norteamericana, afirmará «desde *fuera* » de ella misma *componentes esenciales de las propias culturas excluidas*, para desarrollar una nueva política futura, la del siglo XXI. (2007: 143–5)
>
> is not a cultural globalization of the valued daily life of the majority of humanity. From that non-included potentiality, the alternative 'exteriority' (never assumed; scorned and not valued), arises a project of 'trans'-Modernity, 'far from' Western Modernity. ... To speak of 'trans'-Modernity will demand a new interpretation of the whole phenomenon of Modernity, to count on moments which were never incorporated into European Modernity, and which subsuming the better of European and north American Modernity, will affirm 'from outside' itself essential components of the excluded cultures, to develop a new political future, that of the twenty-first century. (Dussel 2011: 129–31)

And that 'trans'-Modernity is the decolonial difference to which Caribbean and South American transculturation takes us.

II

By the beginning of the twenty-first century, two centuries of anti-Hegelianism seemed finally to have won through. The decline and reconceptualization of dialectical and binary thinking has been the philosophical marker of the postmodern age, indeed the fundamental characteristic of 'postmodernism' itself, most evident and indeed fully elaborated with respect to 'difference', whether in semantics, philosophy, 'culture', art, or gender and sexuality. Non-binary concepts of difference have undermined binary thinking so much that difference itself has been transformed according to the protocols of transitivity, a schema already anticipated many years ago in the realm of linguistics, not simply in Saussure's theory of the sign, but also, for example, in Nikolai Troubetskoy's *sprachbund* (Jakobson 1962–71: I.137–43). Since we no longer have discrete binary genders, on the same principles we no longer have discrete cultures or languages or literatures. In that sense, translation, as some have suggested, has become at once superfluous and the continuous state of being for language and culture, not in the traditional sense of moving from source to target language across a binary divide, but rather through invoking its extended resonances of unsettlement – the transitional, the transient, *la traversée*, the crossing. What would it mean to focus on, to trace, the transitory trail of the trans rather than competing (non) concepts of difference? To think such crossings from the perspective of its agents rather than those already living in place trying to come to terms with suffering its opposite? The *attraversamento* rather than the *contrappasso*?

But not, perhaps, the 'transcultural'. The difficulty in conceptual terms is that just as the decline of binary oppositions has undone the basis of older forms of identity politics so too culture as such becomes hard to conceptualize at all if it is no longer bounded, since concepts by definition are developed through the creation of boundaries. In that situation, the prefix 'trans' becomes meaningless when attached to culture. Much contemporary critical writing in the literary sphere avoids this theoretical problem by simply celebrating evidence of 'cross-cultural' interactions, interventions, sensibilities, in contemporary literary texts that evidence the disruption and decline of monocultures (if they ever really existed). Outside the realms of gender and sexualities studies, we have been less adventurous in thinking through new theoretical models that reconceptualize the trans. In this landscape, the term difference as such obviously no longer cuts the mustard, but one element that the trans still emphatically retains at the level of the connotations of the signified is that of the transgressive. Breinig and Lösch reject or seek to subsume theories that are subversive or bear marks of 'normative value judgment' (2006: 114), but the hovering connotation of the aura of trespass and the transgressive will never disappear from the trans which cannot be subsumed in such a way as to lose its transgressivity. The word 'transgress' derives from the Latin *transgress-*, participial stem of *transgredī* to step across (*Oxford English Dictionary* [*OED*]), and thus operates as a deliberate act of translation in its guise of moving across, transferring, *sconfinare*. Transgress means to pass over or beyond, to go beyond the limits (of the law), to trespass. Given its relation to traditional social norms, trans will always remain associated with this transverse unsettling edge, just as the term 'queer' has been reworked to mean not simply gay but has become a way of rethinking and re-reading by erasing the borders between gay and straight as well as other conceptual distinctions that are symptomatic of normative binary thinking. Obliquity and movement are all. This allows us to rethink the differential in terms of the trans as a transgressive structure working against or, especially, at a tangent to the norm.

What if we begin by thinking of globalization as fundamentally disruptive, producing unevenness, disparities, inequalities, rather than in terms of smooth flows? The idea of flows, of peoples, of commodities, offers an unsituated process without ascribed agency or direction appropriate to a society of *affluence*: An abundance of words, feelings, riches, possessions, all pouring in. At the same time, that affluence itself sets up the possibility of migration and immigration in the noun's more literal if less common meaning of a 'general movement of people in a particular direction, a moving crowd' (*OED*). Flows may be imagined as taking place globally in a general model, but actual flows, whether of goods, or capital, or people, operate in a particular direction or directions that are sometimes haphazard, doubled, back and forth. All of these things only 'flow' metaphorically, for the word flow applies specifically to liquids. When the metaphor gets invoked to describe people, and in particular migrants, it begins to mix with the affective everyday language of racism: '[M]igrants are flowing in!' and then, 'migrants are pouring/flooding in!', at worst accompanied by the language of being 'swamped'.

But migrants, refugees, asylum seekers are not water. They are individual human beings who do not amount collectively to any form of liquid. Only seas or currents in rivers flow. The 'flow' of goods does not generally conjure up phobic responses: that is reserved for people. If individuals, refugees, illegal migrants are obliged to move from one place, one country to another, then that transitive movement will have to involve some form of passage, crossing, recrossing across a plethora of thresholds, impasses, openings. Migrants do not flow, unencumbered, in a single direction. Passage, *carrefours*, traversals, transient though they may be, can be the perduring tormented situation of migrants, the transitus, for many remain on the move, never reach what might have been their imagined final destination, never know when they have 'finally' arrived, or perhaps within the necessary short-term thinking that comes with suddenly having to leave your country and your home under some form of duress, any destination remains vague and unresolved as you are bounced to and fro by the ebb and flow of political strife and economic instability. Either way, as Fanon observed, the only thing that is permanent for the refugee is insecurity (2011: 648). The majority of migrants and refugees from the global South remain within the global South, often in the vast camps on the fringes of cities such as Cairo or mazed, packed right inside them in unbelievable density as in Beirut. Only a small fraction of migrants and refugees make their way to that part of the world known as 'the West'. Arriving in some country of the global North, let us say in Europe, may form part of the haphazard journey, but even that does not by any means end the experience of crossing and passage, either because the migrant continues to move from one country to another, or because even if he or she stops in one place (perhaps for a moment, a week, a month, a year, a life…), the traversal only takes on different forms, the crossings continue, ricocheting from one place to another in perpetual motion. The migrant must encounter, navigate changing environments, experiencing the practices and institutions of an already situated population at every point of arrival and departure. Now the chance and dangers of constant physical movement are transformed into a different form of threat: The migrant becomes the site of 'cultural difference' and the object of analysis of the 'transcultural'. Never the agent because such processes are always described from the outside, in other words from the perspective of those already domiciled in the host nation.

In earlier days, the situated migrant who has settled, perhaps temporarily who knows, certainly not the migrant herself, would be characterized as an 'exile'. But 'exile' as a term has a certain dignity and nobility to it, and de facto if not de jure, the connotation and aura of a certain class. Exiles, to put it bluntly, tended to be aristocrats, or at least middle class, like Prince Nikolai Troubetzkoy or Walter Benjamin or Edward Said. Modern migrants, many of whom may well in fact be middle class, are not given the dignity of being described as exiles, even if they too have no choice. Arguably, however, this is in its own way a positive development, for calling migrants exiles, as sometimes still happens in France, also implies that they are temporary, that they will ultimately be going back to wherever they came from, that they do not form a part of the settled community. Far from the glamour of the exile, the terms used today to describe migrants are typically negative and derogatory, 'illegal aliens', or simply 'illegals' as they say in the United States. Even among more liberal circles, the experience of migrancy is reduced to the jostle of differences. The 'cultural difference' that migrants are commonly thought to bring with them, to represent, always forms part of a power relation. Outside of texts, as soon as we move to speech, difference will always be embedded in structures of power, which is why difference, whether binary or non-binary, is never simply difference, and why the act of invoking difference will always remain a stranger to genuine hospitality, which seeks, sees, discerns no difference.

René Descartes' trajectory from France to the Netherlands to Sweden did not, still does not, mean that he was or is classified as a migrant. Internal migrants are fulfilling the capitalist ideal of freedom of the movement of labour. 'Migrants' have also fulfilled that attribute viewed so positively in economic terms, but they are 'migrants' because, whether exilic or not, they will in all likelihood have literally crossed an international border, and it is the traversal of that border that gives rise to the various undignified forms of objectification to which they are routinely subjected. For the migrant, however, that border represents only one stage among many crossings, so that crossing itself takes on something of an ontological foundation. *Los atravesados* repeatedly find themselves at crossings where 'Schmerz versteinerte die Schwelle', crossroads where no supernatural power is available to be conjured up. Anyone who has come over land or over water will have endured a journey not only of borders but also of continual barriers, impasses of one sort or another as they navigate the passage from place to place on the way, invoking cunning and ingenuity to turn the impasse into a passageway, the dead end aporia into a porous border (Young 2021). Once temporarily 'settled', a different kind of crossing supervenes: In relation to the particular institutions, bureaucracies, legal systems and practices of the place, at which new kinds of barriers must be negotiated. The migrant always comes in at an angle to the mental and physical topography of a city, an established form that he or she will have to traverse along the oblique slant of the one who does not know or belong. And yet, that traversal will always be transformative, precisely because the migrant cuts across hierarchical levels dialogically to form new assemblages, new points of contact, chiasma, visible and invisible, from components that have hitherto been arranged in other more fixed or established forms.

Let us think the relation of such crossings to other forms of *traversal* that have been mapped out, such as Kristeva's re-accentuation of Mikhail Bakhtin through the radical avant-garde writers who cut across the structures of bourgeois nineteenth-century writing, 'la traversée des frontières', in *La*

Révolution du langage poétique (1974: 525–43). Kristeva shows that traversal can enable potential subject positions for those who arrive athwart social or cultural formations obliquely, even though they may not necessarily think of themselves in terms of being others, or as different, for any minoritarian relations in short. The traversal involves an active intervention by the individual subject 'qui prend en écharpe les institutions sociales dans lesquelles il s'était précédement reconnu, et coincide ainsi avec les moments de rupture, de rénovation, de révolution d'une société' (Kristeva 1975: 11) ['who attacks from an oblique angle the social institutions in which he had previously recognized himself, and thus coincides with the moments of rupture, of renovation, of revolution of a society' (translation by the author)]. Except that for the migrant, he or she has likely never previously recognized themselves in such structures, so the transgressive dialogization may be less planned than an inevitable effect of daily life experiences in transient places. And this is why *la traversée, il attraversamento, die Überfahrt, die Überschreitung*, crossings, cannot but also be *transversal*, intersecting and going beyond the limits of the parallel lines of established institutional and urban geographies. The oblique transversal, lying athwart, will always be transgressive in some form, as indeed it has been for the migrant by the singular act of crossing the border which has been set up to keep him or her out. The indirect slanted approach will always structure ways of cutting through, of sidestepping the impasse, of discovering hidden forms of porosity. So too for anyone who finds themselves at odds with social structures and institutions, or wishes to position themselves in that way, and it is in this context that 'transversality' has been invoked by Félix Guattari who summons up the traversal as a means of cutting across the embedded hierarchies of the psychiatric institution in order to form new unthought of assemblages (2003). Versions of this concept, in fact, have a long genealogy in terms of the theorization of relations set obversely to dominant structures, not brushing directly against the grain, but working crossways to it. A closely related form of intersectional crossing that enables a perspective on multiple forms of being that are too complex, too multifaceted, too fleeting, to be reduced to sameness and alterity can be found in Deleuze. Deleuze's source beyond Guattari's essay (which was originally published in the same year) was probably Husserl and Sartre, but he characteristically transforms the concept into his own distinct modality, developing his understanding of the transversal as the eruption of desubjectified oblique points of connection in his analysis of Marcel Proust.

Proust, Deleuze argues, invents a structure of memory which is gradually revealed as a general principle of how to make chiasmatic connections between incompatible disparate elements, including those in individual characters, or between them, or within the caverns of memory, according to transverse logics, without assimilating them into a totalized form. Proust, according to Deleuze, himself offers a way out of the problem of the iniquities of difference whereby subjects are transformed into objects because such a structure allows an elaboration that is 'ni dans le point de vue ni dans la chose vue, mais dans la transversale' (Deleuze 1964: 153). ['neither in the viewpoint nor in the thing seen, but in the transversal' (Deleuze 2000: 185).] He cites the following example from Proust's description of the landscape seen through the windows of a train:

> Or nous avons vu précédemment, dans les directions les plus diverses, l'importance d'une *dimension transversale* dans l'œuvre de Proust: la transversalité. C'est elle qui permet dans le train, non pas d'unifier les points de vue d'un paysage, mais de les faire communiquer suivant sa dimension propre, dans sa dimension propre, alors qu'ils restent incommunicants d'après les leurs. C'est elle qui fait l'unité et la totalité singulières du côté de Méséglise et du côté de Guermantes, sans en supprimer la différence ou la distance: « entre ces routes des transversales s'établissaient ». (Deleuze 1964: 201–2)
>
> Now, we have previously seen, in the most diverse directions, the importance of a transversal dimension in Proust's work: transversality. It is transversality that permits us, in the train, not to unify the viewpoints of a landscape, but to bring them into communication according to the landscape's own dimension, in its own dimension, whereas they remain noncommunicating according to their own dimension. It is transversality that constitutes the singular unity and totality of the Méséglise Way and of the Guermantes Way, without suppressing their difference or distance: 'between these routes certain transversals were established'. (Deleuze 2000: 168)

Transversals affirm connections between irreconcilable fragments without uniting them. The key element in Proust's description of the landscape seen from the train is that any totality that is created resides in the provisionality of the transversal:

> quand je l'aperçus de nouveau, mais rouge cette fois, dans la fenêtre d'en face qu'elle abandonna à un deuxième coude de la voie ferrée; si bien que je passais mon temps à courir d'une fenêtre à l'autre pour rapprocher, pour rentoiler les fragments intermittents et opposites de mon beau matin écarlate et versatile et en avoir une vue totale (Proust 1919–27: 4.69).
>
> I was lamenting the loss of my strip of pink sky when I caught sight of it afresh, but red this time, in the opposite window which it left at a second bend in the line,

so that I spent my time running from one window to the other to reassemble, to collect on a single canvas the intermittent, antipodean fragments of my fine, scarlet, ever-changing morning, and to obtain a comprehensive view of it and a continuous picture. (Proust 1919–27: 4.69; 1941: 3.325–6)

Proust the traveller collects and puts together the fragmented views on a single canvas in somewhat the same way as Wittgenstein describes his *Philosophical Investigations* – as an assemblage of necessarily disjointed 'remarks' which in a comparable way are not reducible to a particular point of view:

> meine Gedanken bald erlahmten, wenn ich versuchte, sie, gegen ihre natürliche Neigung, in *einer* Richtung weiterzuzwingen. – Und dies hing freilich mit der Natur der Untersuchung selbst zusammen. Sie nämlich zwingt uns, ein weites Gedankengebiet, kreuz und quer, nach allen Richtungen hin zu durchreisen. – Die philosophischen Bemerkungen dieses Buches sind gleichsam eine Menge von Landschaftsskizzen, die auf diesen langen und verwickelten Fahrten entstanden sind.

> my thoughts soon grew feeble if I tried to force them along a single track against their natural inclination. – And this was, of course, connected with the very nature of the investigation. For it compels us to travel criss-cross in every direction over a wide field of thought. – The philosophical remarks in this book are, as it were, a number of sketches of landscapes which were made in the course of these long and meandering journeys. (Wittgenstein 2009: 3, 3ᵉ)

In both Proust and Wittgenstein, journey time has been turned into forms of cavernous space, a transversal that involves crisscrossing leaps across time and multiple points of view that cannot add up to a single perspective, creating communications, or links, between heterogeneous elements according to counter-intuitive or non-normative forms that never totalize objects or subjects. Proust's transversality offers a way of thinking those secreted potentialities of contemporary society hitherto conjured up in terms of difference without positioning anyone according to reductive or demeaning subject–object positions – they, them, the different, the Other – making fleeting chiasmatic connections between irreducible heterogeneous elements.[6]

Proust himself brings the traversal together with the transversal from the moment that he tastes the madeleine, where traversal, which he always associates

---

[6] In Germany, the transversal was invoked by Welsch in the 1990s with respect to identity and rationalities (1992: 177–81; 1995). Today in Austria, Gerald Raunig is a notable contemporary theoretician of transversality. His Deleuzian machinic assemblages which offer a plethora of provocative proactive disassemblages, providing an unruly conceptual ecology of structures which do not suppress difference by invoking connections (2021).

with impulses across immense distances in space or time, initiates the power of forms of memory outside the individual's control. The fundamental Proustian experience, remarkably, is conjured up in terms of surpassing the limits of one's own consciousness, of going beyond, breaking through boundaries, journeys, migration and, if reading after Benjamin, translation: 'Grave incertitude, toutes les fois que l'esprit se sent dépassé par lui-même; quand lui, le chercheur, est tout ensemble le pays obscur où il doit chercher et où tout son bagage ne lui sera de rien. Chercher? pas seulement: créer' (Proust 1919–27: 1.66). ['What an abyss of certainty whenever the mind feels that some part of it has strayed beyond its own borders; when it, the seeker, is at once the dark region through which it must go seeking, where all its equipment will avail it nothing. See? More than that: create' (Proust 1941: 1.59).]

The straying Dantesque migrant mind travels beyond its own confines, at once creator, trespasser and translator, and in going beyond the limits of the law brings something new to the light of day from that darkness, giving reality and substance to an entity that has hitherto never been articulated: 'je sens tressaillir en moi quelque chose qui se déplace, voudrait s'élever, quelque chose qu'on aurait désancré, à une grande profondeur; je ne sais ce que c'est, mais cela monte lentement; j'éprouve la résistance et j'entends la rumeur des distances traversées' (Proust 1919–27: 1.67). ['I feel something start within me, something that leaves its resting-place and attempts to rise, something that has been embedded like an anchor at great depth; I do not yet know what it is, but I can feel it mounting slowly; I can measure the resistance, I can hear the echo of great spaces traversed' (Proust 1941: 1.60).]

It is not the alternation of the possible walks or 'ways' that is so important as the mental traversals of the spaces, the routes between them: 'Déjà entre ces deux routes des transversales s'établissaient' (Proust 1919–27: 15.207) ['already between these two routes transversals were established' (Proust 1941: 12.411; translation modified)], routes so distinct that they had hitherto seemed like diametrical opposites, 'si opposés qu'on ne sortait pas en effet de chez nous par la même porte, quand on voulait aller d'un côté ou de l'autre' (Proust 1919–27: 1.183) ['so diametrically opposed that we would actually leave the house by a different door, according to the way we had chosen' (Proust 1941: 1.183).] Proust links the traversal of memory across abandoned objects and relics, outwardly indifferent but impalpably embedded within the vast structures of recollection, with the dynamics that arise from 'un courant transversal' (Proust 1919–27: 14.50) ['a transversal current' (Proust 1941: 12.44)] that erupts to flow back and forth between the two ways, Méséglise and Guermantes, between which the mind or the work of art creates disembodied links among their disconnected objects, memories, encounters, retranslating, reinterpreting the hitherto inaccessible and invisible pivots in the dark regions of lost, unforeseen encounters.

The process of traversal will always interconnect and mesh with the transversal, as with the uprooted lily that drifts helplessly from bank to bank of the Vivonne which the current never lets rest for a moment, 'refaisant éternellement la double traversée' like an anguished figure endlessly repeating its particular torment in Dante's *Inferno* (Proust 1919–27: 1.228) ['eternally repeating its double journey' (Proust 1941: 1.232)]. Traversal and transversal involve oblique movements tracing unenvisaged connectivities across material, social and linguistic formations, not the crystallization of a new form, disjunctive or otherwise. It begins to seem that transversal and traversal themselves describe two 'ways' between which they make hitherto unimaginable connections: The intimate Méséglise Way of Guattari and Deleuze, where the work of transversal takes the form of establishing transverse forms of communication, and the estranging Guermantes Way of Kristeva's modernists traversing the space of writing. Transversal connects and re-accentuates the two ways dialogically, of Guermantes and Méséglise, of Don Tabaco and Doña Azúcar, with their incompatible elements of distance and desire, of strangeness or estrangement and intimacy, in the migrant's or migrating mind's unpredictable encounter with lost or unfamiliar landscapes and social and cultural practices, or in the revisionary translation which seeks to estrange that society, its social and aesthetic practices, from the toxicity of its past. And even if it is finally revealed that they connect together in the far distance, the aberrant links between the embedded objects laid out along disjunctive paths remain to be made. The two ways offer practices of decolonial detonation, not through explicit *controversia* between them and not as harmony either, as they brush sideways unpicking the well-tempered tricks and slights of hand of established harmonies. Travelling 'en écharpe', passing through and across customary social and cultural formations, the migrant, the refugee, effect and trace transversals that shape unthought of connections while their traversals fire off obliquely at a tangent, disassembling the entrenched lines of custom into hitherto inconceivable aggregations and unobserved porosities. Together, the two ways make up a dissonant synesis as they cross and hook up obliquely disconnected points of the social – creating, catalysing, aggregating, transposing and translating the given into new, revolutionary possibilities, and in that spiralling leap opening up unbounded new potentialities for the future, liberating flights into the blue of dreams.

References

Allolio-Näcke, L., B. Kalscheuer and A. Manzeschke (2005), *Differenzen anders denken: Bausteine zu einer Kulturtheorie der Transdifferenz*, Frankfurt: Campus.

Anzaldúa, G. (1987), *Borderlands/La Frontera: The New Mestiza*, San Francisco: Aunt Lute Books.

Balibar, É. (2002), 'What Is a Border?', *Politics and the Other Scene*, 75–86, trans. C. Jones, J. Swenson and C. Turner, London: Verso.

Beckett, S. (1959), *Molloy. Malone Dies. The Unnamable*, London: Calder & Boyars.

Benjamin, W. (1972), 'Die Aufgabe des Übersetzers', *Gesammelte Schriften* 4 (1): 9–21.

Benjamin, W. (1996), *Selected Writings: I, 1913–1926*, ed. M. Bullock and M. W. Jennings, Cambridge, MA: Harvard University Press.

Breinig, H. and K. Lösch (2002), 'Introduction: Difference and Transdifference', in H. Breinig, J. Gebhardt and K. Lösch (eds), *Multiculturalism in Contemporary Societies: Perspectives on Difference and Transdifference*, 11–36, Erlangen: Universitätsbund.

Breinig, H. and K. Lösch (2004), 'Lost in Transdifference. Thesen und Antithesen', in L. Allolio-Näcke, B. Kalscheuer and A. Manzeschke (eds), *Differenzen anders denken: Bausteine zu einer Kulturtheorie der Transdifferenz*, 454–5, Frankfurt: Campus.

Breinig, H. and K. Lösch (2006), 'Transdifference', *Journal for the Study of British Cultures* 13 (2): 105–22.

Butler, J. (1990), *Gender Trouble: Feminism and the Subversion of Identity*, London: Routledge.

Cassin, B. (2004), *Vocabulaire européen des philosophies: Dictionnaire des intraduisibles*, Paris: Éditions du Seuil.

Cixous, Hélène (2010), *Le Rire de la Méduse et autres ironies*, Préface de Frédéric Regard, Paris: Galilée.

Coronil, F. (1995), 'Introduction' to F. Ortiz, *Cuban Counterpoint: Tobacco and Sugar*, ix–lvi, Durham, NC: Duke University Press.

Deleuze, G. (1964), *Proust et les signes*, Paris: PUF.

Deleuze, G. (2000), *Proust and Signs*, trans. Richard Howard, Minneapolis: University of Minnesota Press.

Derrida, J. and M. Ferraris (2018), *Le goût du secret*, Paris: Harmann.

Dussel, E. (2007), *Política de la Liberación. Historia mundial y crítica*, Madrid: Editorial Trotta.

Dussel, E. (2011), *The Politics of Liberation: A Critical World History*, trans. Thea Cooper, London: SCM Press.

Fanon, F. (1952), *Peau noire, masques blancs*, Paris: Éditions du Seuil.

Fanon, F. (2011), *Œuvres*, Paris: La Découverte.

Glissant, E. (1990), *Poétique de la relation*, Paris: Gallimard.

Guattari, F. (2003), 'La Transversalité', in *Psychanalyse et transversalité. Essais d'analyse institutionnelle*, 72–85, Paris: La Découverte.

Hall, S. (1988), 'New Ethnicities', in K. Mercer (ed.), *Black Film British Cinema*, 27–31, London: Institute of Contemporary Art.

Hannerz, U. (1996), *Transnational Connections: Culture, People, Places*, London: Routledge.

Jakobson, R. (1962–71), *Collected Writings*. 2 vols. Vol. I: Phonological Studies; vol. II: Word and Language. The Hague: Mouton.

Kristeva, J. (1974), *La Révolution du langage poétique. L'avant-garde à la fin du XIXe siècle: Lautréamont et Mallarmé*, Paris: Éditions du Seuil.

Kristeva, J. (1975), *La traversée des signes*, Paris: Éditions du Seuil.

Lentz, C. (2017), 'Culture: The Making, Unmaking and Remaking of an Anthropological Concept', *Zeitschrift für Ethnologie* 142: 181–204.

Marggraf, A. S. (1747), 'Expériences chimiques faites dans le dessein de tirer un véritable sucre de diverses plantes, qui croissent dans nos contrées', *Histoire de l'académie royale des sciences et belles-lettres de Berlin*, 79–90, Berlin: Haude et Spener.

Marty, E. (2021), *Le Sexe des modernes. Pensée du neutre et théorie du genre*, Paris: Éditions du Seuil.

Nancy, J.-L. and I. Goh (2021), *The Deconstruction of Sex*, Durham, NC: Duke University Press.

Ortiz, F. ([1940] 2002), *Contrapunteo cubano del tabaco y azúcar*, ed. Enrico Mario Santí, Madrid: Música Mundana Maqueda.

Ortiz, F. (1950), *La Africanía de la música folklórica de Cuba*, Habana: Publicaciones del Ministerio de educacíon.

Ortiz, F. (1995), *Cuban Counterpoint: Tobacco and Sugar*, trans. Harriet de Onís, Durham, NC: Duke University Press.

Proust, M. (1919–27), *À la Recherche du temps perdu*, 15 vols, Paris: Gallimard.

Proust, M. (1941), *Remembrance of Things Past*, trans. C. K. Scott Montcrieff, 12 vols, London: Chatto & Windus.

Rama, Á. (1982), *Transculturación narrativa en América Latina*, Mexico: Siglio XXI.

Raunig, G. (2021), *Ungefüge. Maschinischer Kapitalismus und molekulare Revolution*, Band 2, Vienna: Transversal Texts.

Reichardt, D. (2020), 'Creating Notions of Transculturality: The Work of Fernando Ortiz and His Impact on Europe', in E. Sturm-Trigonakis (ed.), *World Literature and the Postcolonial*, 69–83, Berlin: Metzler.

Said, E. W. (1983), *The World, the Text, the Critic*, Cambridge, MA: Harvard University Press.

Santí, E. M. (2005), *Ciphers of History: Latin American Readings for a Cultural Age*, New York: Palgrave Macmillan.

Saussure, Ferdinand de (1971), *Cours de linguistique générale*, ed. Charles Bally et Albert Séchehaye, Paris: Payot.

Saussure, Ferdinand de (2002), *Écrits de linguistique générale*, ed. Simon Bouquet, Rudolf Engler, avec la collaboration d'Antoinette Weil, Paris, Gallimard.

Schulze-Engler, Frank (2006), 'What's the Difference? Notes towards a Dialogue between Transdifference and Transculturality', *Journal for the Study of British Culture* 13 (2): 123–32.

Smith, Zadie (2000), *White Teeth*, London: Hamish Hamilton.

Stein, M. (2008), 'The Location of Transculture', in F. Schulze-Engler and S. Helff (eds), *Transcultural English Studies: Theories, Fictions, Realities*, 249–66, Amsterdam: Rodopi.

Welsch, W. (1992), 'Subjektsein heute: Zum Zusammenhang von Subjektivität, Pluralität und Transversalität', *Studia Philosophica* 51: 153–82.

Welsch, W. (1994), 'Transkulturalität – die veränderte Verfassung heutiger Kulturen', in *Sichtweisen: Die Vielheit in der Einheit*, 83–122, Weimar: Stiftung Weimarer Klassik.

Welsch, W. (1995), *Vernunft: Die zeitgenössische Vernunftkritik und das Konzept der transversalen Vernunft*, Frankfurt: Suhrkamp.

Welsch, W. (1996), 'Transculturality – the Form of Cultures Today', in *Le Shuttle: Tunnelrealitäten Paris-London-Berlin*, 15–30, Berlin: Künstlerhaus Bethanien.

Welsch, W. (1999), 'Transculturality – the Puzzling Form of Cultures Today', in M. Featherstone and S. Lash (eds), *Spaces of Cultures: City, Nation, World*, 194–213, London: Sage.

Wittgenstein, L. (2009), *Philosophical Investigations*, revised 4th edn, ed. P. M. S. Hacker and Joachim Schulte, trans. G. E. M. Anscombe, P. M. S. Hacker and J. Schulte, Oxford: Wiley-Blackwell.

Young, R, J. C. (1995), *Colonial Desire: Hybridity in Theory, Culture and Race*, London: Routledge.

Young, R. J. C. (2012), 'Postcolonial Remains', *New Literary History* 43 (1): 19–42.

Young, R. J. C. (2021), 'Irrecoverable Histories', *Recherche littéraire/Literary Research* 37: 33–60.

3

On transcultural globalectics: Ngũgĩ meets Schulze-Engler

Tanaka Chidora
Goethe University Frankfurt
University of the Free State

Introduction

The debate on what constitutes African Literature is old, going as far back as the Makerere Conference of 1962.[1] It continues to be significant, however, as revealed by Taiye Selasi's rejection of the category of 'African Literature' (2013). The Makerere Language Debate, itself a part of the Makerere Conference, and the question of what African Literature is, are central to the cumulative development of Ngũgĩ's position concerning African Literature and 'globalectics' (a term Ngũgĩ[2] coined in 2012) and to the central arguments in Schulze-Engler's iterations on transculturality and World Literature. Ngũgĩ's early Afrocentric and decolonial writings take their cue from his dissatisfactions, not only with the way the so-called language debate panned out, but also with the assumptions upon which the conference was premised. A major issue, the first in fact, on the agenda of the conference was a discussion of the question: 'What is African Literature?' Ngũgĩ would capture this issue many years later in *Decolonising the Mind* (1986a) when he asks more questions: 'Was it literature written by Africans? What about a non-African who wrote about Africa: Did his work

---

[1] The Makerere University Literature Conference, titled 'A Conference of African Writers of English Expression', and popularly known for the Language Debate, took place in 1962. It was a conference where African writers gathered to debate what African Literature was, and the language it was supposed to be written in. On one side were writers whose approach was that of completely rejecting European languages and using languages that were in existence before colonialism. It is to this group that Ngũgĩ belonged. On the other side was Achebe, whose approach involved using English in ways that captured African experiences in their cultural settings. This meant 'localizing' English.
[2] While ideally, Ngũgĩ wa Thiong'o should be cited as wa Thiong'o in in-text references, he has popularly been cited as Ngũgĩ.

qualify as African literature? What if an African set his work in Greenland: Did that qualify as African literature? Or were African languages the criteria?' (Ngũgĩ 1986a: 6). For Ngũgĩ, the Makerere University Literature Conference had already, by the time writers from Africa gathered in 1962, assumed that African Literature was that which was written in English. As the conference was titled 'A Conference of African Writers of English Expression', those writers who wrote in Kiswahili, Yoruba, Gĩkũyũ and other African languages were not included. Thus, even though one of the main issues on the agenda involved a discussion of what African Literature was, the exclusion of literatures written in non-English African languages revealed that the convenors somehow already had an idea of how they wanted African Literature to be defined. However, the questions that animated the conference concerning the definition of African Literature would prove vital in subsequent conversations concerning World Literature.

Instead of pursuing these enriching complexities in order to unravel the transcultural nature of human experience, Ngũgĩ pursued the route of condemning English in a move that was meant to decolonize the mind or delink the African from a global modernity that Ngũgĩ considered European. Thus, *Decolonising the Mind* (1986a) and *Moving the Centre* (1993) represent this Ngũgĩ who operates from a position that dichotomizes the world into Europe (especially English Europe) and the rest of us. This is different, however, from the Ngũgĩ of *Globalectics* (2012), whose position takes into account the complexity of human experiences, cultures and literatures, and proposes a globalectical approach to World Literature. This Ngũgĩ comes close to Schulze-Engler in many ways, particularly in the way he abandons his earlier nativist and culture-specific conceptions and categories of literature. The earlier position of Ngũgĩ is based on the notion that cultures are self-contained and have internal homogeneity. Because of colonialism, Ngũgĩ saw what he termed African culture as a victim of imperial culture. For the earlier Ngũgĩ, the way to disentangle from colonialism, especially for literature, involved saving national literatures from a totalizing colonialism. This also involved writing in local languages and abandoning what Ngũgĩ called languages of colonialism. His globalectical vision is, however, and as I will demonstrate, different from this earlier position, for it is based on the recognition of World Literature. This is where Ngũgĩ comes close to Schulze-Engler. However, Ngũgĩ's globalectical vision for World Literature is also based on a postcolonial position and, therefore, retains certain aspects of his earlier writings. In contrast to this, Schulze-Engler's position is based on a transcultural vision that is disenchanted with postcolonialism's misconception of modernity as European and its belief that European modernity must be challenged by writing back to the empire, or, alternatively appropriated, translated, rehistoricized and read anew in order to produce something hybridized, or understood and deconstructed through colonial discourse analysis (Schulze-Engler 2007). Central to Schulze-Engler's position is disenchantment with postcolonialism's continued use of the victim paradigm. The main argument of his position is that one should move from 'enchanted solidarity', by which he means unconditional solidarity with (whoever claims) victimhood to the more differentiated 'disenchanted solidarity'. All of these postcolonial approaches that Schulze-Engler shuns are based on the erroneous view that the former colonizer's modernity is what constitutes the globe, the categorization of literatures and the degree of eminence given to literary works from all over the globe. This, too, is the position that Ngũgĩ strongly operates from in his early writings, a position that also feebly remains somewhere in the background of his globalectical approach in his 2012 publication.

The arguments of Ngũgĩ and Schulze-Engler are important in understanding what the category of what is considered as African Literature is, or has become since the days of the anti-colonial struggle, to the more contemporary times of migrant narratives by writers who are considered African. The anti-colonial aesthetic that animated Ngũgĩ's earlier literary and non-fictional writings has also given way to writings that are being produced in the context of complex movements and transcultural connections. The anti-colonial movements that Ngũgĩ intellectually supported have morphed into ruthless regimes that use the rhetoric and grand ideas of liberation to sustain tyrannical rule. What African Literature is, or has become, is best captured in the declarative title of Taiye Selasie's article: 'African Literature Doesn't Exist' (2013). This declaration is based on Selasie's view that the category is an 'empty designation' (2013: 1) which disregards the complexities of African cultures and the fact that literature transcends geopolitical borders within which we try to imprison it. The category, African Literature, as Selasi declares, is a designation that invents a monolithic Africa. It is this invention of a monolithic Africa that animates Ngũgĩ's neat categorization of literature in his earlier writings when he maps the order in which literature should, in the Kenyan context, be studied: Kenyan Literature, East African Literature, African Literature, Caribbean and Afro-American Literature, Asian Literature and European Literature (Ngũgĩ 1986a). Thus, Ngũgĩ, writing in the context of the anti-colonial movement, falls back on these neat categories, a position that, as I will demonstrate, later gives way to a globalectical vision that comes close to Schulze-Engler's transcultural approach to World Literature.

I will particularly argue that Ngũgĩ's globalectical approach, though a marked departure from the essentialist approach of his earlier writings, relies heavily on postcolonialism. Thus, even though Ngũgĩ's new approach recognizes World Literature, it is a recognition that still relies on the organization of the world into centre/periphery. It is, therefore, a globalectics that still sees some literatures as more privileged than others, with the globalectical theory a way of challenging this privilege. I argue that Schulze-Engler's transcultural approach to World Literature can enrich Ngũgĩ's globalectical theory. It is on the basis of this intersection that I propose a transcultural globalectical approach to literature.

Ngũgĩ's earlier writings

Ngũgĩ's earlier writings, especially *Decolonising the Mind* (1986a) and *Moving the Centre* (1993), are based on a decolonial vision that agitates for the delinking of Africa from Europe. This decolonial vision arose from the view that African people, victims of imperialism in its colonial and neocolonial forms, needed to restore their communal self-determination, liberate their culture, politics and economy from a Euro-American stranglehold and use their own languages to escape the linguistic encirclement of the continent (Ngũgĩ 1986a). Ngũgĩ's belief then was that writing in English was a colonial act that should be shunned because even if one were to use African proverbs in ways that would carry the weight of the African experience in English, one was merely allowing a European language to prey on an African language and be enriched by it. According to Ngũgĩ, '[i]n my view language was the most important vehicle through which that [colonial] power fascinated and held the soul prisoner. The bullet was the means of the physical subjugation. Language was the means of the spiritual subjugation' (1986a: 9). The 'fatalistic logic' of English's presence, as Achebe famously declared (qtd in Ngũgĩ 1986a: 7) was not supposed to justify a betrayal of such magnitude!

By linking language to culture, by saying that Gĩkũyũ was the language of his culture and English the language of his education (therefore mental colonization), Ngũgĩ created a neat taxonomy that was based on the belief that there was culture on one side and education (and by extension, colonization) on the other. Thus, Ngũgĩ saw his education as taking him further and further away from his culture because the language of his education was a carrier of another culture from another geopolitical space and a tool of colonial oppression. Language, for him, carried the specific culture of a specific community of human beings with a specific form, character, history and relationship to the world. By learning and writing in English, Ngũgĩ believed that a writer suffered a disconnect from that specificity. English could never 'as spoken or written properly reflect or imitate the real life of [the African writer's] community' (1986a: 16). Thus, Ngũgĩ here linked people, languages and literature to specific geopolitical locations.

Ngũgĩ also believed that the use of English in education in African states produced a class of writers called 'the petty bourgeoisie' (Ngũgĩ 1986a: 20), who, while recognizing the evils of colonialism, failed to identify with the class that, in his view, mattered because they were using English in their writing instead of the language of that class. For Ngũgĩ, the class was that of the peasantry. Even though the 'petty bourgeoisie' (Ngũgĩ 1986a: 20) class of writers expressed disillusionment with post-independence governments and excesses, for Ngũgĩ, it could not become organic or authentic enough to be one with the peasants because 'its quest was hampered by the ...language choice, and in its movement toward the people, it could only go up to that section of the petty bourgeoisie – the students, teachers, secretaries, for instance – still in closest touch with the people. It settled there, marking time, caged within the linguistic fence of its colonial inheritance' (Ngũgĩ 1986a: 21–2). Thus, this class was viewed as representing the petty bourgeoisie's interests and could not achieve 'authentic' African-ness in its writings. Ngũgĩ here moves from language as a marker of culture to language as a marker of class, betraying the socialist basis of his analysis. The peasant class, the masses, for Ngũgĩ, was the one that carried true revolutionary potential to delink Africa from Europe, but how could that be done when the vanguard – the writer and intellectual – was using a language of colonialism? The irony that the transformative power of socialist politicking had already been tested and had come short was, however, lost on Ngũgĩ; hence, Ngũgĩ thought that the post-independence tyrannies could be challenged through another socialist, peasant-led revolution. The question is, what would have changed this time around to necessitate such positive hope? This romanticization of the peasantry as a class that is central to a socialist struggle is extended when Ngũgĩ links these struggles to the struggles of people in 'South Africa, Namibia, Kenya, Zaire, Ivory Coast, El Salvador, Chile, Philippines, South Korea, Indonesia, Grenada, Fanon's "Wretched of the Earth", who have declared loud and clear that they do not sleep to dream, but dream to change the world' (Ngũgĩ 1986a: 3). Writing in 1986, one wonders why Ngũgĩ would continue holding on to a socialist rhetoric of Africa's liberation that had already proven that it was just that: rhetoric. In 1986, Kenya had been independent for twenty-three years!

Ngũgĩ's socialist rhetoric was based on a dichotomy between Europe and the colonized. By characterizing modernity as European, he portrayed the formerly colonized as either neocolonized or excluded because of belonging to a modernity that was not of their own creation, to the extent that even technology 'always appears to us as external, their product and not ours' (Ngũgĩ 1986a: 16–17). By locating the peasant outside modernity and, therefore, outside of literature in English by writers of African origin, Ngũgĩ conceived of modernity as the work of Europe only, in which the colonized had played no part. This depiction of the formerly colonized as lacking agency also disregards their contribution to literature, contributions that were being made in what Ngũgĩ regarded as colonial languages. What Ngũgĩ failed to admit was that the so-called colonial languages had become local. By claiming that characters speaking in English in novels written by Africans were not really peasants but falsifications of history and reality (Ngũgĩ 1986a: 22), Ngũgĩ was, in fact, negating reality and severely simplifying the experiences of the Kenyan peasantry. He was reducing Kenyans to a simplified dichotomy that can be captured thus: English/written literature = petty bourgeoisie; Gĩkũyũ and other Kenyan languages/orature = peasant. Ngũgĩ's romanticization of the peasant (his version of the working class in the international language of socialism) allowed him to both praise the peasant for Africanizing English and to laugh at Achebe and Okara for attempting the same. In ridiculing Okara and Achebe for attempting to 'localize' English, Ngũgĩ (1986a: 8) says, 'Why, we may ask, should an African writer, or any writer, become so obsessed by taking from his mother-tongue, to enrich other tongues? Why should he see it as his particular mission? We never asked ourselves: how can we enrich our languages?'

Yet, in the same breath, he praises those who have 'Africanized' English and French:

> In fact when the peasantry and the working class were compelled by necessity or history to adopt the language of the master, they Africanised it without any of the respect for its ancestry shown by Senghor and Achebe, so totally as to have created new African languages, like Krio in Sierra Leone or Pidgin in Nigeria, that owed their identities to the syntax and rhythms of African languages. (Ngũgĩ 1986a: 23)

Thus, Ngũgĩ's focus on a socialist path led him to disregard Anglophone literature by African writers while romanticizing the peasant for creating new languages out of English. Here, Ngũgĩ misses the opportunity, in his politics of language, to explore the creative contributions of authors of African origins (whom he calls the bourgeoisie) to World Literature; in his socialist politics, they did not constitute a class that was malleable enough for his simplified reduction of the world into the oppressor versus the peasant.

In *Decolonising the Mind*, Ngũgĩ is at pains to distinguish between the educated intelligentsia, whom he looks down upon, and the peasants. For him, peasants are more authentic creators of African Literature because they kept alive endangered African languages 'in the daily speech, in the ceremonies, in political struggles, above all in the rich store of orature – proverbs, stories, poems, and riddles' (Ngũgĩ 1986a: 23). They also produced singers and attracted to their ranks intellectuals from the petty bourgeoisie class who would go on to write in African languages. Thus, the peasant must play a central role in the creation of national literature:

> It is therefore too early to make any conclusion about the character of the language of the African fiction and particularly the African novel. And here I am also talking of fiction as a language. But I am convinced that it will find its form and character through its reconnection with the mainstream of the struggles of African people against imperialism and its rooting itself in the rich oral traditions of the peasantry. (Ngũgĩ 1986a: 85-6)

It is clear that Ngũgĩ sees himself as a bourgeois intellectual who committed class suicide by identifying with peasants and writing in Gĩkũyũ. Therefore, for Ngũgĩ, you were either a peasant creating literature in African languages or Africanized colonial languages, or a bourgeois intellectual committing class suicide to write in African languages. That peasants can come up with Africanized English but the educated intelligentsia cannot write any true African Literature if they continued to use English, French and other languages of European origin once more betrayed Ngũgĩ's own socialist biases. By claiming that the writer who wrote in English was merely enriching the modernity of the conquering nation, Ngũgĩ placed the writer of African origin outside modernity and, therefore, outside World Literature, consequently reproducing the same colonialist line of thinking that saw Europe as the centre of literature. This assumption is one of the most glaring flaws of the decolonial movement today, a weakness that is central to Olúfẹ́mi Táíwò's critical approach in his latest book, *Against Decolonisation: Taking African Agency Seriously* (2022). Táíwò argues that the premise of the decolonial debate is colonialist in nature because it assumes that the formerly colonized have no agency and are eternal victims of the machinations of the former colonizers. Like the current decolonial movement that Táíwò critiques, Ngũgĩ's obsession with categorization drove the spirit of the time he wrote *Decolonising the Mind*. Ngũgĩ himself was a central intellectual contributor to that spirit, and he continues to be cited as a central figure even in today's decolonial movement, a movement that has continued with dividing the world into the West and the rest of us. It is a movement that, in the field of literature, has also been spawned by such critics as Chinweizu in *Toward the Decolonisation of African Literature* (1983).

Ngũgĩ also argued that writers of African origins writing in European languages were not producing African Literature (Ngũgĩ 1986a: 26). He called it Afro-European Literature and defined it as 'literature written by Africans in European languages in the era of imperialism' (1986a: 27). For him, 'African literature can only be written in African languages, that is, in the languages of the African peasantry and working class' (1986a: 27). Thus, we see here Ngũgĩ's approach to language, literature and culture as that of locating language, literature and culture in specific geopolitical settings and ignoring the complexities that exist within these cultures, languages and literatures. If we follow the thinking of Schulze-Engler (2008: xi, xii), then what Ngũgĩ called the 'environment' of the Kenyan child, to which that child could only be restored by using the mother tongues of Kenya, was based on 'the "separatist" idea of "cultures" as self-enclosed entities' which failed 'to acknowledge the fact that in an increasingly interconnected world, cultures are increasingly intertwined and people often constitute their cultural identities by drawing on more than one culture'. In that regard, the role of English 'cannot be analysed by simply condemning English, but only by a careful analysis of its actual functions in an emerging world society, to which literary studies can undoubtedly make a major contribution' (Schulze-Engler 2012: 12).

While *Moving the Centre* (1993) represents a slight change from how Ngũgĩ approached his vision in *Decolonising the Mind* and recognizes the effect of globalization, even seeing globalization in more favourable light, it continues to treat cultures as discrete and homogenous entities, hence Ngũgĩ's reference to pluralism of cultures, itself a subtle nod towards multiculturalism. He argues that African cultures are an integral part of the world and should be respected as equal entities in a globalized world comprising discrete, homogenous and self-contained cultures. It is a vision that is closely related to multiculturalism, whose conceptual flaws have been criticized. For instance, Kymlicka (2014: 2) has observed multiculturalism's tendency to essentialize the identities and practices of minority groups, while Philips (2007) has criticized multiculturalism's reification of culture. The assumption that cultures have internal harmony is also at the centre of Welsch's criticism of multiculturalism. Cultures, according to Welsch, are not islands or autonomous spheres, and any notion that they are discrete, homogenous entities is both 'factually incorrect and normatively deceptive' (1999: 4). Ngũgĩ, on the other hand, assumes that cultures have internal harmony, thereby stressing the differences of cultures instead of the complex fluidity that challenges discreteness and homogeneity. These ideas animate Ngũgĩ's philosophy concerning culture and literature, leading him to categorize literature in terms of country, region and continent, and even proposing a method of studying literature that begins at country level (in his case, Kenya), regional, continental and ideological (socialist literature first, for instance, before the literature of Western capitalists). Unlike Ngũgĩ, Schulze-Engler sees transculturality as a concept that captures the condition of literature today. It is a literature that is concerned with 'negotiating intimate questions of personal identity, gender relations and family life that turn out to be as decisive for the dynamics of modern societies as the macropolitics dominating public discourse, which focus on questions of economic policy, political systems and ideological conflicts' (Schulze-Engler 2007: 28). Where Ngũgĩ privileges a reading or creation of literature that challenges what he sees as the centre, that is, North America and Europe, Schulze-Engler opts for a multi-polar, decentred dynamic that lies at the heart of transcultural communication.

Towards transcultural globalectics

Ngũgĩ's *Globalectics* can be seen as a cumulative output of his shifting approach to the decolonial debate over the years, coming twenty-six years after *Decolonising the Mind*. On the literary front, *Wizard of the Crow* (2006) represents that same cumulative output, coming twenty years after declaring his final farewell to English in *Decolonising the Mind*, but representing the impossibility of a complete break from English in a transcultural globalectical world, even when writing in Gĩkũyũ. This has led Mwangi to observe:

> Readers will note that Ngũgĩ uses the novel to reposition himself on his pet issue of the language of African literature. Despite his spirited campaign to conserve African languages from the hegemony of English, Ngũgĩ's original is so much haunted by English that his Gĩkũyũ readers would have to be competent in English to comprehend the novel in their own mother tongue. By borrowing words directly from English, even when there are equivalents from other African languages, and by reproducing long sentences in English without translation, Ngũgĩ may be backtracking in the novelistic form from his hard-line [1986a] position against Europhone literature, a position he has gradually abandoned

> in his essays and teaching practices as a professor in the West, where he has had to conduct his duties in English. The characters' discursive fields, and perhaps Ngũgĩ's own, demand that the indigenous language in the novel be interlaced with English to express a more globalized world order. (2007: 256)

Thus, Gĩkũyũ mingles with the same English that Ngũgĩ delinked himself from in that famous declaration in *Decolonising the Mind*. What comes out clearly in *Globalectics* is that while Ngũgĩ has not departed from his anti-colonial perspective, he has managed to connect it to a more globalized order that relies on the fluidity and mixing of cultures. It is in that regard that Ngũgĩ comes close to Schulze-Engler's transcultural iterations.

Ngũgĩ's globalectical imagination builds on Goethe, on whom Schulze-Engler builds, and beyond whom he develops his thesis on transculturality and World Literature (see Ngũgĩ 2012; Schulze-Engler 2007). Goethe's idea is that creative products like literature cannot be national property but are global products. Thus, literature belongs to the world, hence the category of World Literature. According to Ngũgĩ (2012: 49), this category 'must include what's already formed in the world as well as what's now formed by the world, at once a coalition, a cohesion, and coalescence of literatures in world languages into global consciousness'. This marks a departure from Ngũgĩ's insistence on systematically studying literature according to nations, regions and continents, and according to internationalist solidarities based on the socialist idea. It is here that the ideas of Ngũgĩ come close to those of Schulze-Engler. For Ngũgĩ, writing in English does not, therefore, mean enriching Europe, as was his previous stance in *Decolonising the Mind* and *Moving the Centre*: 'When Asians and Africans write in English, their product is surely part of the English language cultural universe. Can this writing be defined within a purely national boundary? Is Naipaul a Caribbean or an English writer? Does Salman Rushdie belong to Europe or Asia?' (Ngũgĩ 2012: 53).

Ngũgĩ is here invoking globality by going beyond the national or continental territory. In the same vein, he sees African Literature as going 'beyond the national territorial state, assuming, at the bare minimum, the continent for its theater of relevance and application' (2012: 54). In *Decolonising the Mind*, Ngũgĩ sees relevance as how 'we see ourselves […] in relation to ourselves and other selves in the universe' (Ngũgĩ 1986a: 101). Further, in *Decolonising the Mind*, this quest for relevance is possible only in the context of the anti-imperialist struggle. In that regard, African Literature is supposed to be at the centre so that all other literatures are viewed in relation to it. But in this anti-colonial struggle, the orature of the peasant and worker was supposed to be at the centre.

This means class sympathies and the tenets of socialist solidarity influenced the philosophical standpoint of Ngũgĩ. According to Ngũgĩ's then ideology, no critic (or student) was supposed to be suspicious of idealized portrayals of literary characters fighting a liberation war. These characters, in many ways, become the ventriloquists through whom Ngũgĩ sermonized. One can think of *Matigari* (1986b), translated into English in 1989, a novel with a character by the same name. Matigari represents the Mau-Mau, whom Ngũgĩ naively idealized. The reduction of literature to this political, ideological standpoint, and the assertion that African Literature is only relevant in the context of the liberation struggle is, in the words of Schulze-Engler (2007: 25), 'a little out of place' because there are other literary motivations that have come to the fore 'such as the critique of social and political ills in newly independent societies or of dysfunctional gender norms, or the dialogue with new movements for democracy in the late 1980s and early 1990s', including diasporic and post-diasporic experiences.[3] Moreover, this approach to the teaching of literature that always locates it in the context of intellectual opposition to the West 'represents a simplifying mode of wishful thinking that can hardly do justice to the cultural and social complexity of contemporary societies around the world' and privileges 'the colonial past' (Schulze-Engler 2007: 25–6). In *Globalectics*, however, Ngũgĩ's approach to relevance is different. It is postcolonialist. In fact, the postcolonial is the basis of Ngũgĩ's globalectical vision, but he uses it in a way that is markedly different from his earlier investment in anti-colonial politics.

In *Globalectics*, Ngũgĩ chooses the postcolonial because for him,

> it is the closest to that Goethian and Marxian conception of world literature because it is a product of different streams and influences from different points of the globe, a diversity of sources, which it reflects in turn. The postcolonial is inherently outward looking, inherently international in its very constitution in terms of themes, language, and the intellectual formation of the writers. (Ngũgĩ 2012: 49)

In his choice of the postcolonial, Ngũgĩ is aware of its limitations besides its widespread use. As a period marker, it 'raises more questions than it answers. Periodization of any sort in science or history ... is wrought with conflicting histories, geographies, ideologies, and perspectives, depending on who – where, when, and how – is setting the different markers of events and time' (Ngũgĩ

---

[3] In my doctoral thesis (Chidora 2017), I introduce the concept of 'postdiaspora' to refer to the explosion of boundaries between 'home' and 'diaspora'.

2012: 49). The fact that every postcolonial must include the *posts* of both the former colonizer and formerly colonized and the various colonialisms that have occurred in human history means that the *post* cannot mean the same thing. Conceptually, it centralizes the colonial and peripheralizes, in a Hegelian sense, everything that happened before the colonial or outside it. Regardless of these shortcomings and many others of the postcolonial, Ngũgĩ prefers it in his globalectical vision because it 'embodies [a] new synthesis. While having its own particularity, like all other tributaries to the human, the postcolonial is an integral part of the intellectual history of the modern world because its very coloniality is a history of interpenetration of different peoples, cultures, and knowledge' (Ngũgĩ 2012: 51). Thus, in reality, the postcolonial has no geographical location in the Third World but in the 'intertextuality of products from all the corners of the globe [and] its universality tendency is inherent in its very relationship to historical colonialism and its globe for a theater' (2012: 53). Because of this, Ngũgĩ sees the postcolonial as constituting the heart of Goethe's World Literature. World Literature, then, implies that 'organizing the teaching of literature on the principle of national boundaries is outmoded, and even more so the export of national literatures as superior knowledge' (Ngũgĩ 2012: 53). It is around this principle that Ngũgĩ organizes his globalectical vision. There is, here, a marked departure from Ngũgĩ's earlier conceptions of literature that centralized the peasant and idealized the Mau Mau guerrilla. His acceptance of universality over his earlier culture-specific and socialist conceptions and categorizations of literature is also interesting. Could it be that Ngũgĩ had come to terms with Schulze-Engler's observation concerning socialism today? According to Schulze-Engler, '[it] is hard to imagine who in the twenty-first century should actually be the carrier of the socialist "counter-modernity" that was championed by the so-called socialist world during what Eric Hobsbawm has called "the short twentieth century"' (2015: 21–2). Or could it be that the outcomes of the revolutions Ngũgĩ had romanticized were discouraging?

The globalectical, therefore,

> is a way of approaching any text from whatever times and places to allow its content and themes form a free conversation with other texts of one's time and place, the better to make it yield its maximum to the human. It is to allow it to speak to our own cultural present. It is to read a text with the eyes of the world; it is to see the world with the eyes of a text. (Ngũgĩ 2012: 60)

In this globalectical vision, Ngũgĩ eschews the myopic tendency to look at literature and the languages in which it is written hierarchically, that is, entertaining the notion that some literatures and languages are inherently more superior than others. This discomfort is shared by Schulze-Engler when he ridicules the thinking that 'this world literary space is hierarchically ordered; the old literatures of the centre, which have been hoarding cultural capital for centuries and have managed to establish a sphere of "literary autonomy", dominate the newer, impoverished, and deprived literatures of the peripheries where "literary autonomy" has not yet been achieved' (2012: 9). A globalectical vision therefore breaks these walls of myopia that assume that there are a privileged few whose languages and literatures are classified, 'open only to a few' (Ngũgĩ 2012: 73). Breaking these walls will make literature accessible, 'a tool for clarifying interactive connections and interconnections of social phenomena and their mutual impact in the local and global space, a means of illuminating the internal and the external, the local and the global dynamics of social being' (Ngũgĩ 2012: 59). In this regard, Ngũgĩ's approach agrees with that of Schulze-Engler except, as I will demonstrate in more detail later, in Ngũgĩ's use of postcoloniality as the basis of globalectics.

Schulze-Engler's conception of World Literature is against categorizing literature and studying it according to national space (Schulze-Engler 2012). According to Schulze-Engler, such an approach is flawed because literature is erroneously seen in relation to a centre of which the West, especially Paris, is the 'meridian', a notion popularized by Casanova in 1999 (Schulze-Engler 2012: 9).[4] This also means that modernity, when viewed from this erroneous perspective, is unitary and has a centre. Such an approach, according to Schulze-Engler (2012: 11), assumes that all other literatures are aspiring towards this centre and ignores the complex articulations of human experience which cannot be reduced to perspectives that are national in character. According to Schulze-Engler:

> First and foremost, once English-language literatures worldwide are seen as a discursive field rather than as an imaginary assembly of national literatures, a genuinely transnational and transcultural perspective can emerge that is capable of encompassing both the literary practice of writers who can no longer be related to one particular 'national literary space' and the complex articulations that link individual works of literature not only to local or regional modernities with their specific social, linguistic, and cultural constellations, but also to the worldwide

---

[4] Schulze-Engler's 2012 chapter can be regarded as a riposte to Casanova's flawed assumptions in *The World Republic of Letters* ([1999] 2004), in which World Literature is defined as a world republic of letters yet continues to be organized according to national spaces, with the centre being the West, especially Paris.

field of English-language literatures and specific forms of communicative interaction and political conflict engendered by it. (2012: 11)

In Schulze-Engler's position, we perceive an awareness of the multiplicity of modernities that is absent, for instance, in the postcolonial perspective that animates Ngũgĩ's globalectical vision.

The postcolonial, according to Schulze-Engler, has shortcomings that should position us to move towards a perspective that is truly relevant to the spirit of World Literature. The postcolonial perspective, in Schulze-Engler's words, poses 'the danger of a renewed homogenisation of very diverse literatures by means of a quasi-universalistic model based on a highly abstract notion of "colonial experience" that suggests an immediate comparability of the literatures of, for example, Canada or Australia with those of Nigeria or Jamaica' (2007: 25). This is the same criticism that Ngũgĩ, regardless of his continued use of the postcolonial, also directs at this perspective in *Globalectics*. More importantly, the use of postcolonial to define cultures and literatures that are intellectually opposed to the West also ignores the intellectual and social complexities of these same cultures and literatures. As Schulze-Engler warns, 'If postcolonial perspectives on contemporary literatures and cultures focus exclusively on the latter's potential for resisting "Western discourses of power," they run the risk … of playing down other forms of political oppression and neglecting their importance for contemporary literatures' (2007: 26). The anticolonial politics that seems fashionable in some postcolonial theorizations, which is at the heart of *Decolonising the Mind* and *Moving the Centre*, and whose vestiges remain in the more advanced *Globalectics*, assumes that modernity is solely a product of the colonial experience and the West the centre of that modernity. The centrality of the West is even apparent in postcoloniality itself: 'On the other hand, criticism has focused on the close link between postcolonial theory and a Western "theory industry" from which parts of the so-called "postcolonial world" (such as Africa) have largely been excluded' (Schulze-Engler 2007: 26). By extension, this theory conveniently ignores the existence of multiple modernities and how the world is being rapidly transformed by globalization. In that regard, Schulze-Engler suggests a transcultural approach to World Literature that takes all these issues into account.

The transcultural approach takes into consideration how societies and cultures have been altered by globalization, thereby altering our own perceptions of them. This means our understanding of literary texts can no longer be moored to frameworks that contextualize them to discrete traditions and cultures. Culture has for a long time now been viewed with suspicion as a category with which to organize people and things. While culture was important in challenging Eurocentrism in Ngũgĩ's anticolonial struggle, it cannot remain central 'as a heuristic category for describing contemporary modes of living in and making sense of the world' (Schulze-Engler 2007: 27). Its nation-centric obsession is against the spirit of World Literature. This is why there is need to move beyond the postcolonial, without totally ignoring some of its useful approaches, towards the transcultural. Transculturality has more to offer to World Literature because of its awareness of the complexity of human experiences. These experiences cannot be categorized in terms of discrete, internally homogenous cultures and societies. Thus, instead of an *intercultural* approach that is based on how discrete, internally homogenous cultures interact, Schulze-Engler prefers the *transcultural* approach that recognizes 'a radically altered state of "culture" and "difference" in the contemporary world – for those engaged in cultural practices (including the production of literature) as well as for those seeking to develop analytical categories to describe and understand these practices' (2007: 28). Thus, instead of a bipolar approach that sees, for instance, African Literature as a creative and intellectual opposition to Europe or the United States, a more useful approach will be multipolar and decentred, recognizing writers as communicators of complex changes within and across cultures.

Thus, while Ngũgĩ's globalectical vision represents useful intersections with approaches to World Literature, it is limited by its over-reliance on postcoloniality. It is in that regard that I propose a revision of globalectics that utilizes transculturality. Such a globalectical approach would depart from seeing cultures as self-contained, postcolonial frameworks. In such a transcultural globalectical approach, 'African Literature [indeed] doesn't exist' (Selasi 2013).

Conclusion

This chapter began by exploring the centrality of the issues raised at the Makerere Conference in 1962 to Ngũgĩ's lifelong commitment to the advancement of African literatures, languages and cultures in the context of colonialism and neocolonialism. I discussed these issues through reference to *Decolonising the Mind* and *Moving the Centre*. I concluded that while it is prudent to understand the context and times of these two works, they have their shortcomings that have to do with Ngũgĩ's centralization of culture and the contextual study of literature. I argued that literature can no longer be read and criticized in ways that tie it to a geographical location or a culture. Culture is not a homogenous and discrete category. In a rapidly globalizing world, such a view of culture is unhelpful. The delinking venture that drives Ngũgĩ's rejection of English is based on an erroneous approach to culture which also informs that categorization of literatures of the world according to national spaces. In *Globalectics*, we see Ngũgĩ departing from this approach and accepting World Literature as a category that best captures the spirit of writing and reading literature in a globalized world. *Globalectics* is an approach that is wary of nation-centric categories that previously informed Ngũgĩ's approaches. However, Ngũgĩ based his globalectical approach on postcoloniality, whose shortcomings have been well explored by various critics, including Schulze-Engler. Schulze-Engler's transcultural approach to World Literature, therefore, offers more critical awareness because of its rejection of a dichotomous approach to literature that only recognizes the West as a centre against which literature from the formerly colonized must be read. Schulze-Engler argues that the world is more complex than Europe and the rest of us. Europe is not the centre of modernity to which all societies are being drawn; rather, multiple modernities constitute today's world. In that regard, any study of literature must take a multipolar approach. I finally argued that Ngũgĩ's globalectical approach is more enriching from a transcultural perspective than from a postcolonial one, hence my suggestion for a transcultural globalectical approach to World Literature.

References

Casanova, P. (1999), *The World Republic of Letters*, trans. M. B. Debevoise (2004), Cambridge, MA: Harvard University Press.

Chidora, T. (2017), 'Out of Crisis: Discourses of Enabling and Disabling Spaces in Post-2000 Zimbabwean Literary Texts in English', PhD Thesis, University of the Free State. Available online: http://hdl.handle.net/11660/9183 (accessed 31 October 2022).

Chinweizu, I., J. Onwuchekwa and M. Ihechukwu (eds) (1983), *Toward the Decolonisation of African Literature: African Fiction and Poetry and Their Critics*, Washington, DC: Howard University Press.

Kymlicka, W. (2014), 'The Essentialist Critique of Multiculturalism: Theories, Ethos, Policies', Robert Schuman Centre for Advanced Studies Research Paper No. RSCAS 2014/59, Florence: European University Institute, EUI/RSCAS.

Mwangi, E. (2007), 'Wizard of the Crow (Ngugi wa Thiong'o)', *Tydskrif Vir Letterkunde* 44 (2): 253–6. https://doi.org/10.17159/2309-9070/tvl.v.44i2.4551.

Phillips, A. (2007), *Multiculturalism without Culture*, Princeton, NJ: Princeton University Press.
Schulze-Engler, F. (2007), 'Theoretical Perspectives: From Postcolonialism to Transnational World Literature', in L. Eckstein (ed.), *English Literatures across the Globe: A Companion*, 20–32, Paderborn: Wilhelm Fink Verlag.
Schulze-Engler, F. (2008), 'Introduction', in F. Schulze-Engler and S. Helff (eds), *Transnational English Studies: Theories, Fictions, Realities*, ix–xvi, Amsterdam: Rodopi.
Schulze-Engler, F. (2012), 'The Commonwealth Legacy: Towards a Decentred Reading of World Literature', in B. Ashcroft, R. Mendis, J. McGonegal and A. Mukherjee (eds), *Literature of Our Times: Postcolonial Studies in the Twenty-First Century*, 3–14, Amsterdam: Rodopi.
Schulze-Engler, F. (2015), 'Once Were Internationalists? Postcolonialism, Disenchanted Solidarity and the Right to Belong in a World of Globalized Modernity', in P. K. Malreddy, B. Heidemann, O. B. Laursen and J. Wilson (eds), *Reworking Postcolonialism: Globalisation, Labour and Rights*, 19–35, London: Palgrave Macmillan.
Selasie, T. (2013), 'African Literature Doesn't Exist'. Available online: https://www.literaturfestival.com/medien/texte/eroeffnungsreden/Openingspeach2013_English.pdf (accessed 31 October 2022).
Táíwò, O. (2022), *Against Decolonisation: Taking African Agency Seriously*, Bloomsbury: C. Hurst & Co.
wa Thiong'o, N. (1986a), *Decolonising the Mind: The Politics of Language in African Literature*, London: Heinemann.
wa Thiong'o, N. (1986b), *Matigari*, London: Heinemann.
wa Thiong'o, N. (1993), *Moving the Centre: The Struggle for Cultural Freedoms*, Nairobi: EAEP; London: James Currey.
wa Thiong'o, N. (2006), *Wizard of the Crow*, London: Harvill Secker.
wa Thiong'o, N. (2012), *Globalectics: Theory and the Politics of Knowing*, New York: Columbia Press.
Welsch, W. (1999), 'Transculturality: The Puzzling Form of Cultures Today', in M. Featherstone and S. Lasch (eds), *Spaces of Culture: City, Nation, World*, 194–213, London: Sage. Available online: http://www.westreadseast.info/PDF/Readings/Welsch_Transculturality.pdf (accessed 16 February 2023).

Part Two

Transgressive kinships

4

Not-so-happy families: Durrell, Goodall and the myth of Africa

Graham Huggan
University of Leeds

The *Festschrift* is a loose and baggy monster, to be sure: half fly-by-night academic essay, half confirmatory mark of lasting respect and friendship.[1] The second is more important than the first, though *Festschriften* are a great deal more than just ceremonial occasions, still less professional opportunities for (and I'm wincing already at the wishing-you-well-in-retirement idiom) 'passing on the torch'. The philosopher Alan Soble (2003) probably gets it right with his tongue-in-cheek list of criteria for his own possible *Festschriften*. Suffice to mention two criteria here. First, advises Soble, the essays should be written by 'cherished teachers (if any are still alive), students, colleagues and, perhaps in a few cases, famous strangers who have clandestinely admired my work'. Second, 'all of the essays [should] deal directly with my important published work'. This makes *Festschrift* sound like a vanity project, which they may well be except for the fact that their recipients aren't usually involved in them. Nor are they necessarily expecting them: Indeed, another of Soble's criteria is that a *Festschrift* should come as 'a great surprise' to those who receive it, though this possibly confected surprise may be dampened by the rather less welcome realization that one has reached a certain, valedictory stage of one's career. (Frank, I can only say that I know how this feels ...)

I somehow doubt that Frank will be surprised by any of this, but that doesn't mean that his case is any less deserving. And it certainly doesn't mean that the

---

[1] Some material in this chapter has been reprinted from chapter 3 of Will Abberley, Christina Alt, David Higgins, Graham Huggan and Pippa Marland's book *Modern British Nature Writing, 1789–2020: Land Lines* (Cambridge University Press, 2022). Thanks to the publishers for allowing the work to be reproduced here.

collected tributes in this volume are anything other than wholly genuine acts of friendship – a friendship which, in my own case, extends over virtually the entirety of our respective academic careers. Frank is the most generous of men in what, by definition, is a generous field, shaped and subsequently reshaped by people all over the world who may not always be inclined to agree with one another (and may often be keen to be given the chance to *dis*agree with one another), but who are nearly always welcoming of one another when their paths do eventually cross. I would call this the 'postcolonial' field, Frank probably wouldn't. This non-confluence probably already tells you something, but though I suspect that Frank has latterly relented (ha! another private battle won), his obstinate reluctance to use the 'p' word has been a mark of his career. He has his reasons. 'Postcolonial' has always been a troublesome term, involuntarily cancelling out differences even as it vigorously asserts them. It is also a conflict-ridden term: One that welcomes internal dissent and more-than-occasional bouts of abject hand-wringing, and one that is always spoiling, given even half the opportunity, for a fight. A more congenial term, at least on the surface, is the one that I associate first and foremost with Frank's work: 'transcultural'. Although 'transcultural' is no more transparent a term than 'postcolonial', it is easy enough to define its dominant characteristics. If 'transculturality' ostensibly describes the 'dynamic structure of human cultures', it simultaneously insists on the complexity and diversity of the processes that make up these cultures, which are less bounded entities than ragged-edged amalgams composed of repeated acts of local/global transfer and exchange (Anastasijevic et al. 2020: n.p., *Keywords in Transcultural English Studies*; see also Schulze-Engler and Helff 2009).

'Transculturalism', the *modus operandi* for this syncretic view of cultural exchange, involves two rather different conceptions of the *family*. For Regina Kessy, transculturalism is tantamount to 'thinking as a human family', building support for 'tolerant communities' that are appropriately 'mindful of human dignity' and respectful towards social and cultural differences without seeking to pigeonhole them in territorial, linguistic, or racial/ethnic terms (2018: n.p.). A different view of transculturalism, however, involves thinking *beyond* the family, or at least beyond normative, biogenetic understandings of the family as a social unit. My Leeds colleague John McLeod, in his important work on transcultural adoption, stresses affiliative over filiative ties as the ethical basis for human relations, challenging those models of 'biogenetic attachment, racial genealogy, cultural identity and normative family-making' that have tended to dominate most thinking about the family in modern times (McLeod 2015: n.p.). Although she doesn't use the term 'transcultural' as far as I know, Donna Haraway has been influential as well, both in critiquing normative conceptions of the family and, in her own particular case, positing more bio-egalitarian alternatives to it. These she sees primarily in terms of *kin*, her umbrella term for 'webs of affective and material relationships' (Haraway 2016: 216) that extend beyond the human species and are not circumscribed by anthropocentric (and often patriarchal) paradigms of ancestry or genealogical descent. Family, Haraway insists, cannot do the work of kin, which stretches well beyond the family unit, crucially contesting the self-perpetuating logic of reproduction on which most heteronormative understandings of the family are solidly based (2016: 202–3). Family is by definition a domesticating term, whereas kin is 'a wild category that all sorts of people [can only] do their best to domesticate' (2016: 2). Kinship *defamiliarizes* in the sense that it implicitly represents an uncoupling of 'kin' from the domestic protocols of 'family', but it also explicitly discards such universalizing ideas as 'common humanity' – hence Haraway's emphasis on the performative act of 'kin-making' as an inevitably selective formation of alliances which, while border-crossing to some extent, also 'recognizes specificities, priorities, and urgencies [...]. Kinships exclude as well as include, and they should do that' (2016: 207).

The rest of this chapter picks up briefly on some of these ideas, which I see as being folded, whether directly or not, into the capacious concept of the 'transcultural', and while I have my own issues with the term (and will come back to these), I recognize its value and salute Frank's work in applying it to a wide range of different examples from all corners of the world. Taking my cue from this work, I now want to look more specifically at what 'family' means in works by two twentieth-century British celebrity conservationists: Gerald Durrell and Jane Goodall. As will be seen, this involves a crossover postcolonial/transcultural approach that potentially opens up alternative, non-human-specific ideas of the family, but also challenges some of the ideologies lurking behind them: the family as multispecies collective; the ancestral family; the Family of Man. Part of my purpose is to gauge the extent to which transcultural ideas/ideals, which tend to blur the boundaries between the familiar and the foreign, are compatible with those of the family, or whether they require a broader, more affiliative understanding of human and non-human relations in which even those most intimate to us remain unknown to us – as we remain largely unknown to ourselves.

Gerald Durrell is widely acknowledged to be one of the most accomplished nature writers of the twentieth century, both within and beyond Britain, as well as 'one of the great conservation leaders of the modern world' (Botting

2000: xvii). Although Durrell's star has arguably waned since his death in 1996, many of his books are still in print and *My Family and Other Animals* ([1956] 1971), in particular, remains popular more than half a century after it was first published. Similarly, Durrell's wide-ranging conservation work continues to be influential. The Durrell Wildlife Preservation Trust, established after his death, is one of the world's most recognized wildlife charities, while Jersey Zoo, one of his most treasured conservation projects, remains operational more than sixty years after it was first set up. During his lifetime, Durrell – a larger-than-life figure in almost every sense – identified himself as being in the vanguard of the international conservation movement, for which, according to his biographer Douglas Botting, he believed himself to be one of the 'standard bearers in a new moral crusade' to save wildlife from the extinction that threatened it worldwide (Botting 2000: 240). He also became a global celebrity at a time when conservation – now widely seen as being a major conduit for celebrity – emerged as the media-driven, capital-intensive global phenomenon that we recognize it as today (Brockington 2009; Huggan 2013).

Durrell was a contemporary of David Attenborough's, and the two men shared several characteristics: A life-long love of wildlife, a good understanding of the ways in which this love might be transmitted to a wide audience, and a charismatic presence, both in front of the camera (Durrell, much like Attenborough, was a tireless, globetrotting broadcaster) and in other aspects of public life. Perhaps the biggest connection between the two, however, was (and, in Attenborough's case, remains) their self-presentation as *amateur naturalists*. Durrell, again like Attenborough, had few professional zoological credentials and never claimed as much; instead, he identified himself as an amateur in the British natural-historical tradition: A self-taught animal lover, committed to educating others about the need to protect endangered animals and convinced by the intrinsic value of wildlife.

Durrell's focus on extinction seems up to the minute today, and in some ways he was a quintessentially modern figure, well aware of the uses that might be made of his own celebrity and by no means averse to mixing the profit motive of corporate capitalism with the moral imperative to save threatened wildlife. However, in other respects (and once again the comparison with Attenborough is apt) he was something of a throwback, not just in terms of his indebtedness to the natural-historical tradition, but also in his cultivation of what might uncharitably be described as a colonialist sensibility in both his life and his conservation work. The connections between conservation and colonialism are well documented (see, e.g., Drayton 2000; Grove 1995), while there is evidence to suggest that modern-day conservation, however well intentioned, serves predominantly First World political and economic interests, or provides the rationale for top-down forms of social and environmental control (Adams and Mulligan 2003; Duffy 2010). Durrell's conservation work is not unsusceptible to this critique, and it seems significant that much of it was done in the twilight of empire, while his ancestral connections (he was born in India) link him clearly to the heyday of the Raj (Botting 2000: xvii).

A never seriously shaken belief in the superiority of the British also emerges periodically in his writing, especially in early works such as *The Overloaded Ark* (1953) and *The Bafut Beagles* (1954), which recount his African expeditions as a young man in language that cannot help but strike contemporary readers as racist, even if it was also very much a product of its time. To some extent, this attitude also appears in by far his best-known work, *My Family and Other Animals* ([1956] 1971), which in keeping with most of his early books is travel writing masquerading as natural history rather than the other way round. Certainly, the text has more in common with British travel writing of the time by the likes of, say, Eric Newby than it does with the natural-historical writing of his contemporaries. And like much of Newby's work, *My Family* – ostensibly a retrospective of the Durrell family's enchanted years in Corfu (1935–9) – offers a slapstick account of the misadventures of the English abroad, featuring many of that now dated subgenre's classic ingredients: locals with funny habits and even funnier accents, throwaway remarks about the 'native temperament' and, perhaps above all, a seemingly automatic deference towards the British. As the narrator says early on, tongue only half in cheek, 'The fact that I was English was sufficient [to be trusted], for the islanders had a love and respect for the Englishman out of all proportion to his worth. They would trust an Englishman where they would not trust each other' (Durrell 1971: 47).

My Family is redeemed, to some extent, by its instinct for self-parody and, more particularly, by its wry and at times even melancholy awareness of its own escapism, with its uncomplicated childhood perspective licensing old-school natural-historical pursuits which, even back in the 1930s, were well past their sell-by date. Ten-year-old Gerald is described gleefully stealing eggs and, in one case, snatching baby magpies straight out of their nest, while the island's bountiful natural environment reveals itself without too much effort and seems not to object over much to being disturbed. The childhood perspective also allows for exaggeration, with every family outing seen as an expedition, and every new natural-historical discovery opening up a different (animal) world. People are included among these discoveries, and are assessed using similar behavioural criteria; often they are explicitly likened to animals and vice versa, as when young Gerald examines the courtship rituals of his teenage sister Margo's numerous Greek suitors, or introduces us to three visiting British artists, one of whom 'looked and sounded like a cockney owl with a fringe', and another of whom 'looked like a well-boiled prawn with a mop of dark, curly hair' (1971: 121).

Durrell's gift for caricature is joined here to what might be called a juvenile form of sociobiology, the study of the biological basis for social behaviour which, a couple of decades later, would come to be associated with the Harvard-based entomologist E. O. Wilson's work. Mostly, though, *My Family* contents itself with shifting between 'older', natural-historical ways of describing and acting upon the natural world, and 'newer' ecological perspectives. A good example is the chapter 'The World in a Wall', which reveals a wealth of life hidden within the crumbling wall of the Durrells's sunken garden. In scientific terms, this might be described as an ecological niche, a mixed biotic community of plants and animals; but scientific terms are beyond the self-taught Gerald, for whom the wall and its inhabitants are, instead, a 'rich hunting ground' (1971: 129). Still, the descriptions the narrator provides are accurate enough and, anthropomorphisms aside, the chapter gives a good sense of the autonomy of a miniature world – one to which an impressionable young boy is granted privileged access, but also one which operates independently of him, its hybrid blend of predators and prey difficult for him to distinguish as 'everything seemed to feed indiscriminately off everything else' (1971: 130).

This is nature writing in classic observational mode, yoked to a childhood idyll in which the 'secret' island of Corfu, still largely shielded from the outside world in the 1930s, offers a seemingly inexhaustible source of astonishment through its rich profusion of native wildlife. Nature functions alternately as spectacle and (adventure) playground, and often both of these at once, with the antics of its human and animal inhabitants amplified to the level of comic opera as the text, scattered lyrical interludes apart, moves at pace from one manic set piece to the next (1971: 7). Though it wouldn't be published until a couple of decades later, one suspects that Durrell would have heartily agreed with the tone and spirit of Joseph Meeker's pioneering 1974 study *The Comedy of Survival*, where comedy, seen by Meeker as a 'mode of action common to many animal species and deeply rooted in evolutionary history', registers 'a valuable contribution to survival and a habit that promotes [individual and social] health' (Meeker [1974] 1997: 9–11). Comedy, for Meeker, means 'muddling through [rather than] progress or perfection' (1997: 160); oriented as it is towards the evolutionary advantages of cooperation and adaptation, it tends to avoid the types of polarized conflicts that characterize a tragic view of life (1997: 37).

This might help account for the fact that *My Family*, in keeping with most of Durrell's written work, is anything but a conventional conservationist vehicle; in fact, as Botting points out, 'there is not a glimmer to be found [in any of Durrell's early writings] of [his] views on the proper role of zoos, on animal conservation in general, and on the captive breeding of endangered species in particular', all issues that were central to his life's work (Botting 2000: 206). It might also help explain why Durrell's writing, allied to this work, was paradoxically effective in raising awareness of conservation issues, drawing attention to conservation precisely by *not* attending to it, and by choosing to focus instead on 'feel-good' accounts of the wonder and beauty of the natural world. Not that Durrell was shy of advertising the tragedy of extinction in the public domain, as evidenced in his typically forthright views at the 1976 World Conference on Breeding Endangered Species in Captivity: 'Mankind is creating false extinctions caused by over-population. All species are being pushed to one side by the damage we are doing to their habitats. Mankind continues to act as if there were another world just around the corner which we can use when we have ruined this one. But there isn't' (480). As Botting observes, the sheer scale of animal extinctions worldwide would cast a long shadow over Durrell's life, which had its own fair share of losses. His father died of a brain aneurysm when he was just three, and much of his early writing emerged out of *that* shadow. The epigraph to *My Family*, taken from Shakespeare's *As You Like It*, references a 'humorous sadness' that is never far beneath the surface of his work, and indeed one of the many ironies that surround Durrell's life and work is that, while no one could have been more committed than he was to the protection of endangered animals, he was never particularly good at protecting himself (1971: 4).

Durrell's writing, like Durrell himself, is marked by a restless energy that is always on the point of tipping over into excess, and that routinely mocks its own extravagances. If its charms are faded today, that's probably because the Durrell brand is so obviously designed to be old-fashioned. In *My Family*, the anachronistic qualities of Durrell's work, filtered through a childhood persona, are strategically magnified, allowing him to present a view of a real place that exists partly in memory, but also partly in the imagination: a looking-glass world. The unreality of the text (as in the Alice books) is produced out of an exaggerated sense of innocence, supporting a light-hearted study of cross-species family ties in which, ironically, non-human animals are taken *away* from their families, seconded to a young boy's fantasy mission to bring as much of the natural world indoors as he can.

My Family, in this and other respects, offers a wry but still largely self-justificatory account of an assimilated multispecies family – one whose hierarchical and domesticating tendencies are reminiscent of another long-outdated natural-historical paradigm, the Family of Man. The Family of Man, as is well known, was a vast Victorian natural-historical project aimed at establishing a pattern by which human beings and other living creatures could be assigned an orderly place within a pre-set classificatory grid arranged, evolutionary adaptations notwithstanding, along rigidly hierarchical lines (Norcia 2010: n.p.). Usually traced to Darwin's *Origin of Species* (1859), the Family of Man effectively licensed several generations of white-British imperialists to take a familial responsibility upon themselves to 'improve their colonial children [by exposing them] to English cultural ideals, manners, government and religion' (Norcia 2010: n.p.). In Anne McClintock's words, 'Britain's emergent national narrative took increasing shape [during the second half of the nineteenth century] around the image of the evolutionary Family of Man. The family offered an indispensable metaphorical figure by which national difference could be shaped into a single historical genesis narrative' (1995: 23).

Within the overarching logic of the Family of Man, colonized people could be welcomed into the family fold as long as they agreed to keep their place and to behave themselves; the nuclear family unit, as Richard Phillips argues, thus became one of the essential building blocks upon which colonial systems, embedded within the larger Family of Man structure, could sustainably be based (2009: 1).

While it would be going too far to see Durrell as subscribing to this openly racist model of interspecies/intercultural relations, it is worth challenging the conciliatory humour that he uses to mask the aggressive privileges on which the model is based. What is largely missing from his work, it could be said, is a *trans*species/*trans*cultural perspective in which the material and imaginative possibilities of relating to unfamiliar others is weighed against the dangers of assimilating their differences; in which, in Haraway's terms, the entrenched power differentials that block a view of kinship as *itself* unfamiliar are simply wished away. Kin, in Haraway's revisionist terms, are 'unfamiliar (outside what we thought was family or gens), uncanny, haunting, active': They make us as much as we make them (2016: 103). Families, for Haraway, work according to the self-privileging logic of recognition and resemblance, whereas kin afford no such securities: Ancestors are interesting, not in spite of the fact, but *because* of the fact, that they are passing strange (2016: 103). Transculturalism, at its best, offers just such an uncanny perspective, not least in its insistence that the familiar and the foreign, far from being mutually exclusive, are productively cross-contaminating terms (Schulze-Engler and Helff 2009).

Published some fifteen years later than *My Family* (1971), Jane Goodall's *In the Shadow of Man* could hardly be more different in its approach, but its extended account of Goodall's pioneering *in situ* study of chimpanzee social relations – which would itself extend over a period of ten years – shares Durrell's basic aim of extending the human family to include other animals, while its aura of innocent idealism would feed into a 'Goodall legend' that proved every bit as durable as Durrell's, turning this unlikeliest of duos into the foremost celebrity conservationists of their times. In Goodall's case, the legend emerged out of a timely conjunction of mutually influencing factors, notably her subject (primatology) and her gender (female) – a combination which, almost unheard of at the time (the 1960s), would have a dramatically galvanizing effect on the international media reception of her work (Fedigan 2001). Meanwhile, it can also be attributed to her celebrity status as a twentieth-century white-British 'environmental saviour' who, albeit in a very different mould to Durrell's, became iconically associated with the global protection of endangered wildlife (Huggan 2013: 7).

Now in her late eighties, Goodall remains as popular a figure as ever, as do the various 'rehabilitant narratives' which, featuring chimpanzees and other apes as surrogates for humans, look to offer relief for the turbulent times we live in by rescuing endangered animals in order that humanity might be rescued from itself (Haraway 1989: 156). Conciliatory scenarios of human–simian contact are integral to these narratives, as they are throughout *In the Shadow of Man*, with one particular scene having become iconic in its own right. In the scene, Goodall, reacquainted a decade after establishing contact with one of her original primate subjects, David Greybeard, holds hands with him in an intimate 'drama of touch' (Haraway 1989: 149) that not only peels away the years, but also reaches out across differences of all kinds (sex, race, species) in a semi-mythical setting in which 'both are rehabilitated to a natural wildness to which Man, their ultimate stand-in, is [serendipitously] reconciled and restored' (Huggan 2013: 108). Donna Haraway reads the scene as emblematic for Goodall's 'message of natural peace' (1989: 127), harnessing it to what she sees as one of primatology's most striking mythic narratives, in which the figure of Woman, mediating between animal 'nature' and human 'culture', is conscripted for the task of mending the broken link between both of them and the master figure of Original Man (Huggan 2013: 108; see also Haraway 1989: 150).

Allied to these myths is what might loosely be called the myth of 'wild Africa'. This myth, which still feeds into some popular Western conservation narratives, represents the African continent as a 'refuge from the technological age' and a 'glorious Eden for wildlife' (Adams and McShane 1992: xii); it also engages the contradictions inherent in colonial Africa as at once a field for the free play of conquistadorial fantasy (Hammond and Jablow 1975) and a site to be reverentially protected, 'held in trust for future generations [...] as a reminder of our savage past' (Adams and McShane 1992: 8; see also Huggan 2009: 71). Finally, the myth of 'wild Africa' taps into another powerful myth, that of human origins, which celebrates Africa as ancestral presence (site of Original Man) even as some versions of it simultaneously imply that Africa still is what Europe is no longer: A 'dark' place of deficit from which today's modern Europeans have triumphantly evolved (Mudimbe 1990). (Suffice to mention here that Frank's work, much of which centres on Africa, painstakingly debunks these pernicious colonial myths, positing in their place a pluralistic view of the continent as an internally differentiated site in which 'transcultural modernities' are continually reshaped and renegotiated, and colonial legacies, even as these periodically resurface, are repeatedly faced down [see, e.g., Schulze-Engler and Riemenschneider 1993; also Bekers et al. 2009].)

As I have already implied, Durrell's work – particularly his early work – is hardly immune from these myth-making tendencies, and while Goodall's is significantly more nuanced, it remains deeply entangled in the mythic narratives that surround the field of primatology, which posits the great apes, not just as human ancestors, but as 'shadow' members of the larger human family: the Family of Man. One of the points of such mythic narratives, Haraway suggests, is to blur the uneven relations of power that made the post–Second World War study of primates possible in the first place. Chimpanzees, *pace* Haraway, exist in the shadow of man in more senses than one, and the scientific breakthroughs of the 1960s – the discovery that chimpanzees and other apes were more like us than we could ever have thought – provided a powerful if also powerfully mystifying antidote to an era marked by the major social upheavals that accompanied decolonization and the civil rights movement, and that was stalked by the potentially world-ending spectre of nuclear war. It is certainly true that popular-scientific works like *In the Shadow of Man* convey little sense of the world outside of their own immediate sphere of influence, and it is particularly telling that Goodall's text makes so little of the coming-into-being of Tanzania as a fully independent nation in 1961, only a year after her own field studies began. However, at another level, the text is seemingly aware of its own ambivalent status as a late-colonial artefact. When Stephen Jay Gould, in attempting to rescue Goodall's work from the criticism it received at the time, rightly celebrates it as 'one of the great achievements of twentieth-century scholarship', he slightly spoils the point by denying that it is 'a dying gasp from the old world of romantic exploration' (Gould, qtd in Goodall 1993: vii); in fact, the text derives much of its narrative power from the fact that it is an accomplished piece of modern scientific writing and a late-romantic travelogue *at the same time*. It is also a typically anxious piece of animal writing, with its anxieties evenly distributed between Goodall's keen awareness of her own vulnerability in the face of her animal subjects, who are immeasurably more powerful than she is, and her nagging uncertainty about the validity of her scientific research, which asks more questions than it can possibly answer and is hedged about with qualifications of all kinds (Goodall 1993: 57).

To some extent, the care Goodall takes with the text, notably her reluctance to over-claim, is of a piece with the respect she shows towards the animals, who are socially and individually differentiated in ways that only a prolonged period of intense scrutiny – Goodall is adamant throughout that her field research should not be mistaken for casual observation – allows. However, their surface similarities aside, the emotional lives of animals are *not* equated with those of humans, and while Goodall acknowledges that the lasting relationships that some of them develop with one another 'may be [seen as] shadowy forerunners of human love affairs, I cannot conceive of chimpanzees developing emotions, one for the other, comparable in any way to the tenderness, the protectiveness, tolerance, and spiritual exhilaration that are the hallmarks of human love in its truest and deepest sense' (122, 126, 196). 'Chimpanzees', she goes on to suggest, 'usually show a lack of consideration for each other's feelings which in some ways may represent the deepest part of the gulf between them and us. For the male and female chimpanzee there can be no exquisite awareness of each other's body – let alone each other's mind' (187).

Remarks like this imply that while Goodall granted her animal subjects life histories of their own, she also saw them as lacking the intellectual and emotional complexity of their human counterparts; they also indicate that, like today's animal biographers, she was fully aware of the pitfalls of projecting human thoughts and emotions onto non-human animals, of attempting to account for animals' individuality without resorting to 'reconstruct their feelings [or] read their minds' (Krebber and Roscher 2018: 2). Indeed, Goodall's support for conservation in *In the Shadow of Man* appears to be based on her recognition of animals' *differences* from humans: Differences only further illuminated when, as is demonstrably the case with the great apes, they share several similarities with our so-called primitive ancestors as well as with our contemporary selves. Modern animal writing tends to support this view, which is based less on the alterity of animals than on the fact that we continue to know so little about them while so readily claiming some sort of emotional connection with them. Modern animal writing – and I will close on this point – thus offers interesting opportunities to join transcultural to transspecies perspectives without necessarily subscribing to *either* the unifying myths of family *or* the hierarchical kinship networks that tend to accompany uncritical applications of these two terms. The multipurpose prefix 'trans', functioning at its best, challenges such hegemonic relational structures and the supposedly reassuring explanations they seek to provide. It permits the recognition of shared properties and characteristics that work *beyond* prescriptive classificatory systems, but also *across* them, allowing for productive boundary-crossings of different kinds. There is a danger, of course, that the sometimes improbable affiliations that these crossings produce can end up offering their own kind of reassurance, and as Haraway rightly reminds us, even the unlikeliest discoveries of 'kin' are subject to potentially violent exclusion processes, just as 'family' ties work to hide the coercive practices that help maintain their inclusivity – nowhere more so than in such supposedly all-encompassing structures as the Family of Man.

As Frank knows only too well, I have difficulties accommodating 'mild' versions of transculturalism (though these are not, to be fair, his own) that simply replace competition with cooperation, or that downplay the issues of power that postcolonialism highlights – including the abusive power to define what 'culture' is, and to whom it 'rightfully' belongs. I also suspect that there are good reasons why the particular form of transcultural English studies that Frank has done so much to develop and promote has proved so popular in Germany; that there are not always acknowledged links between, for example, its situated approach to colonialisms worldwide and their far-reaching, sometimes devastating consequences: broader Kantian understandings of cosmopolitanism and global community, and Habermasian liberal–pluralist initiatives to extend democracy beyond the potentially imprisoning (and often tacitly ethnocentric) context of the modern nation-state. Hence Frank's admirable view, consistently upheld, of literature as a rich reservoir of cross-fertilizing transcultural values that refuse to be circumscribed by any one culture, nation, race or ethnicity, in so far as *any* of these pseudo-familial categories can warrant being seen in singular terms. I'm not a cultural nationalist either, and these days it seems almost ridiculous for a British citizen (albeit of Scottish descent!) to be one. Perhaps

I'm a 'transculturalist', too, though a 'postcolonialist' first and foremost. Put that down to an unseemly family squabble: You and I are kin, Frank, and I value your friendship as much as I ever have – may it last for another thirty years!

Acknowledgement

Part of this chapter was previously published in Will Abberly, Christina Alt, David Higgins, Graham Huggan and Pippa Marland, *Modern British Nature Writing, 1789-2020: Land Lines*, published in 2022 by Cambridge University Press. My thanks to the publishers for allowing material to be reprinted here.

References

Adams, J. S. and T. O. McShane (1992), *The Myth of Wild Africa: Conservation without Illusion*, New York: Norton.

Adams, B. and M. Mulligan (eds) (2003), *Decolonizing Nature: Strategies for Conservation in a Post-Colonial Era*, London: Earthscan.

Anastasijevic, S. et al. (2020), *Keywords in Transcultural English Studies – The Glossary*, Frankfurt: Goethe Universität. Available online: www.transcultural-english-studies.de (accessed 14 October 2020).

Bekers, E., S. Helff and D. Merolla (eds) (2009), *Transcultural Modernities: Narrating Africa in Europe*, Amsterdam: Rodopi.

Botting, D. (2000), *Gerald Durrell: The Authorised Biography*, London: HarperCollins.

Brockington, D. (2009), *Celebrity and the Environment: Fame, Wealth and Power in Conservation*, London: Zed Books.

Drayton, R. (2000), *Nature's Government: Science, Imperial Britain, and the 'Improvement' of the World*, New Haven, CT: Yale University Press.

Duffy, R. (2010), *Nature Crime: How We're Getting Nature Wrong*, New Haven, CT: Yale University Press.

Durrell, G. (1953), *The Overloaded Ark*, London: Faber & Faber.

Durrell, G. (1954), *The Bafut Beagles*, London: Rupert Hart-Davis.

Durrell, G. ([1956] 1971), *My Family and Other Animals*, reprint, London: Penguin.

Fedigan, L. (2001), 'The Paradox of Feminist Primatology: The Goddess's Discipline?', in A. Creager, E. Lunbeck and L. Schiebinger (eds), *Feminism in Twentieth-Century Science, Technology, and Medicine*, 47–72, Chicago: University of Chicago Press.

Goodall, J. ([1971] 1993), *In the Shadow of Man*, London: Weidenfeld & Nicolson.

Gould, S. J. ([1993] 1988), 'Introduction to the Revised Edition', in J. Goodall, *In the Shadow of Man*, vii–xi, London: Weidenfeld & Nicolson.

Grove, R. H. (1995), *Green Imperialism: Colonial Expansion, Tropical Island Edens and the Origins of Environmentalism, 1600–1860*, Cambridge: Cambridge University Press.

Hammond, D. and A. Jablow (1975), *The Myth of Africa*, New York: Library of Social Sciences.

Haraway, D. (1989), *Primate Visions: Gender, Race, and Nation in Modern Science*, New York: Routledge.

Haraway, D. (2016), *Staying with the Trouble: Making Kin in the Chthulucene*, Durham, NC: Duke University Press.

Huggan, G. (2009), *Extreme Pursuits: Travel/Writing in an Age of Globalization*, Ann Arbor: University of Michigan Press.

Huggan, G. (2013), *Nature's Saviours: Celebrity Conservationists in the Television Age*, London: Routledge/Earthscan.

Kessy, R. (2018), 'What Is Transculturalism?' Available online: www.transculturalfoundation.org/what-is-transculturalism (accessed 14 October 2020).

Krebber, A. and M. Roscher (2018), *Animal Biography: Re-framing Animal Lives*, London: Palgrave Macmillan.

McClintock, A. (1995), *Imperial Leather: Race, Gender and Sexuality in the Imperial Contest*, Chicago: University of Chicago Press.

McLeod, J. (2015), *Life Lines: Writing Transcultural Adoption*, London: Bloomsbury.

Meeker, J. W. (1997), *The Comedy of Survival: Literary Ecology and a Play Ethic*, Tucson: University of Arizona Press.

Mudimbe, V. Y. (1990), *The Invention of Africa: Gnosis, Philosophy, and the Order of Knowledge*, London: James Currey.

Norcia, M. A. (2010), 'The Dysfunctional "Family of Man" – Mary Venning and Barbara Hofland Classify Human Races in Pre-Darwinian Primers'. Available online: www.victorianweb.org/history/norcia1.html (accessed 14 October 2020).

Phillips, R. (2009), 'Settler Colonialism and the Nuclear Family', *Canadian Geographer* 53 (2): 239–53.

Schulze-Engler, F. and S. Helff (eds) (2009), *Transcultural English Studies: Theories, Fictions, Realities*, Amsterdam: Rodopi.

Schulze-Engler, F. and D. Riemenschneider (eds) (1993), *African Literature in the Eighties*, Amsterdam: Rodopi.

Soble, A. G. (2003), 'Review of Fact and Value: Essays on Ethics and Metaphysics for Judith Jarvis Thomson, ed. A. Byrne, A. Stalnaker, and R. Wedgwood', *Essays in Philosophy* 4 (1): 70–5.

5

The 'makings of a diasporic self': Transcultural life writing, diaspora and modernity in Stuart Hall's *Familiar Stranger* (2017)

Katja Sarkowsky
Augsburg University

Theory, relationality and the voice(s) of memoir

Familiar Stranger: A Life Between Two Islands, cultural theorist Stuart Hall's posthumously published memoir, is in many ways a genre hybrid. Early on, Hall formulates both a disclaimer and a programmatic statement: 'I never want to write a memoir.' Instead, he explains, 'I am more concerned here, as I have been in much of my more professional academic writing, with the connection between "a life" and "ideas"' (2017: 10). What follows is, indeed, not a 'memoir in a formal sense' (Hall 2017: 10), and even though the book is centrally concerned with the development of Hall's ideas as a theorist, it is also not a straightforward intellectual autobiography. Rather, it presents a hybrid format that seeks to understand the life story of the autobiographer in its intertwinement with political, social, historical and intellectual processes; long passages of the book do not deal with Hall's individual life but sketch, for instance, the history of Jamaica or the social structure of post-war Britain. Yet, these socio-historical – deindividualized – 'digressions' do not only provide an important framework for placing 'Stuart Hall' and his life story, but they are also, as the text makes clear, an integral part of Hall's intellectual becoming. Writing his life is thus not merely a sketch of said life and the emergence of the theoretical concepts that have been so important for his overall work, such as diaspora or cultural identity; what is more, these concepts at the same time serve as an analytical matrix for understanding his life: *Familiar Stranger* performs the mutual illumination of life, life story and theory.

But Hall's memoir is a hybrid in another way as well. It emerged out of dialogues and conversations, with other texts and with other people, and while there are important intertextual dialogues to be discussed later in this chapter, the dialogical emergence of *Familiar Stranger* is to be understood very literally so. It was co-written with British historian Bill Schwarz, who – as Hall's long-time friend, interlocutor and, with Catherine Hall, literary executor – arranged the material and edited the book three years after Hall's death. In his preface, Schwarz retraces how a set of commissioned interviews on Hall's intellectual development some twenty years ago turned into a manuscript of over 300,000 words by the time of Hall's death in 2014. 'The book had evolved as a shared manuscript, which changed hands between Stuart and myself over many years for revision and emendation', he explains. 'Over time the authorial provenance of many passages slipped from view' (Schwarz 2017: xv). The explicitly dialogical structure of the interviews was replaced by a first-person narrative late in the process, as Schwarz relates, but it continues to organize both the structure of the narrative and its tone. *Familiar Stranger* is thus, in more than one way, a deeply relational text. Life writing – autobiography and memoir in particular – tends to be considered a solitary genre, the expression of an autonomous subjectivity, but, as Paul John Eakin reminds us, 'the subject of autobiography to which the pronoun "I" refers is neither singular nor first', insisting 'that the first person of autobiography is truly plural in its origins and subsequent formations' (1999: 43). Collaborative memoirs such as *Familiar Stranger* can therefore be regarded as texts that explicitly showcase the fundamental relationality inherent to the genre.

There are, of course, highly problematic or even exploitative examples of collaborative life writing, depending on the power asymmetries between the collaborators, the control or 'author-ity' over the text in question, and (often) the financial and reputational benefit that come of its publication.[1] The purpose of

---

[1] Since *Familiar Stranger* was published posthumously, there is clearly the problem of final authorization of the text, a problem Schwarz addresses at the end of his preface: 'For me the outstanding difficulty is that Stuart himself was unable to adjudicate on the finished draft. I can imagine his many reservations. He could never return to his writing without being tempted to take it apart and to drive the argument on, or take it in new directions. This certainly would have been no exception' (Schwarz 2017: xvii). This, I would think, pertains also to the structure of the overall text, the selection and narrative combination of textual elements that characterize self-narration as much as any other kind of text; my reading of *Familiar Stranger* pays close attention to the memoir's 'emplotment' and hence to an aspect of the text over which Hall himself had no final control. I regard the text as a form of dual-voiced auto/biography based on trust and dialogue in which the autobiographical voice is, to

devoting some space to this issue in this introductory section is not to call into question the authority of Hall's autobiographical voice; on the contrary, given the way in which Hall worked as a theorist and activist, the collaborative form and the tone of this memoir seems programmatic, the autobiographical voice self-reflexively plural and dialogical. David Scott's epistolary explorations of Stuart Hall's voice in his eponymous monograph have important implications for reading Hall's memoir as a dialogical text. Scott highlights the centrality of dialogue for Hall's theoretical work, and he sees the responsiveness and necessary openness of dialogue manifest in Hall's writing – the written text preserving the type of address of the talk from which it often originated. Addressing Hall, Scott acknowledges 'the vivid sense one has in your writing that you are *speaking*, and speaking to *someone*, namely, the reader', immediately clarifying that this is more than the address to an implied reader that every text necessarily performs: 'These essays are *addresses*, literally. What they *do* is verbally attend to others – that is what their linguistic action is. They presume – or perhaps more properly, they mimetically reconstruct – the *relationality* of your spoken discourse' (2017: 33; emphases in the original). Scott's emphasis on the discursive orality of Hall's theoretical work applies to some extent to *Familiar Stranger* (which was published in the same year as *Stuart Hall's Voice*) as well, and the initial conceptualization of the memoir as a series of interviews is very much in line with this reading. Scott calls interviews a form of 'thinking with' (2017: 5), and while the first-person narrative on which Hall, Schwarz and the publishers eventually settled suggests a more conventional, seemingly monological autobiographical narrative, the text nevertheless retains that sense of 'thinking with' which, I suggest, links Hall's theorizing and life writing. Both, theory and life narration, tend to be conceptualized as solitary and monological endeavours; in Hall's memoir, by way of its collaborative format, the tone and the way in which the text engages with other texts and concepts, autobiographical narration and social theory co-emerge. The intertwinement of life and theory that *Familiar Stranger* both reflects upon and performs is a relational, dialogical process.

The link between autobiography and theory is an important, but largely under-researched branch of the study of life writing; it has received more attention in biographical writing than in scholarly research, despite what Dieter Thomä, Vincent Kaufmann and Ulrich Schmid in *Der Einfall des Lebens* have called the 'autobiographical turn of theory' (2015: 13). In this book, they propose

an extent, a reconstructed one. I will refer to the autobiographer's voice as Hall's throughout this contribution and use 'Stuart Hall' in the few instances where I refer to the narratively constructed persona.

to read the link between autobiography and theory neither as a 'projection', in which autobiography is understood as a form of self-construction in line with the author's theoretical models, nor as a 'reduction', in which theory becomes a mere expression of the author's life struggles (2015: 8). Rather, they seek to capture the 'interface', the 'juncture between life and writing' (2015: 8; my translations). I understand this as the moments in either life writing or theory (or both), in which an autobiographer reflects upon and theorizes the ways in which life – or rather: a specific life, the writer's life – can be told, and how this life and its possibilities of narrativization are conditioned (not: determined!) by social, cultural, and historical structures and dynamics. This overlaps with what C. Wright Mills has called the 'sociological imagination' and its acute, even embodied awareness of the connection between biography, history and social structure as the 'most fruitful form of self-consciousness' (Mills 2000: 7). But it is amended by a theoretical notion of how not only one's life, but also the *narration* of this life – not just its world-reflecting, but also its world-making capacities – are grounded in the social and historical conditionality of its being and becoming.

The considerations offered in the following pages are tentative in scope: From the perspective of a life-writing scholar, I want to think about the link between self-representation, self-construction and theoretical reflection, and the ways in which transcultural life writing by its own means offers a way of theorizing both transculturality and the possibilities of life writing. Taking Hall's memoir as the text around which to centre such considerations is no accident; not only are questions of cultural identity, diaspora and representation central to his overall work, but *Familiar Stranger* offers important reflections on how these questions intersect with and shape an individual life and its conditions of narrativization, and there are obvious intersections with Hall's theoretical discussions of identity and identity construction. When Hall writes in his essay 'Cultural Identity and Diaspora' that 'who speaks, and the subject who is spoken of, are never identical, never exactly in the same place', he might as well be speaking of the memoir that he was to write. 'Identity', he continues, 'is not as transparent or unproblematic as we think. Perhaps instead of thinking of identity as an already accomplished fact, which the new cultural practices they represent, we should think, instead, of identity as a "production", which is never complete, always in process, and always constituted within, not outside, representation' (1990: 222). Hall's understanding of identity, of its processual character and of its constitution through representation can be read as a conceptual framing of writing one's life and the self-reflective representational processes this entails. As Judith Butler has argued,

> [w]hen the 'I' seeks to give an account of itself, it can start with itself, but it will find that this self is already implicated in a social temporality that exceeds its own capacities for narration; indeed, when the 'I' seeks to give an account of itself, an account that must include the conditions of its own emergence, it must, as a matter of necessity, become a social theorist. (2005: 7–8)

Hall *was* a social theorist (as well as a literary scholar) and very much aware of how not only autobiographical subjects, but also the conditions of self-narration are necessarily implicated in specific social and historical formations. His memoir thus presents a particularly instructive example of a text that seeks not only to combine self-life-writing with theory, but that also writes the autobiographical as a form of theoretization, a work-in-progress that intimately connects self-consciousness with the development and ongoing modification of theoretical concepts and categories – ethnicity, diaspora, race and modernity prominent among them.

In this contribution, I set out to read *Familiar Stranger* as an exploration of the very tension in its title. Obviously, it cannot and does not claim to provide a comprehensive reading of Hall's memoir or to do his important work justice. My aim is modest; what I hope to offer is a sense of *Familiar Stranger*'s conceptualization and actualization of the link between theorizing and transcultural life writing and of some of the broader implications that such a link might have. The section 'Transcultural Life Writing' enquires into the dynamics and characteristics of transcultural life writing in relation to transcultural fiction. Tying in with the question of how such dynamics can be narrated, the section 'Emplotting the Emergence of a Diasporic Subject' looks at ways of 'emplotting' the diasporic self and subject in the memoir. The section 'Ongoing Passages: Displacement, Diaspora and the "Familiar Stranger"' asks how such emplotment brings together displacement as an individual experience, an analytical category and a theoretical concept. The concluding section '"Conscripts of modernity"? The worlding of transcultural life writing' seeks to connect this to another concept central to Hall's memoir, modernity, and – reconnecting to the question of fiction – asks how life writing such as Hall's can productively be understood as an alternative form of literary worlding. Hall's memoir, I suggest, exemplifies how life writing can contribute to our understanding of the constitution not only of a 'social self' in a seemingly monologic genre, but also of how the relationality of this self thus narratively constituted – over and over again – can help reflect upon the very categories of its constitution.

Transcultural life writing

The 1990s saw a number of related important shifts in the social sciences as well as in literary and cultural studies and the newly established academic field of postcolonial studies. A previous focus on the nation gave way to an emphasis on transnationalization; notions of culture and questions of belonging increasingly shifted from an emphasis on 'roots' to one on 'routes' (to use James Clifford's juxtaposition [1997]) and from 'culture' to 'transculturality', picking up both on the insights of cultural anthropology regarding cultures as dynamic systems of practice and on the concepts of writers and theorists such as Éduoard Glissant, Homi K. Bhabha and others who emphasized creolization and hybridity against notions of cultural essence, authenticity or purity.[2] The simultaneous revival and expansion of a theoretical concept of 'diaspora' with its tension between ideas of 'homeland' and transnational and local community building is in this context not accidental and became an important – if at times inflationarily used – touchstone for conceptualizing forms of belonging shaped by tensions between place, mobility, cultural identification and collective historical experience. Such notions of transculturality in the widest sense helped understand processes that might have originated in and shaped by colonial histories, but that also expanded, transcended and transformed the effect and ascribed meaning of these histories and drew attention to the changes that both formerly colonized countries *and* the metropolitan 'centres' underwent during colonialism as well as in the course of decolonization processes. In this context, 'postcolonial Europe', as Frank Schulze-Engler has argued, 'signifies more than cleavages, exclusions, and the legacies of Europe's colonial past; it also signals the permanent presence in Europe, often extending over several generations, of millions of people of non-European origin' (2013: 676), and an ongoing, intimate entanglement of Europe with other parts of the world, as well as of 'western' modernity with other manifestations of it. This has a significant impact on cultural practices and production. With regard to Anglophone fiction, Schulze-Engler has emphasized elsewhere how transnational relations to 'real or imagined "homelands" outside

---

[2] Hall's own work was very implicated with such considerations, see for instance his 'Creolité and the Process of Creolization' (2003).

Europe are inextricably linked to a transcultural dynamic that changes the understanding of British society, culture, and literature not anymore just from its margins, but increasingly also from its midst' (Schulze-Engler 2019: 368–9; my translation).

At first glance, there appears to be a contrast between the explicit constructedness and the imagination of fiction, on the one hand, and memoir and autobiography, genres that are perceived as 'expressing' a self and relate the 'true' events of a life, on the other. Yet, Schulze-Engler's observations regarding the shift in changes from the 'margins' to the 'midst' of British society equally apply to these genres and they relate to the same social and cultural processes that have triggered such shifts in fiction and the transcultural dynamics manifest in it. Given their association with depicting 'true life', one might think that autobiographical genres do so even more than fiction, but life writing, too, involves processes of conscious construction, of selection, omission and combination, and how transcultural dynamics come into play varies as much as it does in fiction. While memoirs and autobiographies often have conventional structures, these structures are neither cast in stone nor are they self-evident. The way in which a memoir (or other kinds of life writing) is structured, its choice of beginning, ending and thematic foci, and not least how it combines its different elements, is crucial for what kind of story it tells. This applies particularly to cross- or transcultural life writing in which, as Rebecca Hogan and Joseph Hogan have put it, the subject 'unfolds/discovers itself in the crossing of cultural boundaries and through the encounter of two or more cultures. The self is explored in the encounter with the other and as the other in this "borderland" or "frontier" or "contact zone" (Anzaldúa; Krupat; and Pratt)' (1997: 149).[3] *How* such an encounter is emplotted – to use Hayden White's term (1973) – as how strongly juxtaposed or potentially intertwined the cultures in question are presented or as how closed or porous a system 'culture' is understood in the first place may vary significantly, though. A life story of

---

[3] Most systematic considerations of cross- or transcultural life writing focus on the narration's content, on its thematic emphasis on travel, migration, displacement, exile or diaspora as constellations of cultural encounter, and this is certainly a decisive aspect of it. A related and complementary way of identifying transcultural life writing is by paying attention to form. Critics have acknowledged that narrating one's life tends to follow culturally available models and thus may vary significantly across cultural contexts (Eakin 1999). Many autobiographers draw on more than one cultural convention of life narration and such a 'hybridization' of form presents an important aspect of life writing's transculturality. While Hall's memoir is, as discussed, in many ways a formal hybrid in its mixture of historiography, theory, autoethnography and autobiographical recollection, I will focus in my discussion of the memoir on the chosen structure, content and references in how processes of transculturation in particular are narrated.

migration can be narrated as one of arrival, transformation, tension, perpetual alienation or return, for instance, and cultural encounters can be presented as stories of conflict, of assimilation, or hybridization; either can be narrated as an individualized story, one of family, or community, in one or more than one voice. While such narrative and structural choices are clearly grounded in how autobiographers remember, understand and interpret their own life and past, they conversely are, as I want to suggest, crucial for that very remembrance, understanding and interpretation. Experience, to paraphrase Joan Scott (1991), is an act of interpretation and is always mediated; life writing does not merely represent but narratively structures the recollection of the past; and identity, to come back to Hall's insight quoted above, is produced within the structures of representation. In other words, life writing documents and reflects transnational and transcultural dynamics not because of its supposedly mimetic character of 'true' events and the depiction of 'real' lives, but precisely because of the *tension* between the constructedness that links it to fiction, on the one hand, and the genre expectations of 'truthfulness', on the other.

Emplotting the emergence of a diasporic subject

Hall is very much aware that his autobiographical recollections in *Familiar Stranger* present an attempt at interpretation of his development, both his life's and his ideas' – a dual act of interpretation, a reconstruction of the emergence of his thinking and a reflection of this emergence in the very terminology of that thinking. The memoir's structure is already indicative not only of a life course – 'from Jamaica to Britain' – but also of a self-reflective narrative order. It is divided into four parts of different lengths, each of which encompasses between one and four chapters, and what at first glance appears as a straightforward journey is, however, much more complicated. Both the issues covered in each part and the section and chapter titles showcase the complexity of developing what Hall later in the memoir calls a 'diasporic self'. So while 'Part I: Jamaica' centres on Hall's childhood and youth in Jamaica, it also retraces Jamaican history and includes extensive theoretical discussions on the category 'race'; 'Part II: Leaving Jamaica' – which I will discuss in more detail in the final section of this chapter – ends with the departure for Britain but largely thinks about education and literature; 'Part III: Journey to an Illusion' deals mostly with Hall's years at Oxford, but connects the recollection of this time to considerations of Caribbean migration to the UK; and 'Part IV: Transition Zone', finally, revisits his move away from Oxford and his increasing politization, but also discusses some of the fundamental concepts that became so important in his later work in more detail, too. Note that the titles of parts III and IV shift away from naming geographical locations, potentially gesturing towards the notion of discursive spaces, and that three of the four section headers indicate movement and transformation; the title's 'life between two islands', we might say, is cast here as a story of becoming, with the two islands – Jamaica and Britain – as both geographical and symbolic locations inscribed by their past and present entanglements and as presenting complex reference points for Hall's identification processes and reflections.

Not surprisingly, then, as a life narrative, the memoir stresses migration, notions of exile and diaspora; it focuses on the first three decades of Hall's life: growing up in a middle-class 'coloured' or 'brown, mixed-race' (2017: 15) family in colonial Jamaica in the 1930s and 1940s, his move to the UK in 1951 on a Rhodes Scholarship to study English at Oxford's Merton College, his increasing political activism and his move to London in 1958. It is the time periods to which Hall attributes formative experiences and it ends with his move to Birmingham. It thus does not cover his subsequent work at the Centre for Contemporary Cultural Studies and his prominent role in expanding the scope of cultural studies and the work done at the centre to attend to race and gender as well as to the initially central category of class. By focusing on the personal and intellectual formation of 'Stuart Hall' up to that point, Hall retrospectively marks a moment of 'emergence', if you will. He writes:

> I have chosen to close the narrative in the early 1960s, when I was entering my thirties. By then I had stepped outside the immediate impress of colonial subjugation, discovering the means of becoming a different sort of person. ... These changes didn't magically resolve the unease which had been incubated as I grew up in a racially subordinate position in colonial Jamaica. It was not an ending like the fabled closure of a Victorian novel. They marked the moment when I came to understand that my life was my own to make, and that obeisance to either colonial Jamaica or to metropolitan Britain, or England, was not the only choice before me. Other spaces opened up. These were, I saw, spaces to be made. (Hall 2017: 3–4)

This passage on the first page of the memoir sets the tone for a narrative that stresses a process of transformation as well as of agency and that rejects a binary juxtaposition of Jamaica and Britain in favour of what might be called with Homi Bhabha a 'third space' which 'though unrepresentable in itself ... constitutes the discursive conditions of enunciation that ensure that the meaning and symbols of culture have no primordial unity or fixity; that even the same signs can be appropriated, translated, rehistoricized and read anew' (Bhabha 1994: 37).[4] In the cited passage, Hall shifts from geographical locations to discursive spaces, and these include the kinds of spaces mapped by the terminology which he developed in his work and which he in this memoir applies to his own life.

It is noteworthy that in this passage, Hall juxtaposes 'colonial Jamaica' to 'metropolitan Britain' and hence the Jamaica of Hall's youth, not the postcolonial Jamaica of his potential future. The time period that ends Hall's memoir was a time of fundamental transition for Jamaica: It had joined the West Indies Federation – a polity Hall was very much in favour of – but left the federation and became an independent nation in 1962. Between 1958 and his departure for Birmingham in 1964, Hall left Oxford for London, worked as a teacher, co-launched and edited the *New Left Review*, married Catherine Hall – and decided to remain in Britain. Hall does not describe this as a conscious decision, though, when he writes: 'By the time I thought I really had to decide, I discovered the decision had already been made' (2017: 203); the decision or rather realization that he would stay in the UK marks the end of a transition period in which, as he describes it, is one of 'disenchantment', a 'shattering of false illusions' (2017: 203) and the realization that 'in ways that are very profound, you can never go home again' (2017: 134).

The 'third spaces' that Hall sees opening up (or rather, that he sees could be *made*) in the early 1960s turn out to be inextricably interwoven with the development of theoretical concepts; thus, the memoir's focus on Hall's formative period explores the basis of many of the concepts that came to play a central role for his later work. One of these concepts is cultural identity, and particularly in the first sections of the memoir, Hall narrates his early life in close intertwinement with considerations of identity and identification in the context of colonial structures and postcolonial subjectivity. The migration story from Jamaica to Britain that 'Stuart Hall' undertakes is one 'of a life-long escape attempt' (2017: 61) and of impossible arrival. 'Escape' is personal: In *Familiar Stranger* as well as in a number of interviews before (and in some of them, even more explicitly), Hall highlights the role of his family's, particularly his mother's investment in a kind of colonial nostalgia, a 'gross colonial simulacrum' (2017: 31) even, and their internalization of and subscription to a strictly hierarchical racial regime – a 'pigmentocracy', to use Edward Telles's term (2014), that results not

---

[4] Hall does not use this term here, but he deploys the concept of 'third space' explicitly at a later point when he speaks about his generation of Caribbean migrants who realize that there is no necessity to choose between the 'viewpoints of colony and metropole. New spaces – third spaces – were in the process of opening up and giving us a life line. This was certainly so for me' (2017: 92).

only in class differences, but also in a division of 'two Jamaicas' (as the second chapter is entitled), a 'European-orientated governing elite' and the 'coloured middle-class' on the one hand and the 'mass of Jamaica's black people' on the other (Hall 2017: 25). 'Plantation life constituted the aspirational model of her hopes and fears, which she recast for her own family to adopt', he writes of his mother (2017: 5), who, as he continues elsewhere in the text, 'had imbibed all the habits of her adopted class' and 'improbably … continued to think of England as her real home' (2017: 27). As such, the sense of estrangement that the young Stuart Hall – whose skin colour, as Hall points out, is 'one of the blackest' in his family (2017: 16) – develops is not only personal, but historically embedded, by implication political, and with a direct effect on the categories with which he eventually comes to order his perception of the world, also as a cultural theorist. 'Partly as a result of this experience [the destructiveness and trauma of his family's colonial simulacrum; clarification added], I have never been able to make that distinction on which so much conventional social science depends, between the "objective" and the "subjective" aspects of social processes, the interior and exterior social worlds', Hall writes (2017: 59). What is of particular interest in the context of this chapter is how he explicitly ascribes this intellectual insight, at least in part, to his lived experience. Early on, the memoir creates the sense of 'displacement' – familially, racially, historically – that is central to the way Hall thinks about and places himself in the world; narratively, this is presented in a number of passages, of which the migration from Jamaica to Britain is only one, as will be discussed in the next section.

Ongoing passages: Displacement, diaspora and the 'Familiar Stranger'

As indicated, the memoir does not narrate Stuart Hall's migration from the Caribbean to Britain as a straightforward journey of departure and arrival. Not only is the story of migration complicated by the intertwinement of emotional ambivalence of the departure as both educational opportunity and escape, the alienating experiences in the UK and the long period in which a return to Jamaica seemed a distinct possibility, but it also involves a process of 'becoming' that encompasses Jamaica and Britain in a complex entanglement of 'here' and 'there' that does not always fully align with geographical locations. The overall narrative trajectory of such becoming, of stepping out of a historically conditioned position into one of self-positioning, can be tentatively cast as one from colonial to West Indian to postcolonial to diasporic. This narrative trajectory does not project a straight line of 'development', either, of course. But it serves as a matrix to understand, as will be discussed further below, the increasing analogization of subject and society in the memoir and its function for Hall's own reconstruction of his social and cultural theoretical framework. The passages described in the memoir are constantly doubled, on different levels – they are geographical and intellectual, but they are also descriptive and interpretative. Passages, 'routes' (Hall 2017: 76), serve as the central conceptual metaphor not only to capture a 'life's journey', but also as interpretative matrix for the understanding of social and cultural constellations; diaspora is not only an experience, but also an 'emergent space of inquiry' (2017: 143).

One central strategy of what I will discuss in the final section as the memoir's 'worlding' is its constant intertextual cross-referencing. Throughout his memoir – and very much in line with its dialogical character as discussed above – Hall references a number of other theorists and texts, including autobiographical texts. Two works that he comes back to time and again are George Lamming's *The Pleasures of Exile* (1960) and Edward Said's *Out of Place* (1999). These references obviously document the engagement with texts that continued to be important for Hall, but beyond the question of personal resonance, they also place his memoir in a particular life-writing tradition. With Lamming, Hall did not only share the West Indian migration experience to the UK (if under different circumstances), but his memoir also shares with *The Pleasures of Exile* the hybrid character in terms of genre; the essays collected in *Pleasures* combine the autobiographical with considerations of politics and particularly literature. Also, Lamming's text was published during the very time period that Hall describes, making it part of a then contemporary reflection on the experiences described in both Hall's and Lamming's texts. Said's memoir *Out of Place* – which refers to a very different migration context and was published during the time when Hall and Schwarz were already conducting the interviews that would eventually result in *Familiar Stranger* – serves, I believe, a different function. Hall references the title more than once, and it is relevant that the 'out-of-placeness' in Said's memoir – like in Hall's own narration – refers to the situation of exile (a notion that Hall adopts at times for his own narrative and that echoes Lamming as well as Said's more general work on the generative power and ambivalence of 'exile') as well as to a familial estrangement. In the course of the memoir, Hall appears to shift slightly from notions of the colonial and postcolonial and the exiled subject to that of the diasporic – but what remains important, also for the relevance of Said as a reference, is that the story of diasporarization begins already in Jamaica: Not only does Hall repeatedly stress the notion of the 'two Jamaicas' where he questions his place in light of his family's history and his own position within his family, but he also points to the already diasporized space of Caribbean societies. Linking his own narrative of place and displacement to these broader historical and cultural processes highlights once more Hall's programmatic attempt to embed his own story in them. But rather than merely illustrating that the individual life is shaped by its historical context, Hall narrates this embeddedness both as a necessary condition and as an analogous process.

The question of cultural identity becomes a crucial intersection of individual and collective dynamics; not only does the centrality of history for the constitution of cultural identity move to the foreground, but also – as discussed more generally above – its processual and provisional character. In 'Cultural Identity and Cinematic Representation', Hall argues that in one important sense, cultural identity

> is a matter of 'becoming' as well as of 'being'. It belongs to the future as much as to the past. It is not something which already exists, transcending place, time, history and culture. Cultural identities come from somewhere, have histories. But, like everything which is historical, they undergo constant trans-formation. Far from being eternally fixed in some essentialised past, they are subject to the continuous 'play' of history, culture and power. Far from being grounded in a mere 'recovery' of the past, which is waiting to be found, and which, when found, will secure our sense of ourselves into eternity, identities are the names we give to the different ways we are positioned by, and position ourselves within, the narratives of the past. (1989: 70)

Hall's thoughts on the ongoing identity formation process of groups apply also to the individual and to individual life narration, where the construction of such 'narratives of the past' takes a slightly different form, with the individual's identificatory choices marked by being positioned as well as self-positioning. Read thus, using other writers' – particularly Lamming's and Said's – autobiographical work as a narrative framing for one's own life story presents an alignment with their experience and their interpretation of it, but by so doing also positions Hall's self-narration in a convention of transcultural life writing that stresses the ambivalence or even impossibility of belonging, that does not 'sublate' the encounters of the contact zone that is so characteristic of this genre (cf. Hogan and Hogan 1997) into a notion (or even desirability) of eventual arrival – let alone, return. The 'diasporic subject' that Hall writes has to constantly re-evaluate and redefine their identificatory alignments, but such alignments continue to have their specific historical moment. At one point, Hall observes: 'I think the form of belonging known now as black British … makes perfect sense for younger generations born in Britain, but of Caribbean descent and background. But I cannot own it. I am of a different generation' (2017: 172), and generation, for Hall, is, as he argues earlier in the book, 'more than chronology. It's symbolic rather than literal', conveying a shared vision and background of experience (2017: 44).

If these considerations of identity and identification are specifically formulated with regard to the Caribbean and/or to Black Britain, the references to Lamming and Said, but also to the work of C. L. R. James, James Baldwin, Henry James and others, at the same time establish transnational and transcultural connections that place the historicized individual experience in a broader interpretative framework of displacement. The title of the memoir is a clear nod towards the notion of the stranger as conceptualized by Georg Simmel, as the one who 'comes today and stays tomorrow', as 'the potential wanderer, so to speak, who, although he has gone no further, has not got over the freedom of coming and going' (Simmel 1971: 143). The 'stranger' in Simmel's understanding becomes familiar without ever fully ceasing to be a stranger, and in an interview with Kuan-Hsing Chen, Hall uses the 'familiar stranger' in explicit reference to Simmel (1996: 490), a reference to which he returns in his memoir when, at some point, he calls himself 'an uneasy traveller between conflicting symbolic homes' and characterizes his 'particular brand of being "out of place" as the product of a diasporic displacement'. This is, he continues, 'the insider/outsider perspective of Georg Simmel's "stranger", the terrain of Homi Bhabha's "in-between", the controlled doubling of Ashis Nandy's "intimate enemies", W. E. B. DuBois's "double consciousness" and Edward Said's "out of place"' (Hall 2017: 172). The diasporic position is thus precisely not the outsider's perspective, but characterized by the *tension between* what is cast as inside and outside.[5]

But Hall's considerations of the 'familiar stranger', as the diasporic subject, do not stop with this subject: The trajectory of 'becoming' that the memoir traces

---

[5] In this context, 'familiar stranger' does not only refer to the diasporic subject; Hall also evokes the discussed tension between the strange and the familiar to narrate his experience of the UK after arrival:

> England seemed simultaneously familiar and strange, homely and unhomely, domesticated, but at the same time a thoroughly dangerous place for the likes of me. I know a lot about it, and yet I did not really know it at all. Encountering the metropole at first hand, not through the screen memory of the colonial displacement, it now seemed populated with unquiet graves and ghosts that wouldn't lie down to rest. … Far from 'coming home' – as I suppose my mother's class and generation must have fondly imagined – I felt all together more dislocated, literally out of place. (2017: 204)

is at once a personal, an individual one *and* the trajectory of a theory of culture and society. Not only is the subject conditioned by their historical, cultural and economic circumstances; conversely, the subject's becoming also serves as the 'prism' through which to analogously understand society and culture – as dynamically evolving, as necessarily hybridized and shaped by displacement as manifestations of a multiple modernity. While this line of thought, as will be discussed in the following final section, starts with the Caribbean, it eventually extends to a more broadly conceived notion of modern society.

'Conscripts of modernity'? The worlding of transcultural life writing

'Part II: Leaving Jamaica' of the memoir encompasses one single chapter, entitled 'Conscripts of Modernity'. In this chapter, Hall recalls his education in Jamaica, the Eurocentric syllabus, but also his encounter with modernism in art and particularly literature, and with jazz music. He describes a process of both discovery and transformation that is shaped by an increasing awareness – and retrospective evaluation – of how that encounter constitutes the colonial subject, but also how society is configured by its constant engagement with modernity and its artistic forms, modernism in particular. 'Modernism, however we choose to understand it' he writes, 'was one of the resources which allowed me to assemble another life, at one remove from the diktats of the colonial order, as I experienced them. Not without contradictions and the occasional cul de sac, of course' (2017: 121).

These contradictions are evoked in the chapter's title which is borrowed from the eponymous monograph that Hall's friend and interlocutor David Scott published in 2004 (Hall 2017: 122), and I suggest that this choice provides a relevant framing not only for this section, but also for Hall's understanding of culture and society developed throughout the memoir. Responding to the debate about multiple modernities in the late 1990s and early 2000s, Scott criticizes what he sees as the substitution of a narrative of submission to colonial modernity with a narrative of resistance to colonial modernity in the debate, and he calls for closer attention to 'the extent to which the transformed terrain on which these creative responses [resistance to dominant notions of modernity and the constitution of "alternative" modernities; clarification added] are being enacted is itself positively constituting (or rather, reconstituting) these subjects' (Scott 2004: 114), and thus how these 'transformations ... *constitute* the making of colonial modernities and the subjects who find themselves conscripts of that structure of power' (2004: 115; emphasis added). The colonial 'conscripts of modernity' are thus indeed inserted into a modernity shaped by power asymmetries, but it is this framework itself that brings forth an alternative terrain of modern existence and subjectivity which might not be in line with hegemonic understanding of what constitutes 'the modern'. Scott's *Conscripts of Modernity* focuses on *The Black Jacobins*, C. L. R. James's 1938 book on Toussaint L'Ouverture and the Haitian Revolution; his analysis highlights the seeming contradiction of using modern concepts of, for instance, freedom against manifestations of that very modernity, such as, colonial structures or slavery, but it is that very contradiction that brings forth alternative forms of modern existence. Hall creates an analogy to his own generation by way of constitution of subjectivity in this 'modern terrain' shaped, but not determined by colonial structures. His memoirs exemplify what Schulze-Engler has referred to as the 'micropolitics of modernity', that is, 'renegotiations, struggles, and changes revolving around intimate questions of personal identity, gender relations, and family life that are less significant for the way in which modernity is experienced than the "big" issues' of individualization, differentiation and rationalization' (2007: 24). But it also exemplifies how the individual's experience and interpretation of it can enable a conceptual reconfiguration of the very conditions of its emergence. In a section on Jamaican language and culture, Hall explains at one point: 'My experience of these Jamaican linguistic practices undoubtedly came to inform my later understanding of how cultures work *in general*' (2017: 75; emphasis in the original); in an important conceptual reversal of conventional understandings of 'standard' and 'deviation' in the development of modern societies and cultures, the Caribbean becomes paradigmatic.

In this context, the processes of displacement and alienation narrated in this memoir become characteristics of a late modern existence. Elaborating in the above-mentioned interview with Kuan-Hsing Chen on the relation between the diasporic, the postmodern and the postcolonial, Hall explains: 'Nowadays it [i.e., alienation or deracination; clarification added] comes to be the archetypal late-modern condition. Increasingly, it's what everybody's life is like. … Since migration has turned out to be *the* world-historical event of late modernity, the classic postmodern experience turns out to be the diasporic experience' (1996: 490; emphasis in the original). Analogously, one might argue that a particular type of life writing – of which I regard Hall's as exemplary – is a manifestation of a late modern condition and positionality. Anthony Giddens has regarded contemporary autobiographies as 'interpretative self-histories'

(1991: 76) closely intertwined with the institutional processes of late modernity. In his memoir, Hall not only programmatically elaborates on the link between individual positioning and concepts and dynamics of culture and society, but also frequently reflects on how to write such a connection and how to write a or one's life. Hall's elaborations on the importance of narrative form shift diaspora, disruption, displacement centre stage and they apply to fiction as well as to life writing:

> The great value of diasporic thought, as I conceive it, is that far from abolishing everything that refuses to fit neatly into a narrative – the displacements – it places the dysfunctions at the forefront. In the imaginary it is possible to condense different persons in a single figure, to alter places, to substitute different time frames, or to slip 'irrationally' between them, as dreams frequently do. Montage is its lifeblood. We have to work *with* such ways of telling and speaking, with no attempt to iron out the disruptions. There are no alternative, direct routes. In historical reality, we cannot turn back the ever-onward flight path of time's arrow. We can never go home again, and we need to fashion narrative forms able to catch the full complexities – the displacements again – of this collective predicament. (2017: 171; emphasis in the original)

But this collective predicament is mirrored and configured in the individual, too. Coming back to my initial emphasis on the self-reflexive constitution of subjectivity in and through life writing, then, I want to turn in closing to the question of the kind of 'cultural work', to use Jane Tompkins's term (1986), that transcultural memoirs such as Hall's do or can do. Without doubt, *Familiar Stranger* provides important insights into Hall's personal and intellectual development, the emergence of concepts central to his theoretical work and important insights into his view on Jamaican and British history and society. The way in which the memoir offers such insights, however, its selection of foci, structure of narration, intertextual connections and theoretical framings, also presents, I want to suggest, a form of 'worlding'. The title of this collection, 'The Many Worlds of Anglophone Literatures', suggests the necessity of attention to processes of imaginative 'worlding' in the study of literature, and the work by scholars such as Pheng Cheah, Birgit Neumann, Stefan Helgesson or Frank Schulze-Engler analytically and conceptually attests to the importance of world-making processes in literature. Literature 'construes imaginative worlds and configures new worldly spaces, alternative geographies, contact zones and transitory spaces that, thriving on both transcultural entanglements and local differences, may offer readers new visions of the world' (Neumann and Rippl 2017: 9).

Life writing usually has not been included in such discussions, and given the kind of claim and audience address of life-writing texts there are plausible reasons for this exclusion. Fiction offers processes of worlding by way of the 'what if'; by so doing, it offers its own way of theorizing sociability and being in the world. By contrast, life writing, memoir and autobiography in particular, lays a generic claim to at least a subjective 'truth', or better: '[T]ruthfulness', of one's being and thus seems to be invested rather in world reflection rather than world-making. Yet, life writing – maybe counterintuitively so – can be seen as offering forms of worlding, too. Memoirs such as Hall's highlight how an individual's recollection and reconstruction of life and self is bound up not only with a sense of 'how things were and are' from an individual's perspective, but also of what they might have been or even be in the future, against all odds; intertextual connections, constitutive relationality and – in Hall's case – the paradigmatic link between 'a life' and 'ideas', as he has put it (2017: 10), are processes of framing and interpretation. The 'world-reading' process of life writing is not merely receptive, but creative and productive; as such, it has 'world-making' capacities, too. This is nowhere more evident than in transcultural life writing which constitutively tests, challenges, transgresses and reconfigures what is perceived – and by whom – as 'cultural boundary', and the weight such an inscription might have. In Hall's memoir, 'displacement' and 'diaspora' are not only shaping experiences but also central ways for framing thought. As he writes in a chapter aptly entitled 'Creolizing Thinking' on Caribbean intellectuals: 'Nothing was ever codified as having its correct place and time. In a suitably paradoxical formulation, displacement moved to the centre of things. To think in this manner enabled us to catch the world in all its unpredictabilities. Out of our subaltern position, there emerged the possibility of engaging with history anew' (2017: 62). By offering the narrative of such an engagement, by connecting the development of a life and the ideas that in turn allow understanding it, Hall's memoir invites readers into a self-critical dialogue of their own about what constitutes their understanding of the 'world' and their shifting – racialized, gendered, classed – places in it.

References

Bhabha, H. (1994), *The Location of Culture*, London: Routledge.

Butler, J. (2005), *Giving an Account of Oneself*, New York: Fordham University Press.

Clifford, J. (1997), *Routes: Travel and Translation in the Late Twentieth Century*, Cambridge, MA: Harvard University Press.
Eakin, P. J. (1999), *How Our Lives Become Stories: Making Selves*, Ithaca, NY: Cornell University Press.
Giddens, A. (1991), *Modernity and Self-Identity: Self and Society in the Later Modern Age*, Stanford, CA: Stanford University Press.
Hall, S. (1989), 'Cultural Identity and Cinematic Representation', *Framework: The Journal of Cinema and Media* 36: 68–81.
Hall, S. (1990), 'Cultural Identity and Diaspora', in J. Rutherford (ed.), *Identity: Community, Culture, Difference*, 222–37, London: Lawrence & Wishart.
Hall, S. and K.-H. Chen (1996), 'The Formation of a Diasporic Intellectual: An Interview with Stuart Hall by Kuan-Hsing Chen', in D. Morley and K.-H. Chen (eds), *Stuart Hall: Critical Dialogues in Cultural Studies*, 484–503, London: Routledge.
Hall, S. ([2003] 2015), 'Creolité and the Process of Creolization', reprinted in E. Guitérrez Rodríguez and S. A. Tate (eds), *Creolizing Europe: Legacies and Transformations*, 12–25, Liverpool: Liverpool University Press.
Hall, S. with B. Schwarz (2017), *Familiar Stranger: A Life between Two Islands*, London: Allen Lane.
Hogan, R. and J. Hogan (1997), 'Introduction: Cross-Cultural Autobiography', *a/b: Auto/Biography* 12 (2): 149–50.
Lamming, G. (1960), *The Pleasures of Exile*, London: Michael Joseph.
Mills, C. W. (1959), *The Sociological Imagination*, Oxford: Oxford University Press. Kindle edition (2000).
Neumann, B. and G. Rippl (2017), 'Anglophone World Literatures: Introduction', *Anglia* 135 (1): 1–20. doi: https://doi.org/10.1515/ang-2017-0001.
Said, E. (1999), *Out of Place*, New York: Vintage.
Schulze-Engler, F. (2007), 'African Literature and the Micropolitics of Modernity: Explorations of Post-Traditional Society in Wole Soyinka's *Season of Anomy*, Nuruddin Farah's *Sardines* and Tsitsi Dangarembga's *Nervous Conditions*', *Matatu* 35: 21–35.
Schulze-Engler, F. (2013), 'Irritating Europe', in G. Huggan (ed.), *Oxford Handbook of Postcolonial Studies*, 667–91, Oxford: Oxford University Press.
Schulze-Engler, F. (2019), 'Erkundungen einer dezentrierter Moderne: Transnationalität und Transkulturalität in anglophonen Literaturen', in D. Bischoff and S. Komfort-Hein (eds), *Handbuch Literatur und Transnationalität*, 366–83, Berlin: De Gruyter.
Schwarz, B. (2017), 'Preface', in S. Hall with B. Schwarz, *Familiar Stranger: A Life between Two Islands*, xiii–xvii, London: Allen Lane.
Scott, D. (2004), *Conscripts of Modernity: The Tragedy of Colonial Enlightenment*, Durham, NC: Duke University Press.
Scott, D. (2017), *Stuart Hall's Voice: Intimations of an Ethics of Receptive Generosity*, Durham, NC: Duke University Press.
Scott, J. W. (1991), 'The Evidence of Experience', *Critical Inquiry* 17 (4): 773–97.

Simmel, G. ([1908] 1971), 'The Stranger', reprinted in D. Levine (ed.), *On Individuality and Social Form: Selected Writings*, 143–9, Chicago: University of Chicago Press.

Telles, E. (2014), *Pigmentocracies: Ethnicity, Race, and Color in Latin America*, Chapel Hill: University of North Carolina Press.

Thomä, D., V. Kaufmann and U. Schmid (2015), *Der Einfall des Lebens. Theorie als geheime Autobiographie*, München: Hanser.

Tompkins, J. (1986), *Sensational Designs: The Cultural Work of American Fiction, 1790–1860*, Oxford: Oxford University Press.

White, H. (1973), *Metahistory: The Historical Imagination in Nineteenth-Century Europe*, Baltimore, MD: Johns Hopkins University Press.

6

Toward re-centring the senescent: Pedagogical possibilities of Anglophone short fiction

Mala Pandurang and Jinal Baxi
Dr. BMN College Mumbai

This chapter stems from a proposed project on 'promoting intergenerational interactions through literary interventions' by the English Department of Dr. BMN College, Mumbai (India).[1] The project has been conceived with two primary objectives in mind. First, we intend to explore innovative pedagogical methods that would facilitate the language proficiency of undergraduate students in English through literary appreciation skills. Secondly, the Government of India enforced stringent norms due to the COVID-19 pandemic in March 2020, wherein all institutions of education were compelled to immediately discontinue physical classes and shift to an online mode of instruction. The lockdown severely restricted the mobility of students to the spaces of their homes, as a consequence of which several students shared instances of intergenerational conflicts due to the intensified interaction with senior family members within the joint family structure,[2] common to many Indian homes. A shared narration of women students was of the conflict of tradition and modernity with senior family members, as well as the responsibility for caregiving of the elderly which is increasingly perceived as an imposed burden. Sociological studies indicate that one of the biggest contemporary problems that many older people encounter is that of perceptions of ageing from younger populations, rather

---

[1] https://www.bmncollege.com/ home-3/. Dr. BMN is an exclusive women's college (Autonomous) under the SNDTW Women's University, Mumbai.
[2] The term 'joint family' is used to indicate a consanguineal family unit that includes two or more generations of kindred related through either the paternal or maternal line who maintain a common residence and are subject to common social, economic and religious regulations (*joint family*, n.d.).

than the process of ageing itself (Segal 2013, qtd in Dowey 2015: n.p.) and that emerging attitudes of 'ageism', or the act of treating people unfairly because of their age, is becoming 'an increasingly widespread form of discrimination fuelled by negative perceptions of old age' (AGE Workshop 2020). We recognized the circumstances of the lockdown, which had enforced intergenerational interactions within the proximity of restricted domestic spaces, as offering an opportunity to evolve a curriculum wherein we could engage young adults with postcolonial creative writing as an entry point to explore subjective aspects of ageing (Dowey 2015). In a study on 'Globalization and Ageing in India', Joshi points out how the consumerist market economy of the twenty-first century has had its long-term implications on Indian local cultures. In particular, there has been a shift from traditional-/community-based support systems to more individualized structures (Joshi 2011), which, in turn, has impacted upon the fast-changing social fabric of urban India wherein our target group of students is located.

Könönen (2020) discusses contemporary narratives of ageing in today's globalized world in terms of two categories. First, there is the 'decline narrative' which is preoccupied with the degeneration of cognitive and physical faculties with high dependency on others, resulting in the 'end of the story and the end of a person's life.' (Bjursell 2019: 1) Alternatively, narratives of 'successful aging' (Könönen 2020: 176) emphasize on the absence of diseases and maintenance of physical and mental functioning resulting in predictable descriptions of the senescent,[3] which presuppose relations of dependence associated with disability and ill health. Such images are commonly propagated through advertisement campaigns in the global marketplace which promote a universalist desire to be forever young (Clarke 2010), especially through images that celebrate youth and vitality on the one hand and denigrate and de-sexualize older people on the other hand. As academics from the field of postcolonial studies, we make a conscious effort to integrate discourses of class, gender, caste and sexuality into the teaching of Anglophone narratives as a means of addressing power structures. The subject of ageing, on the other hand, tends to remain largely side-lined and unexplored. We, therefore, felt the need to evolve a framework for classroom activities wherein postcolonial narratives could be explored for insights into the range and complexity of issues related to the diversity of the ageing experience, and also invite generational perspectives to the same.

---

[3] The term 'senescent' means becoming old, and therefore in less good condition and less able to function well (*senescent*, n.d.).

We commenced the project with an extensive review of available material on the social constructions of ageing including interdisciplinary resources in the domains of literature, sociology and psychology. Our quest was for Anglophone short fiction from the Global South that featured elderly individuals, but which can also serve as literary gerontological 'antidotes to the toxin that is ageism' (Woodward 2019: 375; see also Gaidash 2014). Critical gerontology is based on the argument that stereotypical perceptions and stories about age are cultural constructions that have to be challenged (Könönen 2020: 176). As a conceptual framework, literary gerontology draws upon creative narratives as a resource to better understand representations of the cultural construction of the physiological and psychological impact of growing older, and also provides the tools to interrogate and deconstruct ageing as a category of social difference. It facilitates a closer examination of thematic concerns such as bodily functions, repressed sexual desire and perceptions of mortality in relation to the processes of ageing.

As we began to collate instructional material for classroom interactions, we faced a perceptible gap in the availability of literary gerontological material on aspects of old age in locations of the Global South – we choose to use the term Global South as a point of reference to locations and communities that have been negatively impacted by contemporary capitalist globalization.[4] While there is a growing body of critical reading available that offers complex analyses of literary texts from the perspective of ageing, such resources mostly draw their working examples from Anglo-American and European literature located in the Global North, with little attention being paid to literary production by non-Western writers. In a special issue of the *Journal of Aging Studies*, Van Dyk draws attention to how key postcolonial concepts derived from postcolonial theorizing such as 'othering', 'exile' and 'subaltern positions' can be applied to the analyses of the stages of later life (van Dyk 2016: 110). In an explorative essay in the same issue, Kunow suggests a postcolonial reading of American author Eudora Welty's *A Visit of Charity* (1933) as a text 'which keeps aged otherness at an observable distance', comparing the protagonist Marian's visit to the old age home to that of a Western explorer's curious visit to the jungles of the uncivilized. In his reading, Kunow points out that old age is seen as 'the

---

[4] According to Mahler, critical scholarship that falls under the rubric of Global South Studies can include the analysis of, 'the study of power and racialization within global capitalism in ways that transcend the nation-state as the unit of comparative analysis, and in tracing both contemporary South–South relations – or relations among subaltern groups across national, linguistic, racial and ethnic lines – as well as the histories of those relations in prior forms of South–South exchange' (Mahler 2017: n.p.).

heart of darkness' and the aged characters of the texts such as Eudora Welty are developed 'to be looked at' or observed instead of being the pivotal character of the story (Kunow 2016: 3). According to Kunow, a postcolonial perspective can be used to draw out connections between Marian's visit to the home for old people and Joseph Conrad's *Heart of Darkness* as 'a translocation from the normative spaces of Western culture into another domain in terms of an assault on the senses' thus leading to 'a general sense of vague and oppressive wonder' (2016: 507). However, as Rajan-Rankin observes, the application of postcolonial theoretical concepts to aspects of ageing discussed therein in this special issue remains relatively static in application and falls short of being translated into lived experiences in postcolonial spaces (Rajan-Rankin 2018).

Carmen Concilio takes up the challenge to deal with this lacuna through a close reading of Anglophone texts in *Imagining Ageing: Representations of Age and Ageing in Anglophone Literatures* (2018). With the inclusion of critical analysis of the works of Alice Munro, J. M. Coetzee and Patricia Grace, Concilio attempts to establish the relationship between gerontology and literary postcolonial works in terms of how 'ageing can become an issue of an ongoing negotiation of cultural concepts, social practices, ideals and behaviours between social and ethnic groups' (Concilio 2018: 10). Additionally, two significant publications from postcolonial locations in the Global South that contribute to the gap in the conceptualization and theorizing of old age in Global South literary production are Ira Raja's *Grey Areas: An Anthology of Indian Fiction* (2010) and Pepetual Mforbe Chiangong's *Old Age in African Literary and Cultural Contexts* (2021). Raja's analysis extends to excerpts from Amitav Ghosh's *The Shadow Lines* (1988), Upamanyu Chatterjee's *The Last Burden* (1993) and short stories of Chaman Nahal's 'The Womb' (2005) among others. Similarly, Chiangong attempts to present how old age is conceptualized from literary, cultural and linguistic perspectives through an analysis of elderly characters in African literature located in varied geographical locations across the continent (Chiangong 2021). The essays in this collection tackle vacillations of conceptions of old age in relation to culture, agency, esteem, prejudice and history (Chiangong 2021: 2).

In order to formulate theoretical tools for the analysis of aspects of ageing in select narratives from Global South locations, we further drew from a range of interdisciplinary inputs, including Reddy and Sanger's 'Matters of Age: An Introduction to Ageing, Intergenerationality and Gender in Africa' (2012), Lawrence Cohen's *No Aging in India: Alzheimer's, The Bad Family, and Other Modern Things* (2006, Sarah Lamb's *Aging and the Indian Diaspora: Cosmopolitan Families in India and Abroad* (2009, qtd in Kunow 2016), William J. Edwards's

'Taupaenui Māori Positive Ageing' (2010) and Mere Kēpa's 'Bring "Me" Beyond Vulnerability. Elderly Care of Māori, by Māori' (2006). What emerges from our readings of the discussions of 'ageism' is a constant reminder that age-related experiences are culturally determined/culturally framed or transculturally available (Reddy and Sanger 2012; Woodward 1999, qtd in Kunow 2016) and that the 'life histories of older people are intricately intertwined with the histories of their families, communities, nations as well as global trends' (Mehta and Singh 2008: 1). For instance, traditional approaches to ageing in the Global South often differ widely from official classifications of when a person is to be considered older than others in the community. Dowd suggests that while traditional African definitions of an elder may correlate with the chronological ages of fifty to sixty (Kowal and Dowd 2001), organizations such as the United Nations do not offer a standard criterion of old age, though it falls back on the criteria of sixty-plus years to refer to an older population. In the Indian context, Kakar draws from the Hindu Dharmasastras which describes a human's life course as consisting of three main phases: childhood, youth and old age (1997). He points out that as per Hindu social practices, the marriage of one's eldest child, which is assumed to lead to the beginning of the reproductive career of the next generation of the family, is considered to be a mark of the onset of old age (Menon 2018). While the materiality of the human body and its physical decline is a recurrent trope in narrations on ageing in Western literature (Twigg and Martin 2014), Saurav Kumar explains how Hindu philosophical traditions consider biological ageing as an opportunity for the individual to accumulate the knowledge which will help her/him to attain 'moksha' or freedom from the continuous cycle of births and deaths (Kumar 2021). It therefore follows that the older members of the family are traditionally assigned a pivotal role in the decision-making processes. In Jhumpa Lahiri's 'The Third and Final Continent' (1999), the idea of old age as perceived by the narrator, who has newly immigrated from India, is challenged when he realizes that his landlady Mrs. Croft is a hundred and three years old and not in her eighties, as he had initially imagined. He is struck by her independent existence in opposition to that of his own widowed mother. His attitude to age is based on the perception that the life course of the female Hindu is defined in terms of her role in the family as daughter, wife, mother or grandmother. His mother therefore being widowed, and aged, is triply marginalized.

Keeping in mind Fondo's suggestion that both postcolonial and ageing studies are interested in interrogating and deconstructing the process of cultural othering (2018: 135), the next step of our project was to collate narratives which are associated with the conventional canon of postcolonial writing, but which also offer themselves to interpretation from an ageist perspective. Ngũgĩ wa Thiong'o's 'Gone with the Drought' (1975) is generally taught as a short story that is about severe conditions brought about by a series of droughts in colonial and post-independence Kenya, and its long-term impact of subsequent economic hardships on the narrator's family and their livelihood. The story can, however, also be read in terms of an intergenerational encounter with 'otherness' of the child narrator with an old woman, who is given to bouts of 'uncontrollable paroxysms of laughter for no apparent reason' (Ngũgĩ 1975: n.p.) and is considered 'mad' by everyone else (Raja 2010: xix). The narrator, however, empathizes with the unnamed old woman protagonist who is deeply affected by the death of her only son from the dire circumstances of the drought. The child-narrator associates her mental condition with the impoverishment and the diminished power of the land, and its loss of greenness and white bareness. He seeks her out with yams and *njahi* beans but his gifts of food remain untouched as an assertion of her refusal to give in to acts of perceived charity, despite her age and helplessness. The boy reacts in sharp anger when one of the brothers makes an ocular remark about her madness: '"Mad indeed" I almost screamed. And everybody stared at me in startled fear. All of them, except my father who kept on looking at the same place' (Ngũgĩ 1975: n.p.). In doing so, the young boy individualizes the old woman, lending her a subjecthood hitherto denied to her, and in turn, challenges the dominant gaze of the community that can perceive only fragility and degeneration of the mind when looking at the old woman.

Similarly, Ama Ata Aidoo's short story 'The Girl Who Can' (1997) is more often than not read solely from a feminist perspective as a critique of imposed gendered roles of women. Adjoa is a young girl of seven who is mocked for her thin legs, and inability to articulate words. The narrative centres on the interaction between women of three generations (Adjoa, her mother and grandmother) who view her physical condition as indicative of an inability to marry and bear children at a later stage of life – a woman's legs must 'have meat on them with good calves to support solid hips … to be able to have children' (Aidoo 1997: 14). The story can be re-read in terms of how the character of Nana subverts established stereotypes associated with the traditional perceptions of the role of a grandmother. Nana's eventual delight at Adjoa's victory in countless school races suggests that an elderly person's mind is not always as rigid as is perceived. The grandmother ultimately shares in the triumph of the little girl, carrying the 'gleaming cup on her back' (Aidoo 1997: 16) as if it were her own. Yet another narrative that lends itself well to discussions of de-stereotyping and assigning agency to female seniors is Ondaatje's 'The Passions of Lalla' (1982) set in Sri Lanka, wherein the elderly Lalla is portrayed as a woman who constantly attempted to fulfil her role as a caregiver in her youth as well as middle age, for her children as well as 'a mad aunt' to other children in the community. Therefore, in her old age, she asserts her right to take anything from anyone as 'all her life she had given away everything she owned to whoever wanted it' (Ondaatje 1982: 112). Unlike stereotypical descriptions of grandmothers, who are believed to constantly enjoy the embrace of children and grandchildren and who are pious, religious, frown upon indulgences such as drinking, Lalla is projected as a woman 'full of passions' (Ondaatje 1982: 111) who seeks freedom at sixty-eight years of age from pre-defined age-related gender roles. Lalla creates her own opportunities of living well within her given location and community, thus asserting agency and free will.

Patricia Grace's short story 'Journey' (1980) is often read in terms of its description of the impact of colonization and urbanization on the local Maori community. This has also resulted in the marginalization of traditional roles of the elderly within the Maori sociocultural ecosystem wherein individuals in large families have traditionally coexisted with extended family members in the same households (Edwards 2010: 133). The 71-year-old protagonist, once revered for his position as an elder, has to now contend with the family's perceptions of him as transiting towards physical and mental decline (Grace 1980: 89). He is particularly pained that family members who had once needed to be taken care of by him now have no utility value for his presence. His reminiscences allow for an analysis of the societal changes that have taken place in Māori culture wherein care does not imply only health-related matters 'but also cultural, political and social relationships and is grounded in whānau (extended family), whanaungatanga (connectedness) and kanohi (extended participation) (Kēpa 2005, qtd in Valle 2018: 175). The elder reflects on how the Pākehā[5] have built everything over land and sea (Grace 1980: 100). He however refuses to remain a passive protagonist and he travels to the city to assert the right of his family over their ancestral land, only to find that the Pākehā plan to turn it into an off-street parking lot. Moeke-Maxwell points out, for a Maori individual, home is the preferred site for burial, surrounded by whānau (Moeke-Maxwell 2015, qtd in Valle 2018: 176). In his declaration after dinner with his family, the protagonist counters this preference when he voices his wish to be cremated as 'it is not

---

[5] 'Pākehā' is a New Zealander of European descent or a foreigner. *Māori Dictionary* 'Pakeha' (*Te Aka Online Māori Dictionary*, n.d..), https://maoridictionary.co.nz/search?keywords=pakeha (accessed 23 February 2023).

safe in the ground' (Grace 1986: 108), indicating his frustrating acceptance of the postcolonial world around him but bearing no wish to be a part of a world in which he finds no place of his own. While Grace's narrative describes the marginalization of the aged protagonist who was once a valuable contributor to his society, it also presents strategies of resistance wherein the old man attempts to counter the process of double marginalization, first as an indigenous native and secondly as a senior.

In the Indian context, caring for the old is perceived as the moral responsibility of the family and community and this is a notion that tends to be celebrated in terms of a positive aspect of a traditional value system as compared to the more modern functioning of the 'nuclear' family. It is ironic however that while there is an idealized projection of respect accorded to the aged on the one hand, organizations such as HelpAge India[6] and Dignity Foundation[7] draw our attention to the growing lack of recognition of the experience, knowledge and the vital contributions of elder persons to society including caring for loved ones. The presence of retirement homes and private institutional care for the elderly is slowly gaining visibility in Indian cities, but, by and large, the concept of a private institution to care for the aged is still viewed as 'a deplorable Westernization' leading to a loss of traditions and values (Lamb 2009: 56, qtd in Kunow 2016: 5). We shortlisted two short stories that problematize the position of the elder while presenting conflicting notions of interdependence and intergenerational reciprocity within cultural and social discourses of middle-class Indian homes. The elderly protagonists are placed in a joint or extended family in the domestic space of the Indian middle-class home, allowing for an analysis of the complex interactions between family members in the context of caregiving and care receiving, particularly central to the context of the genesis of our project.

Gita Hariharan's 'The Remains of the Feast' (1994) is a first-person account of twenty-year-old Ratna's vivid memories of the last days in the life of her great-grandmother Rukmani who is in the terminal stages of cancer. Ninety-year-old Rukmani is being cared for by her grandson and his wife who regard their cancer-stricken dying grandmother as an invalid, and therefore by implication, a burden on the family's living space and financial resources (Hariharan 1994: 284). They consider their role as caregivers as obligatory and duty-bound.

---

[6] www.helpageindia.org. (n.d.). *NGO India: Charity in India, Elderly or Senior Care Non Profit Organization - HelpAge India.* [online] Available at: https://www.helpageindia.org/ (accessed 24 October 2022).

[7] Dignity Foundation. (n.d.). *NGO for elderly in India.* [online] Available at: https://www.dignityfoundation.com/?gclid=Cj0KCQjw0IGnBhDUARIsAMwFDLmdqjtUxO7JJSsQHhS8u6L6SWvU94MkhVwTo1JXX3tKodzx4F4VDDYaAki3EALw_wcB (accessed 22 October 2022).

Ratna, on the other hand, defines her great-grandmother beyond her illness and celebrates the ninety-year-old's sense of humour and zest for life. A pre-medical student, she regards Rukmani's body as still 'a solid, reliable thing' and 'a wonderful resilient machine' until it starts to degenerate due to the ravages of cancer (Hariharan 1994: 284). The old woman becomes increasingly determined to defy gender and caste restrictions in her last days, after having lived a life of the continuous denial and suppression of her innate desires as a Hindu Brahmin widow. Instead, her body is wrapped with a pale brown sari or 'her widow's weeds' (Hariharan 1994: 284). Ratna's attempt to fulfil all of Rukmani's wishes, including smuggling in hair removal creams so as not to be 'an ugly old woman', is an acknowledgement of the old woman's final attempt to reclaim agency of the self and to context the myth that physical degeneration implies a dimming of natural desires. 'A Devoted Son' (1983) by Anita Desai centres upon the strained relationship between a father (Varmaji) and his 'dutiful' doctor son (Rakesh). As in Hariharan's story, the denial of desired food stuff is central to the plight of the elderly protagonist (Desai 1983: 4). His diet is under the surveillance of the ever-watchful eyes of his dutiful doctor son who is determined to control his diet by enforcing a strict schedule of pills and tonics. The family caters to him as they would a child and he gradually becomes trapped in a definitive role associated with old age. Varmaji interprets his son's actions as 'cold heartlessness' and 'tyranny in disguise'. Rakesh, on the other hand, is lauded for being a dutiful son who fulfils societal expectations of caring for his elderly father and thereby repaying his debt for the education given to him. Whereas Hariharan's narrative centres on the resistance of the ninety-year-old widow, albeit in the last stages of her life, Desai's protagonist Varmaji is unable to exert any agency, despite his repeated desire to do so.

The two short narratives by Hariharan and Desai challenge the perception that emotions, innate desires and decision-making powers of the elderly necessarily diminish and are weakened by age and time. Rukmani and Varmaji's yearnings are suppressed by caregivers under the assumption that it is for their physiological good. The onus on their well-being is undertaken by the comparatively younger family members as caregivers who are unable to acknowledge that 'even in frail old age, there is the possibility of an opening up of life' (Wallace 2011: 394). We are thus reminded to keep room for those 'whose voices have the most to contribute to our understanding of them' (Heier 2018: n.p.). The question arises of variations of societal definitions of 'need' according to age. The sense of responsibility of Rakesh, as well as Ratna's parents, towards Varmaji and Rukmani, respectively, is based on assumed accountability reinforced by the perception that they are duty-bound to look out for the health and best interests of the cared. The stories draw our attention to moral dilemmas and quandaries on notions of caregiving and the conflict between the carer and the person being cared for. While one is sympathetic to the plight of the ageing Rukmani and Varmaji, the reader is also made empathetic to overtaxed emotionally and physically drained caregivers. The narratives achieve a fine balance of drawing attention to the cared on the one hand, while also creating empathy for the caregiver who is overtaxed emotionally and physically by the very processes of caring.

In the third stage of our project, we moved towards offering a seminar programme to undergraduate students who inhabit spaces that encompass the complexity of cultures in a world increasingly characterized by global modernities. Our intention was to engage students in a critical exploration of how subjectivities of the elderly are 'othered', so that they can subsequently reconstitute subject positions of those who are de-centred due to their life's progression. As part of the exercise, we used the five literary interventions discussed in the above section (Ngũgĩ, Grace, Ondaatje, Desai and Hariharan) as a counter-discourse to the deficit model of ageing 'as a dull, dreary dead-end' (Clarke 2010, qtd in Reddy and Sanger 2012: 5; Kunow 2016: 2). The students' discussions focused on the impact of ageing on both the protagonist as well as on their family members, in the context of the short stories from Kenya, Ghana, Sri Lanka, New Zealand and India. An analysis of responses therein brings out a positive ethics of connectedness wherein the engagement of the student groups is simultaneously governed by empathy for the marginalized elderly on the one hand and for the protagonists' family members who are placed in the unavoidable position of caregivers, on the other. Respondents attribute their empathetic dual position to their own cultural value systems, but equally to the transformative effects of a consumerist economy linked to globalization processes which 'now extends to all areas of the earth and all areas of life and invades our inner world as never before' (Joshi 2011: 1). We propose to conduct a similar exercise with a partner department in a corresponding Global South location to compare how students in other cultural locations respond to the shared history of global modernities. Such an exercise, we believe, will allow us to explore patterns of similarity and difference in the experiences of ageing across settings as well as to formulate a framework for transcultural comparisons of constructions of age. It is important to stress that this approach goes beyond examining literary texts merely in terms of their geo-cultural locations. It will also attempt to explore a decolonial framework that draws from indigenous philosophies of life courses situated in readings that are outside the domain of Anglophone knowledge systems. Such an intention can be connected to the reminder placed on the webpage of The Centre for Transcultural Studies of the University of Pennsylvania ('Centre for Transcultural Studies: Who We Are' n.d.) that in today's age, we cannot take a single culture's problems as our departure point. Rather, we must seek to conceptualize global processes as emerging from interconnections among specific localities. Such an approach will not only facilitate a comparativist understanding of related issues in our contexts and will also augur an understanding of such processes in diverse global locations and contexts. This view resonates with Mary Louise Pratt's position on comparative literature as a tool to cultivate 'deep intercultural understanding and genuinely global consciousness' (1995: 62). Our proposed framework draws from the work of Frank Schulze-Engler who has long advocated for a change in perspective in pedagogical approaches to postcolonial Anglophone literature from a narrow focus on a shared British colonial history to more contemporary transcultural contexts. In the introduction to *Transcultural English Studies*, Schulze-Engler and Helff discuss the work of Wolfgang Welsch who posits that 'transculturality cannot be understood as a process related to a specific hierarchical relationship of societies and cultures (such as colonialism or imperialism), but instead needs to be perceived as a specific quality of contemporary cultures that necessitates the development of new theoretical concepts' (2008: xii). Similarly, the thrust of our argument in this chapter is to suggest that any attempt to understand ageism in the context of an increasingly globalized work requires an acknowledgement of shared human commonalities within a framework of larger diversities. Such a move, we are confident, will enrich any endeavour to address global interconnections of the future, and is especially relevant in contexts wherein the 'target cultures' under consideration 'refuse to sit still for pedagogical purposes' (Schulze-Engler and Helff 2008: 10).

References

AGE Internal Workshop (24 November 2020), 'Tackling Ageism after COVID-19'. Available online: https://encorenetwork.org/wp-content/uploads/2022/03/AGE_Workshop_a-PowerPoint-Presentation.pdf (accessed 24 October 2022).

Aidoo, A. (1997), 'The Girl Who Can', in *The Girl Who Can and Other Stories*. Sub-Saharan. Available online: https://blackfeministreadinggroup.files.wordpress.com/2017/02/aidoo-the-girl-who-can.pdf.

Bjursell, C. (2019), 'Growth through Education: The Narratives of Older Adults', *Frontiers in Sociology* 4. doi: 10.3389/fsoc.2019.00011

'The Center for Transcultural Studies: Who We Are' (n.d.), Upenn.edu. Available online: https://www.sas.upenn.edu/transcult/whoweare.html (accessed 24 October 2022).

Clarke, L. H. (2010), *Facing Age: Women Growing Older in Anti-Aging Culture*, Lanham, MD: Rowman & Littlefield.

Cohen, L. (2006), *No Aging in India: Alzheimer's, the Bad Family, and Other Modern Things*, Berkeley: University of California Press.

Concilio, C. (ed.) (2018), *Imagining Ageing: Representations of Age and Ageing in Anglophone Literatures*, Bielefeld: transcript.

Desai, A. (1983), 'A Devoted Son', *Games at Twilight and Other Stories*, 1–9, New York: Penguin Group USA. Available online: https://digestablewords.wordpress.com/short-story-a-devoted-son-by-anita-desai/ (accessed 24 October 2022).

Dowey, C. (1 October 2015), 'What Old Age Is Really Like', *The New Yorker*. Available online: https://www.newyorker.com/culture/cultural-comment/what-old-age-is-really-like (accessed 24 October 2022).

Edwards, W. J. (2010), 'Taupaenui Māori Positive Ageing', PhD thesis, Massey University. Available online: https://mro.massey.ac.nz/handle/10179/1331 (accessed 24 October 2022).

Fondo, B. (2018), 'Coming to Terms Ageing and Moral Regeneration' in *J. M. Coetzee's Age of Iron and Elizabeth Costello*, in C. Concilio (ed.), *Imagining Ageing: Representations of Age and Ageing in Anglophone Literatures*, 127–39, Bielefeld: transcript.

Gaidash, A. (2014). 'Discourse of Ageing in Tina Howe's *A Marriage Cycle*', in K. Kozak and J. Kolbusz-Buda (eds), *Novel Approaches in Language, Literature and Culture Studies*, 11–23. Available online: www.researchgate.net/publication/283146806_DISCOURSE_OF_AGEING_IN_TINA_HOWE%27S_A_MARRIAGE_CYCLE.

Grace, P. (1980), 'Journey', in *The Dream Sleepers and Other Stories*. [online] Passeggiata Press, pp.95–108. Available online: https://englishwithmisschenery.weebly.com/uploads/1/7/8/1/17814047/journey.pdf (accessed 24 October 2022).

Hariharan, G. (1994), 'The Remains of the Feast', *Kunapipi* 16 (1): 282–7. Available online: https://ro.uow.edu.au/kunapipi/vol16/iss1/56

Heier, J. (8 July 2018), 'The Relevance of Critical Insights of Postcolonial Theory', *Ethics of Care* (blog). Available online: https://ethicsofcare.org/the-relevance-of-critical-insights-of-postcolonial-theory/ (accessed 24 October 2022).

'Joint Family', Thesaurus, Cambridge Advanced Learner's Dictionary (n.d.). Cambridge University Press. Available online: https://dictionary.cambridge.org/dictionary/english/joint-family?q=Joint+family (accessed 24 October 2022).

Joshi, A. K. (2011), 'Globalization and Ageing in India', *International Journal of Social Quality* 1 (1): 33–44. Available online: https://www.jstor.org/stable/23971680 (accessed 24 October 2022).

Kakar, S. (1997), 'The Search for Middle Age in India', in R. Shweder (ed.), *Welcome to Middle Age! (And Other Cultural Fictions)*, 75–98, Chicago, IL: University of Chicago Press.

Kēpa, M. (2006), 'Bring "Me" Beyond Vulnerability. Elderly Care of Māori, by Māori', *Gerontologist* 45 (special issue II): 542. doi: 10.1093/geront/45.Special_Issue_II.1.

Könönen, M. (2020), 'Contemporary Narratives of Senility', *Laboratorium: Russian Review of Social Research* 12 (2): 169–86. doi: 10.25285/2078-1938-2020-12-2-169-186.

Kowal, P. and J. E. Dowd (2001), *Definition of an Older Person: Proposed Working Definition of an Older Person in Africa for the MDS Project*, Geneva: World Health Organization. doi: 10.13140/2.1.5188.9286.

Kumar, S. (2021), *Fiction as Gerontological Resource: A Critical Study of Select Novels*, Banaras Hindu University. Available online: http://hdl.handle.net/10603/371786.

Kunow, R. (2016), 'Postcolonial Theory and Old Age: An Explorative Essay', *Journal of Aging Studies* 39: 101–8. doi: 10.1016/j.jaging.2016.06.004.

Lahiri, J. (1999). 'The Third and Final Continent', in *Interpreter of Maladies*, Boston, MA: Houghton Mifflin.

Mahler, A. (2017), 'What/Where Is the Global South?' in E. O'Brien (ed.), *Oxford Bibliographies in Literary and Critical Theory*. Available online: https://globalsouth studies.as.virginia.edu/what-is-global-south.

Mehta, K. and A. Singh (2008), 'Introduction: The Search for Voices among Indian Diasporic Elderly', in K. Mehta and A. Singh (eds), *Indian Diaspora: Voices of the Diasporic Elders in Five Countries*, 1–12, Leiden: Brill. doi: https://doi.org/10.1163/9789087904074

Menon, U. (2018), 'Old Age and Hinduism', *Oxford Bibliographies*. Oxford University Press. Available online: https://www.oxfordbibliographies.com/display/document/obo-9780195399318/obo-9780195399318-0211.xml.

Moeke-Maxwell, T. (2015), 'Homedeathscapes: Maori End-of-Life Decision-Making Processes', in M. Kēpa, M. McPherson and L. Manu'atu (eds), *Home: Here to Stay*, Wellington: Huia.

Ngũgĩ wa Thiong'o (1975), 'Gone with the Drought', in *Secret Lives and Other Stories*, 15–20, New York: Lawrence Hill. Available online: https://Ngugiwanyongoshort storiesblog.wordpress.com/2019/02/06/gone-with-the-drought/ (accessed 24 October 2022).

Ondaatje, M. (1982), 'The Passions of Lalla', in *Running in the Family*, 95–112, Toronto: McClelland & Stewart.

Pratt, L. M. (1995), 'Comparative Literature and Global Citizenship', in C. Bernheimer (ed.), *Comparative Literature in the Age of Multiculturalism*, 58–65, Baltimore, MD: Johns Hopkins University Press.

Raja, I. (ed.) (2010), *Grey Areas: An Anthology of Indian Fiction on Ageing*, New York: Oxford University Press.

Rajan-Rankin, S. (2018), 'Race, Embodiment and Later Life: Re-Animating Ageing Bodies of Color', *Journal of Aging Studies* 45: 32–8. doi: 10.1016/j.jaging.2018.01.005

Reddy, V. and N. Sanger (2012), 'Matters of Age: An Introduction to Ageing, Intergenerationality and Gender in Africa', *Agenda* 26 (4): 3–14. doi: 10.1080/10130950.2012.793062.

Schulze-Engler, F. and S. Helff (eds) (2008), *Transcultural English Studies: Theories, Fictions, Realities*, Leiden: Brill/Rodopi. doi: 10.1163/9789042028845.

'Senescent', Thesaurus, Cambridge Advanced Learner's Dictionary (n.d.), Cambridge University Press. Available online: https://dictionary.cambridge.org/dictionary/english/senescent (accessed 24 October 2022).

Subramanian, S. B. (2001), 'The Zamindar of Pallipuram', in M. Mukherjee (ed.), *Let's Go Home and Other Stories: An Anthology of Indian Short Stories in English*, 83–9, Hyderabad: Orient Longman.

Twigg, J. and W. Martin (2014), 'The Challenge of Cultural Gerontology', *Gerontologist* 55 (3): 353–9. doi: 10.1093/geront/gnu061.

Valle, P. D. (2018), 'Representing Age and Ageing in New Zealand Literature', in C. Concilio (ed.), *Imagining Ageing: Representations of Age and Ageing in Anglophone Literatures*, 165–82, Bielefeld: transcript.

van Dyk, S. (2016), 'The Othering of Old Age: Insights from Postcolonial Studies', *Journal of Aging Studies* 39: 109–20. doi: 10.1016/j.jageing.2016.06.005.

Wallace, D. (2011), 'Literary Portrayals of Ageing', in I. Stuart-Hamilton (ed.), *An Introduction to Gerontology*, 389–415, Cambridge: Cambridge University Press.

Welty, E. (1993), 'A Visit to Charity', in *Anthology of American Literature*, 1476–9, New York: Macmillan.

Woodward, K. M. (ed.) (1999), *Figuring Age: Women, Bodies, Generations*, Bloomington: Indiana University Press.

Woodward, K. M. (2019), 'Afterword: Literary Antidotes to the Toxin That Is Ageism', *Studies in American Fiction* 46 (2): 373–81. doi: 10.1353/saf.2019.0016.

7

Notes from a classroom: Teaching Anglophone transculturality amidst environmental devastations

Kathrin Bartha-Mitchell and Michelle Stork
Goethe University Frankfurt

Introduction

In this chapter, we outline the role of transcultural approaches to teaching as well as to reading Anglophone texts under conditions of increasing environmental devastations. Our insights and argumentative strands regarding the need for conversations across Transcultural English Studies, Mobility Studies and the Environmental Humanities result from a seminar we co-taught in the summer term of 2022. This seminar, entitled '"Running from Both the Living and the Dead": Imagining Environmental and Mobility Justice in Transcultural Anglophone Texts', was one of the first to take place in-person after the COVID-19 pandemic had taken teaching into the virtual realm. It can therefore be understood as located in a context of 'environmental devastation' caused by the novel coronavirus. As recent studies indicate, '[t]here is a strong link between climate change and infectious disease outbreaks' (Cohut 2022). Of course, other environmental issues, many direct results of increasingly extreme climate, loom large, such as large-scale flooding in Pakistan and record temperatures and forest fires across Europe in the summer of 2022.

Taking on board student feedback, we argue in this chapter that transculturality becomes most relevant to students in conjunction with recognizable societal issues, such as migration, climate change and extinction. Rather than as an abstract term, transculturality and its implications become relevant to life worlds and lived experience when embedded into these larger sociocultural developments. Alongside in-class discussions, we conducted a short class survey[1] that supports this observation. The student responses led us to conclude that debates around terminology, such as 'transculturality vs. postcoloniality' – while highly relevant for experts in the field – seem to engage students at BA level far less than pressing concerns related to climate change, sustainable mobility and various forms of migration. We found that urgent issues surrounding environmental justice and mobility justice, as portrayed and interrogated in literature and film, can become useful entry points for students into the realm of Transcultural English Studies. Indeed, our students quickly picked up on connections drawn between these fields.

Environmental and mobility justice were leading concepts in our seminar. Mimi Sheller has connected these two concepts, arguing that '[e]nvironmental injustices and mobility injustices are two faces of the same problem, each contributing to the other, and they are intertwined with the uneven distribution of access to transport, energy, and the fundamental life requirements of clean air, water, food and shelter' (2018: 25). Both environmental justice and mobility justice approaches therefore draw attention to the social and historical dimension of human and more-than-human mobilities – for example, of energy and waste – something that Transcultural English Studies pays little attention to.[2] Thus, we ask: What do new fields, such as the Environmental Humanities and Mobility Studies, have to offer transculturality? And what does a conversation between these approaches open up for the study of literature?

A reading of the seminal transcultural theorist Wolfgang Welsch, which will be expanded upon later in the chapter, illustrates some of these interconnections that interest us. In his essay 'Transculturality: The Puzzling Form of Cultures Today' (1999), Welsch contrasts transculturality with earlier models of cultures as self-contained (after Johann Gottfried Herder), but also with concepts like inter- and multiculturality, which both still presume a clear demarcation between cultures. Welsch uses the metaphor of 'islands' to contest the 'container theory' of cultures and to argue that this metaphor is unhelpful: '[T]he description of today's cultures as islands or spheres is factually incorrect and normatively deceptive. Cultures *de facto* no longer have the insinuated form of homogeneity and separateness. They have instead assumed a new form, which is to be called

---

[1] See survey questions in the appendix to this chapter.
[2] The Energy Humanities might need to adopt a transcultural perspective to move beyond the Eurocentric notions that inform some of the field's most influential studies, such as Cara Daggett's *The Birth of Energy* (2019). Daggett centres on European notions of energy in large parts and assumes a postcolonial lens in others.

transcultural in so far as it *passes through* classical cultural boundaries' (1999: 197; emphases in the original).

Welsch uses the metaphor of islands to show how cultures can no longer be conceived, yet with this image, he indirectly points to the water surrounding the islands as a much more apt metaphor to capture the increasing movement of cultures in modern processes of transculturation.³ Further in the essay, moreover, Welsch quotes the German-Swiss writer Carl Zuckmayer, who also draws on water imagery to illuminate the long history of transcultural thought. Describing Goethe's, Beethoven's, Gutenberg's and Mathias Grünewald's ancestry as composed of various people passing through Europe, such as the Romans, Jews, Christians, Greeks, Celts, Swedes, and the like, Zuckmayer writes: 'They were the best, my dear! The world's best! And why? Because that's where the peoples intermixed. Intermixed – like the waters from sources, streams and rivers, so, that they run together to a great, living torrent' (qtd in Welsch 1999: 200). Although Welsch himself does not draw attention to the water metaphor, he comments: 'This is a realistic description of a folk's historical genesis and constitution. It breaks through the fiction of homogeneity and the separatist idea of culture as decreed by the traditional concept' (1999: 200). As Welsch here conveys – albeit implicitly – this imagery is 'realistic', suggesting not only that he believes Zuckmayer is right, but also (and this might not be the intended meaning) that the image of water is more than a metaphor. Paying attention to the material properties of water, then, as material ecocritics have proposed with the idea that matter is expressive – 'storied matter', as Serenella Iovino and Serpil Oppermann (2012: 451, 468) have put it – seems to enable a fresh perspective on transculturality, as we later show.

In the first part of this chapter, we argue that there is a need to further reflect the theory of transculturality in practical university teaching methodologies. Building on similar questions raised in *Transcultural English Studies* (2009c) and *Beyond 'Other Cultures': Transcultural Perspectives on Teaching the New Literatures in English* (Doff and Schulze-Engler 2011b), both co-edited by Frank Schulze-Engler, we engage with Frank's teaching practice, as he has remained devoted to teaching throughout his career, and propose ideas for methodological and structural renewal on how to teach transculturality amidst environmental destruction.⁴ In the second part, we propose further directions in the field of

---

³ For the sake of a clear focus, we omit an engagement with Welsch's image of 'spheres'.
⁴ A useful and evolving resource for teaching the Environmental Humanities is available at https://www.asle.org/teach/teaching-resources-database/. There is an increasing number of publications on 'eco-pedagogies': see for example the special issue of *Anglistik* entitled 'Focus on Ecological English Language Teaching' (2022), edited by Roman Bartosch and Christian Ludwig, as well as volumes on

transcultural theory, arguing that 'transculturality' can be supplemented by a more sustained engagement with ecocriticism, as expressed in the notion of 'transcultural ecocriticism'. This term serves multiple purposes: One central aim is to start extending transculturality beyond its focus on 'human' cultures and to open it to the fields of the Environmental Humanities and Mobility Studies. With a close reading of the element of water in various creative and theoretical texts concerned with transculturality, we show that the concept becomes highly relevant when understood environmentally. By paying attention to the way water is used metaphorically, materially and metaphysically, we argue that water aptly captures the ways in which transculturality can be understood as a cultural and an environmental phenomenon. As we suggest with the term transcultural ecocriticism, the example of water enables us to understand transculturation as a life form itself: An elemental force with its own will, trajectory and flow that has strong agency.

Teaching transculturality revisited

The seeds of the questions posed above can partly be traced back to Frank's teaching and research. His 2017 seminar entitled 'Ecocriticism, Environmental Justice and Cli-Fi: Anglophone Literatures in the Anthropocene' already combined transcultural and environmental concerns. We also take up his interest in (cultural) mobilities, of which his seminar 'Travellers' (summer term 2021) and his essay on 'Automobilität in der afrikanischen Literatur' (2018) are only two pertinent examples. Writing this chapter as Frank's former and current (PhD) students, his research and teaching have, of course, thoroughly influenced our own. Kathrin Bartha-Mitchell was a PhD researcher with Frank Schulze-Engler and Sue Kossew (Monash University) and is currently a postdoctoral fellow at the Department for New Anglophone Literatures and Cultures at Goethe University Frankfurt (NELK). Thanks to Frank's supervision and her stay at NELK, her ecocritical work was challenged to bring transcultural approaches into conversation with the Environmental Humanities, with the outcome of a transcultural reading of the concept 'cosmos' (her PhD thesis *Unsettling the Anthropocene: Cosmological Readings of Contemporary Australian Literature*

Multispecies Futures (2022), edited by Andreas Hübner et al., on *Ahuman Pedagogy* (2022), edited by Jessie L. Beier and Jan Jagodzinski and on *Pedagogy in the Anthropocene* (2022), edited by Michael Paulsen et al.

was published online with open access and is forthcoming as a monograph with Routledge, 2023). Her current postdoctoral research pursues transcultural perspectives on Intergenerational Justice. Michelle Stork was first taught by Frank in 2012. Her PhD project combines transcultural and Mobility Studies approaches for the study of contemporary Anglophone road narratives. She also attended a number of Frank's seminars, in which the selected texts were never confined by national borders or geographical location; in fact, travelling texts usually took centre stage. New publications quickly found their way into Frank's seminars and his passion for literature transpired in our in-class discussions. In the few instances where Frank launched into monologues, it was to vividly and emphatically illustrate the shortcomings of postcolonial theory (Schulze-Engler 2015: 20) vis-à-vis transcultural approaches – a legacy we shall turn to in part two.

To gauge where *our* students' greatest interests lay, we conducted a simple questionnaire (attached as an appendix to this chapter) in which we asked for short definitions of the three key terms – transculturality, environmental justice and mobility justice – and whether students use these terms beyond the classroom (the short answer was 'no' for all three terms). While this was a simple questionnaire that produced mainly qualitative feedback, it nonetheless resulted in a number of insights. One student noted that 'the term Environmental Justice was the most interesting to [them] because it includes other concepts like transculturality and transspecies'. Another student expressed the wish for more seminars on ecocritical approaches, saying 'I think it would be nice if the University would focus on environmental justice in its seminars'. Since one of the concerns of our seminar was to bring cultural and literary studies to bear on the Environmental Humanities and Mobility Studies, we were also thrilled to see that most students commented on particular texts as salient entry points into deeper reflections on these overlapping concerns.

In our seminar, we started out with broad questions that aimed at bringing environmental and mobility justice into dialogue, looking at their potentialities, differences and limitations. At the same time, we were keen on drawing out the transcultural dimension of these debates, using examples that we referred to as 'transcultural Anglophone texts'. These included Myron Dewey's *Awake: A Dream from Standing Rock* (2017), George Miller's *Mad Max: Fury Road* (2015), Amitav Ghosh's *The Hungry Tide* (2004), Jesmyn Ward's *Sing, Unburied, Sing* (2017) and Behrouz Boochani's *No Friend But the Mountains* (2018). Although we limited the linguistic variety to the Anglophone world, the examples we chose countered a 'methodological nationalism' (Beck 2007) by being thoroughly located in geopolitical, sociocultural and environmental contexts (rivers, deserts, roadscapes, wetlands, oceans, prisons). Next to providing a global comparative perspective, this focus on Anglophone texts also allowed for deep and complex discussions: In contemporary Germany, university classes in English departments usually presuppose a high level of language competency that allow for a concentration on content, rather than language acquisition.

In our seminar, we addressed the transcultural dimension of the classroom by drawing on a variety of teaching methodologies as one way of addressing multiple experiences and forms of knowledge. At Goethe University, our students came from a variety of cultural backgrounds, many of which lent the seminar's topic even more relevance. Throughout our hybrid seminar (mostly taught in person, but also online), we experimented with a range of teaching methods, including different forms of group work, individual reflections, the formulation of a thesis statement in preparation for writing a term paper, short input presentations and discussion questions brought by the students, as well as regular anonymous and non-anonymous opportunities for feedback on the seminar. As bell hooks reminds us, and as we can confirm after spending time together with our students, 'the classroom remains the most radical space of possibility in the academy' (1994: 12). Given our own student experience of seminars that largely consisted of student presentations and often unstructured discussions, we see an urgent need to employ varied activities and methodologies in university settings that reflect the diversity of the classroom, which not only includes a range of cultural and socioeconomic backgrounds, but also refers to different learning preferences (Woolfolk 2021: 167).[5] According to Leask and Carroll, 'teaching [ideally] encompasses a broad range of activities' and '[p]rinciples for effective teaching across cultures need to be equally broad ranging' (2013: 6). Similarly, transcultural theorist Mary Louise Pratt has argued that part of the idea of the term 'contact zone'[6] (a central idea of Transcultural English Studies) was 'to contrast with ideas of community that underlie much of the thinking about language, communication and culture that gets done in the academy' (1991: 38). She continues:

---

[5] Woolfolk distinguishes between learning preferences and learning styles (2021: 167). She argues that while learning styles may not have as strong an impact on learning outcomes as routinely expected, 'presenting information in multiple modalities might be useful' (2021: 168).
[6] Pratt has defined a 'contact zone' as a social space that enables the intermingling of two or more cultures. They are 'spaces where cultures meet, clash, and grapple with each other, often in contexts of highly asymmetrical relations of power, such as colonialism, slavery, or their aftermaths as they are lived out in many parts of the world today' (1991: 33).

> We are looking for the pedagogical arts of the contact zone. These will include, we are sure, exercises in storytelling and in identifying with the ideas, interests, histories, and attitudes of others; experiments in transculturation and collaborative work and in the art of critique, parody, and comparison (including unseemly comparison between elite and vernacular cultural forms); the redemption of the oral; ways for people to engage with suppressed aspects of history (including their own histories), ways to move into and out of rhetorics of authenticity; ground rules for communication across lines of difference and hierarchy that go beyond politeness but maintain mutual respect; a systematic approach to the all-important concept of cultural mediation. (Pratt 1991: 40)

While Pratt lists these vital elements of transcultural teaching methodologies, we would add that there is a great need to further extend this area of research (Hartwiger 2011; Singh and Doherty 2004; Wolff 2002): We need more knowledge, sensibility and practical approaches for how to cultivate classrooms as transcultural contact zones.[7] We suggest that the transcultural conditions in the classroom could be addressed through an adequate breadth of methodologies that are sensitive to the students' backgrounds and that support transcultural knowledge production (Barnhardt 2000: 7; Leask and Carroll 2013: 6).

The way we framed the content of our class was also informed by transcultural theory. While postcolonial approaches seem to be more prominent in larger social debates and in popular culture, Frank's investment has been, and continues to be, in transculturality. Frank himself has noted that 'it seems ... unconvincing to regard transculturality as a methodological panacea for cultural and literary studies' (2009a: xiii), and yet the concept is well suited for an engagement with specific geographical contexts and locations and their respective 'micropolitics' (Schulze-Engler 2007a: 21). As opposed to 'distant reading' (Moretti 2013), Frank zooms in on 'the nitty-gritty details of the raw material it [literature] is feeding into its epistemological gristmill' (Schulze-Engler 2007b: 10). In his essay 'From Postcolonialism to Transcultural World Literature', he makes the important point that 'transculturality ... is not specific to the New Literatures in English, but the New Literatures in English are specifically suited to explore the dynamics of transculturality in the contemporary world' (2007b: 28). He also investigates transculturality's postcolonial legacies, such as taking 'the political

---

[7] Annika Kreft's study *Transkulturelle Kompetenz und literaturbasierter Fremdsprachenunterricht: eine rekonstruktive Studie zum Einsatz von 'Fictions of Migration' im Fach Englisch* (2020) shows that transculturality has not yet properly taken hold in school classrooms, for example, where both teachers and students tend to affirm binary and nation-based understandings of culture. Kreft proposes that teachers can actively influence pupils' development of transcultural knowledge by providing the right conditions and cues that will allow them to challenge these simplistic binaries.

dimensions of literature seriously' (2007b: 28). In contrast to postcolonial approaches, Transcultural English Studies place greater 'emphasis on local and regional contexts of literature, on their intertextual and dialogical relationships to a multiplicity of intellectual debates, cultural movements and oral traditions' (2007b: 28); they open 'English-language texts to a wider comparative perspective that acknowledges the manifold "transnational connections" shaping English-language literatures everywhere in the world' (2007b: 28–9); and they stress literature's concern 'with internal conflicts within cultures' (2007b: 29). Following Frank's approach, we share an interest in locality and regionality that is embedded in a global perspective which stresses exchange and mobility. We build on and extend his work by initiating conversations between Transcultural English Studies and ecocriticism, moving transcultural theory beyond human-centred approaches and placing greater emphasis on the material dimensions underlying transculturality. Building on Doff and Schulze-Engler (2011b), we draw concrete connections between transculturality as a cultural phenomenon and suitable teaching practices. To this end, we also need to critique the problematic conditions for teaching in the current (German and global) academic system and plead for more support of teaching efforts. Even as early-career researchers are expected to gain teaching experience and formal training (i.e. through teaching certificates), academic teaching remains profoundly undervalued and underpaid in Germany and beyond. Through the prevalence of 'Lehraufträge' (lectureships), initially introduced to offer more practical courses run by experienced professionals but now widely used to cover core elements of the curriculum (see Neumann 2019), universities are reinforcing a structure in which teaching privileges those who can afford to do under- and unpaid work: Only the time spent teaching is compensated – preparatory work, student support and marking are unpaid. Access to teaching is intransparent, as 'Lehraufträge' are usually not advertised, but 'given' from professor to PhD candidates or Postdocs. Importantly, this structure renders diversity in teaching less likely.

We now turn to previous takes on teaching transculturality to clarify crucial divergences. The focus is on Sabine Doff's contribution to *Transcultural English Studies* on 'Inter- and/or Transcultural Learning in the Foreign Language Classroom? – Theoretical Foundations and Practical Implications'. Her essay is part of a section entitled 'Teaching Transculturality' and raises the question whether 'understanding a foreign culture' (2009: 362) is possible. She delineates two answers, each provided by different theoretical 'camps': One, understanding is impossible because the foreign remains out of grasp in its essential difference;

two, 'an understanding among cultures is possible "because we all inhabit a common world"' (2009: 362). Doff proceeds to sketch the position of the second camp as follows:

> In interacting with other cultures, scholars of the latter group claim that students do not have to forget their prior experiences and knowledge but, rather, have the chance to become aware of their values, clarifying and relativizing them. In this line of thought, cultural symbols: i.e., areas of experience that are universal to humankind – for example, concepts of space, love, and friendship, death or illness – play an important role, since they can facilitate understanding between cultures when learners are aware of them. (2009: 362)

This quote suggests that Doff understands transcultural phenomena as 'anthropological universals', which aligns with the most general use of transculturality identified by Daniel G. König and Katja Rakow (2016: 93).[8] For Doff, emotional 'human' experiences are transcultural, but as König and Rakow note, 'such a definition is not only considered too broad by most scholars, but is also rejected because it still builds on the premise that cultures constitute macro-milieus characterised by fixed frameworks of human thought and behaviour' (2016: 93–4). Such a broad definition, they suggest, does not pay attention to how culture shapes thoughts and actions, and therefore 'fails to acknowledge the observable complexity of processes of cultural interaction and identification' (König and Rakow 2016: 94).

Doff argues that transcultural teaching practices should 'stress ... the culture-general rather than culture-specific features and that simultaneously critically investigates the roles of stereotypes in interactions between members of different cultures' (2009: 364). Doff illustrates her theoretical considerations with a Native American example, which allegedly affords EFL (English as a Foreign Language) teachers 'opportunities to investigate Native and non-Native cultures living *side by side* in North America. This encompasses the differences, social practices, values and their meaning across these cultures as well as people who mediate

---

[8] They summarize four uses of the term 'transcultural', which are first, 'phenomena that transcend cultural boundaries' (2016: 93); secondly, 'a specific variety of phenomena that transcend cultural boundaries' (94); thirdly, 'phenomena that are situated between cultural milieus separated by linguistic, religious, normative, or other kinds of boundaries' (94); and fourthly, to 'describe a particular method of approach that [...] deconstructs concepts such as "society", "class", "nation", "culture", or "civilization"' (95) and highlights the 'multipolarity, multiple perspective, and transformative dynamics inherent to the research subject' (95). The latter comes closest to Welsch's definition, but it foregrounds methodology, while Welsch highlights the transformative power inherent in cultures in contact and therefore goes beyond methodology to describe lived realities.

more or less successfully *between* them' (2009: 364–5; emphases added) – features of *inter*cultural models.

However, we disagree with this approach of transculturality as closely linked to universality in some crucial points that are important to outline because of their implications for classroom methodologies. First, while Doff conceives the transcultural as universal (e.g. she understands 'respect' as a transcultural value, 2009: 369–70), transcultural approaches can be understood as being attentive to cultural *specificities* and to how these become mobile, moving beyond the specific into the shared realm that is not necessarily universal. Transcultural processes occur in contact zones, where cultural-general ideas (e.g. the slogan 'Water is Life') can coexist with culturally specific knowledges and belief systems (e.g. the notion that water is sacred, water protectors attribute if not personhood then agency to the river). Secondly, this approach still remains very much rooted in container thinking, as her opening question regarding 'foreign cultures' indicates.[9] Welsch's model is instructive here: Since culture is thought of in rhizomatic, connected terms, there are no absolutely 'foreign cultures': While some cultural elements may be unfamiliar, others will be recognizable, especially under conditions of global modernity. Although Doff moves away from this position in the 2011 publication *Beyond 'Other Cultures'*, her 2009 essay still tends to emphasize separate cultural spheres. Such are precisely the fallacies of intercultural approaches outlined by Welsch: While well-intentioned, intercultural approaches fall short of overcoming container thinking. It is precisely the concept of interculturality that '*creates* by its primary trait – the separatist character of cultures – the secondary problem of a structural inability to communicate between these cultures' (1999: 196; emphasis in the original). Instead, Welsch's approach seems more helpful, as this model places more emphasis on the 'trans', which designates 'across and beyond', challenging this notion of 'foreignness' and absolute difference. As Frank Schulze-Engler has noted, 'culture per se can be argued to be transcultural' (2009a: xii). However, in order to put Welsch's concept to use, specific instances of transculturality need to be scrutinized.

---

[9] Doff's stance on this issue has shifted somewhat in the introduction to *Beyond 'Other Cultures'*, where she and Schulze-Engler suggest that engagements with the so-called New Literatures in English 'allow insights into the complexity of culture rather than laying bare "other cultures", and they challenge readers to come to terms with cultural difference without falling back into the conventional wisdoms produced by a global alterity industry. It is this "constitutive transculturality" that makes the New Literatures in English particularly valuable for teaching about culture in the EFL classroom' (2011a, 4).

Similar to Doff, our approach to teaching transculturality was informed by the conviction that 'we all inhabit a common world' (Klippel 1994: 54, qtd in Doff 2009: 362), enabled by the English language which allows for 'one global conversation with limited participation open to all, and full participation available to none' (Philips 2001: 5). We tried to embrace a form of engagement in the classroom that pays attention to culturally specific and complex processes by drawing out the respective geopolitical contexts in which the films and novels are set. As Doff would have done, we also encouraged students to keep in mind prejudices and fallacies. However, we aimed at framing the filmic and literary material as fertile ground for interrogating stereotypes: These stereotypes can be reinforced, thoroughly challenged or both within the same text. In this sense, we understood our seminar not as a space for learning about 'other cultures' but rather about various knowledge systems, travelling ideas and common concerns across geographies – namely, the environment and mobilities. After all, Welsch has argued that 'trans' stands in for inscribing cultural processes with a sense of motion and mobility (see 1999: 200). In our class, we used commonalities to draw attention to global challenges in a world where environmental devastations will lead to forced migrations. We also contemplated what role fossil-fuelled, harmful modes of mobility play: If environmental injustices are caused by destructive modes of mobility and the degrees and types of mobilities vary across cultures, then what is at stake is one of the central paradoxes of globalized modernity – the ongoing need for mobility. Since the distribution of fossil-fuelled mobilities is unequal, with colonial legacies informing extraction logics, their use is nonetheless historically complex and ongoing.[10] Therefore, a transcultural lens that moves beyond the colonial binaries of 'victims vs. perpetrators' remains insufficient a model for identifying culprits in the form of collectives (e.g. the Global North). Although the postcolonial lens is prevalent in the Anglophone world – given that the British Empire was the largest in the world – transculturality enables a much more nuanced and contemporary exploration of the ways in which English has also become a lingua franca – or 'multilingua franca' (Jenkins 2018: 601) – and a mode of expression in new contexts (consider for example Arab Anglophone Studies).

---

[10] Important studies on automobility, for example, show the historical involvement of 'locals' in colonial contexts. Automobility and the 'progress' it promised turned it into a powerful symbol and in an 'era of easy oil' (Wenzel 2014: 157) its lure was extensive. See for example Lindsey Green-Simms's *Postcolonial Automobility: Car Culture in West Africa* (2017), Joshua Grace's *African Motors: Gender, Technology and the History of Development* (2021) and Georgine Clarsen's 'Revisiting "Driving While Black": Racialized Automobilities in a Settler Colonial Context' (2017: 55).

As Mita Banerjee argues in her contribution to this volume, in settler colonial contexts, it seems difficult to embrace a transcultural perspective when reparations require the identification of responsible parties (188). The same dialectics seem to apply to environmental and mobility justice debates. There is no denying that many environmental injustices have colonial roots, as underlined in the 2022 IPCC report 'Mitigation of Climate Change' (Mercer 2022). Yet, reducing debates to colonialism and blaming former colonizers reduces contemporary complexities. Transcultural theory has been particularly attuned to complex, multiple modes of cultural belonging, internal diversity within and across communities and the active participation of Indigenous groups in global modernity. As transcultural theory makes clear, communities that have traditionally been assumed to be monolithic can no longer be conceived as such. In this sense, a transcultural lens shows that individual perpetrators may be difficult to trace. In more conceptual terms, what is perceived as an injustice may vary based on culturally specific conceptions of 'nature' and is likely to be subject to debate *within* a particular community.

Thus, while concerns over environmental and mobility justice apply to humanity at large (and obviously not only to humans but also to the environment), transcultural specificities soon become evident and cannot be overlooked. As our close reading below shows, the cultural understanding of water as sacred, which is common to many Indigenous cultures across the globe (see Banerjee in this volume), can function as a corrective to colonial notions of nature as a resource and demonstrates different cultural understandings of 'nature'. However, a transcultural lens also emphasizes that animist/anthropomorphizing notions of nature *do* also exist in settler colonial (e.g. North American) and European contexts – if also arguably much more neglected and suppressed. Moreover, while such notions may be more prevalent in Indigenous cultures, notions of 'the sacredness of Mother Earth and the interdependence and unity of all species' (Di Chiro 2016: 104) inevitably travel across cultures, as a result of global movements. Of course, narratives also render these imaginaries and ideas mobile.[11]

Thus, environmental justice and mobility justice debates can themselves be understood as transcultural processes. Not only do they interrogate the different responsibilities for previous damages done to the environment, they also require

---

[11] The wide circulation of bestsellers like Robin Wall Kimmerer's *Braiding Sweetgrass: Indigenous Wisdom, Scientific Knowledge and the Teachings of Plants* (2013) is just one example in a time in which Indigenous knowledges are undergoing a positive revaluation.

communication across cultures (see Butt in this volume) in terms of what 'environment', 'mobility' and 'justice' mean in general, but, most importantly, for particular local contexts. Indeed, alongside local specificities, translocal and global dimensions – also emphasized in transcultural approaches – play a key role. Di Chiro stresses that environmental justice movements are '"seeking a global vision" for healthy, resilient, and sustainable communities rooted in *translocal* "grassroots realities"' (2016: 101; emphasis in the original). This is illustrated in the slogan, 'think global, act local', which has long been prevalent and arguably efficient for various environmental movements.

Towards teaching a transcultural ecocriticism

As fertile a field as Transcultural English Studies has proven to be, teaching this seminar, it became clear to us that it is important that we develop transculturality further, bring it into conversation with urgent social and environmental challenges, as well as think carefully about the importance of teaching. After having reflected on our seminar and suggested the need for more practical teaching methodologies that cultivate the classroom as a transcultural contact zone, we now turn to consider what Transcultural English Studies has to offer to the fields of Environmental Humanities and Mobility Studies; vice versa, we ask how an environmental lens can animate transcultural theory anew. In the following discussion, along with Sheller's definition above, we understand mobility issues as one central concern of ecocriticism, but these interrelations must still be brought into full focus in scholarship emerging in both Mobility Studies and the Environmental Humanities. The quest to bring together Transcultural English Studies with concerns in ecocriticism and Mobility Studies is in line with our earlier mentioned hypothesis that transcultural issues become more graspable and relevant to students when considered as part of recognizable contemporary issues, such as climate change and various forms of travel and migration. In the following, we show how the notion of 'transcultural ecocriticism' has so far been discussed and propose avenues for where scholarship may go. Reading the cultural and environmental significance of water in two creative texts we taught, as well as in transcultural theory, the aim is to strongly advocate for the benefits of an ecocritical lens for transculturality and beyond.

Although an ecocritical engagement with transculturality is certainly already underway, the interrelationship between the two has not been sufficiently theorized. In fact, similar to the problematic equation of 'transculturality' with 'universality' critiqued above, the concept of the transcultural is often used so broadly (e.g. often synonymously with 'transnational') that it loses its specific meaning. Moreover, there is little ecocritical engagement with transcultural theorists such as Wolfgang Welsch and Mary Louise Pratt. An engagement with these thinkers, however, enables a crossover of helpful cultural concepts for environmental theory. Cultural concepts such as 'contact zone' (Pratt), 'liminal space' (Turner) and the 'rhizome' (Glissant/Welsch) can cross-fertilize environmental concepts and illuminate the interconnectedness of nature and culture. Although there is much emerging work, as of yet, there is little overview and understanding for how much these cultural terms interrelate with environmental phenomena or similar environmental terms.[12] For reasons of scope, in this chapter we focus on two of these terms that are especially prominent in transcultural theory: the contact zone and liminal space. To show how fruitful an engagement can be between transcultural theory, ecocriticism and Mobility Studies, we read Welsch and Pratt in conjunction with the element of water in the documentary film *Awake!* and the novel *The Hungry Tide*. The multifarious meanings and elemental properties of water, we argue, enable a complex yet sensory understanding of transculturality.[13]

Research into the concepts of *Liquidity, Flows, Circulation*, to cite the title of a recent publication, suggests that we are currently witnessing a 'cultural logic of environmentalization' (Denecke et al. 2022: 7). This logic describes a tendency to attribute 'environmental' terminology, particularly water-related imagery, to art, media and cultural production (21–2). Denecke, Kuhn and Stürmer's study aims at delineating possibilities and limitations of these metaphors, while also addressing the tension between material conditions and the metaphorization of water's various characteristics to describe 'our contemporary world as a world in flow' (21). Our study shares a similar point of departure; however, we are particularly interested in how the environmental properties of water are portrayed in different media as facilitators of transculturality.

Coined in the context of increasing concern about the destruction of the biosphere during the Cold War, the term 'ecocriticism' emerged in North

---

[12] These terms are examples we discuss in this chapter; however, there are more connections to be made. Another example is the notion of 'alien species'.

[13] Here, our work intersects with much of the research that has been emerging in the Blue Humanities, a field that focuses on the literary and cultural importance of different forms and bodies of water. Here, transculturality is somewhat present, as Arnaud Barras's 2015 article 'The Aesthetics of the Tide: The Ecosystem as Matrix for Transculturation in Amitav Ghosh's *The Hungry Tide*' indicates. We engage with his argument later.

America in the 1970s,[14] aimed at challenging 'ecocidal attitudes' (Garrard 2016: 61). Since these early formulations (often called 'first-wave ecocriticism', which designates a focus on 'nonfiction "nature-writing", non-human nature and wilderness experience, American and British literature, and "discursive" ecofeminism' (Slovic 2010: 4)), the 2000s saw an increased interest in *global* concepts of place 'in fruitful tension with neo-bioregionalist attachments to specific locales', which came to be known as Ecocriticism's 'second wave' (Slovic 2010: 7). In 2009, Scott Slovic and Joni Adamson then ventured to formulate what they thought represented a 'third wave', which, while focusing on cultural background and ethnic identity more intensely than had been the case in early ecocriticism, 'also seek[s] to overcome the limiting, isolating focus on specific cultures as unique phenomena. The impulse to study human experience in relation to the more-than-human world and to compare human experience across cultures, in particular, struck us as an altogether different tendency than we had observed during the first two "waves" of the field' (qtd in Slovic 2010: 4). This third wave thus brought about an interest in transcultural approaches, genres, green cultural studies and a decidedly more activist tendency. As Slovic writes, its main conceptualizations include 'such neologisms as "eco-cosmopolitanism", "rooted cosmopolitanism", "the global soul", and "translocality"' (2010: 7).

Although 'trans-cultural' (Slovic 2010: 6) understandings evidently present a strong feature of this third wave, transcultural *theory* has scarcely been brought into dialogue with ecocriticism. The recent volume *Transcultural Ecocriticism* (Cooke and Denner 2021) is a case in point: Although espousing the concept in its title, the volume does not engage with the history of the term, its theorists and its various significations. Instead, the volume employs transculturality mainly as synonymous with 'transnationalism' and as a welcome widening of Anglo-American contexts. As the editors Stuart Cooke and Peter Denney argue, transculturality refers to a more-than-human global ecocriticism. However, their volume still centres Indigeneity, and thus settler-colonial contexts: 'We urge readers to consider a burgeoning diversity of First Nations scholarship as a central component of any ecocritical method, and in order to avoid the "fetishised landscape[s]" of an imperial ecological aesthetics' (5). Although the title's transculturality aims at a diversification of contexts, it still seems to centre colonial history and could therefore be understood as a form of 'postcolonial

---

[14] It was first used in William Rueckert's 'Literature and Ecology: An Experiment in Ecocriticism' (1978).

ecocriticism' (Huggan and Tiffin 2010).[15] As we suggest in this part, however, there is much to be gained from bringing transcultural theory into contact with ecocriticism, precisely because this helps in broadening the field to wider contexts. As the focus of our class lay not so much on transcultural theory than on applied readings of the intersections of transculturality and environmental and mobility themes, we now turn to these teaching examples to point to the deep reservoir enabled by these overlapping thematical foci.

Our first example discussed in class was the multi-authored documentary film *Awake! A Dream from Standing Rock* (2017) about the protest movement that became known as #NODAPL (short for 'No Dakota Access Pipeline') against the construction of an oil pipeline under and across the Missouri and Mississippi rivers – the drinking water source for over 17 million people. The protest camp was largely organized by the Standing Rock Sioux Tribe in North Dakota, who were able to create a broad movement that supported the protest camp on the ground and beyond. The hashtag #NODAPL, which began trending during the protest camp, testifies to the widespread movement that was able to mobilize attention and solidarity across the world. The camp lasted from April 2016 until February 2017, but was eventually violently cleared up, and the pipeline was completed in 2017.

Awake! was directed by several filmmakers and activists/'protectors',[16] both Indigenous and non-Indigenous, and presents four different short films and styles, ranging from lyrical and affective to fact-based neutrality. Nevertheless, the different parts blend together well: The first part, directed by Josh Fox and narrated by Lakota activist Floris White Bull, presents an affective collage of the Standing Rock protests, providing cultural and personal perspectives on the significance of the Missouri river and employing many landscape shots that feature various streams of water and rivers. While this part includes a cosmological, material and spiritual reflection on the significance of water, the second part, directed by James Spione, contrasts in tone by focusing on the more mundane life at the Oceti Sakowin camp and by showing the impressive everyday camp organization and daily tasks executed by the protectors. In the third part, which again changes significantly in style, Myron Dewey presents footage taken mainly on his mobile phone on the way to or at the protest camp,

---

[15] Recent attempts at moving beyond postcolonial ecocriticism include Shazia Rahman's 'The Environment of South Asia: Beyond Postcolonial Ecocriticism' (2021) and Timothy Clark's chapter '"Postcolonial Ecocriticism"... and Beyond?' in *The Value of Ecocriticism* (2019).
[16] From here on, instead of 'protestors' or 'activists', we use the term 'protectors' which is the self-designation used in the film.

during which confrontations and conversations with the police are especially prominent. In the Coda, Floris White Bull then provides an affective poetic conclusion. These different documentary styles, many of which combine multi-scalar landscape shots with narrative voiceover, enable diverse perspectives on water and its required protection, embedding the river in multi-perspective storytelling.

As the makeup of multiple filmmakers of *Awake!* suggests, the film depicts the shared effort of global, 'trans-Indigenous' (Allen 2012) solidarities. Indeed, in the United States, we can observe a reappraisal of Indigenous knowledges beyond Indigenous communities, which leads to transcultural processes of knowledge production that also inform various environmental movements. Notably, *Awake!* includes a scene in which a young woman brings candy to the baton-bearing army, highlighting that the binary of 'Indigenous people vs. settler police' (19:00) may still exist, but that a conscious effort at overcoming this divide is made by the protectors, who reiterate that the slogan 'Water is Life' also applies to those across the barricade.

While teaching, it was interesting to note the different layers the film presented: Whereas it is likely that most viewers are drawn to the film because of their interest in environmental activism, aspects of mobility and transculturality are, perhaps, less obvious but generated enriching discussions. Although getting to know some basic cultural characteristics of various Indigenous cultures was doubtlessly part of the viewer experience, our focus in class here was not on 'learning about' Indigenous American cultures, but on problematizing the reductive notions of authenticity, purity and essentialism of various identities. The modern mobility of trans-indigenous groups, which could, for instance, be seen in scenes that involve getting to and from the camp by car, shed light on the perhaps obvious but nevertheless paradoxically interesting fact that, today, activists rely on petroleum culture to challenge the fossil fuel industry. Automobility and petroculture are rewarding lenses through which to study the film because they provide a distinct image – the car – as a simple yet memorable symbol of the nature/culture contact zone: The car signifies both an environmental problem *and* the mobility needed for environmental protection. With the help of Sandy Grande's critical essay 'Refusing the Settler Society of Spectacle' (2019), our class discussed issues inherent in essentialist notions of Indigenous cultures as pre-modern and immobile, as well as the fact that more often than not, contemporary activist movements rely on transcultural solidarity, which can imply various forms of fossil fuel use – impure as it may be – in order for the protest to become effective. Problematizing the still all-too-prominent ideas of purity and authenticity is arguably not only helpful in the context of ecocriticism and activist movements in general, but it also represents a central concern of transculturality. In this way, our discussion highlighted the ways in which environmental themes can be aptly understood as a palimpsest: Once the surface has been scratched, the protection of a river reveals many more interesting layers fanning into such diverse aspects as automobility and purity-fixation in environmentalism.

As the central slogan of the NODAPL movement was 'Water is Life', or *mni wiconi*, the Lacota term from which it derives, it is worth contemplating the significance of water in relation to transculturality, mobility and ecocriticism. The elemental properties and the cultural imagery of water can be read to speak to transcultural solidarity: Not only has the rallying-cry 'Water is Life' travelled widely (this motto has, as we pointed out in class, also been used by Indigenous Australian activists in relation to fracking),[17] but the representation of the Missouri river in *Awake!* can also be read to have become a 'contact zone', or a 'liminal space', in which people were able to engage in rich transcultural exchange, and in which natural resources (such as oil and water), and diverse peoples came together in unique ways. As quoted above, Pratt has described the contact zone as a significant *social* space, yet in *Awake!* the significance of the *material* and spiritual place – the river – suggests that the river cannot be neglected for understanding the workings of this particular contact zone. As the many landscape shots and the poetic reflections on the river reveal, water was a central element of this contact zone – one that brought people together in the first place. A liminal zone, as theorized by Victor Turner (1995), describes a threshold or passage 'characterized by the dissolution of order and the creation of fluid, malleable situations that enable new institutions and customs to become established' (Lehmkuhl et al. 2015: 7). Similarly, a liminal period describes a special moment in time that harbours a fluid social order and a portal for societal change (see Lehmkuhl et al. 2015: 16). While Pratt's contact zone describes a significant social *space* of exchange, and 'liminality' refers to a special *spacetime* in which possibilities open up, both seem to neglect the *materiality* of time and space – in other words, the environmental manifestation of liminality and the contact zone. Bringing these concepts into conversation with the film's

---

[17] See, for instance, the short activist film by the Indigenous environmental organization SEED: *Water Is Life* (dir. Cam Suttie): https://nt.seedmob.org.au/water_is_life. Although SEED uses the same slogan, it would of course be nonsensical to argue that notions of the sacredness of water do not exist in other cultures. Although we may be able to locate the origin of this very protest slogan in the Lacota expression *mni wiconi*, the same cannot be true for the idea behind it.

proposition as water being 'sacred' reveals that cultural theory has, by and large, neglected the ecosystem in which liminal processes and contact zones occur. Similarly, social and cultural scholars Ursula Lehmkuhl, Hans-Jürgen Lüsebrink and Laurence McFalls draw on the contact zone and liminality, in order to show how transculturation is spatially constituted: '[B]oth concepts, contact zones and liminality, address core elements of the spatial dimensions of diversity' (2015: 7). Although transculturation and space are connected, space is mainly understood as social. This is perhaps unsurprising, since key geographical ideas influential in literary studies after the so-called spatial turn focused on the social production of space (Cresswell 2004: 10; Lefebvre 1991: 73).[18]

As we can see, important cultural theories of liminality and the contact zone, firmly rooted in the humanities, have yet to be brought more in touch with environmental theory. Moreover, material, environmental conditions and their cultural significance need to be accounted for, which will help move transcultural theory beyond its hitherto largely human-centric focus.[19]

Teaching *Awake!* and engaging with the strong presence of the river – it is repeatedly called and evoked as sacred in the film – drew our attention to the idea that the process of transculturation in the film can be understood in relation to the eco-systemic properties and cultural understanding of water. *Awake!* conveys that it is the liveliness, nurturance and vulnerability of the river that mobilizes people to come together and, as a by-product of this pragmatic and urgent task, transcultural processes unfold. In the unique context of twenty-first-century environmental disasters, such as oil spills,[20] Indigenous cultural traditions of place-reverence are reflected upon and engaged with in novel ways. *Awake!*, which arose from the protest camp, can be regarded as such a reflection of – or a direct expression of – a modern contact zone that engenders not just the transculturation of different cultures, but also of different understandings of 'nature' (resources and elemental properties that cannot neatly be mapped onto

---

[18] It is now also widely accepted that cultural difference is 'socially produced' and 'spatially expressed' (Harris 2017: 263). Harris calls this the 'spatiality of social difference' (Harris 2017: 263).
[19] Héctor Hoyos's *Things with a History: Transcultural Materialism and the Literatures of Extraction in Contemporary Latin America* (2015) takes a promising step in this direction by drawing attention to the environmental and material dimensions of transculturality, turning to rubber trees, soil and discarded objects as they become protagonists in contemporary literature. As he argues, '"[c]ulture" here is a concrete and, again, not just a human affair—think of how the etymology of the word relates to fermentation. These aspects will all come together more clearly through examples, including […] the retelling of the socio-botanical history of sugar and tobacco in Fernando Ortiz (who coined the term *transculturación*)' (2019: 24–5; emphasis in the original). Hoyos effectively points to the material and more-than-human elements implicit in transcultural theory that remain yet to be fully explored.
[20] The film quotes that there have been 1000s of oil spills in the past six years or so.

one or another culture). Although strongly tied to Lakota Indigenous culture with its indebtedness to the Missouri river, the film also invokes that the protest camp by the river is transspatial and transtemporal: transspatial because it brings together a diverse group of activists and protectors from across the United States and beyond; transtemporal because it activates the incorporation of ancestors, historical knowledge, and future generations. In short, in *Awake!*, the river cannot be understood as 'background' to the contact zone. Rather, it can be read as an active agent that drew people together and that marked the liminality of the protest camp in a particular manner, which influenced the ways in which people moved, conversed and experienced the event. The film shows, for instance, how protectors went in and out of the river during confrontations with the police; in one scene, a protector recounts the physical sensation of joy that came from having stood in the freezing river for over ninety minutes without getting hypothermia (15:00). In this sense, this particular process of transculturation and the events at the camp cannot be separated from the eco-systemic significance and corporeal experience of the water, as it is the very threat the oil pipeline poses to the quality of the water that caused people to gather there in the first place.

Of course, not every cultural theory necessarily has to be understood in relation to particular ecosystems. Indeed, in one of the seminars taught by Frank, this question came up in relation to Homi Bhabha's notion of 'Third Space' articulated in *The Location of Culture* (2004). As for Bhabha's concept, it is key that a Third Space is not spatially defined and delineated. While some literary scholars have tried to *locate* 'Third Space', as John McLeod does in 'Living in Between: Interstitial spaces in Timothy Mo's *Sour Sweet*' with regard to an alley in London (1997: 117), Frank emphasized that this is not where the value of Bhabha's concept lies. Instead, Third Space usually describes an imaginary, creative contact zone, beyond a specific geographic location. While we see the value of imaginary and imagined contact zones, we want to add that this interest in imaginary spaces needs to be supplemented by paying greater attention to narrative engagements with different material localities and environments of transculturation – a dimension ecocritical approaches are attuned to.

Teaching *Awake!* thus illuminated each of our seminar's key concepts: the river and its people as a vulnerable ecosystem (environment), the modern engagement with (trans-) Indigenous culture(s) that engendered the solidarity of a highly diverse crowd (transculturality), and the car as the sign of a petrol-fuelled culture that, nevertheless, enables transculturation and environmental activism (mobility/mobilization). Although we discussed each of these three aspects separately to illustrate their specific meaning, they cannot be separated from one another. The film presents all of these aspects in subtle ways with one pragmatic aim: resistance to further environmental devastations in the United States and beyond. As can be illuminated with *Awake!*, therefore, the socio-environmental significance of water is able to point towards complex interactions with cultural difference, while still providing a transcultural site that points to cultural diversity as well as to biodiversity as a value to be protected. Of course, choosing to focus on the mobility and transculturality of this film provides just one reading; the film could also be read along other lines, such as the strategic (self-)exoticization of Native Americans. However, in a film that is decidedly 'about' the protection of this foundational element of life, water also constitutes a figuration that enables new perspectives on mobility and transculturality.

Something similar emerged from our engagement with Amitav Ghosh's novel *The Hungry Tide* (2004). In this novel, which has become somewhat of a classic in ecocriticism, Ghosh explores the complex culture and ecosystem of the biggest wetlands on the planet, the Sundarbans, which are located in the Bay of Bengal in today's Bangladesh and India. *The Hungry Tide* draws a parallel between the lively ecosystem and the cultural diversity of the area. This parallel then illuminates not only historical events, such as the displacement of poor and marginalized communities anew, but also problematizes twenty-first-century concerns of environmental conservation. With the help of Arnaud Barras's illuminating essay 'The Aesthetics of the Tide: The Ecosystem as Matrix for Transculturation in Amitav Ghosh's *The Hungry Tide*' (2015), our class discussed the ways in which the representation of water reflects cultural processes. To illustrate the way 'Ghosh uses the semantic field of water to describe the transformative episodes affecting the foreign focalizers', Barras traces the many parallels the novel draws between water and its influence on characters, such as 'his mind was swamped by a flood of pure sensation' (citing Ghosh 2015: 329, in Barras 2015: 184). As Barras writes:

> The aesthetics of the tide in Amitav Ghosh provides an analogy between the eco- and cultural systems of the Sundarbans: when the rivers of silt meet the tide of the Sea of Bengal, it causes a proliferation of life; in a similar fashion, when the foreign cultures meet the culture of the tide, it causes a proliferation of cultural life, here envisaged as transculturation. ... Ghosh's clever analogy between ecosystem and cultural system allows us to conceive of transculturation in original ways. ... Indeed, the meeting of two cultures does not result in a homogenous new culture; some elements of each are mixed, while some others remain distinct. The most important element that the Aesthetics of the Tide

reveals is that transculturation is a spatio-temporal process that cannot be taken out and analysed independently of the ecosystem it takes place in. (2015: 174)

Importantly, then, the novel explores the ways in which transculturation can be understood 'as much [as] a cultural as an environmental phenomenon' (Barras 2015: 179). Barras uses the image of rhizome, after Deleuze and Guattari, and Edouard Glissant's 'poetics of the mangrove' (from *Poetics of Relation*, 1990 [trans. 1997]) to illustrate these processes of transculturation: 'There is an implication that cultures and actants are not so much rooted and unchanging (vertical) as rhizomatically linked and malleable (lateral), in keeping with the ultimately stabilizing presence of the mangroves' (2015: 180). This has important implications: If transculturation can also be observed in the more-than-human world, we can understand cultural diversity to present a key concern for fostering environmental transformation and, ultimately, protection. As Barras puts it: 'Ghosh's analogy means that cultures are part of the physical world because they shape both environment and organism; they are not on another ontological level, a level of abstraction, but, rather, take part in the concrete construction of the world, just as rivers and humans do. Cultures have a tangible transformative power' (2015: 174).

While Barras's enticing reading evinces that ecocritical readings have engaged with theories of transculturality, there is further work needed to bring this cross-fertilization of transculturality and ecocriticism to the fore and provide accessible overviews. The transcultural theorist Wolfgang Welsch (a staple in Frank's classrooms), for instance, has hardly been engaged with. Apart from water, Welsch uses further environmental tropes that are meant to capture the aliveness and movement of cultures: Cultures can be conceived of as 'multi-mesh[s]' (1999: 200), 'web[s]' (1999: 203), 'life-form[s]' (1999: 201), 'reserves' and 'practice[s]' (1999: 203). What Welsch conjures up here is, thus, culture as a kind of elemental force with agency, evoking Barras's earlier-cited point that transculturation can be understood 'as much a cultural as an environmental phenomenon' (1999: 179). Whereas Barras argues that transculturality cannot be analysed out of the specific eco-systemic context it occurs in, Welsch, however, detaches transculturality from particular geographies: 'The mechanics of differentiation has become more complex, but it has also become genuinely cultural for the very first time, no longer complying with geographical or national stipulations' (1999: 204). Although Barras and Welsch evince slight differences in the understanding of how much attachment to particular 'geographies' is needed to analyse transculturation, the point here is that Welsch's theory casts transculturation as a life form, an evolutionary force with its own will, trajectory and flow: '[The concept of transculturality] does so quite naturally, from the logic of transcultural processes themselves' (1999: 205).

Moreover, in later works, such as 'On the Acquisition and Possession of Commonalities' (2008), Welsch is concerned with the nature/culture dichotomy and the idea of cultural evolution – notions that have also become prevalent in the Environmental Humanities.[21] This points to the deeply relevant interests transculturality shares with ecocriticism: Both fields foster an understanding of culture as a strong, perhaps elemental force that plays a significant role in evolution, and that can therefore be read as deeply relevant for changing the trajectory of ecological collapse the world community is facing. Paying attention to creative texts, in this sense, enables us to contemplate the transformative potential of culture at large, but also of ordinary moments, or of the 'micropolitics of globalised modernity', which Frank has often investigated (Schulze-Engler 2009b). Therefore, as presented in *Awake!*, *The Hungry Tide* and Welsch's theory, it is possible to read the fluidity and mobility of water as a key for these texts' explicit or implicit interest in transculturality.

These examples serve to show that, surprisingly or not, a conversation between transculturality and ecocriticism does not have to be forced, as this cross-fertilization is already evident, even if somewhat neglected by scholars whose work is located in the respective fields. Transcultural theory already evinces engagements with scientific theories and uses – unwittingly or not – environmental metaphors to make itself understood. What is lacking, however, is a more explicit understanding of a transcultural ecocritical agenda. As we have thus argued, the focus on transculturality, mobility and ecocriticism enables productive engagements in classrooms with the benefits of what Rob Nixon calls a 'transnational ethics of place' (2011: 245), which draws attention to the transcultural solidarity needed for activist movements.

Conclusion

Transculturality was never conceived of as a 'purely' theoretical term, and its usefulness lies in its ability to open up new perspectives on literary texts and cultural phenomena. We have adopted Frank's stance that transculturality

---

[21] See, for instance, Dorion Sagan (2016), who describes the complexity of evolution and the departure from Darwinist and neo-Darwinist theories of evolution.

is a highly fruitful phenomenon to be explored through teaching creative texts: 'While transculturality is clearly a perspective that can be applied to an almost limitless number of social constellations throughout human history, it becomes particularly relevant under the more circumscribed conditions of globalised modernity' (2007b: 28). It is therefore not too surprising, perhaps, that our group of students was not extremely interested in discussing transculturality as an abstract, theoretical term. Teaching transculturality, as Frank's teaching has shown, and as we also experienced in our seminar, goes beyond providing definitions of the term and the theoretical debates around it. In this sense, transculturality can be understood as a *practice* that informs readings of primary texts which are able to illuminate the complexity of contemporary issues that go far beyond the postcolonial binaries. As Frank often taught, even in settler colonial contexts, a transcultural lens seeks to refuse a simple division of colonizer/colonized in order to unveil how they permeate one another, mix and mingle in dynamic contact zones.

Moreover, with the help of Pratt's framing of the contact zone as also existing in the classroom, we have argued that transculturality can be useful for developing methodological teaching approaches to culturally diverse groups. Here we have suggested that university teaching has often neglected to incorporate new scientific insights into teaching methodologies, so a reflection on and a diversification of teaching methodology is long overdue. Of course, this point warrants the acknowledgement that this is a structural issue, as university administrations and globalized academia in general largely fail to acknowledge the centrality of teaching.

Throughout our seminar, then, it became clear to us that transculturality is indeed not a utopian concept or an end in itself; rather, it enabled the exploration of transcultural side effects of environmental activism – side effects which were nevertheless highly relevant. Moreover, the focus on transculturality allowed us to grapple with ongoing transformations of globalized modernity under particular material and environmental conditions – in this example, the mobility of Indigenous cultures which were so long problematically defined as immobile, 'local and static' (Lester and Laidlaw 2015: 6, qtd in Standfield 2018: 2), rather than participants in and active shapers of 'transcultural modernities' (Schulze-Engler 2009b). Here, we suggest that a postcolonial ecocriticism can be complemented by a transcultural ecocriticism that pays attention to power dimensions, but discards simple binaries in favour of more nuanced readings of contemporary texts.

Moreover, our discussion of the potentials of a transcultural ecocriticism focused on water as an apt figuration of transculturality. As our readings have shown, transculturation also needs to be understood in reciprocity with environmental conditions and beyond human cultures. Transcultural ecocriticism, then, could mean that we become more conscious of the materiality of language and culture, of the ways in which language and cognition are strongly tied to particular environments. It signifies the potential of learning about the more-than-human world, which can generate new notions of culture and occasionally correct reductive ones. Most important for our times of environmental devastations, however, a transcultural ecocriticism enables us to conceive of culture as a powerful elemental force that has always shaped environments and thus holds a key agency (a key – but not the only one) to halt and repair socio-environmental devastations.

Appendix: Student Questionnaire

1. **What does transculturality mean to you?**

    Write a quick definition.
    Did you know the term before class?
    If yes, did you use it?
    If no, what related terms do you use in everyday life?

2. **What does mobility justice mean to you?**

    Write a quick definition.
    Did you know the term before class?
    If yes, did you use it?
    If no, what related terms do you use in everyday life?

3. **What does environmental justice mean to you?**

    Write a quick definition
    Did you know the term before class?
    If yes, did you use it?
    If no, what related terms do you use in everyday life?

4. **Thinking about the films and novels we have been discussing, which one of these three terms was the most interesting to you and why?**

5. **Have you attended the New English Literatures and Cultures (NELK) Introduction?**

    Yes / No

References

Allen, C. (2012), *Trans-Indigenous: Methodologies for Global Native Literary Studies*, Minneapolis: University of Minnesota Press.

Awake: A Dream from Standing Rock (2017), [Film] Dir. Myron Dewey, James Spione and Josh Fox, USA: Bullfrog Films.

Banerjee, M. (2024), 'Transculturality and the Law: Witi Ihimaera's *The Whale Rider* and a River with Personhood', in Silvia Anastasijevic, Magdalena Pfalzgraf and Hanna Teichler (eds), *The Many Worlds of Anglophone Literature: Transcultural Engagements, Global Frictions*, 187–208, London: Bloomsbury Press.

Barnhardt, R. (2000), 'Teaching/Learning across Cultures: Strategies for Success', in R. Neil (ed.), *Voice of the Drum*, 167–76, Brandon, Manitoba: Kingfisher.

Barras, A. (2015), 'The Aesthetics of the Tide: The Ecosystem as Matrix for Transculturation in Amitav Ghosh's *The Hungry Tide*', in J. Kuortti (ed.), *Transculturation and Aesthetics*, 171–86, Leiden: Brill.

Bartha, K. (2020), *Unsettling the Anthropocene: Cosmological Readings of Contemporary Australian Literature*, Dissertation, Monash University and Goethe University Frankfurt.

Bartosch, R. and C. Ludwig (eds) (2022), 'Focus on Ecological English Language Teaching', *Anglistik* 33 (3). doi: 10.33675/ANGL/2022/3/3.

Beck, U. (2007), 'The Cosmopolitan Condition: Why Methodological Nationalism Fails', *Theory, Culture and Society* 24 (7–8): 286–90.

Beier, J. L. and J. Jagodzinski (eds) (2022), *Ahuman Pedagogy: Multidisciplinary Perspectives for Education in the Anthropocene*, Cham: Springer International.

Bhabha, H. K. (2004), *The Location of Culture*, Abingdon: Routledge.

Boochani, B. (2018), *No Friend But the Mountains: Writing from Manus Prison*, trans. O. Tofighian, London: Picador.

Butt, N. (2024), '"Mobility at Large": Anglophone Travel Writing as a Medium of Transcultural Communication in a Global Context', in Silvia Anastasijevic, Magdalena Pfalzgraf and Hanna Teichler (eds), *The Many Worlds of Anglophone Literature: Transcultural Engagements, Global Frictions*, 209–32, London: Bloomsbury Press.

Clark, T. (2019), *The Value of Ecocriticism*, Cambridge: Cambridge University Press.

Clarsen, G. (2017), 'Revisiting "Driving While Black": Racialized Automobilities in a Settler Colonial Context', *Mobility in History* 8: 51–9. doi: 10.3167/mih.2017.080107.

Cohut, M. (2022), 'In Conversation: Why Climate Change Matters for Human Health', *Medical News Today*, 22 April. Available online: https://www.medicalnewstoday.com/articles/in-conversation-why-climate-change-matters-for-human-health

Cooke, S. and P. Denner (eds) (2021), *Transcultural Ecocriticism: Global, Romantic and Decolonial Perspectives*, London: Bloomsbury Academic.

Cresswell, T. (2004), *Place: A Short Introduction*, Malden, MA: Blackwell.

Daggett, C. N. (2019), *The Birth of Energy: Fossil Fuels, Thermodynamics and the Politics of Work,* Durham, NC: Duke University Press.
Denecke, M., H. Kuhn and M. Stürmer (2022), 'Introduction: The Cultural Logic of Environmentalization', in M. Denecke, H. Kuhn and M. Stürmer (eds), *Flows, Liquidity, Circulation: The Cultural Logic of Environmentalization,* 7–38, Zurich: Diaphanes.
Di Chiro, G. (2016), 'Environmental Justice', in J. Adamson, W. A. Gleason and D. N. Pellow (eds), *Keywords for Environmental Studies,* 100–5, New York: New York University Press.
Doff, S. (2009), 'Inter- and/or Transcultural Learning in the Foreign Language Classroom? Theoretical Foundations and Practical Implications', in F. Schulze-Engler and S. Helff (eds), *Transcultural English Studies: Theories, Fictions, Realities,* 357–71, Amsterdam: Rodopi.
Doff, S. and F. Schulze-Engler (2011a), 'Beyond "Other Cultures": An Introduction', in S. Doff and F. Schulze-Engler (eds), *Beyond 'Other Cultures': Transcultural Perspectives on Teaching the New Literatures in English,* 1–17, Trier: WVT.
Doff, S. and F. Schulze-Engler (eds) (2011b), *Beyond 'Other Cultures': Transcultural Perspectives on Teaching the New Literatures in English,* Trier: WVT.
Garrard, G. (2016), 'Ecocriticism', in J. Adamson, A. Gleason and D. Pellow (eds), *Keywords for Environmental Studies,* 61–4. New York: New York University Press.
Ghosh, A. (2004), *The Hungry Tide,* London: HarperCollins.
Glissant, É. (1997), *Poetics of Relation,* Ann Arbor: University of Michigan Press.
Grace, J. (2021), *African Motors: Gender, Technology and the History of Development,* Durham, NC: Duke University Press.
Grande, S. (2019), 'Refusing the Settler Society of the Spectacle', in E. McKinley and L. Smith (eds), *Handbook of Indigenous Education,* 1013–29, Singapore: Springer.
Green-Simms, L. (2017), *Postcolonial Automobility: Car Culture in West Africa,* Minneapolis: University of Minnesota Press.
Harris, A. L. (2017), 'Spaces of Difference in Subterranean Toronto', in R. T. Tally Jr. (ed.), *The Routledge Handbook of Literature and Space,* 260–72, London: Routledge.
Hartwiger, A. (2011), '"Multiple Possibilities and Multiple Lives": Mediating Transcultural Encounters through Cosmopolitanism', in S. Doff and F. Schulze-Engler (eds), *Beyond 'Other Cultures': Transcultural Perspectives on Teaching the New Literatures in English,* 97–110, Trier: WVT.
hooks, b. (1994), *Teaching to Transgress: Education as the Practice of Freedom,* New York: Routledge.
Hoyos, H. (2015), *Things with a History: Transcultural Materialism and the Literatures of Extraction in Contemporary Latin America,* New York: Columbia University Press.
Hübner, A. et al. (eds) (2022), *Multispecies Futures: New Approaches to Teaching Human–Animal Studies,* Berlin: Neofelis Verlag.
Huggan, G. and H. Tiffin (2010), *Postcolonial Ecocriticism: Literature, Animals, Environment,* London: Routledge.

Iovino, S. and S. Oppermann (2012), 'Theorizing Material Ecocriticism: A Diptych', *Interdisciplinary Studies in Literature and the Environment* 19 (3): 448–75. doi: 10.1093/isle/iss087.

Jenkins, J. (2018), 'The Future of English as a Lingua Franca?' in J. Jenkins, W. Baker and M. Dewey (eds), *The Routledge Handbook of English as a Lingua Franca*, 594–605, Abingdon: Routledge.

Klippel, F. (1994), 'Cultural Aspects in Foreign Language Teaching', *Journal for the Study of British Cultures* 1: 49–61.

König, D. G. and K. Rakow (2016), 'The Transcultural Approach within a Disciplinary Framework: An Introduction', *Transcultural Studies* 7 (2): 89–100. doi: 10.17885/heiup.ts.2016.2.23642.

Kreft, A. (2020), *Transkulturelle Kompetenz und literaturbasierter Fremdsprachenunterricht: eine rekonstruktive Studies zum Einsatz von 'Fictions of Migration' im Fach Englisch*, Berlin: Peter Lang.

Leask, B. and J. Carroll (2013), *Learning and Teaching across Cultures Good Practice Principles and Quick Guides*, Melbourne: International Education Association of Australia (IEAA).

Lefebvre, H. (1991), *The Production of Space*, trans. D. Nicholson-Smith, Oxford: Blackwell.

Lehmkuhl, U., H. Lüsebrink and L. McFalls (2015), 'Spaces and Practices of Diversity: An Introduction', in U. Lehmkuhl, H. Lüsebrink and L. McFalls (eds), *Of 'Contact Zones' and 'Liminal Spaces': Mapping the Everyday Life of Cultural Translation*, Münster: Waxmann.

Lester, A. and Z. Laidlaw (2015), 'Indigenous Sites and Mobilities: Connected Struggles in the Long Nineteenth Century', in A. Lester and Z. Laidlaw (eds), *Indigenous Communities and Settler Colonialism: Land Holding, Loss and Survival in an Interconnected World*, 1–23, London: Palgrave Macmillan.

Mad Max: Fury Road (2015), [Film] Dir. George Miller, Australia: Village Roadshow Pictures, Roadshow Entertainment and Warner Bros. Pictures.

McLeod, J. (1997), 'Living In-Between: Interstitial Spaces of Possibility in Timothy Mo's *Sour Sweet*', in S. Earnshaw (ed.), *Just Postmodernism*, 107–28, Amsterdam: Rodopi.

Mercer, H. (22 April 2022), 'Colonialism: Why Leading Climate Scientists Have Finally Acknowledged Its Link with Climate Change', *The Conversation*. Available online: https://theconversation.com/colonialism-why-leading-climate-scientists-have-finally-acknowledged-its-link-with-climate-change-181642#:~:text=Colonialism%2C%20the%20report%20asserts%2C%20has,on%20climate%20change%20since%201990 (accessed 25 October 2022).

Mo, T. (1982), *Sour Sweet*, London: Vintage Books.

Moretti, F. (2013), *Distant Reading*, London: Verso.

Neumann, D. (2019), 'Was ist ein Lehrauftrag und wie wird man Lehrbeauftragter?', *Academics*. Available online: https://www.academics.de/ratgeber/was-ist-ein-lehrauftrag (accessed 25 October 2022).

Nixon, R. (2011), *Slow Violence and the Environmentalism of the Poor*, Cambridge, MA: Harvard University Press.

Paulsen, M., J. Jagodzinski and S. M. Hawke (eds) (2022), *Pedagogy in the Anthropocene: Re-Wilding Education for a New Earth*, Cham: Palgrave Macmillan.

Philips, C. (2001), *A New World Order: Selected Essays*, London: Secker & Warburg.

Pratt, M. (1991), 'Arts of the Contact Zone', *Profession*, 33–40.

Rahman, S. (2021), 'The Environment of South Asia: Beyond Postcolonial Ecocriticism', *South Asian Review* 42 (4): 317–23. doi: 10.1080/02759527.2021.1982613.

Rueckert, W. ([1978] 1996), 'Literature and Ecology: An Experiment in Ecocriticism', in C. Glotfelty and H. Fromm (eds), *The Ecocriticism Reader: Landmarks in Literary Ecology*, 105–23, Athens: University of Georgia Press.

Sagan, D. (2016), 'Evolution' in J. Adamson, W. A. Gleason and D. Pellow (eds), *Keywords for Environmental Studies*, 113–18, New York: New York University Press.

Schulze-Engler, F. (2007a), 'African Literatures and the Micropolitics of Modernity: Explorations of Post-Traditional Society in Wole Soyinka's *Season of Anomy*, Nuruddin Farah's *Sardines* and Tsitsi Dangarembga's *Nervous Conditions*', *Matatu: Journal of African Culture and Society* 35 (3): 21–35.

Schulze-Engler, F. (2007b), 'From Postcolonialism to Transcultural World Literature', in L. Eckstein (ed.), *English Literatures across the Globe: A Companion*, 20–32, Paderborn: Wilhelm Fink Verlag.

Schulze-Engler, F. (2009a), 'Introduction', in F. Schulze-Engler and S. Helff (eds), *Transcultural English Studies: Theories, Fictions, Realities*, ix–xvi, Amsterdam: Rodopi.

Schulze-Engler, F. (2009b), 'Transcultural Modernities and Anglophone African Literature', in E. Bekers, S. Helff and D. Merolla (eds), *Transcultural Modernities: Narrating Africa in Europe*, 87–101, Amsterdam: Rodopi.

Schulze-Engler, F. (2015), 'Once Were Internationalists? Postcolonialism, Disenchanted Solidarity and the Right to Belong in a World of Globalized Modernity', in P. K. Malreddy, B. Heidemann, O. B. Laursen and J. Wilson (eds), *Reworking Postcolonialism: Globalization, Labour and Rights*, 19–35, Basingstoke: Palgrave Macmillan.

Schulze-Engler, F. (2018), 'Automobilität in der afrikanischen Literatur', in S. Scholz and U. Vedder (eds), *Handbuch Literatur und Materielle Kultur*, 313–23, Berlin: De Gruyter.

Schulze-Engler, F. and S. Helff (eds) (2009c), *Transcultural English Studies: Theories, Fictions, Realities*, Amsterdam: Rodopi.

Sheller, M. (2018), 'Theorising Mobility Justice', *Tempo Social* 30 (2): 17–34. doi: 10.11606/0103-2070.ts.2018.142763.

Singh, P. and C. Doherty (2004), 'Global Cultural Flows and Pedagogic Dilemmas: Teaching in the Global University Contact Zone', *TESOL Quarterly* 38 (1): 9–42. doi: 10.2307/3588257.

Slovic, S. (2010), 'The Third Wave of Ecocriticism: North American Reflections on the Current Phase of the Discipline', *Ecozon@: European Journal of Literature, Culture and Environment* 1 (1): 4–8. doi: 10.37536/ECOZONA.2010.1.1.312.

Standfield, R. (2018), 'Introduction', in R. Standfield (ed.), *Indigenous Mobilities: Across and Beyond the Antipodes*, 1–33, Acton, A.C.T.: Australian National University Press.

Turner, V. (1995), 'Liminality and Communitas', in V. Turner, R. Abrahams and A. Harris (eds), *The Ritual Process: Structure and Anti-Structure*, 94–130, New Brunswick: Aldine Transaction Press.

Wall Kimmerer, R. (2013), *Braiding Sweetgrass: Indigenous Wisdom, Scientific Knowledge and the Teachings of Plants*, Minneapolis, MN: Milkweed Editions.

Ward, J. (2017), *Sing, Unburied, Sing*, London: Bloomsbury Circus.

Water Is Life (2018), [Film] Dir. Sam Cuttie, Australia: Know Studio.

Welsch, W. (1999), 'Transculturality: The Puzzling Form of Cultures Today', in M. Featherstone and S. Lash (eds), *Spaces of Culture: City, Nation, World*, 194–213, London: Sage.

Welsch, W. (2008), 'On the Acquisition and Possession of Commonalities', in F. Schulze-Engler and S. Helff (eds), *Transcultural English Studies*, 1–36, Leiden: Brill.

Wenzel, J. (2014), 'How to Read for Oil', *Resilience: A Journal of the Environmental Humanities* 1 (3): 156–61. doi: 10.5250/resilience.1.3.014.

Wolff, J. M. (ed.) (2002), *Professing in the Contact Zone: Bringing Theory and Practice Together*, Urbana, IL: National Council of Teachers of English.

Woolfolk, A. (2021), *Educational Psychology*, 14th edn, Harlow: Pearson.

Part Three

Transversal readings

8

Transculturality and the law: Witi Ihimaera's *The Whale Rider* and a river with personhood

Mita Banerjee
Johannes Gutenberg University Mainz

In 2017, New Zealand saw a remarkable verdict. For the first time in New Zealand history, a river was granted the status of 'personhood'. This chapter sees the court ruling as a potential climax in a development which goes all the way back to the founding of the nation of Aotearoa/New Zealand itself. At the same time, the court decision can also be seen as part of a process of reconciliation, in which white New Zealanders or Pākehā attempted to 'right' the ways of the past. The court ruling that grants personhood to the Whanganui River can be seen as being part of translation: the translation of Māori epistemology into New Zealand law. This epistemology, which was at the core of the court petition, has in turn been articulated not only in the court, but also in the pages of literature.

In this chapter, my aim is to put the court case in dialogue with Witi Ihimaera's groundbreaking text, *The Whale Rider*. I argue that, in its articulation of Māori identity, *The Whale Rider* can itself be seen as a form of petition, or rather, of laying claim to a redefinition of New Zealand epistemology. The recent court decision hence puts into practice what *The Whale Rider* advocates. From a perspective akin to law and literature studies, Ihimaera's novel and the court case can be said to be in conversation with each other. As Richard Posner notes in the introduction to his study on *Law & Literature*, '[this book] brings together two overlapping bodies of thought, the legal and the literary, that have much in common, including an emphasis on rhetoric. ... Law itself is formulated and announced in writings, such as statutes, the Constitution, and judicial opinions that sometimes exhibit a density, complexity, and open-endedness comparable to what one finds in literary works' (2008: 1).

In this chapter, my aim is to map the idea of this 'kinship' between law and literature onto the terrain of Māori–Pākehā relations in Aotearoa/New Zealand. I am interested in what I see as a continuity between a specific piece of legislation – the granting of the status of 'personhood' to the Whanganui River in 2017 – and a literary novel that precedes this legislation by thirty years: Witi Ihimaera's *The Whale Rider* (1987). In the context of Māori–Pākehā relations in New Zealand, the task of the legislature is to decide to what extent Māori signification (i.e. the 'cultural' and epistemological elements at the core of Māori self-definition) can be translated into law. Reconciliation, in turn, may depend on the legislature's ability to incorporate Māori epistemologies into law in a way that it is on par with Pākehā norms, values and assumptions.

At the same time, I would like to bring the notion of transculturality into this debate on a potential reconciliation in law and in literature. As Frank Schulze-Engler has observed, 'transculturality' sets out to complicate both the notion of 'culture' and of the nation-state. According to him,

> [t]he first and most obvious consequence is that we start to question the widespread assumption that societies and cultures should be primarily seen in terms of the nation-state. The German sociologist Ulrich Beck has formulated a classical critique of this idea, which he refers to as 'the container theory' of society and culture: according to this theory, the power-space of nation-states is the ultimate container of societies, and any kind of social practice is defined and determined by the conceptual frame constituted by the nation-state. (Schulze-Engler 2009: 91)

In the context of the reconciliation debate that links New Zealand to other settler colonies such as the United States, Canada and Australia, however, the concept of transculturality may at first sight seem counterintuitive. Transculturality, in some of its uses, may be seen to counter clear-cut dichotomies. It shifts the scenario of the 'clash' between different cultures, conceived as distinct from one another, to the overlapping spaces through which these cultures may actually be interconnected. Moreover, it seeks to understand not so much what cultures 'are' than the ways in which individuals deal with and negotiate the cultures that they come into contact with. Schulze-Engler points out, '[u]nderstanding culture and literature in terms of a transcultural framework shifts the focus of attention away from the quasi-diplomatic "international" relations between cultures and towards the productive communicative processes by which individuals and social groups make sense of culture in the contemporary world' (2009: 93). Striving to transcend pre-given dichotomies, the concept of 'transculturality' is interested in the fluidity of cultures as well as in the fluidity of the spaces in-between these cultures. What transculturality argues against is the notion of 'culture' as a clearly circumscribed 'container'. As Schulze-Engler goes on to note, '[t]he challenge is thus to move beyond this dysfunctional "container theory" and to become aware of the new, complex realities created by transnational and transcultural processes in the contemporary world' (2009: 91).

Yet, this notion of fluidity, fruitful as it may be in different contexts, may seem contestable in the context of the relationship between the (former) colonizer and the colonized. In order for injustices of the past to be addressed, the boundary between the colonial power and the colonized people has to be upheld. To speak of fluidity here, it may at first be assumed, would be to sabotage the very project of 'redress' (Henderson and Wakeman 2013: 3), of seeking compensation for the injustices of the past.

Transculturality and redress: From literature to the courtroom

As I read the contemporary process of reconciliation in Aotearoa/New Zealand through *The Whale Rider* and the court decision, however, I will try to show how transculturality can in fact coexist with the politics of redress. Both Ihimaera's novel and the court decision recognize the power relationship between Pākehā and Māori in New Zealand, and they recognize the need for reconciliation. This need, at first sight, seems to be predicated on the delineation or contours of the parties involved. Reconciliation is predicated on opposition, an opposition between clearly circumscribed antagonists, even as it seeks to bridge the gap between the two. If reconciliation can be understood as a process of translation and dialogue, the languages of the parties involved, it would seem, have to be distinct from one another. How, we might ask, would transculturality figure in this context?

I would like to argue in this chapter that this dilemma between clear-cut definition and the changeability and fluidity of culture is where Ihimaera's novel *The Whale Rider* is at its most powerful. It is predicated on the evolving, the dynamic change and the contemporaneity of Māori culture in Aotearoa/New Zealand. At the core of *The Whale Rider*, there is the concept of tradition. For years Koro Apirana, the custodian, has been looking for an heir. This heir, however, can only be male according to Māori custom: '"A girl," Koro Apirana said, disgusted. "I will have nothing to do with her. She has broken the male line of descent in our tribe." He shoved the telephone at our grandmother, Nanny

Flowers, saying, "Here. It's your fault. Your female side was too strong"' (Ihimaera 1987: 10). Koro's great-granddaughter, Kahu, thus seems an unlikely candidate for the position, even as she is utterly devoted to her great-grandfather:

> Under these conditions, the love which Kahu received from Koro Apirana was the sort that dropped off the edge of the table, like breadcrumbs after everybody else has had a big feed. But Kahu didn't seem to mind. She ran into Koro Apirana's arms whenever he had time for her and took whatever he was able to give. If he had told her he loved dogs I'm sure she would have barked, 'Woof woof'. That's how much she loved him. (Ihimaera 1987: 36)

In *The Whale Rider*, transculturality is mapped onto gender relations. Even as these debates take place within a Māori culture that is still recognizable as such, this culture, internally, is nevertheless fluid, evolving. In the narrative, this dynamism is also mapped onto the tumultuous marriage between Koro and his wife, Nanny Flowers: 'Nanny Flowers and Koro Apirana had finished their argument by the time I returned home, but the atmosphere was as frozen as the Antarctic wasteland … "He's sleeping in the bunkhouse with you tonight," Nanny Flowers told me, jerking her head at Koro Apirana. "I've had enough of him. Divorce tomorrow, I mean it this time"' (Ihimaera 1987: 34).

One of the central themes of the novel, it could be argued, is female pragmatism. Because she knows that her husband will be reluctant to acknowledge a girl as his rightful successor, Nanny Flowers covertly takes precautions of her own. First, she sees to it that her great-granddaughter is named after Kahutia Te Rangi, the ancestor whose successor she wants Kahu to become, despite the fact that she was born a girl. Second, she makes sure that Kahu's umbilical cord is buried in a place that will ensure the girl's ongoing connection to her ancestors. In this endeavour, she enlists Kahu's uncle Rawiri, the narrator in *The Whale Rider*:

> 'This is where the birth cord will be placed,' she said, 'in sight of Kahutia Te Rangi, after whom Kahu has been named. May he, the great ancestor, always watch over her. And may the sea from whence he came always protect her through life.' Nanny Flowers began to scoop a hole in the loose soil. As she placed the birth cord in it, she said a prayer. When she finished, it had grown dark. (Ihimaera 1987: 17)

Transculturality, seen from this perspective, does not only emerge between cultures, erasing the clear-cut boundary between the two, but it also takes place within a single culture. Trying to hold on to the notion of a stable, fixed culture and tradition, Koro keeps trying to find a male successor. When the contest is over and once again, no successor has been found, Kahu goes on a dive herself: 'Before we could stop her she stood up and dived overboard. Until that moment I had never even known she could swim' (Ihimaera 1987: 71). As she goes on the dive in which none of the male contestants had been able to succeed, Kahu realizes that the animal world supports her in her quest to retrieve the pebble that Koro had tossed into the ocean. This support prefigures the fact that Kahu is indeed the 'whale rider' and serves as a foreshadowing of the end of the narrative:

> They were dolphins. They circled around Kahu and seemed to be talking to her. She nodded and grabbed one around its body. As quick as a flash, the dolphins sped her to another area of the reef and stopped. Kahu seemed to say, 'Down here?' and the dolphins made a nodding motion. Suddenly Kahu made a quick, darting gesture. She picked something up, inspected it, appeared satisfied with it, and went back to the dolphins. (Ihimaera 1987: 72)

In *The Whale Rider*, however, recognition is not only at stake within Māori culture, in Kahu's quest for being recognized by her great-grandfather, but it also takes place between cultures. It could be argued that this is transculturality at its most powerful. As I will elaborate below, Ihimaera explores spaces and contexts in which Māori culture is in fact being recognized by Pākehā institutions. At the same time, however, the Māoriness that Kahu seeks recognition for is a hybrid, evolving and dynamic one.[1] It is a Māori cultural articulation which has evolved in its negotiation with Pakeha signification and Pākehā frameworks. It is this complex intersection between transcultural recognition and intracultural change that Ihimaera's narrative dramatizes by having Kahu win in an essay contest at her high school. The essay is to be read out at the graduation ceremony. As Kahu enters the stage to read out her prize-winning essay, the concept of translation is crucial. How can Māori culture be translated to a Pākehā audience? Remarkably, Kahu gets up on stage and reads out her essay, that, surprisingly for both Māori and Pākehā audiences, is entirely in Māori. The headmaster's surprise thus mirrors that of the audience: 'What was remarkable, he said, was that the student had given it entirely in her own tongue, the Māori language. He called for Kahutia Te Rangi to come forward' (Ihimaera 1987: 68).

---

[1] There may be a danger here to suggest that Kahu's understanding of Māori culture is a hybrid one, while her great-grandfather Koro's notion of Māoriness is non-changing and essentialist. This is clearly not the case; as Brendan Hokowhitu has emphasized (2008), Koro's conceptualization of Māori practices is no less hybrid, even if he may not fully be aware of implicitly masculinist frameworks.

Kahu thus refuses to translate her essay that will hence be understandable only for Māori in the audience and for those Pākehā who speak Māori. For those who do not, the essay will be seen as a cultural performance that will remain opaque. This, as I will argue in more detail below, is a powerful space for Māori to inhabit: Kahu's performance forces a Pākehā audience to bear the burden of the untranslated: They witness a performance which they do not understand, but must respect nevertheless. As I will show in the second part of this chapter – 'A River with Personhood and Talking to Whales', – the scenario which Ihimaera's narrative evokes here prefigures an actual court case surrounding the Whanganui River. This court case, as I will elaborate below, similarly hinged on the notion of untranslatability. In both instances, there is an act of translation that is at once a refusal of translation. The same is true, I will try to show below, in the granting of personhood to the Whanganui River.

As Kahu is reading out her essay on the stage, Māori signification comes into its own. It asks to be recognized by Pākehā New Zealanders without being translated:

> There were stars in her eyes, like sparkling tears. 'Distinguished guests, members of the audience, my speech is a speech of love for my grandfather, Koro Apirana.' Nanny Flowers gave a sob, and tears began to flow down her cheeks. Kahu's voice was clear and warm as she told of her love for her grandfather and her respect for him. Her tones rang with pride as she recited his whakapapa and ours. She conveyed how grateful she was to live in Whangara and that her main aim in life was to fulfil the wishes of her grandfather and of the tribe. (Ihimaera 1987: 69)

The novel itself may be seen to act as a mediator here. Since the narrator, Kahu's uncle, understands the meaning of her words, the meaning of Kahu's essay is being conveyed to the reader. The narrative thus manages to convey translation and the absence of translation at one and the same time. Within the narrative Kahu refuses to provide an English translation for the text she is reading out on the stage. The novel itself, on the other hand, conveys both the refusal of translation and the meaning of Kahu's prize-winning essay. What is so significant, however, is that despite this refusal of translation, Kahu gets the prize: The jury hence recognizes what it potentially does not understand. The same is true, I will suggest below, of the granting of personhood to a river. In Western epistemology, such an act may seem inconceivable. With the 2017 Whanganui River Claims Settlement Act/ Te Awa Tupua Act, New Zealand law thus acknowledges and honours a Māori concept it does not understand. For Māori, the Whanganui River is related to humans in a way that is inconceivable in Pākehā epistemology. For this concept, there is neither equivalent nor translation. Just as Kahu's untranslated essay wins the prize, the Whanganui River Claims Settlement Act thus honours a concept that is both untranslated and, to an extent, untranslatable. Both Ihimaera's novel and the court case negotiate the line between what can and what cannot be translated. As I will show below, the granting of personhood to the Whanganui River is a legal approximation to Māori cultural and religious signification; it can hence be situated half-way between translation and untranslatability.

Up on stage, Kahu celebrates her Māori culture in a language which Pākehā audiences will not understand. It is at this juncture that Ihimaera's novel may be seen to hark back to the origins of historical injustice. For the very notion of New Zealand is based, historically on an act of mistranslation. It is an injustice inflicted through translation gone awry. The Treaty of Waitangi (1840), the very treaty upon which the nation of New Zealand was founded, contained two versions, one in English and one in Māori. What was so pernicious, however, is that the Māori version deliberately mistranslated the British text. While the Māori version assured Māori that they would retain sovereignty over the land, the English version held that they would cede this sovereignty. As Ulf Tiemann notes,

> [a]n examination of the treaty texts shows that the two treaty texts differ in significant respects. The British assumed that the Māori had ceded sovereignty over New Zealand to them through the treaty. The Māori, on the other hand, concluded the treaty on the assumption that they would retain their sovereignty and merely cede governmental powers to the British Crown by signing the kawanatanga. (1999: 29)[2]

Quite literally, then, Māori did not know what they were signing when they accepted the Treaty of Waitangi (McHugh 1991) that would literally turn them into a colonized people.

To return to Ihimaera's novel, we may well read Kahu's reading of her essay on a white stage as harking back to this original injustice. In 1840, the settlers forced Māori not only to listen to but to sign a text that had been wrongly translated. Through this trick, which was both legal and linguistic, Māori signed an English document which they did not understand, misguided by a translation that was deliberately unfaithful to the original. Here as in other settler colonies, what

---

[2] Original German: 'Die Untersuchung der Vertragstexte zeigt, dass die beiden Vertragstexte in wesentlichen Punkten voneinander abweichen. Die Briten gingen davon aus, die Maori hätten ihnen durch den Vertrag die Souveränität über Neuseeland abgetreten. Die Maori schlossen den Vertrag hingegen in der Annahme, sie würden ihre Souveränität behalten und mit dem kawanatanga lediglich Regierungskompetenzen an die britische Krone abgeben.' Translation by the editors.

ensued was hence what legal scholar Lindsay Robertson has called a 'conquest by law' (2005: x).

It is this failure or refusal of translation that Kahu forces her audience to repeat in reverse. Her Pākehā audience has to sit through a reading they do not understand. It is this bearing of that which is not understood, which is not translated, which may lie at the heart of the project of reconciliation. Unlike in the Treaty of Waitangi, however, there is no violence done, no harm inflicted by Kahu's reading. Yet, what remains is the space of respect, and of recognition. By reading to her Pākehā audience a text that they cannot understand, Kahu implicitly asks this audience to observe Māori customs and protocol (Frame 2002: 13), even if it cannot understand this protocol. The same, as I will point out in the next section of this chapter, is at stake in the court case granting personhood to the Whanganui River.

To return to the novel and the image of Kahu up on the stage, this is a space which cannot be overestimated: It is the refusal to translate. What is so remarkable in the context of transculturality, however, is that this refusal of translation is by no means synonymous with the idea that what is being translated is itself stable. There is hence a difference between the act of refusing translation, on the one hand, and the dynamism of the content of the text, on the other. In refusing to translate her text into English, Kahu may stress Māori protocol, and may ask the audience to observe this protocol, even if they cannot understand the text that is being read out on stage. Yet, within the essay itself, there is cultural dynamism and cultural change; there is transculturality in the sense of the fluidity of Māori culture. Ultimately, cultural dynamism and cultural change are at the heart of the essay, described to the reader through Rawiri's narrative. The essay thus has both a transcultural and an intracultural function. As an essay delivered in the Māori language (Te Reo Māori), it asks a Pākehā audience to respect Māori culture even if it cannot understand some of its protocols. As the essay is also addressed to Koro Apirana, however, it takes up the concept of intracultural change: It is Kahu's way of asking her great-grandfather to accept her as a female successor.

In the essay and through its language politics, Kahu asks Pākehā New Zealanders to recognize Māori culture. In this call for recognition, in turn, Kahu proves a worthy successor to Koro Apirana, her great-grandfather. She demonstrates the legitimacy that he is unwilling to grant her. Kahu is all the more devastated, then, when she realizes that her great-grandfather for whose sake she wrote and performed the essay, refuses to come to the graduation event. As the narrator notes, '[t]he sadness and the joy swept us all away in acknowledging Kahu, but we knew that her heart was aching for Koro Apirana' (Ihimaera 1987: 69).

What is equally remarkable, however, is that it is with this untranslated essay that Kahu wins the prize. This, too, can be seen to be in line with reconciliation: Pākehā New Zealand bears its inability to understand. The nation that was once founded on a deliberate distortion of meaning, on an act of mistranslation, now stands in silence as it witnesses a performance it cannot understand. Reconciliation and translation are interrelated here in a highly complex process.

At the same time, Kahu's reading out of her essay in Māori can be related to yet another historical space: the space of the Waitangi Tribunal. The Waitangi Tribunal has been a key part of reconciliation in New Zealand. Founded in 1975, its aim was to redress the injustices of the past. Māori claimants could bring before the Crown all the instances in which the Crown could be demonstrated to have breached the Treaty of Waitangi. The Waitangi Tribunal has been related by some observers to frameworks created by the Truth and Reconciliation Commission in South Africa (Winter 2013). According to Tiemann, '[i]t is not only the courts that have defined Māori rights from the Treaty of Waitangi (Ehrmann 1999). The Waitangi Tribunal has also influenced this development. Since its inception in 1975, it has dealt with various claims from different tribes. In this way, it has investigated over 150 years of colonial injustice' (Tiemann 1999: 134).[3]

From the beginning, however, the Waitangi Tribunal was hampered by its cultural framework. First, since its creation in 1975, the hearings of the Waitangi Tribunal had been held in a meeting room of the Intercontinental Hotel in Auckland (Tiemann 1999: 134). To Māori petitioners, this setting seemed highly inappropriate as the site of the redressing of historical wrongs and cultural injustice (134). Petitioners found themselves unable to convey their concerns in the space of the (Pākehā) Intercontinental Hotel, that they saw as a form of cultural insensitivity. Second, they were required to give their testimony in English, and the hearings followed the regular protocol of a New Zealand courtroom. Translation – in both linguistic terms and in terms of the framework in which the testimony had to be given – proved to sabotage the very project of the Waitangi Tribunal. As Tiemann observes,

---

[3] Original German: 'Nicht nur die Gerichte haben die Maori-Rechte aus dem Vertrag von Waitangi definiert. Auch das Waitangi Tribunal hat diese Entwicklung beeinflusst. Seit seiner Einführung 1975 hat es sich mit diversen Ansprüchen verschiedener Stämme beschäftigt. Auf diese Weise ist es über 150 Jahren kolonialen Unrechts nachgegangen.' Translation by the editors.

[t]he hearing procedure was particularly problematic. The tribunal was not given any procedural rules. Therefore, the tribunal under its then-chairman, Chief Judge Gillanders-Scott, initially followed the standard court protocol. This formulaic hearing process, however, did not help Māori participants to gain trust in the Tribunal. The hearing venues were also unfamiliar to the Māori and caused discomfort. Temm finds it indicative of the Tribunal's cultural insensitivity that the first two hearings were held in the ballroom of the Hotel Intercontinental in Auckland. (Tiemann 1999: 138)[4]

All this changed, however, when Sir Edward Taihakurei Durie, himself of Māori ancestry, became chairman of the tribunal. Durie proceeded to change both the setting and the protocol of the Waitangi Tribunal. From now on, the hearings were to be held not in a hotel room, but in a marae, a Māori religious site.

Moreover, because of this setting, the hearing now had to follow Māori protocol. This meant that a testimony could not be interrupted, even if it went on for several days, and it could be delivered in Māori. What resulted from this change was that Pākehā were required to observe Māori protocol, and not vice versa. According to Tiemann,

[t]he courtroom atmosphere faded away. Māori were free to speak out about their claims. The tribunal also changed its hearing protocol. The tribunal adapted to the customs of the claimants. It did this by adapting to the protocol in place at that particular marae. Claimants could now speak in Te Reo Māori if they wished. The speech was not translated until the claimant had finished. This is because simultaneous translation would involve interrupting the speaker. This is considered impolite according to Māori custom. (Tiemann 1999: 139)[5]

This change in both the language and the cultural framework which underlay the Waitangi Tribunal proved to be decisive for the outcome of the hearings. Where

---

[4] Original German: 'Problematisch war vor allem das Anhörungsverfahren. Dem Tribunal waren keine Verfahrensregeln vorgegeben. Daher hielt sich das Tribunal unter seinem damaligen Vorsitzenden, Chief Judge Gillanders-Scott, zunächst an das allgemein übliche Gerichtsprotokoll. Allerdings gewannen die Maori angesichts dieses förmlichen Anhörungsverfahrens zunächst kein Vertrauen in das Tribunal. Auch die Anhörungsorte waren den Maori nicht vertraut. Sie führten zu Unbehagen. Temm empfindet es als bezeichnend für die kulturelle Insensibilität des Tribunals, dass die ersten beiden Anhörungen im Ballsaal des Hotel Intercontinental in Auckland stattfanden.' Translation by the editors.

[5] Original German: 'Die Gerichtssaalatmosphäre verschwand. Maori konnten sich zu ihren Ansprüchen frei äußern. Außerdem änderte das Tribunal sein Verhandlungsprotokoll. Das Tribunal stellte sich auf die Sitten der Anspruchsteller ein. Dazu passte es sich dem auf dem jeweiligen marae geltenden Protokoll an. Die Anspruchsteller konnten nun in Te Reo Maori vortragen, wenn sie es wünschten. Der Vortrag wurde erst übersetzt, wenn der Anspruchsteller ihn beendet hatte. Eine Simultanübersetzung wäre nämlich mit der Unterbrechung des Vortragenden verbunden. Dies wird nach Maori-Sitte als unhöflich empfunden.' Translation by the editors.

before Sir Durie's appointment, the majority of the petitions had been rejected, virtually all petitions were granted after the framework had been changed.

It was this untranslated space, moreover, which made it possible for Māori epistemology to be fully understood. In Māori, the petitioner was able to explain and convey the full significance of his claim. As the petition was translated only subsequently to the petitioner's statement which had been delivered without interruption, the translation could no longer sabotage its meaning. In essence, this meant that the audience often had to sit through hours of testimony that it did not understand. Moreover, the petitioner was able to express the full significance of Māori epistemology with regard to the historical injustices he now sought compensation for because the statement could be delivered in a marae, not a hotel room. This scenario may well be said to anticipate current debates about structural equality. If institutions have historically been complicit in perpetuating hegemony through the protocols they require, Judge Durie proceeded to sabotage structural hegemony by having the trial moved from the hotel to the marae, and thus to a space which Māori petitioners would find appropriate for the claims they were making. This change in site, moreover, entailed a change in procedure. From now on, the hearings of the Waitangi Tribunal had to adhere to Māori protocol.

This change in the framework of the Waitangi Tribunal can be seen to be directly connected to the Te Awa Tupua Act of 2017. The claim to grant the status of personhood to a river was brought before the Waitangi Tribunal by the Whangaui Iwi. As commentators have noted, the idea of a river as a 'living being', let alone an ancestor of humans, is unknown in some strands of Western epistemology. At the same time, it is important to distinguish between hegemonic currents in Western cultural, legal and philosophical thought (Dickinson 2016), on the one hand, and, on the other hand, those lines of thought whose conceptualization of the nature–human divide is less rigid. In recent years, as efforts to counter the climate crisis have increased, there have been references to 'ecocide', which implies that ecological destruction is often closely linked to cultural genocide (Raftopoulos and Morley 2019). With a host of critical intervention arguing for the need to move beyond the Anthropocene, there has been a paradigm change within Western thought to think beyond humans and to acknowledge the agency of non-human actors (Clark 2015; DeLoughrey 2019; Huggan and Tiffin 2009).

Similarly, Greek and Roman mythology knows gods and goddesses who personify oceans and rivers, such as the Greek god Poseidon or Celtic River goddesses.[6] Even as in the course of this chapter, I am trying to trace an

---

[6] I am indebted to Silvia Anastasijevic for this point.

opposition between 'Western' epistemologies which revolve around a categorical human–nature divide and Māori thought which rejects such a clear-cut divide, it is important to note that there are oppositions and counter-narratives to this divide within Western philosophy as well.

It may thus have been the change in protocol described above – the fact that the claim could be filed in Te Reo Māori, in Māori language, and that it could not be interrupted – that enabled the claimants to convey the full complexity of the epistemology that underlay their petition. Whether such a settlement would have been possible before the change brought about by Sir Durie is a matter of speculation. Yet, it may nonetheless be assumed that these changes were favourable both to the submitting and the eventual granting of the claim.

A river with personhood and talking to whales

Arguably, all of these instances are also at the core of the most recent court decision, which granted the status of personhood to the Whanganui River in the Te Awa Tupua (Whanganui River Claims Settlement) Act from 20 March 2017. From the vantage point of Western legal epistemology, it may at first seem bizarre to grant a river the status of personhood. As Christopher Finlayson, the attorney general who negotiated the settlement, puts it, 'Section 12, the Recognition of the River: The river is an indivisible and living whole incorporating all its physical and metaphysical elements. And so, people may well look at this and say, "What planet are these New Zealanders living on?"' (*The River Is Me*).

It is important to note at the outset, however, that the court decision is in fact less bizarre than it may at first seem. In its 2017 decision, the court grants the river the status of a legal person, not a human being. As Carstens notes, '"[i]t may seem strange to some at first that a natural object is recognized as a legal entity," explained Finlayson, government negotiator. "But it is no stranger than the status of foundations, companies or corporations"' (Carstens 2017: n.p.).[7] I would like to suggest here that what is at stake in the court decision is both translation and untranslatability. As Finlayson notes, he, as a Pākehā attorney general, does not have to fully understand the concept which underlies the court ruling; he only has to respect it.

---

[7] Original German: '"Es mag manchem zunächst merkwürdig vorkommen, dass ein Naturgegenstand als juristische Person anerkannt wird", erklärte Chris Finlayson, Verhandlungsführer der Regierung. "Aber es ist nicht merkwürdiger als der Status von Stiftungen, Unternehmen oder Aktiengesellschaften."' Translation by the editors.

At the core of the ruling is a recognition of Māori epistemology. This epistemology, as both *The Whale Rider* and the court petition emphasize, hinges on the continuity between the human and the natural worlds. As Geoffrey Hipango, a representative of Māori community development puts it in an interview in David Reid's short film *The River Is Me*, '[t]he river ... we see this as a living entity, that carries our ancestors, that carries their memories. It's meaningful for our history' (*The River Is Me*).

In this instance, too, Ihimaera's novel *The Whale Rider* anticipates the logic of the claim put forward by the Whanganui Iwi. Both literary texts and court petitions can reflect the cultural and social contexts that they emerge from. The beginning of Ihimaera's novel could well have been submitted as evidence in the claim on behalf of the Whanganui River. *The Whale Rider* begins with the close connection between humans and the non-human world:

> The dark shape rising, rising again. A whale, gigantic. A sea monster. Just as it burst through the sea, a flying fish leaping high in its ecstasy saw water and air streaming like thunderous foam from that noble beast and knew, ah yes, that the time had come. For the sacred sign was on the monster, a swirling moko pattern imprinted on the forehead. Then the flying fish saw that astride the head, as it broke skyward, was a man. He was wondrous to look upon, the whale rider. (Ihimaera 1987: 3–4)

If, from the vantage point of Māori epistemology, there is a form of kinship between humans and nature, then it comes without question that nature has to be protected just as human beings do. According to Carstens,

> [i]n fact, the Whanganui River plays a central role in the belief system of the indigenous people, the Whanganui Iwi. They see and revere in it a mythical ancestor. 'The view of the past 100 years is that you can own and manage the river. But for us it is a living being, an indivisible whole,' said Gerrard Albert, the tribe's chief negotiator. 'We are not the rulers of nature, but a part of it,' Albert continued. 'It is according to this fundamental belief that we want to live.' (Carstens 2017: n.p.)[8]

---

[8] Original German: 'Tatsächlich spielt der Whanganui River in der Weltanschauung der Ureinwohner, der Whanganui Iwi, eine zentrale Rolle. Sie sehen und verehren in ihm einen mythischen Vorfahren. "Die Sicht der vergangenen 100 Jahre ist, dass man den Fluss besitzen und managen kann. Doch für uns ist er ein lebendes Wesen, ein unteilbares Ganzes", sagte Gerrard Albert, der Verhandlungsführer des Maori-Stammes. "Wir sind nicht die Herrscher über die Natur, sondern ein Teil von ihr", so Albert weiter. "Dieser Grundüberzeugung gemäß wollen wir leben."' Translation by the editors.

At the same time, the court ruling comes at a time when Western epistemologies, too, have come to acknowledge the need for sustainability. Indigenous studies may well converge with ecocriticism here. At the same time, there is in this court ruling and in the negotiation that preceded it the need for translation. As Finlayson puts it, if indeed the need to protect the river is acknowledged by all parties involved, then a form of translation has to be found. Which concept, in Western legal epistemology, would be best suited to ensure the safety and the integrity of the river? Gerrard Albert, who represented the Whanganui iwi in the claim, describes this need for translation as follows: 'When we were negotiating with the Crown, we said we need to find an approximation at law to how we view and hold this river. Legal personhood was the closest approximation we could find. We knew that saying that the river is both spiritual and virtual wasn't going to be enough. We needed to define what that is' (*The River Is Me*).

It is in this context that the concept of legal personhood emerges. Crucially, it could be argued that this is a space both of translation and of untranslatability. What comes first in this process, arguably, is one of the key tenets of Māori epistemology: The kinship between humans and nature. Carstens observes, '[t]he judges thus followed the Māori argument that the river was not a thing, but a living being' (2017: n.p.).[9] What is significant, however, is that transculturality and modernity also come into play here. As *The Whale Rider* states at the outset, Pākehā and Māori alike betrayed the kinship between human and animal nature. In keeping with transculturality, there is hence also a fluidity of culture. Both Māori and Pākehā have been indelibly affected by modernity. It is with this estrangement that Ihimaera's novel begins. The whale rider terminates his communion with the whale, stating from now on, he will now have to confine himself to the human world:

> 'One last ride, friend,' his master had said. In elation, anger and despair, the whale had taken his golden master deeper than ever before and had sung to him of the sacred islands and of their friendship. But his master had been firm. At the end of the ride, he had said, 'I have been fruitful and soon children will come to me. My destiny lies here. As for you, return to the Kingdom of Tangaroa and to your own kind.' The heartache of that separation had never left the whale, nor had the remembrance of that touch of brow to brow in the last hongi. (Ihimaera 1987: 75–6)

---

[9] Original German: 'Die Richter folgten damit der Argumentation der Maori, der Fluss sei kein Ding, sondern ein Lebewesen.' Translation by the editors.

For both parties, then, a quest for restoring this original connection emerges. The whale, Ihimaera's narrative points out, has remained mournful and nostalgic, waiting for the whale rider to come back. By the same token, subsequent generations of humans have realized that this estrangement from the animal world has been pernicious. When a school of whales has unaccountably been stranded on the beach, Māori and Pākehā collaborate in trying to get the whales back afloat. In order to save the whales, however, it is essential that the ancient ways of human–animal communion be restored. Yet, once the connection between Māori and the whales had been broken by the last whale rider, Māori are at a loss to communicate with the whales. In this estrangement, Māori and Pākehā have come to converge. As the narrator goes on to describe,

> [t]he first sight to greet our eyes was this old European lady who had sat down on a whale that some men were pulling onto the beach with a tractor. They had put a rope round the whale's rear flukes and were getting angrier and angrier with the woman. ... But she would just return and sit on the whale again, her eyes glistening. We came to the rescue and that was the first punch-up of the day. 'Thank you, gentlemen,' the lady said. 'The whale is already dead of course, but how can men be so venal?' (Ihimaera 1987: 81)

What is needed to get the whales back into the water, Ihimaera's narrative emphasizes, is a common effort in which Māori and Pākehā join forces. The same is true, arguably, in the Whanganui River Claims Settlement Act of 2017. The Whanganui River now has both Māori and Pākehā guardians. As Finlayson dryly remarks, '[o]bviously, the river itself wouldn't go into court, it is represented by a number of people. The key thing is the legislation settles all the historical claims that had been brought against the Crown going back over a hundred years' (*The River Is Me*). Similarly to Ihimaera's novel, the Whanganui River Claims Settlement Act stipulates that Māori and Pākehā collaborate in ensuring the safety and well-being of the river. Just as in *The Whale Rider*, the 'European lady' and Kahu's iwi collaborate in order to save the whales, the Te Awa Tupua Act appoints two human guardians, who act on behalf of the river. As David Freid's film notes in the voiceover, '[t]he Whanganui River will soon have two jointly appointed human representatives, one nominated by the Crown and one by Whanganui iwi' (*The River Is Me*). Together, these guardians, Māori and Pākehā, will make sure that the river stays safe. It is through this guardianship, it could be argued, that the kinship between humans and non-humans has been both acknowledged and restored. *The Whale Rider* begins with the loss of this kinship, and it ends in a passage in which this kinship has been restored.

The Te Awa Tupua Act of 2017 serves a similar function, even if this function works differently for Māori and Pākehā, respectively. For Pākehā, it writes into law a kinship between humans and the non-human world that is not known in hegemonic strands of Western epistemology. It thus acknowledges a concept of kinship for which it has neither name nor epistemology. For Māori, on the other hand, the Te Awa Tupua Act restores a connection that in Māori epistemology and belief system, has never been questioned, but which had remained unacknowledged by New Zealand law. In keeping with the aim of the Waitangi Tribunal, then, the Whanganui River Claims Settlement Act redresses a historical injustice. The implications of the Te Awa Tupua Act could thus not be more far-reaching. By granting the river personhood, New Zealand law – seen from a Western perspective – deliberately blurs the boundary between what, in Western epistemology, is seen as 'natural' and what is seen as 'supernatural'.

To dominant strands of Western thinking, the kinship between humans and rivers may seem unimaginable.[10] Yet, it is this kinship that the legislation now acknowledges. In a sense, this piece of legislation incorporates both 'magical' – or rather, spiritual – elements and 'realistic' ones. It translates into law the Māori concept of the kinship between humans and nature; and it is 'realistic' or rather, pragmatic, in that it finds a legal approximation for this kinship: the status of legal personhood.

In this sense, the Te Awa Tupua Act could be described with a concept that is usually reserved for literary texts: the notion of 'magic realism'. This scenario in which the law is described in the terminology of literary studies, in turn, is in keeping with Posner's account of the connection between law and literature. According to Posner, literature can explore legal scenarios, just as legal texts can possess 'literary' qualities. He notes, 'law is a rhetorical discipline, and the judicial opinions of some of the greatest judges, such as Oliver Wendell Holmes, have literary merit and repay literary analysis. Opinions and briefs are like stories; they have a narrative structure' (2008: xi). What could be added to this description in the context of Aotearoa/New Zealand is that the law can express cultural categories, whose expression have usually been reserved for

---

[10] It should be emphasized here that the entire field of ecocriticism has challenged such division from within Western contexts as well. Yet, it may be crucial to note that such ecocritical counter-narratives, too, refer to non-Western epistemologies, especially to Indigenous philosophies (DeLoughrey 2019; Garrard 2011). In keeping with the notion of transculturalism, it must hence be stressed that even as I am referring to the opposition between Pākehā and Māori epistemologies – an opposition around which, arguably, colonialism has revolved – neither of these cultures are monolithic. In this vein, a transculturalist reading of Western epistemologies would stress counter-narratives and anti-hegemonic forces within Western culture as well.

literature. The Whanganui River Claims Settlement Act could thus be said to redress historical injustice through 'legal magic realism'. It restores justice by acknowledging the kinship between the human and the non-human worlds. In a similar vein, *The Whale Rider*, too, ends in the passage that is akin to magic realism. Ultimately, Kahu proves that she is Koro's true successor by riding on a whale: 'Then she felt that same shiver again, and again placed her head against the whale's skin. This time when the whale dived, it stayed underwater longer. But Kahu had made a discovery. Where her face was pressed the whale had opened up a small breathing chamber' (Ihimaera 1987: 106). By proving to her community that she is the true successor of the whale rider, Kahu demonstrates to her great-grandfather that she is the heir that he has been looking for all along. In the end, Koro realizes his own mistake and makes up to his great-granddaughter:

> 'I should have known she was the one,' Koro Apirana said. 'Ever since that time when she was a baby and bit my toe.' 'Boy, if only she had real teeth,' Nanny Flowers agreed. ...
>
> 'You're the best grandchild in the whole wide world,' he said. 'Boy or girl, it doesn't matter.' (Ihimaera 1987: 117–20)

Where the ending of the novel prefigures the present moment, and where it prefigures the Te Awa Tupua Act, is thus precisely in the relationship between magic and realism. Not long ago it might have seemed bizarre to Pākehā New Zealanders to grant the status of personhood to a river. The epistemology which underlay this change in status would have been dismissed as magical, as mere superstition. In 2017, however, this 'superstition' was finally acknowledged as a legitimate epistemology. Even if this epistemology, as in Kahu's remarkable reading of her essay, cannot be fully translated, it has to be acknowledged. In this sense, Ihimaera's novel *The Whale Rider* charts out the space between what is magic and what is real; between what can be translated and what has to remain untranslated but must be acknowledged, nonetheless. As Koro reminds his community,

> '[w]hy did a whale of its appearance strand itself here and not at Wainui? Does it belong in the real world or the unreal world?' 'The real,' someone called. 'Is it natural or supernatural?' 'It is supernatural,' a second voice said. ... Koro Apirana put up his hands to stop the debate. 'No,' he said, 'it is both. It is a reminder of the oneness which the world once had. It is the birth cord joining past and present, reality and fantasy. It is both. It is both,' he thundered, 'and if we have forgotten the communion then we have ceased to be Maori.' (Ihimaera 1987: 94)

In its negotiation of the physical and the metaphysical worlds, the Whanganui River Claims Settlement Act is strikingly similar to the ending of *The Whale Rider*. As Attorney General Christopher Finlayson notes, what underlies the claim by the Whanganui Iwi is the insistence that the natural and the supernatural worlds – to use Ihimaera's terms – cannot be separated. Finlayson notes, '[t]he fact of the matter is you can't divide a river up into the bed, the water column, and the air above the river. I think you can get hung up on these Western concepts of ownership' (*The River Is Me*). As Finlayson emphasizes, the Te Awa Tupua Act subverts Western notions of ownership. It thus departs from 'common law' and Western legal epistemology to create a piece of legislation that deliberately incorporates Māori epistemologies. An interview with director David Freid in the film *The River Is Me* elaborates on this potential transformation of New Zealand law:

[Freid:] Ok, so the river's water comes from the rain, and the rain falls to farmland, on city streets, through a lot of different areas. Because the river now is literally indivisible, I'd imagine then that everything that water touches along the way might eventually gain the same personhood.

[Finlayson:] Yes, I suppose, that's right, insofar as the water is part of this indivisible entity, it can flow in, flow out, yea.

[Freid:] So, then the larger idea would be that all of nature, in some way or another, gets spoken for.

[Finlayson:] When you think about it, why not?

What is so striking in this respect is that the discourse surrounding the eventual ratification of the Whanganui River Claims Settlement Act corresponds almost verbatim to a passage in Ihimaera's novel *The Whale Rider*. In the novel, Koro is certain that the passing of the whale will also be the end of Māori. Before Kahu goes out to save the whale, she has the following conversation with her great-grandfather:

'There is no place for it here in this world. The people who once commanded it are no longer here.' He paused. 'When it dies, we die. I die.'

'No, Paka. And if it lives?'

'Then we live also.' (Ihimaera 1987: 98)

In a similar vein, Geoffrey Hipango remarks in an interview in Freid's film: 'If the river was to pass, if the river was to die – well, we would die also' (*The River Is Me*).

In the courtroom after the verdict has been delivered and the Whanganui River has been turned into a legal person, Māori perform a waiata, a traditional song-performance. This scene, which is still available online, seems both laden with potential and highly ambivalent. What makes it ambivalent, despite the power of cultural expression that it holds, is that the courtroom is almost empty, and only a few Pākehā New Zealanders have remained to witness the performance. Unlike the scene in Ihimaera's novel where Kahu reads out her essay in Māori to a room full of people, few Pākehā New Zealanders are there to listen to the waiata. Yet, what remains is the solace of the ruling itself. By translating Māori epistemology into New Zealand law, white New Zealand has recognized an epistemology which it may not quite understand. In this sense the court decision begins where Ihimaera's novel has ended: on a hopeful note.

In this essay, I have tried to bring the framework of law and literature studies to the discussion of reconciliation in Aotearoa/New Zealand. I have argued that Ihimaera's novel *The Whale Rider* conveys an epistemology which is also at the heart of a recent legislation that grants personhood to the Whanganui River. At the same time, I have also tried to relate these literary and legal scenarios to the notion of transculturality. As I have attempted to show, transculturality is by no means out of place in a context where historical injustices are being addressed. As Ihimaera's *The Whale Rider* illustrates, the politics of redress can coexist with the idea that cultures are always in flux, evolving. Finally, it could be argued that the recent settlement that grants personhood to a river can be situated both in the context of reconciliation and of sustainability. As nations strive to find a new attitude to the non-human environment and to counteract the effects of climate change, the idea that human lives can be sustained only in tandem with non-human life may no longer seem quite as bizarre. It is in the context of the climate crisis, in Aotearoa/New Zealand and elsewhere, that Indigenous epistemologies are finally being acknowledged for the complex cultural and scientific knowledge they provide. This acknowledgement, in turn, has been long overdue. It is in the spirit of this knowledge that, following the cue of the Te Awa Tupua Act, Indigenous and non-Indigenous communities across the globe may have to collaborate in order to safeguard the future integrity of the planet. To end with the last sentence of Ihimaera's remarkable novel: 'Let it be done.'

In this chapter, I have tried to relate the concept of the 'many worlds' of Anglophone literature to Ihimaera's ground-breaking novel *The Whale Rider*.

I have suggested that not only in light of the current climate crisis and notions of 'ecocide', but also with regard to the growing field of ecocriticism, Ihimaera's novel is prophetic. By pointing out the kinship between humans and whales, the novel exemplifies the fact that Indigenous cultures have been premised on maintaining close connections between humans and nature, as well as humans and the land they inhabit. In keeping with this volume's emphasis on space and spatiality, *The Whale Rider* 'allows for the introduction of post-human agents and frameworks into the discussion of what Anglophone worlds consist of' (see introduction to this volume, 19).

At the same time, however, Ihimaera's narrative carefully guards itself against the stereotype of the 'eco-Native': The idea that Indigenous communities are inherently ecocritical (Banerjee 2012; Garrard 2011; Smithers 2015). Rather, and entirely in keeping with the notion of transculturality, Ihimaera's novel firmly locates Māori communities inside modernity. Both Māori and Pākehā groups, the text can be said to imply, have forgotten what it means to connect to the whales. In this sense, the kinship between humans and nature has to be re-established both for Māori and Pākehā New Zealanders alike. At the same time, I have tried to locate this ecocritical and transcultural reading of *The Whale Rider* in the field of law and literature studies. As I have tried to show, it is remarkable that recent New Zealand laws, such as the Whanganui River case, have explicitly incorporated Māori epistemologies in New Zealand law. Moreover, I have tried in this chapter to highlight the role of language in processes of colonization and de-colonization. Crucially, the colonization of New Zealand was founded on a deliberate mistranslation of Māori language and epistemology (Tiemann 1999). This also has far-reaching implications for notions of Anglophone literature. As I have tied to trace in this chapter, Ihimaera inscribes Māori epistemology into his English-language novel; at the same time, a key scene in the narrative – Kahu's reading out her essay, in the Māori language, to a Pakeha audience, who may not understand it – revolves precisely around the notion of untranslatability.

Finally, I have tried to situate such legal reform in the framework of reconciliation. Taking the Waitangi Tribunal as a case in point, I have suggested that a key component of reconciliation is the retrospective and present acknowledgment of Māori epistemology and its legitimacy to the fullest possible extent. In this sense, Ihimaera's novel *The Whale Rider* can also be seen as a literary contribution to processes of reconciliation. Thirty-six years after its publication, Ihimaera's novel is thus more current than ever.

References

Banerjee, M. (2012), 'The Myth of the EcoNative? Indigenous Presences in Ecocritical Narratives', in T. Müller and M. Sauter (eds), *Literature, Ecology, Ethics: Recent Trends in Ecocriticism*, 215–26, Heidelberg: Winter.

Carstens, P. (2017), 'Maori-Fluss erhält Rechte als Person', *Geo* (16 March). Available online: https://www.geo.de/natur/nachhaltigkeit/15997-rtkl-neuseeland-maori-fluss-erhaelt-rechte-als-person (accessed 18 October 2022).

Clark, T. (2015), *Ecocriticism on the Edge: The Anthropocene as a Threshold Concept*, New York: Bloomsbury.

DeLoughrey, E. (2019), *Allegories of the Anthropocene*, Durham, NC: Duke University Press.

Dickinson, E. (2016), 'Ecocultural Conversations: Bridging the Human–Nature Divide through Connective Communication Practices', *Southern Communication Journal* 81 (1): 32–48.

Ehrmann, M. (1999), 'The Status and Rights of Indigenous Peoples in New Zealand', *Zeitschrift für ausländisches öffentliches Recht und Völkerrecht* 59 (2): 463–96.

Frame, A. (2002), *Grey and Iwikau: A Journey into Custom – Kerei Raua Ko Iwikau: Te Haerenga me nga Tikanga*, Wellington: Victoria University Press.

Garrard, G. (2011), *Ecocriticism: The New Critical Idiom*, New York: Routledge.

Henderson, J. and P. Wakeham (2013), 'Introduction', in J. Henderson and P. Wakeham (eds), *Reconciling Canada: Critical Perspectives on the Culture of Redress*, 3–27, Toronto: University of Toronto Press.

Hokowhitu, B. (2008), 'The Death of Koro Paka: "Traditional" Māori Patriarchy', *The Contemporary Pacific* 20 (1): 115–41.

Huggan, G., and H. Tiffin (2009), *Postcolonial Ecocriticism: Literature, Animals, Environment*, New York: Routledge.

Ihimaera, W. (1987), *The Whale Rider*, Kindle edition, Auckland: Raupo.

McHugh, P. (1991), *The Maori Magna Charta – New Zealand Law and the Treaty of Waitangi*, Auckland: Oxford University Press.

Posner, R. (2008), *Law and Literature*, Cambridge, MA: Harvard University Press.

Raftopoulos, R., and J. Morley (2020), 'Ecocide in the Amazon: The Contested Politics of Environmental Rights in Brazil', *International Journal of Human Rights*, doi: 10.1080/13642987.2020.1746648.

Robertson, L. (2005), *Conquest by Law: How the Discovery of America Dispossessed Indigenous Peoples of Their Land*, Oxford: Oxford University Press.

Schulze-Engler, F. (2009), 'Transcultural Modernities and Anglophone African Literature', *Matatu: Journal for African Culture and Society* 36 (1): 87–101.

Smithers, G. (2015), 'Beyond the "Ecological Indian": Environmental Politics and Traditional Ecological Knowledge in Modern North America', *Environmental History* 20 (1): 83–111.

The River Is Me (2018), [Film] Dir. D. Freid, Switzerland: Films for the Earth.

Tiemann, U. (1999), *Rechte der Ureinwohner Neuseelands aus dem Vertrag von Waitangi*, Münster: LIT.

Whanganui River Claims Settlement Act/Te Awa Tupua Act (2017). Available online: https://www.legislation.govt.nz/act/public/2017/0007/latest/whole.html (accessed 28 February 2023).

Winter, S. (2013), 'Towards a Unified Theory of Transitional Justice', *International Journal of Transitional Justice* 7 (2): 224–44, https://doi.org/10.1093/ijtj/ijt004.

9

'Mobility at large': Anglophone travel writing as a medium of transcultural communication in a global context

Nadia Butt
Goethe University Frankfurt

Introduction

Transculturality is currently one of the essential concepts circulating in academic discourse. In the last few years, transculturality has been increasingly recognized as a significant step to understanding cultural overlaps in the face of worldwide travel and mobility in the age of globalization, faced with political, cultural and natural challenges such as the refugee crisis, the emergence of right-wing nationalism across several countries in the Western world, Brexit, the MeToo Movement, the Black Lives Matter Movement and the current Corona pandemic, to name but a few. In our hyperconnected global world, it is almost impossible not to be affected or touched by cross-border changes. Indeed, physical and virtual mobility have transformed not only the different spheres of contemporary existence, but also the way we think, react, interact, behave and above all communicate in the shared space of culture. Not only does mobility create a space of transcultural communication (see Tomas 1996: 9–17), but it also shapes and influences it in several ways. Therefore, in this chapter, my contention is that transcultural communication in the age of global mobility urges us to define 'other cultures' from a new perspective – a perspective that makes us look at cultures as interconnected, interlinked – as relational webs – and thus not as closed containers. To support my contention, I allude to twenty-first-century Asian, African and Arab Anglophone travel writing as 'a hybrid genre' (Holland and Huggan 1998: 8) before moving on to present my case study, namely, a travelogue-cum-reportage *Afropean: Notes from Black Europe* (2019) by the Black British writer Johny Pitts, which communicates cultural fusions, flux and fluidity on the one hand and cultural transcendence, transgressions and translations on the other. My chapter consists of two parts: In the first half, I set out to define transculturality as an increasingly interdisciplinary concept and conceptualize transcultural communication; in the second half, I present my case study.

Conceptualizing transcultural communication: Thinking beyond 'Other' cultures in the age of global mobility and migration

Since Cuban anthropologist Fernando Ortiz's coinage of the term 'transculturation' in 1947 ([1947] 1995) to suggest an alternative for the term acculturation, transculturality has been fervently debated not only in the disciplines of philosophy (Welsch 1999), sociology (Beck 2006), cultural studies (Schulze-Engler 2007), literary studies (Ascari 2011; Kloss 1998), media and communication studies (Hepp 2015), but it has also been discussed in terms of transcultural competence (Glover and Friedman 2015) in the area of teaching and learning foreign cultures and languages (Doff 2009: 357–72; West-Pavlov 2005).

Transcultural approaches are fundamentally shaped by theories of cultural hybridity, syncretism, plural identities, mass migration, diaspora and globalization. 'What these concepts share is a political, philosophical, socio-cultural and pedagogical agenda which aims to reach *beyond* well-established and conventional Eurocentric modes of thinking – *beyond* binary oppositions, hierarchical structures and asymmetries inherent in them' (Volkmann 2011: 113; emphasis in the original). Instead of focusing on paradigms of binarism – that is, 'practices of contrasting clearly defined cultures, transcultural approaches focus on notions of intermingling, the creation of "in-between spaces"' (Volkmann 2011: 113), which Homi K. Bhabha calls the 'Third Space' or 'interstitial passages' (1994: 4) giving rise to something different and new. Virginia H. Milhouse et al. conclude that the transcultural concept is 'based on the principle that a single culture, in and of itself, for maturity requires interaction and dialogue with other cultures' (2001: ix). They add that 'transculturalism' is about 'affirming diverse ways of knowing, communicating and behaving so that when individuals from different cultures come together, there is the potential for each to be enriched by the other' (2001: x). Therefore, in their opinion, the notion of transculture is related to 'other cross-cultural concepts, including intra- and interculturalism, internationalism, and postmodernism – in the sense that it rejects the notion that there is only one way of knowing, behaving, or communicating' (2001: x). Thus, transculturality is not merely a response and a reaction to the representations of 'other cultures' in different media, but a tool and a method to live in a world of cultural connections and conflicts, different opinions, races and religions, languages, and social norms.

Indeed, the twenty-first century is a century of travel and mobility in which the emergence of migrant and diasporic communities tend to unfold not only new cultural configurations across fixed territorial and national borders, but also alternative ways of communication to address and articulate these configurations, which resonate with cross-border realities in our constantly changing world. Hence, transculturality is increasingly discussed in tandem with prominent concepts in literary and cultural theory such as transnational relations (Hannerz 1996), new cosmopolitanisms (Strand 2010: 229–42), nomadic lifestyles (Dagnino 2015: 93–107), global diasporas (Cohen 1997), multiple modernities (Eisenstadt 2000: 1–29), new Englishes (Pennycook 2007), postcolonialism (Huggan 2006: 55–63), memory studies (Erll 2011: 4–18), to name but a few. I argue that transcultural communication not only deviates from treating cultures as singular entities but offers a perspective on culture that is beyond the traditional vision of culture as 'authentic' or 'fixed' – a perspective that presents culture as moving, in flux, in short, a work in progress. Andreas Hepp likewise maintains that the concept of transcultural communication 'involves processes of communication that transcend individual cultures' (2015: 3), which, he believes, confirms the fact that this concept is of great importance to human cooperation in a time of advancing globalization. According to Hepp, '[t]he concept of transcultural communication employs *culture* as outlined by Jan Nederveen Pieterse (1995) as a translocal concept distinct from a territorial conception of culture' (2015: 12; emphasis in the original). As a result, translocal conceptions focus on 'hybridity, translation and ongoing identification. Culture is, here, something that is processual and unfinished' (Hepp 2015: 12). In this way, transcultural communication makes way for an ongoing dialogue, aiming at cooperation and collaborations among members of different cultures who absorb differences, 'otherness' as a key to individual and cultural enrichment despite facing unexpected challenges. In his book, *Transcultural Odysseys: The Evolving Global Consciousness*, Germaine W. Shames (1997) rightly infers that transcultural challenges at home or during our travels abroad tend to broaden our worldview that is determined not by its borders but by its scope. Certainly, such a worldview leads to thinking about culture more creatively and to the fact that travel and mobility are conducive to developing our new cultural horizon.

After many scholars' scepticism towards the theories of biculturality, acculturation, interculturality and multiculturality in the last decades, the transcultural concept has drawn attention in diverse disciplines these days (see McIntyre-Mills 2000; Naficy 2007: xiii–xv). Since Mary Pratt's use of transculturation as a phenomenon of the contact zones 'where disparate cultures meet, grapple with each other, often in highly asymmetrical relations of domination and subordination' (1992: 4), several scholars such as Frank Schulze-Engler, Wolfgang Welsch, Diana Taylor, Mikhail Epstein and Arianna Dagnino have tried to remap transculturation as transcultural or transculturality to detach the concept from its original colonial and nationalistic contexts and propose its use in contemporary settings. Dagnino considers the twenty-first century as marked by a transcultural sensibility; therefore, she opts for the transcultural perspective due to its ability to promote and highlight 'a flexible and fluid manner of enquiry particularly suited to the present context of global mobility, global writing and global languages' (2015: 9; see also Dagnino 2013).

Unlike a number of 'post'-theories such as postcolonialism, postmodernism or poststructuralism, which tend to indicate a 'passage' or 'a phase after' as well as inter- or multiculturalism, which tend to focus on cultures as separate entities, the transcultural approach, which aims at transcendence and fusions, is relatively new. However, proponents of transculturality now claim that transculturality is not a new phenomenon, as cultures have always been in contact and dialogue with each other, and 'culture *per se* can be argued to be transcultural' (Schulze-Engler 2009: xii). As a result, transculturality is not a neologism but a more 'pragmatic turn' in the field of cultural and literary theory (see Bond and Rapson 2014), which calls for not only a broader understanding of contemporary cultural encounters but also different ways of communication between cultures.

In the context of this chapter, the transcultural concept alludes to the new cultural condition of today that worldwide travel and mobility have generated. In this light, Alastair Pennycook proclaims, '[n]otions of the transcultural, transnational and translocal present a way of thinking about flow, flux and fixity in relation to location that move beyond both dichotomies of the global and local, and dialectics between global homogenization and local heterogenization' (2007: 44). Essentially, the term 'transcultural' denotes 'the *trans*versal, the *trans*actional, the *trans*lational, and the *trans*gressive aspects of contemporary behaviour and imagination triggered by the changed and changing dynamics of cultural production and identity building' (Dagnino 2012: 4; emphasis in the original; citing the ideas of Aihwa Ong 1999: 4). Considering the idea of identity, Diana Taylor declares transculturation as a 'shifting process' (1991: 92) that 'involves the shifting of socio-political … borders' and 'modifies collective and individual identity' (1991: 90). Thinking beyond the model of clash of civilizations popularized especially by Samuel P. Huntington (1996) as well as of history as a singular Western domain, as presented by Francis Fukuyama (1992), transcultural theorists such as Wolfgang Welsch, Mikhail Epstein and Diana Taylor broaden the scope of culture and history and seek to place them in a wider, global context. These theorists particularly address culture as a slippery terrain by pointing to the significance of cultural overlaps and interactions rather than that of contestations and antagonism. Thus, Welsch, Epstein and Taylor define the transcultural as a model of cultural development, change and enrichment to understand the present world of mass migration and mobility.

Significantly, the conceptualizations of 'transculturality', 'transculture', 'transculturating transculturation' elucidated by Welsch (1999), Epstein (2009) and Taylor (1991) aim to dissolve the polarities of 'superior versus inferior' cultures, which was believed to be essential to the original concept of transculturation. Frank Schulze-Engler has taken up the transcultural concept to study contemporary Anglophone literatures from a new perspective (2007: 20–32; 2019: 366–83). Indeed, Schulze-Engler's 2009 collection of essays *Transcultural English Studies* shows his substantial efforts to divest the transcultural concept of its postcolonial connotations and present it as a more convincing theoretical model for the study of global cultures than intercultural and multicultural theories, which were further developed by Dagnino and Pennycook in their works in the context of comparative literature and linguistics.

In effect, the transcultural concept, both as a theoretical and methodological tool to understand contemporary cultural trajectories 'across the lines' (Cronin 2000), is increasingly examined by several scholars and writers who seek to think beyond the idea of culture based on the binaries of 'the West' and 'the Rest', 'us' and 'them', 'colonial and colonized'. Rather, they concentrate more on the dialogic aspects of culture as manifested in Gilles Dupuis's interpretations, an expert on migration and literature. According to Dupuis:

> Transculturalism ... does not limit itself to two cultures facing each other, trying to work out what they assume to be their intrinsic discrepancies. Transculturalism takes place when at least two – and sometimes three or more – cultures are not only engaged in dialogue, but partake in a more profound and often contradictory process, in which enlightenment, understanding, and continuous reassessment of identity are at play. The ultimate aim is to transform each other's identity through a long, arduous, and sometimes painful negotiation of Otherness. (2008: 497–508, qtd in Dagnino 2013: 153)

In light of Dupuis's definition, Dagnino reminds us that the transcultural perspective may prove to be a 'more viable alternative concept when dealing with works that might be inscribed within the wide family of "the literature of mobility"' (Dagnino 2012: 6), to which I add literature of travel or 'literature on the move' (see also Ette 2003). According to Dagnino, this kind of literature includes those works of fiction and non-fiction that are particularly affected and shaped by 'migratory flows, exploratory/travelling drives, diasporic/exile conditions, expatriate statuses, postcolonial experiences, transnational movements ... by the multiple trajectories of global nomads' (2012: 6). Thus, they provide deep insight into the changing dimensions and patterns of culture in the age of global travel and mobility, which has blurred the borders of identity and belonging, as more and more people leave home and settle abroad.

My definition of the transcultural draws mainly on Welsch's view of the transcultural as illustrating the 'puzzling forms' of culture today (1999), Schulze-Engler's approach to 'the New Literatures in English' as 'a transcultural field with blurred boundaries' (2009: xvi), Epstein's theorizations of 'transcultural' as transcending 'the borders of traditional cultures' (2009: 330). As a result, in the present context, the transcultural refers to the complex process of cultural metamorphosis which renders both belonging and identity a fluid notion; indeed, the transcultural also refers to the processes of cultural blending and fusions as well as transactions and communication (see Butt 2015). Examining Anglophone travel writing as a potent medium of transcultural communication, I argue that these forms of writing are mostly written by authors who tend to act and think beyond the narrow confines of a nation or nation-state. Consequently, these writers set out to address and explore questions concerning diverse forms of cultural, political and even existential (un)belongings in their work. In short, Anglophone travel writing urges a more innovative view of the age in which transcultural communications are the outcome of global cultural connections and encounters as well as conflicts and challenges.

Anglophone travel writing as a reflection of transcultural communication in a global context

Anglophone travel writing as a burgeoning area of inquiry points to the significance of migratory and diasporic flows that are increasingly dominating the age of globalization. Publications such as *Other Routes: 1500 Years of African and Asian Travel Writing* (2005), compiled by Tabish Khair et al., or *Travel Writing and the Transnational Author* (2014) by Sam Knowles, reveal that travel writing cannot be deemed a solely Western domain. Instead, it is a genre which travels around the globe. In addition, the proliferation of Asian, African, Black or Arab travel writing has caught the attention of scholars and readers alike, confirming the fact that travel is no longer a Western privilege but is undertaken out of curiosity or necessity by several people from the Global South. Finally, travel as a frame of cultural overlaps has played a significant role in generating 'travelling concepts' (see Bal 2002), 'travelling theory' (see Clifford 1989; Said 1983) or the notion of 'moving cultures' (MA programme at Frankfurt University).[1] Admittedly, travel as trope or motif is fundamental in shaping a number of theoretical concepts in different disciplines (see Graulund and Edwards 2012). At the same time, by virtue of its flexible nature, travel writing has also been taken up by mobilities studies to investigate 'mobile lives' (Elliott and Urry 2009; qtd in Aguiar et al. 2019: 5) from a global perspective.

Amitav Ghosh and Pico Iyer are the two most prominent writers in Indian travel writing. Both have transformed contemporary travel writing in terms of genre as well as subject matter. While Ghosh is preoccupied with the idea of travelling histories and memories, Iyer is engaged with transnational and transcultural connections of global travellers (Butt 2021: 331). Ghosh's *The Iman and the Indian* (2002) and Iyer's *The Global Soul* (2001), for instance, are not conventional travel books, which may present a Eurocentric perception of travel; instead, they are a deep meditation on travel and its impact on the human imagination. Indeed, a number of genres such as the (historical) essay, autobiography, memoir, field diary and the private journal certainly come together in these two works. A mere cursory glance at Black travel writing or African travel writing unfolds similar developments. Nigerian-British author Noo Saro-Wiwa's *Looking for Transwonderland* (2012) and Kenyan writer Binyavanga

---

[1] https://www.uni-frankfurt.de/45978567/Moving_Cultures___Transcultural_Encounters___Cultures_en_mouvement___rencontres_transculturelles___Culturas_en_movimiento___encuentros_transculturales___Culture_in_Movimento___Incontri_Transculturali__Master_of_Arts (accessed 15 December 2022).

Wainaina's *One Day I Will Write about This Place* (2011) are interesting cases in point. Saro-Wiwa makes use of humour and irony in documenting her travels through her home country Nigeria as a cultural insider as well as outsider, whereas Wainaina merges the genre of travel writing with life-writing, time travel as well as memoir as he chronicles the process of growing up as a middle-class Kenyan. He seeks to present the Africa of his imagination as opposed to that of Western perception, which is not devoid of cultural biases. The reader accompanies the author to places he has seen and experienced first-hand such as South Africa, the Sudan, Kenya, Lagos, Uganda. Instead of portraying Africa as a 'dark continent', he shares a variety of experiences ranging from pop culture or football to political corruption or famine, all of which provide insights into the author and his world.

Several travel writers have tried to present their epic journeys in the genre of travel writing, experimenting with its form in an unusual way. Iranian writer Behrouz Boochani's *No Friends but the Mountains* (2018) and the other Iranian writer Dina Nayeri's *The Ungrateful Refugee: What Immigrants Never Tell You* (2020) mirror sociopolitical realities of our contemporary times in a very personal account. Boochani's harrowing tale, arduously typed on the mobile phone, moves the reader as he states his dangerous journey to Christmas Island and his illegal detention on Manus Island in Australia. Moving between prose and poetry, the travel account may also be called world prison literature, refugee literature or the diary of a man on the run. Such experiments with form resonate with the extraordinary journey Boochani is compelled to undertake as a refugee who does not seem to possess the basic human right to move freely. Likewise, Nayeri's narrative provides a new insight into modern journeys that refugees are bound to undertake as they simply have no choice but to flee. As Nayeri documents her own process of living in refugee camps before getting asylum in America, she recounts the conversations from refugees and asylum seekers who communicate the perils of travelling across borders in the hope for turning over a new leaf in life. Unfortunately, this hope is marred and crushed by the Western authorities who tend to look upon refugees with great suspicion.

Finally, the example from Arab Anglophone travel writing points out gender conflicts and the move from tradition to modernity against the turbulent political backdrop. Leila Ahmed's autobiography *A Border Passage: From Cairo to America – A Woman's Journey* (1999) not only traces a single woman's journey from the Arab World to the United States but also offers a historical account as socio-political realities shaped Ahmed's imagination from childhood to adulthood. Writing about the process of growing up as a woman in Cairo with rigid patriarchal family structures, her writing becomes a metaphor of life as a journey – a form of travel from innocence to enlightenment. Another dimension of the journey motif is conspicuous in Palestinian writer Raja Shehadeh's memoir *A Rift in Time: Travels with My Ottoman Uncle* (2010), which is a family chronicle as well as a reflection on how the disputed Jordan Rift Valley in Palestine has undergone dramatic changes over the years. The narrative unfolds how a major part of Palestine's history and that of its people has dwindled away as the names of whole villages have been wiped off the map. However, as Shehadeh looks into Palestinians' struggle for freedom, he looks to a future which is free from Israeli or Ottoman atrocities. Through his travels, Shehadeh evokes not merely the forgotten history of Palestine villages, but he also renders voice to its people, whom he considers to have been oppressed for centuries by more powerful enemies, yet are courageously fighting for their rights.

These telling examples of Anglophone travel writing in the twentieth and twenty-first centuries offer spaces of cultural communication in many different ways as each text is a vivid reflection of cultures in conflict as well as in dialogue with each other. These texts also confirm the fact that the literature of travel is 'gigantic' and 'has a thousand forms and faces' (Adams 1983: 281) as each narrative illustrates a certain facet of our age in a distinct narrative form. The more privileged travel writers like Ghosh and Iyer express the more philosophical and intellectual dimensions of travel with reference to history, origins and identity. Also, Saro-Wiwa and Wainaina place the experience of travel in the larger framework of their national histories. However, Boochani and Nayeri are very different kinds of travellers as they do not have the privilege either to travel on or to choose their travel destination without fear and anxiety. Ahmed's and Shehadeh's travel books bring to light undocumented or suppressed histories of the Arab world in relation to the individual and family.

Thus, the various forms of Anglophone travel writing mentioned above are a way of rethinking our globalized world, which seems to create distinct spaces of transcultural communication against heterogeneous political and geographical landscapes. These spaces of transcultural communication, as represented in the genre of travel writing, function as the third space (Schulze-Engler 2009: 155) in which culture and country are not bound to a narrow definition of nationalism (as first modernity; Beck 2006: 6–10) but to the cosmopolitan turn (as second modernity; Beck 2006: 95). Importantly, as narrators-cum-travellers act as storytellers and historians, their narratives become mouthpieces of cultural collusion and collisions, roots and routes (Clifford 1997: 3), all of which provide a critical commentary on the global age in flux.

Criss-crossing Europe and Africa: Transcultural communication on the streets of European cities

Wolfgang Welsch reminds us that '[m]ost of us are determined in our cultural formation by *several* cultural origins and connections. We are cultural hybrids. Contemporary writers, for example, point out that they are not shaped by one home country, but by influences of various origins' (2005: 326; emphasis in the original; qtd in Schulze-Engler 2011: 4). One such author is Johny Pitts, the son of an Irish mother and an African American father, a journalist and a photographer, whose ground-breaking and award-wining travelogue-cum-reportage *Afropean: Notes from Black Europe* (2019), chosen for my case study, is a vivid illustration of transcultural communications. Pitts embarks on a journey and shapes it into a 'book connecting the disparate people and locales of black Europe in a single narrative, allowing each area and community to "speak" to one another on digestible terms' (Pitts 2019: 332). Hepp reminds us that transcultural communication occurs inactively as it 'typically takes place through media' such as newspapers, films and the internet (2015: 3), yet in certain media such as travelogue with pictures, it seems to occur almost actively on the streets, face to face, especially on the streets of European metropolitan cities, which are increasingly inhabited by people of diverse backgrounds.

I argue that the text presents three levels of transcultural communication: First, it emerges with the author's vision of transcultural Europe, which he communicates through the coinage Afropean; second, it surfaces as the real people on the streets, namely Afropeans, whom the author encounters, communicate their transcultural identities and social practices; lastly, it is reflected in the narrative's allusion to significant works by authors who communicate overlapping historical and cultural connections between Africa and Europe. In the following analysis, I will focus on the first two levels of transcultural communication. As Pitts sets out on a journey 'in search of the Afropeans' (2019: 10), he aims to delve into 'black Europe beyond the desk of a theorist, found in the equivocal and untidy lived experiences of its communities' (5). In short, he seeks to map 'black Europe from the street up' (5). As Elleke Boehmer puts it: 'For Pitts, Black history lies not in the past, but all around us; not only in the archive, but in the street' (2020: n.p.).

Pitts's book is the result of 'a low budget five-month-long journey' (Pitts 2019: 6) described as 'five chilly months on the road' (389) by the author, who travels through different European cities investigating the concept of 'Afropean' – that is, both African and European – culture. In other words, Afropean 'resonates somewhere between Africa and Europe' (281). The term 'Afropean', Pitts states on the opening page of his book,

> encouraged me to think of myself as whole and unhyphenated ... Here was a space where blackness was taking part in shaping European identity at large. It suggested the possibility of living in and with more than one idea: Africa and Europe, or, by extension, the Global South and the West, without being mixed-this, half-that or black-other. That being black in Europe didn't necessarily mean being an immigrant. (1)

Travelling with a backpack, notebook and camera, Pitts follows the pattern of Caryl Phillips's 1987 travelogue *The European Tribe*, which 'effectively reversed the black gaze onto white Europeans. Here, Pitts flips the concept on its head, specifically investigating black Europe in the 21st century' (Lecoutteux 2020: n.p.). Like Phillips's work, each chapter of Pitts's book is named after a different city: Sheffield, Paris, Brussels, Amsterdam, Berlin, Stockholm, Moscow, Marseille and Lisbon. In most cases, Pitts deliberately visits the periphery of every city – Clichy-Sous-Bois on the outskirts of Paris, where the racial riots in 2005 took place, or Rinkeby in Stockholm 'where 90 per cent of the local population identified as immigrants' (Pitts 2019: 233), Cova da Moura on the outskirts of Lisbon, an 'unofficial favela-like settlement with its own underground economy' (354) or in transit zones such as train stations and hostels, all the while presenting Afropeans 'as lead actors in their own story' (2). First coined by the British-American musician David Byrne and the Congolese-Belgian vocalist Marie Daulne when their transcultural band Zap Mama released *Adventures in Afropea* in 1993, the term Afropean appealed to Pitts from the time he heard it. The hope that induced him was to see the 'rest of Europe through the eyes of black culture', and find through conversation, music and wandering 'a new configuration of ideas, connected to Africa and Europe but transcending both' (59). According to Pitts,

> The term 'Afropean' was my own object of contemplation, serving as a departure point of investigation and what I hope would be my destination – a coherent, shared black European experience – but the black Europe I'd travelled through had refused to stand still, and I'd begun to think of the myriad experiences of black Europeans as the whole point; 'Afropean' was an opportunity to build bridges among various histories, cultures ad people, but it certainly wasn't absolute or monolithic. (342)

Pitts is someone who virtually and metaphorically travels between cultures. According to Colin Grant, since Pitts is not satisfied with the 'limits imposed on his identity and the framing of his black experience, he is a nomadic writer ... who claims membership of a collective black community in Europe that offers a sense of belonging more nourishing than the reductive nationalism of individual European countries' (2019: n.p.). *Afropean* starts with Pitts's own experiences of growing up mixed-race in a working-class area of Firth Park in Sheffield, which shaped his perception of culture and communication at a young age. Even though he was fully at home in his culturally colourful surroundings, he could not help being irritated to experience racism in a place where immigrants from colonies had settled down as if they saw themselves as 'Brits heading home to the motherland' (Pitts 2019: 12). He concludes:

> I never felt the need to apologise for my presence. The multicultural make-up of Firth Park where I grew up comprised not only a white working-class community but established Yemeni, Jamaican, Pakistani and Indian communities, and later, more recent economic migrants and political refugees from Syria, Albania, Kosovo and Somalia ... From (my childhood bedroom) I've watched everything from Diwali and Eid celebrations to reggae parties ... Yemeni weddings ... It was no multicultural 'utopia' in the conventional sense, but it was alive and convivial, entrepreneurial and dynamic, built upon the tolerant atmosphere that comes with sharing a space daily with other people with diverse beliefs and cultures. (13–14)

It is the idea of 'sharing a space' that is at the heart of the travelogue, for what Pitts observes during his journey through Paris, Brussels, Amsterdam is a perpetuation of dividing the society on racial lines, polarizing Europeans and Afropeans, thus keeping the binaries of 'us and them' – 'culture and its Other' – intact when the reality is that these binaries have long been dissolved, whether people are ready to believe or not. While travelling through Paris, Pitts notices that the French have already absorbed multiple shades of African culture while marginalizing them just as the British, the Dutch or the Portuguese have done. For this reason, Pitts employs the term Afropean to communicate a transformation that has happened and that needs to be accepted as a new cultural reality. The author maintains: 'I choose "Afropean" as a potentially progressive self-identifier (rather than "European") because there is something about the nature of Europe that destroys by assimilation ...' (24). In light of his diverse experiences, he visualizes Europe as a space of cultural liminality, which is conspicuous in everyday existence, yet looked upon suspiciously; therefore, he highlights that he cannot help seeing a Europe that is populated by Egyptian nomads, Sudanese restaurateurs, Swedish Muslims, black French, militants and Belgo-Congolese painters. A continent of Cape Verdean favelas, Algerian flea markets, Surinamese shamanism, German reggae and Moorish castles. Yes, all of this was part of Europe, too, and these were areas that needed to be understood and fully embraced if Europe wanted to enjoy fully functional societies. And black Europeans, too, need to understand Europe and to demand participation in its societies, to demand the right to document and disseminate our stories. (8)

Pitts is particularly interested in the interplay between Black and European cultures to provide new perspectives on the Black diaspora on the one hand and on his own identification with Black Europeans on the other. He reveals that he has travelled extensively, including West Africa, where his blackness is rooted, and Brooklyn, where his father was born, and 'still, nowhere else feels quite as much like home as Europe' (7). Interestingly, it is not a sense of displacement that made him travel, but a sense of being *at home* only in Europe and still treated as an outsider. So, urged by his sense of rootedness in Europe, which seems to be still defined by its 'whiteness', Pitts declares, '[a]s a member of Europe's black community, this Europe I speak of is all part of *my* inheritance, too, and it was time to wander and celebrate the continent like I owned it' (7; emphasis in the original). Thus, he uses his 'own plurality' (5) as the basis of his vision of Afropeans.

Afropean is hence a modern odyssey of a Black man not merely in search of his roots or origins, but someone who is on a quest to understand the image of a heterogeneous Europe as opposed to the projection of a more homogenous Europe. Indeed, Afropean manifests a desire on the part of the author, as a mouthpiece of many others, to imagine blackness not as a trope of alienation or 'otherness' but as part of Europe. While recalling unrest among Black communities in Britain, Pitts declares:

> Looking back at all the violence and death and realizing it wasn't necessarily normal made me want to travel in the name of those who couldn't, or didn't – the working-class black community and children of immigrants – in search of a Europe both they and I might recognize as our own. And so it was that I found myself setting off as that rarest of creatures: the black backpacker. (30)

Pitts's book communicates an alternative view on the condition of contemporary European cultures, which are increasingly dominated by creolization and syncretism. Orienting the reader in the direction of perceiving the image of the Black people in Europe with his usage of Afropean, Pitts points out: 'Initially, then, I saw "Afropean" as something of a utopian alternative to the doom and gloom that has surrounded the black image of Europe in recent years and an optimistic route forward' (2). He adds: 'Afropean had to be more than ... an obsession with an authentic search for the self, and something more like a contribution to a community, with its trade-offs and compromises. It had to build a bridge over that dividing fence that says whether you're in or out and from some sort of informal cultural coalition' (5).

Afropean can be read like a live documentary of areas where Europeans of African descent are shuttling between multiple allegiances and identities. In effect, Pitts's unconventional travel narrative unfolds an alternative map of Europe that does not take centre stage in travel or guidebooks but is absolutely crucial to comprehending the importance of a coherent society rather than a divided one. The text is interspersed with black-and-white photographs that Pitts has taken during his journeys to portray Black Europeans in their everyday existence: riding a bike, taking a train, sitting in a café or simply walking on the streets. Faced with such plurality, Pitts comes to understand the concept of Afropean as a chance to connect rather than disconnect or divide, as an opportunity to build bridges among various histories, cultures and people. Essentially, Pitts is propelled by the possibility that Afropean is a unifying concept, encompassing 'Pan-Africanism, the New Negro Movement, Negritude, the Harlem Renaissance, Marcus Garvey's Back-to-Africa project, Rastafari, Black Power and many others' (Grant 2019: n.p.). According to Paul Gilroy, Black culture in Britain is unique as it is tied to the process of travel and migration and thus to several histories and transcultural origins:

> Britain's Black settler communities have forged a compound culture from disparate sources. Elements of political sensibility and cultural expression transmitted from Black America over a long period of time has been reaccentuated in Britain. They are central, though no longer dominant, within the increasingly novel configurations that characterize another newer Black vernacular culture. This is not content to be either dependent upon or simply imitative of the African diaspora cultures of America and the Caribbean. (1993: 15)

Although Pitts claims that his work is not ethnographical or historical, as he is a journalist and a photographer, I argue that this travelogue presents the history of the modern – a chronicle of 'travelling cultures' (Clifford 1992: 96–116) and communities, moving memories and identities, 'overlapping territories, intertwined histories' (Said 1993: 1). Pitts particularly seeks to unfold the so-called other histories, namely the history of colonial violence and plunder, which cannot be ignored or suppressed from the history of European civilization and glory. Thus, he communicates a view on culture and history which are cross-stitched to such an extent that it is not possible to separate one from the other. In short, he addresses history as '[c]onnective history' (Pitts 2019: 9) in order to contest a linear historical perception. Pitts maintains that '[w]hite history isn't projected as white history because it is simply "history"' (10) dominating TV shows and curricula, but he claims that the history of Black people seems invisible. During his journey on foot, he has discussions with fellow backpackers, activists, students, bouncers, late-night workers, regular folk, friends and strangers he meets by chance to chronicle the visible as well as invisible Afropean. On these journeys, Pitts also becomes increasingly aware of rising nationalism across the continent, as he learns about neo-Nazis in Germany and Russia or about supporters of the National Rally in France, for instance. He cannot help pointing out that he was 'witnessing a slow decline, that the continent was looking backwards, dining out on a wrapped, sentimental view of itself' (207). Yet, the Afropeans seem to thrive on their multiple identities and contribute to enriching cultural forms.

This is most evident when he meets one of the inventors of the term Afropean in Brussels, the Belgian-Congolese singer Marie Daulne. While recounting her story, Marie as a mixed-race woman highlights that '[t]he work I do with Zap Mama brings two cultures together ... Neither one dominates. I take what I have as a European and what I have as an African' (92). In Daulne's story, Afropean becomes a metaphor of cultural encounters and blending, as Pitts declares:

> With this new cultural trajectory, a duality could be celebrated that peered optimistically forward and embraced plurality. It was a place where cultures came together rather than being ripped apart, and where a conscious choice was made to use the power of these two histories in a positive, creative way, rather than dwelling on past tragedies. Daulne's art wasn't about forgetting, more about weaving the cultures into her being in a way that would prevent self-combustion. (92)

Similarly, the story of a hybrid family of Ulli and Ayellet Helmstetter living in Berlin with their adopted daughter Shira Helmstetter inspires the author to understand members of disparate cultures living together in transcultural spaces. Ulli is a white German man married to Ayellet, a Jewish-Israeli woman, both of whom decide to adopt Shira from Kenya after living there for a while and before choosing Berlin their home; to the author, Shira 'the most personified this powerfully global vibe the Helmstetter were giving off' (198).

As he meets such people, he maintains that the term Afropean may embody a complicated, integrated form of blackness in Europe that refused to be bogged down by stereotypes while also refusing to deny its brownness and plurality; the Afropean as a teller of transgressive stories, hybrid histories and complicated cultural allegiances like those so embedded in the personal histories of Pushkin and Abram Gannibal (268).

Notably, Afropean indicates cultural complexity as an outcome of centuries-old historical encounters between Europe and Africa. As Pitts cites Claude McKay's words that '[c]learly, the journeys that need to be made are mental ones' (293), the writing process seems to be a manifestation of the author's travelling imagination. His mental journeys materialize into a new Black identity in Britain, which is not apologetic of its 'impurity' but rather is eager to celebrate it. Pitts is convinced that '[t]here is also no reason for immigrants to think what they are bringing with their own culture can't enrich Europe' (226), making him believe that 'black Europe must be more unified than ever if it is to save its communities from implosion' (263). Pitts observes:

> The future of Europe depends on transparency – governments should clearly state how Europe benefits from diversity, open up and admit when the financial sector has failed society, teach colonial history with nuance and honesty and face up to the past so we can all understand the present and move towards a truly unified future, the potential of which I saw in the eyes and smile of little Shira Helmstetter. (204)

It is interesting for the reader to know that the author does find his Afropea in Marseille which he calls 'métis' or mix: 'a mongrel of a metropolis' (315). What fascinates him about Marseille is not only the fact that it seems to be 'a place of rebellion' (317) but 'its geographical location in Europe' and 'its intrinsic connection to other cultures' (320).

Marseille is 'not a melting pot but a transcultural tagine, the separate ingredients having soaked up the same North African spices, sitting under the same roof' (329). Pitts elaborates that Marseille 'had a bit of Harlem in the 20s, Sheffield in the 90s, splashes of Rio and Marrakech, with Arabic, Italian, Corsican, African and French culture intertwined in the lifestyle' (336). The reader feels as if the author has arrived at his final destination and that Afropea is no longer an imaginary homeland: 'I'd felt I'd found a physical embodiment of Afropea … in Marseille I had found a place I could exist in Europe without any questions of belonging. I knew immediately that I'd found an Afropean Mecca that I would one day return to and make my home' (336). Consequently, unlike Caryl Phillips, Pitts seems more positive and optimistic about the future of Europe as a place of disparate cultural transactions, which are transforming Europe (Schulze-Engler 2013: 685).

Pitts is convinced at the close of his journey in Lisbon that the two continents – Africa and Europe – do share a proximity as continents to which he 'felt most connected' (2019: 380). So, having completed his travels, Pitts deduces, '[t]hese scattered fragments of Afropean experience had formed a mosaic inside my mind, not monolithic, but not entirely amorphous either; rather, the Afropean reality was a bricolage of blackness and I'd experienced an Africa that was both *in* and *of* Europe' (380; emphasis in the original). Indeed, the book demonstrates that the journey to render voice to Afropean is a process, as the book is now part of a larger network, including a website, Afropean.com, which constitutes an important and fast-growing resource for Afropean communities to share their stories, cultures, histories and identities. Thus, the book as a transmedial narrative initiates the ongoing dialogue among Afropeans of diverse origins and becomes a potent medium of transcultural communication.

Conclusion: 'Building bridges, Creating connections'

Just as Caryl Phillips sets out to 'build bridges and dig tunnels between … continents' (Hållén 2014: 7) in his travel books, particularly *The Atlantic Sound* (2000), so does Pitts in his travel text *Afropean* as a sequel of Phillips's travelogue *The European Tribe* (1987; Efoui-Delplanque 2022: 206–39). While rethinking and rewriting European culture and history in his travel book, Pitts suggests alternative ways of comprehending and communicating the image of the New Europe as well as the New Europeans. Through rendering his travelogue as a hybrid genre, Pitts aims to embrace diversity and heterogeneity of societies and cultures of Africa that 'through the mobilities generated by migration, commerce, and communication – has long since become entangled with the "Global North"' (Gremels et al. 2022: 16). Hence, *Afropean* not only maps the personal odyssey of Pitts as a travel writer between cultures and continents, but also sheds light on the fraught relationship and ambivalent cartographies of Europe and Africa, which have been in contact with each other for centuries.

Indeed, *Afropean* as a striking example of Black European travel genre becomes a rich terrain for the representation and development of transcultural reality. The travelogue, having been produced in a transnational space, travels beyond borders literally and metaphorically, enriching our understanding of transculturality. The many journeys of Pitts through different European metropolitan cities, documented in his narrative, resonate with the 'many worlds of Anglophone writing', which demonstrates the dynamics of our interconnected yet conflict-ridden era. Significantly, Pitts's travelogue as a potent vehicle of 'mobile lives' (Elliott and Urry 2009), captured in mobile stories cutting across the neat and clean borders of culture and nation, not only draw our attention to reading 'other' cultures from a broader vantage point but also to experience the so-called cultural exoticism not in a distant geography but next door in the age of global networks of cultures. As the travelogue mixes the author's own views into the interviews he conducts during his journeys through different parts of Europe, the reader gains insights into the new cultural compositions today, as Europe and African criss-cross in multiple ways such as in music, photography, mixed-race couples or children, or simply bilingual Afropean with dual citizenship.

Pitts draws our attention to the fact that in the face of globalization in which travel and mobility are the most prominent features, we are compelled to think beyond the binary opposition of 'primitive' and 'modern', 'self' and 'other' as well as 'home' and 'abroad', for we tend to exist and move in a globally interlinked network of cultures. These networks require us to develop transcultural competence and awareness to communicate effectively in a variety of social setups. Certainly, transcultural communication takes place in different media, but in the medium of twenty-first-century travel writing, it engages with creating connections between cultures and its members in a highly innovative manner in an increasingly globalized world in which a new approach to culture has emerged, particularly suited to exploring hybridity of individual and collective identities. It is with the tool of transcultural communication, as documented in Pitts's travelogue, that we can accept as well as define diversity, 'disjuncture and differences in the global cultural economy' (Appadurai 1996: 27–47) and above all think beyond the idea of 'othering cultures'. In other words, transcultural communication within the frames of Pitt's travel text orients us not only to appreciate pluralism in the world, which is indeed the new normal, but also recognize its significance in the different domains of modern existence. In short, it is flows and fusions, transgression and translation, and flux and fluidity, as delineated in *Afropeans*, that define the condition of both culture and communication in our 'runaway world' (Giddens 1999).

References

Adams, P. G. (1983), *Travel Literature and the Evolution of the Novel*, Kentucky: University Press of Kentucky.

Aguiar, M., C. Mathieson and L. Pearce (2019), 'Introduction: Mobilities, Literatures, Culture', in M. Aguiar, C. Mathieson and L. Pearce (eds), *Mobilities, Literature, Culture*, 1–31, Cham: Palgrave Macmillan.

Ahmed, L. (1999), *A Border Passage: From Cairo to America – A Woman's Journey*, New York: Farrar, Straus & Giroux.

Appadurai, A. (1996), *Modernity at Large: Cultural Dimensions of Globalization*, Minneapolis: University of Minnesota Press.

Ascari. M. (2011), *Literature of the Global Age: A Critical Study of Transcultural Narratives*, Jefferson, NC: McFarland.

Bal, M. (2002), *Travelling Concepts in the Humanities: A Rough Guide*, Green College Lectures, Toronto: University of Toronto Press.

Beck, U. (2006), *Cosmopolitan Vision*, trans. Ciaran Cronin, Cambridge: Polity Press.

Berry, E. and M. Epstein (1999), *Transcultural Experiments: Russian and American Models of Creative Communication*, New York: Palgrave.

Bhabha, H. K. (1994), *The Location of Culture*, London: Routledge.

Boehmer, E. (2020), 'Talking Afropean: Johny Pitts in Conversation with Elleke Boehmer and Simukai Chigudu', *Writers Make World*, YouTube (accessed 20 October 2022).

Bond, L. and J. Rapson (eds) (2014), *The Transcultural Turn: Interrogating Memory between and beyond Borders*, Berlin: De Gruyter.

Boochani, B. (2018), *No Friends but the Mountains: Writing from Manus Prison*, London: Picador.

Butt, N. (2015), *Transcultural Memory and Globalised Modernity in Contemporary Indo-English Novels*, Berlin: De Gruyter.

Butt, N. (2021), 'Cosmopolitan Travellers in a "Deterritorialized" World: Transcultural Encounters in Pico Iyer's *The Global Soul: Jet Lag, Shopping Malls, and the Search for Home* (2000)', in *Prose Studies: History, Theory, Criticism*, 331–48.

Clifford, J. (1989), 'Notes on Travel and Theory', *Inscriptions* 5. Available online: http://humwww.ucsc.edu/CultStudies/PUBS/Inscriptions/vol_5/clifford.html (accessed 21 November 2022).

Clifford, J. (1992), 'Traveling Cultures', in L. Grossberg, C. Nelson and P. A. Treichler (eds), *Cultural Studies*, 96–116, New York: Routledge.

Clifford, J. (1997), *Routes: Travel and Translation in the Late Twentieth Century*, Cambridge, MA: Harvard University Press.

Cohen, R. (1997), *Global Diasporas: An Introduction*, London: UCL Press.

Cronin, M. (2000), *Across the Lines: Travel, Language, Translation*, Cork: Cork University Press.

Dagnino, A. (2012), 'Transcultural Writers and Transcultural Literature in the Age of Global Modernity', *Transnational Literature* 4 (2): 1–14.

Dagnino, A. (2013), 'Global Mobility, Transcultural Literature, and Multiple Modes of Modernity', *Journal of Transcultural Studies* 4 (2): 130–60.

Dagnino, A. (2015), *Transcultural Writers and Novels in the Age of Global Modernity*, Indiana: Purdue Press.

Doff, S. and F. Schulze-Engler (2011), 'Beyond "Other" Cultures: An Introduction', S. Doff and F. Schulze-Engler (eds), *Beyond 'Other' Cultures: Transcultural Perspectives on Teaching the New Literatures in English*, 1–16, Trier: WVT.

Doff, S. (2009), 'Inter- and/or Transcultural Learning in the Foreign Language Classroom? Theoretical Foundations and Practical Implications', in F. Schulze-Engler and S. Helff (eds), *Transcultural English Studies*, 357–72, Amsterdam: Rodopi.

Dupuis, G. (2008), 'Transculturalism and Écritures Migrantes', in R. M. Nischik (ed.), *History of Literature in Canada: English-Canadian and French-Canadian*, 497–508, Rochester: Camden House.

Efoui-Delplanque, R. (2022), 'Towards Afropean Perspectives: Evolving and Conversing Afro-European Narratives from *The European Tribe* (1987) to *Afropean: Notes from Black Europe* (2019)', N. Butt, R. Clarke and T. Krampe (eds), Special Issue 'Rethinking Postcolonial Europe: Moving Identities, Changing Subjectivities', *Postcolonial Interventions* 7 (1): 206–39. doi: https://doi.org/10.5281/zenodo.6069702 (accessed 15 November 2022).

Eisenstadt, S. N. (2000), 'Multiple Modernities', *Daedalus. JSTOR* 129 (1): 1–29. http://www.jstor.org/stable/20027613 (accessed 19 July 2023).

Elliott, A., and J. Urry (2009), *Mobile Lives*, London: Routledge.

Epstein, M. (2009), 'Transculture: A Broad Way between Globalism and Multiculturalism', *American Journal of Economics and Sociology* 68 (1): 327–51.

Erll, A. (2011), 'Travelling Memory', *Parallax* 17 (4): 4–18. doi: 10.1080/13534645.2011.605570 (accessed 20 June 2022).

Ette, O. (2003), *Literature on the Move*, trans. K. Vester, Amsterdam: Rodopi.

Fukuyama, F. (1992), *The End of History and the Last Man*, London: Free Press.

Ghosh, A. (2002), *The Iman and the Indian*, New York: Viking Press.

Giddens, A. (1999), *Runaway World: How Globalization Is Shaping Our Lives*, London: Profile Books.

Gilroy, P. (1993), *The Black Atlantic: Modernity and Double Consciousness*, London: Verso.

Glover, J. and H. L. Friedman (2015), *Transcultural Competence: Navigating Cultural Differences in the Global Community*, Washington, DC: American Psychological Association.

Grant, C. (30 May 2019), 'Afropean by Johny Pitts: Review – Black Europe from the Street Up', *The Guardian*. Available online: https://www.theguardian.com/books/2019/may/30/afropean-by-johny-pitts-review (accessed 30 October 2022).

Graulund, R. and J. D. Edwards (2012), *Mobility at Large: Globalization, Textuality and Innovative Travel Writing*, Liverpool: Liverpool University Press.

Gremels, A., M. Scheurer, F. Schulze-Engler and J. M. I. Wegner (eds) (2022), *Entanglements: Envisioning World Literature from the Global South*, Stuttgart: Ibidem.

Hållén, N. (2014), '"Okay, I am Going to Try This Now." An Interview with Caryl Phillips about *The Atlantic Sounds* and *The European Tribe*', *Journeys* 15 (2): 1–14, Berghahn Books. doi: 10.3167/jys.2014.150201 (accessed 20 January 2023).

Hannerz, U. (1996), *Transnational Connections: Culture, People, Places*, New York: Routledge.

Hepp, A. (2015), *Transcultural Communication*, Malden, MA: Wiley Blackwell.

Holland, P. and G. Huggan (1998), *Tourists with Typewriters: Critical Reflections on Contemporary Travel Writing*, Ann Arbor: University of Michigan Press.

Huggan, G. (2006), 'Derailing the "Trans"? Postcolonial Studies and the Negative Effects of Speed', in H. Antor (ed.), *Inter- und Transkulturelle Studien: Theoretische Grundlagen und interdisziplinäre Praxis*, 55–61, Heidelberg: Winter.

Huntington, S. P. (1996), *The Clash of Civilizations and the Remaking of World Order*, New York: Simon & Schuster.

Iyer, P. (2001), *The Global Soul: Jet Lag, Shopping Malls, and the Search for Home*, New York: Vintage.

Khair, T., M. Leer, J. D. Edwards and H. Ziadeh (eds) (2005), *Other Routes: 1500 Years of African and Asian Travel Writing*, Oxford: Signal.

Kloss, W. (ed.) (1998), *Across the Lines: Intertexuality and Transcultural Communication in the New Literatures in English*, Amsterdam: Rodopi.

Knowles, S. (2014), *Travel Writing and the Transnational Author*, London: Palgrave.

Lecoutteux, F. (11 December 2020), 'Review – Johny Pitts: *Afropean: Notes from Black Europe*', *New Peace*. Available online: https://peacenews.info/node/9723/johny-pitts-afropean-notes-black-europe (accessed 30 October 2022).

McIntyre-Mills, J. (2000), *Global Citizenship and Social Movements: Creating Transcultural Webs of Meaning for the New Millennium*, Amsterdam: Harwood Academic.

Milhouse, V. H., M. K. Asante and P. O. Nwosu (2001), 'Introduction', in V. H. Milhouse, M. K. Asante and P. O. Nwosu (eds), *Transcultural Realities: Interdisciplinary Perspectives on Cross-Cultural Relations*, ix–xx, London: Sage.

Naficy, H. (2007), 'Forward: On the Global Inter-, Multi- and Trans-', in A. Grossman and À. O'Brien (ed.) *Projecting Migration: Transcultural Documentary Practices*, xiii–xv, London: Wallflower Press.

Nayeri, D. (2020), *The Ungrateful Refugee: What Immigrants Never Tell You*, New York: Catapult.

Ong, A. (1999), *Flexible Citizenship: The Cultural Logics of Transnationality*, Durham, NC: Duke University Press.

Ortiz, F. ([1947] 1995), *Cuban Counterpoint: Tobacco and Sugar*, trans. Harriet de Onis, New York: Knopf.

Pennycook, A. (2007), *Global Englishes and Transcultural Flows*, New York: Routledge.

Pitts, Johny (2019), *Afropean: Notes from Black Europe*, Allen Lane: Penguin.

Pratt, M. L. (1992), *Imperial Eyes: Travel Writing and Transculturation*, London: Routledge.

Said, E. W. (1983), 'Traveling Theory', in *The World, the Text, and the Critic*, 226–47, Cambridge, MA: Harvard University Press.

Said, E. W. (1993), *Culture and Imperialism*, London: Chatto & Windus.

Saro-Wiwa, N. (2012), *Looking for Transwonderland: Travels in Nigeria*, New York: Soft Skull Press.

Schulze-Engler, F. (2007), 'Theoretical Perspectives: From Postcolonialism to Transcultural World Literature', in L. Eckstein (ed.), *English Literatures across the Globe: A Companion*, 20–32. Paderborn: Fink.

Schulze-Engler, F. (2009), 'Transcultural Negotiations: Third Spaces in Modern Times', in K. Ikas and G. Wagner (eds), *Communicating in the Third Space*, 149–68, London: Routledge.

Schulze-Engler, F. (2013), 'Irritating Europe', in G. Huggan (ed.), *The Oxford Handbook of Postcolonial Studies*, 669–91, Oxford: Oxford University Press.

Schulze-Engler, F. (2019), 'Erkundungen einer dezentrierten Moderne: Transnationalität und Transkulturalität in anglofonen Literaturen', in D. Bischoff and S. Komfort-Hein (eds), *Handbuch Literatur und Transnationalität*, 366–83, Berlin: De Gruyter.

Schulze-Engler, F. and S. Helff (2009), 'Introduction', in F. Schulze.Engler and S. Helff (eds), *Transcultural English Studies: Theories, Fictions, Realities*, ix–xvi, Amsterdam: Rodopi.

Shames, G. W. (1997), *Transcultural Odysseys: The Evolving Global Consciousness*, Yarmouth: Intercultural Press.

Shehadeh, R. (2010), *A Rift in Time: Travels with My Ottoman Uncle*, London: Profile Books.

Strand, T. (2010), 'The Making of a New Cosmopolitanism', *Studies in Philosophy and Education* 29: 229–42.

Taylor, D. (1991), 'Transculturating Transculturation', *Performing Arts Journal* 13 (2): 90–104.

Tomas, D. (1996), *Transcultural Spaces and Transcultural Beings*, London: Routledge.

Volkmann, L. (2011), 'The Transcultural Moment in English as a Foreign Language', in S. Doff and F. Schulze-Engler (eds), *Beyond 'Other' Cultures: Transcultural Perspectives on Teaching the New Literatures in English*, 113–28, Trier: WVT.

Wainaina, B. (2011), *One Day I Will Write about This Place*, Minneapolis, MN: Graywolf Press.

Welsch, W. (1999), 'Transculturality: The Puzzling Form of Cultures Today', in M. Featherstone and S. Lash (eds), *Spaces of Culture: City, Nation, World*, 194–213, London: Sage.

Welsch, W. (2005). 'Auf dem Weg zu transkulturellen Gesellschaften', in L. Allolio-Näcke, B. Kalscheuer and A. Manzescke (eds), *Differenzen anders denken: Bausteine zu einer Kulturtheorie der Transdifferenz*, 314–41, Frankfurt am Main: Campus.

West-Pavlov, R. (ed.) (2005), *Transcultural Graffiti: Diasporic Writing and the Teaching of Literary Studies*, Amsterdam: Rodopi.

10

The transcultural imaginary: South Asian writing from Aotearoa New Zealand

Janet M. Wilson
University of Northampton

Tourists and visitors to Aotearoa New Zealand today are struck by the visibility of Pasifika/Māori cultures, with te reo spoken fluently on the airwaves, often referring to forms of Māori culture and self-determination like mātauranga Māori (traditional knowledge) and kaupapa (values and principles as basis for action). The media profiling of Māori voices and the Pasifika/Māori presence in areas ranging from fashion, sport, lifestyle, art, literature, film and popular music continues the reframing of New Zealand as Aotearoa. But the growth of ethnic and cultural diversity, due to a surge of migration from Asia and South Asia, is beginning to undo the bicultural framework as burgeoning immigrant communities signify their mixed cultural heritages through glocally oriented and ethnically inflected cultural production. These developments can be traced to the relaxing of the immigration policy in the late 1980s in order to open up the labour market to the global economy, as legislation of 1986–7 changed the preference from source country to skill-based immigration, leading to a new type of highly educated migrant. This chapter argues that immigration of Asians and South Asians to Aotearoa owns a distinctive history and has given rise to distinctive cultural groups whose literary texts actively invoke the phenomenon of the transcultural, one that reflects the immigrant experience.

For instance, the doubling in the number of Indian migrants between 1991 and 2001, leading to media claims of an INV-Asian and 'a problem' between 1993 and 1996, created what Butcher and Spoonley term a 'moral panic' (Butcher and Spoonley 2011: 102).[1] Asian migrants are now the largest migrant groups

---

[1] The play on words in INV-Asian draws on a popular trope that first appeared in the Australian cultural imagination: the threat of being overrun in an invasion from the north, following the Japanese bombing of Darwin in February 1942.

and today comprise 15.1 per cent of the total population.² Refugee migration that has officially favoured South Asian and Pacific nations with most coming from Bhutan, Sri Lanka and Myanmar has added to the ethnically and culturally diverse make-up. Asian and South Asian diaspora communities have expanded and diversified internally through their ethnic affiliations and heritages, and their cultural practices have become more visible in the public sphere, especially the Diwali festivals that feature the global genres of Bollywood dance and Bhangra performance alongside classical, folk and tribal dance and music (Bandyopadhyay 2006: 142–4; Booth 2018: 295–300). A global orientation also appears in the syncretic types of Kiwi Indian cultural production such as the widely acclaimed plays, both at home and overseas, of the Indian Ink Theatre Company.

The hybrid literary output of these migrant communities is still in a fledging state but gaining national exposure as indicated by *A Clear Dawn: New Asian Voices from Aotearoa New Zealand*, a landmark anthology of work by seventy-five emerging writers either Asian or of Asian descent, which indicates the global potential of contemporary New Zealand writing (Morris and Wong 2021). But although the Asian diasporas of Aotearoa New Zealand have received serious scholarly attention in the last two decades, the field of South Asian migrant writing remains underrepresented in critical discourse. Apart from an essay by Dieter Riemenschneider (2016) on the Indian diaspora and cultural production, it is only briefly discussed in recent socio-historical studies (Bandyopadhyay 2006: 145–6; Friesen 2014: 128–34). In examining the emergence of a new transcultural imaginary in New Zealand Aotearoa, this chapter is indebted to Frank Schulze-Engler's legacy in developing the concepts of transculturalism and transcultural theory, building on the work of Wolfgang Welsch and before him Ferdinand Ortiz.

In the current decolonial climate, both intercultural and transcultural frameworks can be used to examine representations in Asian and South Asian cultural production that are exploring the new spaces of diaspora, intersecting the national imaginary with global and transcultural perspectives, and the multiple subject positions in relation to the dominant Pākehā (white New Zealander) norm in New Zealand against which migrant communities continue to be judged. These transworld and transmigration patterns differentiate Asian writers, who are relatively unaffected by the nation's colonial past, from Māori writers as tangata whenua (people of the land or first people), whose historical

---

[2] An increase by 9.2 per cent in 2006. Māori count as 16.5 per cent ('2018 Census Place Summaries' n.d.).

and cultural ties to place (turangawaewae or place to stand), are key to their ethnic identity. These attachments often put homeland in tension with diasporic relocation and global movement in their work.[3] The South Asian migrants also differ ethnically, historically and culturally from migrants from former colonies in the Pacific (Niue, Tokelau, the Cook Islands and Western Samoa) and Fiji, source of a substantial Fiji Indian population that migrated after military coups in 1987 and 2000. Within the category Asian, the response to South Asian migrants from ex-British colonies has differed from that to Asian – specifically Chinese – subjects, who in New Zealand, as in Australia, have been stigmatized as alien, threatening or inferior.

The post-millennial South Asian literary production in Aotearoa New Zealand has a complex genealogy in relation to the postcolonial diaspora writing elsewhere that was influenced by Rushdie's narrative innovations and post-national positioning in *The Satanic Verses*.[4] Like Rushdie's and other forms of globally inflected migrant writing, it is concerned with multiple cultural interactions and world views. But until recently the relatively small numbers comprising the South Asian diasporas and their limited cultural production has meant that diasporic texts of the first generation exemplify this pre-Rushdie stage of the global literary tradition. Issues like racial discrimination and difference, the return home and the ambiguous pull of memory in the individual narrative are all filtered through the problematics of relocation. Such is the more intercultural orientation of the first novel of the Kiwi Indian diaspora, Mallika Krishnamurthy's *Six Yards of Silk* (2005).

In the post-millennial diaspora writing of the Asian and South Asian communities, however, especially that published after 2015, there is a greater complexity in representing these issues. Transcultural perspectives and transnational encounters appear in narrative modes that reflect and refract self-doubt and -reflexivity, represent cultural borders as fuzzy and indeterminate, show ambiguity about the nation-state as container of culture and recognize the text as part of a mobile literary system of production. These ambivalences can be related to the globalized modernity manifest in multi-local concepts of migration, a new spatial flexibility and global technological flows. The recent generation of highly educated, mobile and professional South Asian migrants acknowledges imaginary and virtual homelands which test the powers of

---

[3] For examples of this tension in recent stories by recent Māori writers, see Wilson (2020: 227–8).
[4] In *The Satanic Verses* (1988), Rushdie more decisively breaks with the concept of the nation-state as a container of culture than his earlier novel *Midnight's Children* (1981).

affiliation and memory. Similar states of alienation also appear in the writing of or about refugee and asylum seekers, even though this type principally responds to the pressure of forced migration in ways closer to intercultural writing, and exhibits traumatic memories, states of material and psychological precarity and a consciousness of cultural and ethnic difference.

This chapter examines the more globally inflected narrative modes emerging from the South Asian diaspora that reflect cultural overlap and exchange in the public sphere, and shifting perceptions of the homeland as it is reshaped and renegotiated within the new spaces of the diaspora. It identifies as fictional types two recent novels: *Sodden Downstream* by Branavan Gnanalingam (2017a), about a Tamil refugee family from Sri Lanka, resettled in Naenae near Lower Hutt, and *The Man Who Would Not See* by Rajorshi Chakraborti (2018), about an Indian writer living in Wellington, who is visited by his half-brother from India.[5] These novels can be mapped onto a continuum between intercultural and transcultural concepts that relates to the class, casteist, socioeconomic and political identities of their protagonists. They also reflect contrasting patterns of migration: Refugees from the Civil War in Sri Lanka, on the one hand, and Indian migrants of high economic and professional status, evidence of India's rising economic power, on the other. Such differences affecting identity processes and intercultural exchange are deployed in their distinctive narratologies, although both novels thematically resemble all first-generation diaspora writing: the subject's dislocation in the new space of diaspora, the tensions between past and present homes and homelands.

Interculturalism is based on a binary concept of different cultures – as between Global North and South or European and indigenous – of cultures conceived as singular, distinct and contrastive (Fischer-Lichte 1996: 39). Transculturalism, by contrast, moves away from models of dichotomies, essential difference and incommensurality, of cultures as self-contained entities and linked to a single nation-state, seeing them, instead, as permeable, 'enmeshed webs of cultural relations that extend within and beyond the nation state' (Gilsenan Nordin et al. 2013: x), and as involving cultural processes that are entangled, conflictual and fractured. This differentiation helps distinguish the transnationalism of the South Asian cultural production from that of Māori artists whose work is celebrated as representing New Zealand Aotearoa (as in the Venice Biennale and in European galleries and venues) and whose taonga (highly prized objects)

---

[5] Both were listed for the Ockham New Zealand Book Awards. Gnanalingam's novel was fiction finalist in 2018; Chakraborti's was long listed in 2019.

are being returned from overseas. Multi-located exchanges can open up to the transcultural in indigenous cultural production, but its national/Pacific origins and identity are in no doubt in contrast to the greater deterritorialization of much South Asian art and writing in New Zealand.

The post- or supra-national understanding of culture that underpins transculturalism came to prominence in the work of Cuban theorist Fernando Ortiz, who argued in the 1940s that the transformative interactions between cultures are a way of linking nations of uneven powers; it was revitalized in the work of German critic Wolfgang Welsch (1999) and then by Frank Schulze-Engler (2009), who moved decisively away from concepts of the nation as a bounded entity and container of culture. Used to describe modes of identity formation within cultural interfaces, transculturalism replaces monocultural or multicultural concepts that are now considered as insufficient to describe present conditions. As Sissy Helff claims, transculturality, by contrast to the intercultural, depends on a modernized outlook and contemporary globalized homeworlds, and as the product of 'new transnational social spaces and transcultural identities' has a distinctive narrative self-reflexivity (2013: 31). Both interculturalism and transculturalism, therefore, can be linked to particular phases and kinds of diasporic un/belonging in the negotiation of new identities across multiple categories of the evolving globalized sphere.[6]

In this chapter, *Sodden Downstream* is identified as predominantly intercultural in its differentiations between Sri Lankan and New Zealand homeland spaces, white settler majority and ethnic minority, neoliberal and subaltern perspectives. Focused on the precarity of the refugee protagonist as she struggles through a tropical storm and meets other marginal figures in New Zealand society, the novel's representation of her sense of disempowerment, reinforced by her employer's attitude, might be considered in relation to Judith Butler's definition of precarity as consisting of 'a heightened sense of expendability or disposability that is differentially distributed throughout society' (2011: 3). The story focuses on asymmetrical power relations in society; exclusions from white middle-class heteronormativity due to race, homelessness, delinquency or crime; it implies that social inequality can be resisted by a collective subaltern consciousness reinforced by acts of kindness and sharing and united by condemnations of state and corporate indifference or neglect. The storm throws

---

[6] Interculturalism is associated with the nationalist phase, following the independence of many colonial nations in the latter half of the twentieth century, while transculturalism distinguishes 'cultural areas rather than nations' (Pavis 1996: 5, 6).

disparate characters together with a unifying effect and illustrates Butler's point about human interdependence, that people's 'survival is always dependent on what we might call a social network of hands' (2009: 14): For the refugee protagonist's exposure to the struggles of others induces a sense of community belonging and eventually encourages her 'transcultural' relocation.

The Man Who Would Not See, by contrast, is probably the first example of evolved transcultural fiction produced by the New Zealand Indian diaspora. From the outset it introduces transnational perceptions due to enhanced mobility, the loss of national distinctions and the blurring of borders between old and new homelands. In particular, it exhibits the mode of what Sissy Helf calls 'transcultural narrative unreliability' involving an unreliable narrator,[7] a transnational protagonist whose identity is marked by self-reflexivity and doubt, and a metafictional dimension in the overlapping storylines that intersect its diasporic and national locations. The novel culminates in multiple inflected reconfigurations of home and belonging because the extended family transcends national boundaries.

Despite the socioeconomic differences between their protagonists and their social contexts, the novels share narrative tropes of the individual's entanglement in phenomenological and cultural processes and both point to a rooted potentiality: The tropical storm of *Sodden Downstream* obliterates the landscape and blurs perceptions, projecting the refugee protagonist's sense of dislocation, including asynchronous memories of the Civil War, and enabling a reassessment of her migrant identity. By contrast, the Wellington-based Indian protagonist of *The Man Who Would Not See,* who is accused by his half-brother of ignoring his family in India, becomes associated with the trope of sight loss and fuzzy vision; images of 'not seeing' persuade him that he needs moral reconstitution; the destabilizing of his diasporic locatedness includes deconstruction of his position as narrator. Yet, as in *Sodden Downstream*, unravelling these confusions results in identity reconstruction and a more sedentary and rooted perception of homeland belonging. Such images of disorientation and the implied quest for 'home' in both novels can be read in terms of 'multiple diasporic locations of culture' and the blurring of borders that deterritorialize or decentre the nation-state, dissolve its boundaries and call into question the concept of national cultures (Schulze-Engler 2009: xi).

---

[7] To Helff, the transcultural novel moves between transcultural and intercultural spaces and contains one of the following features: 'first if the narrator and/or the narrative challenge the collective identity of a particular community; second, if experience of border-crossing and transnational identity characterise the narrator's life world; and third, if traditional concepts of home are disputed' (2013: 33).

Reading this diasporic writing heuristically through the lens of transculturalism with its reconfigurations of space and mobility invites revisionary perspectives of different theories of diaspora: The rooted concept of home that is an end point of both texts recalls William Safran's theory of exile, nostalgic longing, and return to the ancestral homeland (1991); yet both novels represent 'grounded' belonging as a subjective realization, dependent on categories of inclusion and exclusion. In *Sodden Downstream* is a relativizing of the new world of the diaspora and the Sri Lanka homeland, while in *The Man Who Would Not See*, the protagonist's renovated belonging to the Indian homeland is sustainable only through continuous movement. In her theorizing of the contested borders of diasporic space, Avtar Brah claims that the 'ideology of return' (2003: 614–15) pertains to all diasporas in keeping with her view of the diasporic journey as about setting down roots elsewhere, and 'the lived experience of a locality' (1995: 192). Brah argues that diasporas are about relational positioning and intersecting 'modalities of gender, race, class, region, language and generation' (618); but her deconstruction of 'discourses of fixed origins, while taking account of a "homing desire" which is not the same as a desire for a "homeland"' (2003: 614–15) does not explicitly extend to contested concepts of home, such as being split between localities, or the reterritorializing implications of the return. This chapter investigates the role of the return in the diaspora space alongside the transcultural negotiation of multiple states of belonging, the subjective states of ambiguity and uncertainty that are traceable to conflicted exchanges in both the original homeland and diaspora. These include the testing of home as a mythic place of desire – Rushdie's 'imaginary homelands and Indias of the mind' (1991: 10) – against the material reality in order to recover rootedness and by that means to construct a homeland in diaspora.

Both novels exhibit in different degrees the 'ambiguities of identities shaped by multiple cultural experiences' (Jacklin 2016: 514), recognition of cultural differences, the finding of common ground between cultures and the individual's discovery of the foreigner within 'in order to be able to comprehend others' (Gilsenan Nordin et al. 2013: x), which are associated with transcultural writing.[8] This comparative analysis aims to identify these novels' analogous representations of the disjunctive world views and temporalities of first-generation migrants from India and Sri Lanka as evidence of an emerging transcultural imaginary of Aotearoa New Zealand.

---

[8] The transcultural novel as defined by Helff (2013) and Dagnino (2015) is a specialized category. Other critics take a broader approach, drawing on the field of transculturalism or identifying a transcultural quality in negotiating new identities across multiple categories: for example, Bekers et al. (2009), Moslund (2010), Ertler and Loschnigg (2004), Kuorti (2014) and Moura-Kocoglu (2011).

Sodden Downstream: Subjectivity and solidarity

Sodden Downstream can be read in the context of the Sri Lankan diaspora in New Zealand, small by comparison to the Indian and Chinese ones, but growing rapidly in the aftermath of the Civil War.[9] As well as referring to a storm's dissolution of outlines and boundaries, the title implies being washed away and is a metaphor for the protagonist's disorientated subjectivity. The story concerns Sita, a Hindu Tamil refugee who lives with her out-of-work husband, Thiru, and son, Satish, scraping by on her meagre income as a contract cleaner. Alienated in New Zealand and constantly remembering her homeland, she is burdened by her refugee past. A sudden tropical cyclone interrupts her journey into Wellington to undertake a work shift, yet her contact with other stranded travellers and motorists from a range of ethnic and social backgrounds involves amicable, conversational exchanges that eventually move her to acknowledge her own suppressed traumatic experiences. But notably her shift to an expanded understanding of alterity does not assume the self-reflexiveness or cultural entanglement found in *The Man Who Would Not See*.

The fact that social and ethnic barriers dissolve in a recognition of shared liminality, encouraging Sita to overcome her abject subjectivity, suggests that such exchanges can be read as a form of cosmopolitanism from below, or as types of the rooted or vernacular cosmopolitanism promoted by Ulrich Beck, Homi K. Bhabha or Anthony Appiah. Thus, cosmopolitan perspectives enable the novel to move away from intercultural relations through the individual transformations associated with transculturalism's utopian potential, regardless of class, caste or social status: As Welsch argues, 'transcultural identities comprehend a cosmopolitan side but also a side of local affiliation' (1999: 205).

Sodden Downstream has a heterodiegetic narration representing a single consciousness that moves between the present moment and memories of the Sri Lankan past, as well as in dialogue with other subjects, both middle-class and professional, such as a prosperous Tamil migrant woman who gives Sita a lift or her son Satish's school teacher, as well as precarious and abject, like many characters she encounters on her journey. The temporal variation in the narrative mode reflects Sita's ambivalence about the material benefits of being resettled in Naenae for more than a year, partly due to her ongoing personal discomfort. The traces of past abuse intrude into her present reality as the buried trauma

---

[9] Migration has doubled from 8313 migrants in 2006 to 16,830 in 2018, when the total number of Asian migrants was 707,598 ('2018 Ethnic Group Summaries: Sri Lankan', *Statistics New Zealand*).

of atrocities suffered in the Civil War, in which her family was suspected of belonging to the Tamil Tigers, threatens to overwhelm her. The fraught legacy of '[t]he past: like a rotting wardrobe that was strapped to her back' (Gnanalingam 2017a: 17) dominates her subaltern female subjectivity, represented through a spatial imagery of dislocation as she struggles along on her journey. Giving birth in a war zone has caused gynaecological problems for which she awaits an operation, resulting in barrenness and preventing marital intimacy; shrapnel is lodged in her arm and thigh. The broken body of the refugee, it is implied, symbolizes her imperfect fit into the national structure. As narrative focalizer, Sita sees her abjection symbolized by the stigma of 'cleaning other people's shit' (10), which causes her obsession with cleanliness, and implies identification with the Dalits, the Indian caste that undertakes such tasks. The ineliminable traces that contact with human defecation causes are conveyed in a metaphor of circulating contamination: 'The smells couldn't be washed from her skin and her clothes. It was as if the smells from Manik had travelled over the Indian ocean ... and deposited themselves in her Naenae flat' (10).

Yet, as a New Zealand citizen with entitlements and rights, her existential experience in the new country separates her from the illegal refugees or asylum seekers of other fictions such as Sanjeev Sahota's Indians hiding out in Manchester in their first year in the UK in *The Year of the Runaways* (2016), or the group of African incomers in Jenny Erpenbeck's novel *Go, Went, Gone* (2018), who move to Berlin in search of work but are eventually sent back to Italy. Despite her discomfort at not belonging, citizenship invokes her gratitude at being taken in, a wish 'to repay New Zealand' (Gnanalingam 2017a: 27).

The novel exhibits some self-reflexivity in the linking of inner and outer disturbance, and imaging the duration of the refugee's suffering through her prolonged journey on foot. Sita's ambivalence and disorientation gain external representation in the turbulence caused by Cyclone Evelyn which hits the Kapiti Coast with hazardous wind gusts and lashing heavy rain, causing a public transport emergency. As she sets out for a night shift in Wellington, chaos and disorder occur: With trains no longer running, and roads closed by floods and traffic jams, she embarks on a circular and haphazard journey through the saturated waterlogged landscape. Her being rerouted from train to bus to road involves encounters with marginal figures of different ethnicities who represent New Zealand's heterogeneous society: A Samoan university student on his way home joins her, and two Māori motorists hospitably offer lifts and invite them home. Their nocturnal conversations encompass issues like racial discrimination (the offer made by a Māori mechanic to help a stranded motorist is rejected) and a fear of migrants competing for local jobs (Gnanalingam 2017a: 92). The Māori/Pasifika with homes to go to are located in a symbolic imaginary of homeland belonging, in contrast to the homelessness of Pākehā fringe travellers: a sex worker, a recently released prisoner hitching to Tokoroa in search of work, a homeless man living in his car who empathizes with Sita's adverse working conditions: 'Fucking cleaning companies. Someone has to crack down on behalf of cleaners' (83), a delinquent teenage boy under police suspicion to whom she tries to 'impart wisdom' when he asks whether there is a God, and feels 'proud' that she had made the effort (120). These socially overlooked figures constitute a local precariat, and the picaresque narrative repeatedly emphasizes precarity as a valid alternative to mainstream perspectives, hence heightening the intercultural division that comprises the novel's moral economy.

The loosening of social and ethnic boundaries on the 21.7 km journey from Naenae to Wellington encourages a more self-reflexive cosmopolitanism in which Sita comes to understand difference as located, mutually informing and relational: That is, she not only ascribes difference to the Other, but also recognizes herself as different (Delanty 2009: 129–30) in unexpected ways. In negotiating her subject position among these marginal figures by finding commonalities with them, she mobilizes a more transcultural perspective. The related tropes of the stranger and the unexpected or strange encounter inform this cosmopolitan approach to alterity that, according to Ulrich Beck, 'essentially means recognition of otherness…differences are neither ranged in a hierarchy nor dissolved into universality, but are accepted' (2006: 67). This recalls Wolfgang Welsch's comment on the interdependence of cultures, that nothing is '*absolutely foreign*' (2009: 7; emphasis in the original), because transculturality requires 'attentiveness to what might be common and connective whenever we encounter things foreign' (1999: 201). The sharing of adverse conditions creates affinities between all the travellers who identify themselves through their sociopolitical circumstances and locations; the othered stranger becomes the cosmopolitan stranger as 'embedded and embodied perspectives that take [the subject's] actual situated location as starting point' (Braidotti et al. 2013: 4) are adopted.

In most of Sita's encounters common ground is found in the shared historical and sporting relations between New Zealand and Sri Lanka. Although her country of origin is little known to her fellow travellers, most of them recall the Sri Lankan cricket team and its star player, Kumar Sangakkara (Gnanalingam 2017a: 61, 35, 84, 124). The global appeal of cricket with its superheroes, therefore, plays a mediating role in opening up what Shemana Cassim calls a 'transnational space of belonging' (2017: 112–13), in which Sita might begin 'to feel at home in the new country' (103). That cricket represents a symbolic attachment to her homeland is suggested by her memory of the Tamil star, Ramalingam Rohit while the future offered by the game is implied by Satish's teacher who is excited by her son's great potential as a cricketer. This new space is 'transformative' (Cassim 2017: 152) both in its linking of cultures and in kindling her hopes for the future: potentially by offering Satish the opportunity to 'become a Kiwi' (Gnanalingam 2017a: 163), to share in New Zealand's sports nationalism and national pride.

These reorienting perceptions catalyse Sita's memories of the atrocities she suffered in Sri Lanka in the final stage of her journey when she walks for two hours along State Highway 2 to Wellington's Central Business District: the murder of family members, her mother killed by shrapnel before her eyes in a refugee camp in Manik in the last days of the war when Satish was a baby, suffering starvation, bombardment and narrowly escaping death. She revises her traumatized subjectivity, in which 'anything that resembled confidence, ambition or self-belief' (Gnanalingam 2017a: 163) was destroyed and faces her abjection by drawing on her new hope for her child's future. Rethinking her past and future by overcoming her earlier determination to forget includes reassessing the public meaning of home, because for all Sri Lankan Tamils the 'homeland' disappeared at the end of the Civil War (Gnanalingam: 2017b: n.p.) and thus lost its diasporic promise as the mythic place of desire. Sita's reflections on the ANZAC commemorations of those New Zealanders who fell in two world wars at first dwell on her alienation from national narratives. She sees stories of sacrifice in Sri Lanka as having been used cynically for political gain in the Civil War, and this encourages her perception that her own suffering cannot be understood within the surviving national context, just as 'she would remain rootless no matter where she stood' (Gnanalingam 2017a: 163).[10] Sita's intercultural perception of the limits of nation-based thinking stresses the need for more globalized narratives, and her negotiation of a subject position involves dismissing the reductive nationalism of global and civil wars or official memorializations. Her journey concludes in establishing a transcultural understanding of home and belonging that comprehends both New Zealand and Sri Lanka national imaginaries, but also moving beyond them.

[10] On the failure to bring Sri Lanka to justice at the International Criminal Court for crimes against humanity and acts of genocide, see the interview with R. Cheran, a Tamil poet living in Canada (2021: 84–5).

Reinforcing the novel's intercultural/transcultural overlap is Sita's self-reconstitution as a precarious subject as she articulates her negativity about the neoliberal institutions and welfare organizations that manage her existence: Politicians who don't give 'a shit for people like her' (Gnanalingam 2017a: 147), and her employer who dismissively patronizes her. In the workplace she is stereotypically represented as one of those disadvantaged 'women, immigrants, people of colour … with a troubled relation to the national state' (Sassen 2007: 125). Her contract offers no securities and she is racialized by her employer, Poleman, who calls her Paddy, an easy-to-remember name he associates with foreign workers. The compensatory $5.00 food voucher he hands out because of her exhausting, protracted journey she passes on to a homeless man who earlier had advised her, 'don't ever let them make you feel grateful' (Gnanalingam 2017a: 172). This self-empowering act also distances her, by implication, from other humiliations: State inspections of the family dwelling by Housing New Zealand and oversight of the family expenditure by the Works and Income manager.

The conclusion rewrites these earlier understandings of home by emphasizing her changed subjectivity in giving away the $5.00 gift voucher, a gesture indicative of a more self-reflexive cosmopolitanism about possession and forms of belonging. The image of the homeless man, a reminder of her former abject life in the Sri Lankan refugee camp, informs her final realization of arrival: 'She was home. … Even if her roots were growing in the dust, she was home' (Gnanalingam 2017a: 178). In making the transition from one subject position to another, of having rerouted through 'a lived sense of locality' (Brah 1995: 192), her provisional homecoming as an 'undecidable belonging' provides space for future negotiation (Dagnino 2015: 203) and some possibility of rootedness.

The Man Who Would Not See: Creating fictional worlds

By contrast to *Sodden Downstream*, a title which points to a catastrophic weather event that in the story elides social and ethnic differences through an intercultural perspective, *The Man Who Would Not See*, with its connotation of blindness and blurred vision, evokes the self-delusion and unreliability of the transcultural novel. The protagonist, Abhay, a middle-class Indian living in Wellington with a Kiwi wife, Lena, a university lecturer, and their four-year-old daughter, is the author of five novels, and this professional identity informs the novel's emphasis on artifice and invention and the intriguing parallel between the contrasts of blindness and sight and the reframing of the 'real' as the 'imaginary'. His half-brother, Ashim, is partly an alter ego. Abhay considers Ashim to be controlling his perception of reality by making provocative statements about his metaphorical blindness, namely his amnesia about his Indian family following his transnational relocation in New Zealand. Their sibling rivalry is played out in the contexts of globalized modernity: the fragmentation of world views in diaspora, the virtual reality of mobile technologies, the unpredictability of memory. In terms of narrative strategy, the metafictional play, juggling facts and the fiction-making process, depends on their entangled identities. In addition is the elision of author and protagonist, for Rajorshi Chakraborti is also an educated, established writer (of five novels in 2018) and a multilocational South Asian diasporan, having arrived in New Zealand from university study in Scotland and Canada (Abhay studied in Edinburgh) after leaving India. These overlapping identities create a textual consciousness about fiction's relationship to reality, about novels as personal and cultural capital, and the global circulation of the diaspora writer's texts as world literature.

The transnational representations of human disorder in *The Man Who Would Not See* – unreliable truths, interrupted plans, changed directions – framed by the guiding metaphor of sightlessness, can be contrasted to the psychic disorientation and confusion about travel routes caused by weather phenomena in *Sodden Downstream*. Chakraborti's novel opens with Ashim's visit to Wellington and, in conversation with Abhay, his version of the breakup of the family home in 1988 following an incident when, as children, they got lost near Howrah Station, Calcutta, and were blamed by their father (Baba) for causing distress. Baba peremptorily separated his three offspring, sending Ashim and his sister, Didi (children of his first wife), to Hazaribargh, while Abhay (the younger son of his second marriage) remained in the family home in Calcutta. Ashim's 'historic grievance' (Chakraborti 2018: 240) at this early injustice leads him to accuse Abhay of manipulating the situation because having '*your house*, and *your father back all to yourself was just too tempting*' (54; emphases in the original).

The political struggle between Self and Other, of inclusion and exclusion in the diaspora space that this encounter dramatizes, are manifested in the destabilizing of Abhay's experience and subjectivity; as Ashim's intervention implies that not only is belonging 'a contested state', as Caryl Phillips asserts (2002: 6), but given the 'warping distance' from which diaspora subjects view the homeland, it has to be revalued (Stierstorfer 2018: 257). Despite his outrage and incredulity at his brother's accusation, Abhay indulges in an 'odyssey of guilt'

(57) and assumes the guise of unreliability. The contested diaspora space is now complicated by the 'bizarre situation' that Sissy Helff associates with transcultural fiction – a questionable view of the world caused by self-doubt (2013: 32), here due to the accusations of 'naivetée' and 'unbelievable blindness' (Chakraborti 2018: 161). Believing Ashim's statement that their sister, Didi, has committed suicide, Abhay moves out of his family home, embarks on an 'atonement plan' and 'self-reform' (240). and begins writing a novel about that branch of the family he has ignored for over twenty years. From here on reality and narrative begin to blur as imagination and the process of writing become an individual social practice (Helff 2013: 35). This also involves a revaluation of reality when, following Ashim's return to India, Abhay then makes a surprise visit to him and his family in Hazaribargh apparently to check him out.

Chakraborti projects his hero's inner turbulence – self-doubt mixed with creativity – through a polyphonic narrative technique in which Abhay and his wife, Lena, as alternating first-person narrators with intersecting yet colliding points of view, speculate on the disconcerting alterity and epistemological difference in Ashim's behaviour in Wellington: his concern for the underdog in supporting a Muslim woman who is being persecuted on a bus, despite the fact that he avoids Muslims socially; his unexplained disappearance as their guest; his sharing of confidences with an elderly Indian friend and neighbour; his favouring of superstitious, pre-colonial rites that Abhay labels as voodoo and black magic, all of which challenge and override the national and ethnic differences associated with intercultural writing. They react differently to Ashim's insistence that Abhay's privileged lifestyle, 'airbrushed of misfortune' (Chakraborti 2018: 62), is unfairly due to his early good fortune to remain in the family home, a claim that initially shocks Lena. Ashim's reported voice creates further doubt and confusion. Not privy to the brothers' exchanges, Lena shifts in her loyalties, saying first that Abhay must 'pay the penance for the rosiness of his life' (57), yet later deciding that Ashim is 'full of poison' (75), telling her husband that his brother 'is cutting you off from your family' (199).

Through these techniques the reader comes to see that Abhay's doubt and guilt and consequent narrative unreliability are functioning as a creative springboard.[11] The novel also associates unreliability with the fragmenting of reality due to transnational movement, and Chakraborti exploits the uncertainty of identity and memory gaps to create an atmosphere of mystery and confusion. Both brothers mislead the reader: Ashim's version of reality is always suspect

---

[11] For the argument that contemporary fictive representations of fallibility echo a social norm, in that 'subjectivity and unreliability are accepted as realities and reliability is regarded as an impossibility', see Zerwick (2001: 170–1, qtd in Helff 2013: 46).

because, as Abhay realizes, it is tactical, designed to lure him back to India. Abhay constructs a new persona as unreliable and guilty, following his theatrical self-accusations that he had perfected the 'art of ignoring' due to 'the family habit of looking away' (Chakraborti 2018: 111, 131), choosing 'smoothness' by living in the West, being supported in his writing by his wife (190), and then using the bizarre situation catalysed by his half-brother as grounds for a new fiction. Finally, given the protagonist-author elision, it seems likely that Rajorshi Chakraborti is teasing the reader about his motives in writing the story.

After Abhay returns to India, 'the concept of "territory", as well as its signifiers and significations' are further destabilized as the focus moves to the world of the text (Brah 2003: 626), when the brothers compete to claim fictional powers: The initial plot of fraternal friction is overlaid by the act of storytelling and metafictional allusions that emphasize the constructedness of the text. Ashim confesses he had lied about their sister's death (she is in fact living in an ashram) in order to offer Abhay an 'irresistible real life plot twist to see what you would do with it' (Chakraborti 2018: 232). Abhay in turn images him as Machiavellian, 'cagey, slippery and downright untrustworthy' (296-7), through intertextual allusions to Patricia Highsmith's Tom Ripley with his 'cold-blooded talent at manipulating others' (238), as analogous to 'a monster egoist' and 'psychopath' (238-9). He then fictionalizes his surprise visit to India as a 'breaking story' (289), one that allows him to participate in Ashim's 'unbelievable performance, a reality show' (284) and to say in collusion: 'I was in it for nothing more than the chance of a sensational book' (233) in which his brother's family would feature (271). Narrative unreliability, therefore, foregrounds Abhay's self-reflexive response to Ashim whose life in Hazaribargh becomes new grounds for storytelling, making Ashim an authorial alter ego. Their overlap as creators and inventors appears in Abhay's perception of a 'pattern of being manipulated' (273), asking: 'Is it entirely my misconception that Dada [Ashim] selects, frames, edits what I see?' (274). His accolade to Ashim, that he is 'the conductor of people [and] an artist ... far greater than you'll ever be' (284) further blurs fraternal identities around the issues of authorial control and manipulation.

Abhay's somewhat implausible rationale for writing a new fiction – to memorialize a (fictitiously) dead sister and 'atone' for the omissions of the past – exposes his performance of mental disturbance and disoriented reality as part of an authorial strategy. Furthermore, framing the novel's fictive space with the reference to its conditions of distribution and readerships, in particular, the cosmopolitan production hubs and global circulation associated with world literature (Damrosch 2003), suggest that Chakraborti the author is articulating a professional dilemma through his proxy the narrator: Abhay's complaint about his books being out of print (Chakraborti 2018: 209) and his diasporic sense of being 'cut off from my professional dreams' (62), because his work is not local enough for the New Zealand market yet lacks circulation in India, has propelled him to expand his fictional scope. The author's lack of access to professional networks exemplifies Rebecca Walkowitz's comment about the marginalization in the market place of migrant writers 'who now participate in a literary system that is different from the system in which they were born, educated, or first published', one that may be inhospitable, for in fact they 'may not fit comfortably into any system' (Walkowitz 2006: 533).

Chakraborti's concern with geographical remoteness revitalizes from a transnational perspective an issue much debated by New Zealand writers throughout the twentieth century: namely that local marketing preferences and the country's distance from cosmopolitan centres in the Global North limited the publishing and marketing of their work.[12] But the protagonist's problematic perception of his Indian past is also an authorial manoeuvre to draw attention to this issue as he 'repatriates' his writing to potential new audiences in India. In any event Abhay reshapes his discourse of blame and guilt and, ever the opportunist, he reframes his brother as 'a lifesaver', the 'flawed messenger who roused me to this journey' (Chakraborti 2018: 227) and inspired 'the subject for my dream book, the one that promised to be the making of me' (65): that is, a transcultural text with appeal to diverse readerships and markets. Unreliability, a catalyst for fiction, enables his protagonist's rediscovery of original belonging and expands the novel's storyworlds and hence its scope.

These oscillations between location and dislocation in Abhay's positioning as a diasporic returnee to India, that from the beginning have determined the novel's 'politics of location' (Brah 2003: 628), begin to stabilize as knowledge of the Hazaribargh family emerges. The irrational attitudes and outrageous accusations that Ashim evinced on his visit to Wellington are reinterpreted in the domestic context, where his homemaking practices show another side: the family's prosperity, his wife Moushimi's successful garden plant business and their care of the missing sister's children. These make Abhay realize his misjudgement, and he experiences the multilingual and cross-cultural perceptions that Emily Hicks associates with border writing and the textual strategy of translation (Hicks 1991, qtd in Brah 2003: 628). In the storyworld, this is anchored to the

---

[12] On this problematic, see Williams (2003), and in relation to transcultural migrant writers, see Thomsen (2008: 62).

psycho-social dimension of the homeland return. Abhay's cultural translation , according to Christine Vogt-Williams, involves, 'a new form of self-perception through a merging of selected cultural aspects whereby lost or nonexistent abilities and convictions and thus a sense of balance can be regained' (2009: 314). India comes to represent a cluster of values that he had previously ignored: 'a primeval and psychological rootedness, perhaps even stability, authenticity and … spirituality' (Vogt-Williams 2009: 314). As Abhay revises his opinion about what is fake or authentic, embracing the 'authenticity' of his nephew, Jhappi, who can perform without faking it, and changing his mind about consulting a tantric astrologer in order to challenge Ashim's 'superstitious' practices, about which he had been sceptical in New Zealand, he relocates into Indian society. Noting that 'the "exiled" half of the family' (Chakraborti 2018: 293–4) – that is, those living in Hazaribargh – live in the rooted way, Abhay discovers a more foundational concept of home in extended family communality, one that enriches and redefines his privileged but remote diasporic life, even though this is sustainable only by continued exchange and travel.

In the family reunion at the end, therefore, Abhay's realignment of his national and family boundaries illustrates the 'increasingly connected life worlds' of the transcultural novel (Helff 2009: 81). The transition from an uprooted Kiwi-Indian identity to a multi-locally located one confirms the value of extended family ties and justifies Abhay's writing of a novel about his entanglement with Ashim and the enmeshing of Kiwi–Indian cultures. The transcultural conception of home is expressed in Lena's email that he receives as he sets out to return to Wellington: 'come home – next time we're all going home together to Hazaribargh' (Chakraborti 2018: 334).

Conclusion: The transcultural imaginary

Despite their differences in class, ethnicity, gender and nation, and despite their disparate narrative strategies, *Sodden Downstream* and *The Man Who Would Not See* can be aligned through tropes of disturbance. These image the ambiguities arising from fragmented familial or cultural affiliations as boundaries dissolve and require reconfiguration. They confirm Welsch's view that the identity formations triggered by new types of cultural contact and networks involve the integration of 'components of different cultural origin' that do not comply 'with geographical or national stipulations' (1999: 204). Notable are their cathartic, affective conclusions in which the confusions and contradictions about belonging coalesce in imaginings of homespace as multilayered and fluidly identifiable both within and beyond the nation. *Sodden Downstream* demonstrates that minority cultures can extend and reshape understanding of what is familiar or strange within the national space, while *The Man Who Would Not See* features a metafictional struggle with the text's transnational content, a decentred image of the nation and a transcultural imaginary. In both novels, consciousness about the constructedness of the text can be attributed to a 'transpatriation' process, a distancing from the cultural and homeland borders in which new forms of creativity emerge through the transcultural lens (Dagnino 2015: 203).

The fictional imaginings of alternative homeworlds and modernities with distinctive practices and lifestyles in these and other fictions by South Asian writers in New Zealand Aotearoa, like the international best-selling Fijian Indian Nalini Singh, the Malaysian Tamil Sugu Pillay and the writers represented in *A Clear Dawn*, suggest that contemporary images of the nation as a social, political and cultural category and container of culture represent a false unity. The country's postcolonial bicultural identity belies its complex ethnic diversity as the national imaginary opens up to multiple global and transcultural revisionings. To this extent the respatializing of world spheres in *Sodden Downstream* and *The Man Who Would Not See* creates interventions into familiar collectivities just as it affirms new solidarities. These fictions and others that inconsistently identify with the spaces of New Zealand show that the South Asian communities in their anti-essentialist transculturalism differ from Māori notions of cultural exchange that are marked by a greater national rootedness. In drawing on experiences of migration and transnational travel, they are establishing a new direction for creative production.[13]

References

'2018 Census Place Summaries' (n.d.), *Statistics New Zealand*. Available online: https://www.stats.govt.nz/tools/2018-census-place-summaries/new-zealand (accessed 26 October 2022).

'2018 Ethnic Group Summaries: Sri Lankan' (n.d.), *Statistics New Zealand*. Available online: https://www.stats.govt.nz/tools/2018-census-ethnic-group-summaries/sri-lankan (accessed 26 October 2022).

---

[13] I would like to thank Anna Smith and other friends who have commented on a draft of this chapter, and the editors of this volume for their helpful suggestions.

Bandyopadhyay, S. (2006), 'Reimagining Indian Identity in Multicultural New Zealand', in H. Johnson and B. Moloughney (eds), *Asia in the Making of New Zealand*, 125–46, Auckland: Auckland University Press.

Bandyopadhyay, S. and J. Buckingham (2018), 'Introduction', in S. Bandyopadhyay and J. Buckingham (eds), *Indians and the Antipodes: Networks, Boundaries and Circulation*, 1–15, Oxford: Oxford University Press.

Beck, U. (2006), *The Cosmopolitan Vision*, trans. C. Cronin, Malden, MA: Polity.

Bekers, E., S. Helff and D. Merola (eds) (2009), *Transcultural Modernities: Narrating Africa in Europe*, Amsterdam: Rodopi.

Booth, A. (2018), 'Negotiating Indianness: Auckland's Shifting Cultural Festivities', in S. Bandyopadhyay and J. Buckingham (eds), *Indians and the Antipodes: Networks, Boundaries and Circulation*, 278–303, Oxford: Oxford University Press.

Brah, A. (1995), *Cartographies of Diaspora*, London: Routledge.

Brah, A. (2003), 'Diaspora, Border and Transnational Identities', in R. Lewis and S. Mills (eds), *Feminist Postcolonial Theory: A Reader*, 613–34, Edinburgh: Edinburgh University Press.

Braidotti, R., B. Blaagaard and P. Hanafin (2013), 'Introduction', in R. Braidotti, B. Blaagaard and P. Hanafin (eds), *After Cosmopolitanism*, 1–7, London: Routledge.

Butcher, A. and P. Spoonley (2011), 'Inv-Asian: Print Media Constructions of Asians and Asian Immigration', in P. Voci and J. Leckie (eds), *Localizing Asia in Aotearoa*, 98–115, Wellington: Dunmore.

Butler J. (2009), *Frames of War: When Is Life Grievable*, London: Verso.

Butler, J. (2011), 'For and Against Precarity', *Tidal Occupy Theory* 1: 12–13.

Cassim, S. (2017), 'Oceans Away: Sri Lankan Migrants in New Zealand. An Exploration of Hybrid Identities, Distance and Everyday Material Practices', PhD thesis, University of Waikato. Available online: https://researchcommons.waikato.ac.nz/handle/10289/11188.

Chakraborti, R. (2018), *The Man Who Would Not See*, Wellington: Penguin Random House New Zealand.

Cheran, R. (2021), 'Poetry as Resistance: R. Cheran in Conversation with Aparna Halpé', in C. Lokuge and C. Ringrose (eds), *Creative Lives: Interviews with Contemporary South-Asian Diaspora Writers*, 74–91, Stuttgart: Ibidem.

Dagnino, A. (2015), *Transcultural Writers and Novels in an Age of Global Mobility*, West Lafayette: Purdue University Press.

Damrosch, D. (2003), *What Is World Literature?* Princeton, NJ: Princeton University Press.

Delanty, G. (2009), *The Cosmopolitan Imagination*, Cambridge: Cambridge University Press.

Erpenbeck, J. (2018), *Go, Went, Gone*, trans. Susan Bernofsky, London: Portobello Books.

Ertler, K.-D. and M. Loschnigg (eds) (2004), *Canada in the Sign of Migration and Trans-Culturalism: From Multi- to Trans-Culturalism*, Frankfurt am Main: Peter Lang.

Fisher-Lichte, E. (1996), 'Interculturalism in Contemporary Theatre', in P. Pavis (ed.), *The Intercultural Performance Reader*, 27–40, London: Routledge.

Friesen, W. (2014), 'The Indian Diaspora in New Zealand: Identities and Cultural Representations', in O. P. Dwivedi (ed.), *Tracing the New Indian Diaspora*, 121–36, Amsterdam: Rodopi.

Gilsenan Nordin, I., J. Hansen and C. Zamorano Llena (2013), 'Introduction: Conceptualising Transculturality in Literature', in I. Gilsenan Nordin, J. Hansen and C. Zamorano Llena (eds), *Transcultural Identities in Contemporary Literature*, ix–xxv, Leiden: Rodopi.

Gnanalingam, B. (2017a), *Sodden Downstream*, Wellington: Lawrence & Gibson.

Gnanalingam, B. (1 October 2017b), 'Interview with Lyn Freeman', *Standing Room Only, Radio New Zealand*. Available online: https://www.rnz.co.nz/audio/player?audio_id=201860709 (accessed 26 October 2022).

Helff, S. (2009), 'Shifting Perspectives – The Transcultural Novel', in F. Schulze-Engler and S. Helff (eds), *Transcultural English Studies: Theories, Fictions, Realities*, 75–91, Amsterdam: Rodopi.

Helff, S. (2013), *Unreliable Truths. Transcultural Homeworlds in Indian Women's Fiction of the Diaspora*, Amsterdam: Rodopi.

Hicks, E. (1991), *Border Writing: The Multidimensional Text*, Minneapolis: University of Minnesota Press.

Jacklin, M. (2016), 'Review of *Transcultural Writers and Novels in the Age of Global Mobility* by Arianna Dagnino', *Studies in the Novel* 48 (4): 513–15.

Krishnamurthy, M. (2005), *Six Yards of Silk*, Wellington: Steele Roberts.

Kuorti, J. (ed.) (2014), *Transculturalism and Aesthetics: Ambivalence, Power and Aesthetics*, New York: Rodopi.

Morris, P. and A. Wong (2021), 'Introduction', in P. Morris and A. Wong (eds), *New Asian Voices from Aotearoa New Zealand*, 1–10, Auckland: Auckland University Press.

Moslund, S. P. (2010), *Migration Literature and Hybridity: The Different Speeds of Transcultural Change*, New York: Macmillan.

Moura-Kocoglu, M. (2011), *Narrating Indigenous Modernities: Transcultural Dimensions in Contemporary Māori Literature*, Leiden: Brill.

Ortiz, F. ([1940] 1975), *Cuban Counterpoints: Tobacco and Sugar*, Durham, NC: Duke University Press.

Pavis, P. (1996), 'Introduction: Towards a Theory of Interculturalism in Theatre?', in P. Pavis (ed.), *The Intercultural Performance Reader*, 1–26, London: Routledge.

Phillips, C. (2002), *A New World Order: Essays*, New York: Vintage International.

Riemenschneider, D. (2016), 'The Persistence and Creation of Internal Borders: India in Aotearoa New Zealand', *Gentle Round the Curves: Selected Essays on Indian Writing in English*, 154–66. Heidelberg: Tranzlit.

Rushdie, S. (1981), *Midnight's Children*, London: Jonathan Cape.

Rushdie, S. (1988), *The Satanic Verses*, London: Viking Penguin.

Rushdie, S. (1991), 'Imaginary Homelands', in *Imaginary Homelands: Essays and Criticism 1981–1991*, 9–21, London: Granta.

Safran, W. (1991), 'Diasporas in Modern Societies: Myths of Homeland', *Diaspora* 1 (1): 83–99.

Sahota, S. (2016), *The Year of the Runaways*, London: Picador.

Sassen, S. (2007), *A Sociology of Globalization*, New York: Norton.

Schulze-Engler, F. (2009), 'Introduction', in F. Schulze-Engler and S. Helff (eds), *Transcultural English Studies: Theories, Fictions, Realities*, ix–xvi, Amsterdam: Rodopi.

Stierstorfer, K. (2018), 'Introduction to "Home and Belonging"', in Klaus Stierstorfer and Janet Wilson (eds), *The Routledge Diaspora Studies Reader*, 255–7, Abingdon: Routledge.

Thomsen, M. R. (2008), *Mapping World Literature: International Canonization and Transnational Literatures*, London: Continuum.

Vogt-Williams, C. (2009), 'Routes to the Roots – Transcultural Ramifications in *Bombay Talkie*', in F. Schulze-Engler and S. Helff (eds), *Transcultural English Studies: Theories, Fictions, Realities*, 309–22, Amsterdam: Rodopi.

Walkowitz, R. (2006), 'The Location of Literature: The Transnational Book and the Migrant Writer'. Special Issue, 'Immigrant Writers: Contemporary Literature in an Age of Globalization', ed. Rebecca Walkowitz, *Contemporary Literature* 47 (4) (Winter): 527–47.

Welsch, W. (1999), 'Transculturality: The Puzzling Form of Cultures Today', in M. Featherstone and S. Lash (eds), *Spaces of Culture: City, Nation, World*, 194–213, London: Sage.

Welsch, W. (2009), 'On the Acquisition and Possession of Commonalties', in F. Schulze-Engler and S. Helff (eds), *Transcultural English Studies: Theories, Fictions, Realities*, 3–36, Amsterdam: Rodopi.

Williams, M. (ed.) (2003), *Writing at the Edge of the Universe: Essays from the 'Creative Writing in New Zealand' Conference, University of Canterbury*. Christchurch: Canterbury University Press.

Wilson, J. M. (2020), 'From National to Global: Writing and Translating the New Zealand Short Story', in P. Fresno-Calleja and J. M. Wilson (eds), *Beyond Borders: New Zealand Literature in the Global Marketplace*, 71–86, Abingdon: Routledge.

Zerwick, B. (2001), 'Historicizing Unreliable Narration: Unreliability and Cultural Discourse in Narrative Fiction', *Style* 35 (1): 151–77.

11

Passages to India: Jewish exiles between privilege and persecution

Flora Veit-Wild
Humboldt University Berlin

'Every story is a travel story,' writes Michel de Certeau famously (1988: 387). Vice versa, every travel writes a story.[1]

In this chapter I am trying to read two stories written by travels my grandparents, Victor and Luise (Lulu) von Leyden, undertook across the Indian Ocean, in 1909 and 1939, respectively. The two journeys took place under very different circumstances. In January 1909, as a young married couple with three children, they set off on a one-year tour around the world. They travelled to Egypt, the Sudan, Ceylon, Japan, Java, China and India. Thirty years later, in March 1939, they crossed the Indian Ocean again. This time they were forced out of Nazi Germany because of their Jewish roots.

Crossing the oceans entails the germ of transcultural experiences. The travellers of my story cannot be said to have been 'mixing' with or 'permeating' the foreign cultures they encountered – this is the definition of transcultural by Wolfgang Welsch (2009: 6–7). And yet their story adds a nuance from aside to the 'Many Worlds of Anglophone Literature'; it resists the usual division of (post) colonial versus Western, subaltern versus privileged and highlights the intricate ways in which history shapes the encounter with foreign worlds. Cosmopolitans with Jewish roots, they were affluent enough to travel the world and open-minded enough to transverse cultures and converse with their proponents. Yet, in their own country they were segregated and persecuted. In my reading

---

[1] 'The journey is universally recognized as a narrative in our culture' (Mikkonen 2007: 286). For the widely discussed narratological interlinking of text and space ('spatial turn'), see Bieger and Maruo-Schröder (2016).

I will explore how my grandparents' travel stories counterpoise each other, how historical fate turns the one into a ghastly mirror of the other.

'A passage to India' – in the literal and the metaphorical sense – entails the liminality of in-betweenness, another aspect linked to the transversal nature of my grandparents' travels. Like the protagonists in E. M. Forster's novel, the travellers are inhabited by the melancholy of not-belonging, and, as I will show in detail, of disrupted communication with the home they left behind, of gaps and silences, and the anguish of being separated from those they left behind.

Furthermore, my grandparents' is also a story of travelling texts in the real material sense, of letters that seemed to vanish 'into thin air'; a journal of exile and separation with first glances through a transcultural window.

Lastly, this chapter writes my own travel story:

> If transnational or transcultural memory brings multiple disparate histories together under one critical umbrella, it does so not only across geographical space, but time too. (Ford 2015: 2)

As I dig into the transgenerational memory of my family, I am travelling across geographical space and a time span of over a century. On this, my own journey, I will encounter unexpected discoveries and will be left to marvel about all that remains hidden (see Figure 11.1).

Letters into the air

'Meine geliebten Kinder,' Marie von Leyden writes on 29 January 1909,

> es ist eine ganze Weile vergangen seitdem ich Euch geschrieben habe, es hat aber etwas so Unbefriedigendes – in die Luft zu schreiben – so ungewiß und ohne Echo. Ich hatte Euch schon nach Port Said durch den Agenten der Lloyd telegraphiert, die Depesche hat er Euch wie es scheint nicht ausgehändigt.[2]
>
> Beloved children, it's been a while since I wrote to you, but I find there's something so unsatisfactory about it – writing into thin air – so uncertain and without echo. I sent a telegram to you in Port Said, through the Lloyd's agent, but apparently, they didn't give it to you.

---

[2] All translations, unless otherwise indicated, are by Flora Veit-Wild, with the assistance of Lucie Velterop von Leyden.

Jewish Exiles between Privilege and Persecution 257

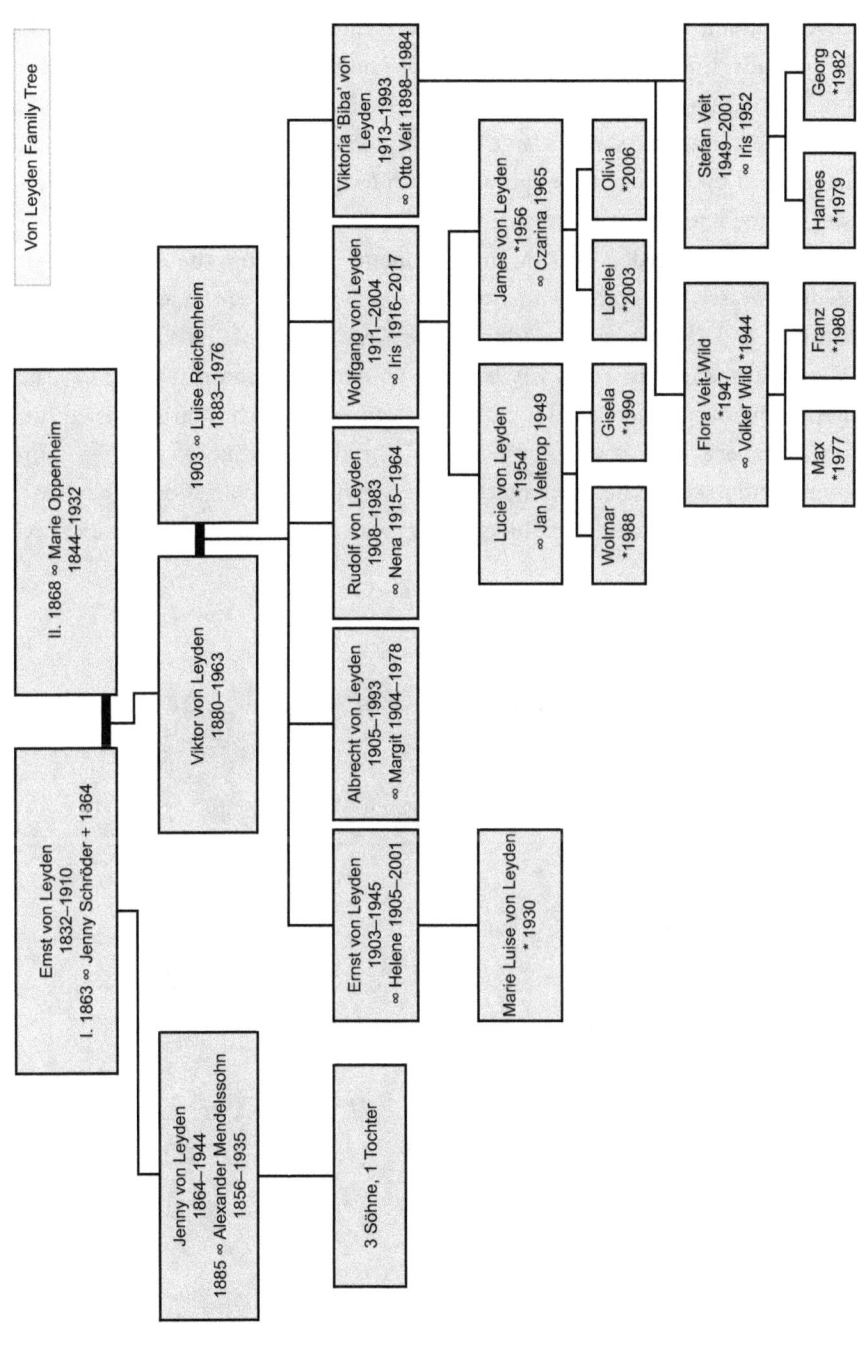

Figure 11.1 The von Leyden family tree.

I see my great-grandmother seated at her writing desk, upright in her brocade covered chair, heavy curtains framing the window, piles of letters under the lamp shade, thick volumes of antique books on the wooden side tables, rows of books lined up on the shelves behind her, leather-bound and gold-rimmed. In the corner, on a brass stand, a large rotating globe. I wonder how often she would have stood up to look at the spinning earth to follow the tracks of her beloved son, Victor, and his wife, Lulu (see Figure 11.2).

Marie von Leyden was a busy woman, managing the large villa in Bendlerstrasse, Tiergarten, the quarter of Berlin where many prominent families had taken residence during the *Gründerzeit* of the German Reich. Marie's husband, Ernst von Leyden, was an eminent authority at the Charité, Berlin's medical school, and a pioneer in cancer research. Marie assisted him in his paperwork, his appointments and the daily routine of life. Yet, more importantly, she had her own multitude of activities and obligations. Apart from entertaining at her salon and dinner parties with up 200 guests, she was an active

Figure 11.2 'Oil portrait of Marie van Leyden.' Courtesy of Lucie Velterop von Leyden, The Hague.

campaigner in the reform movement for women; she founded the first Women's Club in Germany and, at the side of Helene Lange, organized *Gymnasialkurse* (secondary school classes) for girls (Salomon 2019).

The year 1909 must have been particularly demanding for her – emotionally and practically. Victor, born in 1880 after twelve years of childless marriage, and his, wife Lulu (b. 1883), had decided to set out on a one-year tour around the world. Victor had taken leave for that period from the Prussian government, for whom he worked as a junior legal administrator (*Regierungsassessor*), declaring it a study trip to examine the British colonial administration in India (Weiß 2000: 159–60).

Hardly imaginable for us today, the young couple left their three first-born children, aged five, three and four months, behind, in the loving care of their grandmother and two nannies. No wonder Marie's long letters were full of anxiety as to when and if at all her letters and telegrams would reach the travellers. In these letters she reported meticulously about the boys' well-being, especially the baby's – how much weight he had put on; how his diet was changing from milk only to *Apfelzwieback* (rusk with apple); that his first tooth had appeared, and so on. Sometimes she seemed almost overwhelmed with the responsibility she had been given: for instance, when the three-year-old had to have an eye operation and she had to make the decision for the surgery without prior consent of the parents.[3]

However, although the eighteen letters that have found their way, over space and time, into my hands, are to the largest extent filled with everyday nursery reports, they provide me with an, albeit skimpy, outline of my grandparents' trip – against the void left to the imagination about what the letters crossing the Indian Ocean from the *other* side will have contained.

> Die Berichte interessieren uns natürlich ungemein und Luchen [Lulu] schildert so anschaulich und lebendig daß ich die Farbenpracht vor mir sehe und die ersten großartigen Eindrücke mitempfinde (13 Feb).[4]
>
> We find your reports of great interest of course, and Luchen's [Lulu] descriptions are so vivid and lively that I can see the splendour in front of me and live through those magnificent first impressions with you.

---

[3] I remember very well that my uncle Albrecht wore thick glasses and one of his eyes looked sideways. Maybe his second eye did not undergo surgery?
[4] All letter dates, if not stated otherwise, refer to 1909.

While it is a great loss that none of these letters seems to have survived, I am grateful to my grandmother Lulu for keeping all the letters she received from her mother-in-law.[5]

Travelling texts: The envelopes

The most tangible sources of the 1909 tour, legendary in our family lore, are the envelopes. As I see them lined up on my desk, I read them as texts that have travelled alongside my grandparents across water and land. Most of the letters were readdressed multiple times, forwarded from one destination to the next. Displaying my great-grandmother's attempts to keep up with the travellers' movements across the globe, they speak of time and space and speed.

> Meine Geliebten, Es ist so trostlos nicht zu wissen ob unsere Briefe schließlich doch noch in Eure Hände gelangt sind. Daß die Ceyloner Post Euch nicht rechtzeitig erreicht hat ist verwunderlich, daß aber die Briefe direkt nach Peking an die Deutsche Gesandschaft gerichtet von Euch nicht vorgefunden wurden bleibt ganz unbegreiflich. (10 July, sent to Singapore)
>
> My beloved, I feel so miserable not knowing if our letters have finally reached you. How strange that the Ceylon post did not get to you in time; but that you also didn't receive the letters addressed directly to the German embassy in Beijing, is really quite incomprehensible.

Through their different layers of stamps, postmarks and recipients' addresses written by different hands, different pens, in different colours (see Figure 11.3), the envelopes represent palimpsests that give us clues about the route these early international tourists took – they draw a line on the map that Marie, at home, had put up on the wall of her grandchildren's room: 'In dem Spielzimmer hängt jetzt eine große Weltkarte auf der wir Euch verfolgen, Böckchen [nickname of first-born] mit dem größten Interesse und der lebhaftesten Wißbegierde' (21 Jan). ['We are following you on a large map of the world, which now hangs in the playroom. Böckchen [nickname of first-born] is greatly interested, so acutely curious about every detail.'] The last layer of these palimpsests are numbers, added by the sender or the recipient, I presume, to keep some order in that protracted correspondence across time and space.

---

[5] The letters I possess and started to transcribe from my great-grandmother's attractive handwriting in Kurrentschrift (current font), range from 1901, the year of Victor and Lulu's engagement, to 1923.

Figure 11.3 Envelopes of letters sent by Marie von Leyden to the travellers of 1909.

Travelling objects: Hunting trophies and precious objects

My grandparents' house in Partenkirchen, where my brother and I and also our cousins from England used to spend our holidays, was full of material traces of their early world tour. I vividly remember a tall bronze crane (from Japan or China) stretching its long neck up gracefully by the fireplace. Easter eggs could be hidden in the invisible hollow under its wings. A spice jar made of delicate china,[6] in rich colours, stood nearby; and, on the mantelpiece, a Chinese bronze lion sitting on a richly ornamented base; it weighs heavy in my hand when, more than a century later, I lift it up from my piano, its latest habitat.

In her letter of 10 July, Marie acknowledges the arrival of some of those 'travelling objects' but without specifying what they were:

> Dann ist aus Ceylon die Sendung mit den diversen Gegenständen angekommen, wie mir scheint vollkommen intakt, wenigstens schreibt Carl der sie ausgepackt

---

[6] Made in the nineteenth century according to my cousin James von Leyden, who owns the jar now.

> hat nichts von Zerbrochenem, die Jagdbeute aus Ceylon ist noch nicht da. Die Straußfedern von Luchen sind sehr schön geworden.
>
> The consignment with various items has now arrived from Ceylon. It seems perfectly intact, at least Carl who unpacked it, hasn't mentioned any broken items. The hunted loot from Ceylon hasn't arrived yet. Luchen's ostrich feathers turned out to be very pretty.

More childhood memories are evoked when I read about the hunting trophies my great-grandmother had to deal with. The walls of the house in Partenkirchen were full of stuffed animal heads and mounted horns. I presume some were also from the trip to Asia:

> Daß noch ein Büffel zu den Ceyloner Jagdtrophäen kommt ist ja herrlich, es sollen auch sehr bösartige Biester sein. (21 April)
>
> It's wonderful that a buffalo has been added to the Ceylon hunting trophies. They are said to be very vicious beasts.
>
> Daß die Sudanbeute gut angekommen ist, berichtete ich schon. Die Tiere sind in Schwerin beim Präparator, der sich ihrer wie es scheint mit großem Interesse annimmt. ... Hoffentlich werden die Viecher alle nach Wunsch greaten. (22 July)
>
> I've already reported that the Sudan booty arrived safely. The animals are with the taxidermist in Schwerin, who seems to be taking great interest in them. (…) Hopefully the creatures will all turn out as wished.

I wonder whether Marie was happy having to deal with what she called 'Viecher' and 'Biester', and what she thought about her son's hunting sprees in those far-away lands.

Colonial cosmopolitans

'Das Kaiserreich: Verreisen als Privileg', Hasso Spode headlines his blog for Deutsches Historisches Museum:

> Es war die Goldene Zeit des Elitetourismus. (…) [R]iesige Kreuzfahrtschiffe, führend war hier die Hapag, befuhren die Meere von Samoa bis Spitzbergen. Problemlos ließ sich aber auch auf eigene Faust verreisen: Grenzen spielten keine Rolle, Pass- und Visumszwang waren weithin abgeschafft, per Telegraph ließ sich die Suite im Grand Hotel buchen. (Spode n.d.)[7]

---

[7] For details, see also Prein (2005).

The German Empire: Travelling as privilege. – It was the golden age of elite tourism. ... Huge cruise ships, with Hapag leading the way, sailed the seas from Samoa to Spitsbergen. At the same time, it was also possible to travel on your own without problems: borders were irrelevant, passport and visa requirements had been largely abolished and the suite in the Grand Hotel could be booked by telegraph.

The Leydens grew up in cosmopolitan families.[8] For them it was easy to travel on their own initiative – 'auf eigene Faust' as Spode puts it in his article. They had the financial means, spoke English and French, and their families had a wide network of social connections: diplomats, people in politics, arts and science. Ernst von Leyden's medical reputation made him be consulted by high-ranking politicians and monarchs (see E. Leyden 1910). He also got to know prominent colleagues from other countries, some of whom Marie mentions in her letters:

> Von Hermann Weber hatte ich einen Brief, er ist nicht mehr Botschaftsarzt, kennt Wolff Metternich wenig, hat ihm aber geschrieben, er schickte mir auch seine Karte für W.M. falls ich sie benutzen wollte. (3 February)[9]
>
> I had a letter from Hermann Weber, he's no longer the embassy doctor and he doesn't know Wolff Metternich well, but he still wrote to him. He also sent me his card for W.M. in case I need to use it.

In his *Lebenserinnerungen* (memoirs), Ernst von Leyden talks about 'the great joy' of getting to know 'Sir Hermann Weber aus London, einen lieben Kollegen, der, Deutscher von Geburt, in der englischen Metropole zu den gesuchtesten und bedeutendsten Aerzten der vornehmen Gesellschaftskreise gehört' (E. Leyden 1910: 143). ['Sir Hermann Weber from London, a dear colleague; German-born, he belongs to the most sought-after and eminent high-society doctors in the English metropolis.'] The two colleagues met in Pontresina in the Engadin, a prominent place for making or renewing acquaintances. The Leydens spent large parts of their summers there, residing at the renowned Hotel Saratz, where two floors were always reserved for them.[10]

The young Leydens will certainly have travelled in style. I imagine them embarking in Bremen; a handsome couple, Lulu with her slender neck and full

---

[8] The Oppenheims, Marie von Leyden's family, were bankers and art collectors, with ties to the main trading points of the time from Berlin and Hamburg to London. The Reichenheims, Luise's family, had obtained their wealth as factory owners in the textile industry which was closely connected to the British weavers. Cf. Herz (1936); 'Benoit Oppenheim der Ältere' n.d.
[9] Paul Wolff Metterich was German Ambassador in London from 1901 to 1912.
[10] After Leyden's death in 1910, his friends built a memorial for him, at the foot of a mountain where he used to go for his walks ('Memorial Ernst Viktor von Leyden (1832–1910)', n.d.).

brown hair tied at the back; Victor, with his prominent face, short dark hair and a small moustache; young people of the world, self-assured and eager to expand their radius.

The North German Lloyd – to which Marie sent several of her letters – was one of the largest shipping companies of the time. Their high-speed vessels offered the most luxurious first-class cabins; their interiors designed by famous architects of the time ('Norddeutscher Lloyd' n.d.).

All the Leydens had been educated in the arts and were 'amateur' art practitioners with great interest in art.[11] Their hosts will have taken them to places of cultural interest, where they bought the precious artefacts they then sent to Berlin, care of Victor's mother.

More than anything else my grandfather was a great alpinist. Spending his holidays with his parents in the Engadin, he had been introduced to mountaineering at a very early age. Reaching out to prominent summits in the Far East must have been a particular challenge and joy for him. Even Lulu was part of such an undertaking, as my uncle Albrecht, who climbed many mountains with his father, writes in his obituary in the *Alpine Journal*. During their tour of 1909, 'they climbed Smera, the highest volcano on Java, and were told that my mother was the first woman to reach the summit crater. My father also climbed Fujiyama and they ended their tour with a visit to Kashmir, where he shot an ibex and missed a bear' (A. Leyden 1964: 177–8).

Looking at illustrations of an ibex on the internet now, I have a faint memory of an animal head with massive bent horns mounted on the wall above my grandfather's wood-carving studio. Was that the ibex?

Since the late nineteenth century, Japan had shown increasing interest in German culture, politics and science, and an exchange between leading personalities of both countries had started. Marie's envelopes, readdressed and forwarded, provide some clues for the couple's stay in Japan. Miyako Hotel in Kyoto and the Imperial Hotel in Tokyo, to which some of Marie's letters were directed, were created for high-class tourism.[12] The young couple from Berlin's upper class might have dined there with members of the Japanese aristocracy.

---

[11] Victor's uncle was Benoit Oppenheim, a banker and famous collector of art.

[12] In 1900, the Yoshimizuen [in Kyoto] reopened as the Miyako Hotel and has since hosted numerous heads of state and celebrities, from Albert Einstein and Marlon Brando to Ronald Reagan and Andy Warhol' (Ting 2010). '[The Imperial Hotel] was created in the late 1880s at the request of the Japanese aristocracy to cater to the increasing number of Western visitors to Japan. ('The Imperial Hotel, Tokyo' n.d.)

The travellers will have also come with connections from their own social circles and been welcomed by open-minded hosts:[13]

> Für Japan lege ich auf alle Fälle noch eine Karte von Papa an den Generalstabsarzt der Armee Honda ein. Er war zu Papas 70ten hier und schickte ihm nach 2 Jahren ein kleines Geschenk, (Theeserviettten),
>
> For Japan in any case, I'm enclosing a card from Papa to the Army Physician General Honda. He was here for Papa's 70th and 2 years later sent him a small present (tea napkins).

writes Marie in her letter of 21 May, which led me to another interesting trace. After deciphering the name Honda, I identified a Tadao Honda in an online source: He studied medicine in Berlin from 1901 to 1903 (Hartmann 2007: 104). Hence, he must have been Ernst von Leyden's student; he was, like his professor, interested in cancer research (Honda 1903).

Finally, I established, through Marie's letters, a particular clue to a family contact Victor and Lulu had on Ceylon, opening another intriguing window into my transgenerational history (to be followed up in another chapter):

> Lulu's lieber langer Brief aus Kandy und ihr vorhergehender klangen viel begeisterter über Ceylon als dieser letzte. Mit dem kleinen Beychen scheint es wieder zu hapern. Hat er Euch Näheres erzählt? Er sollte nämlich, das war Onkel Benoits ausdrückliche Bedingung, in seinem Kontrakt ausmachen, daß er fest in seinem Bungalo bleiben könne. Jetzt scheinen sie ihn herausgesetzt zu haben als wenn er nur Angestellter und nicht Mitbesitzer sei. Den Kontrakt hat er trotz mehrfacher Mahnung niemals eingeschickt. Mir steigt der Verdacht auf, daß er das bewilligte Geld gar nicht eingezahlt hat, daher nicht Mitbesitzer ist und das Geld verplampert hat. Lulu's lovely long letter from Kandy and the previous one sounded much more enthusiastic about Ceylon than this last one. There seems to be a problem with the little Beychen again. Did he mention any more details? It was Uncle Benoit's express condition that he should state in his contract that he could stay in his bungalow. They seem to have treated him as if he were just an employee and not a co-owner. Despite repeated reminders, he never sent the contract. Therefore, I am fostering the suspicion that he hasn't even paid in the money that his father granted him, which means he's not a co-owner and has squandered the money.

---

[13] Best references might have come from Ottmar von Mohl, who from 1887 to 1889 served as a German diplomat and foreign advisor to the Japanese imperial court ('Ottmar von Mohl' n.d.). His sister Anna was married to Hermann von Helmholtz, renowned physician and scientist, who in turn belonged to the close circles of the Leydens (V. Leyden 1910: 140–1). Von Mohl describes in his Japan memoir how, in 1888, he organized a tour up the Fujiyama for an Austrian alpinist (Mohl 1904: 193–7); he will certainly have had good advice for Victor, who undertook the tour 20 years later.

I was able to identify the name 'Beychen' with the help of Matthias Weniger, an art historian who has worked extensively on Benoit Oppenheim and his art collection (Weniger 2018).

Beychen was a nickname for Benoit Oppenheim Jr, Oppenheim's son, who, so I was told, was undermining his father's expectations by leading an unstable life (i.e. indulging in gambling, relying on his father's wealth). His father bought him a tea plantation on what was then Ceylon, hoping this could help him do something useful and productive (Weniger, personal communication, 31 December 2021). Reading Marie's allusion to 'little Beychen' seems to suggest that this plan might not have worked out. However, presumedly Victor and Lulu visited Victor's cousin on their trip, enjoying what seems to be a very beautiful landscape around the city of Kandy.

Advocating British colonialism

Victor, who had a doctorate in law and worked as a junior legal administrator in a rural town in Silesia, had been granted leave for the year 1909 – partly paid – declaring parts of it as a study trip; he would investigate certain aspects of the British colonial administration in India and present his findings in a study report (Weiß 2000: 158–9).[14]

It was one of the great finds while writing this chapter that a copy of this report turned up in our Leyden archives, a typescript of 174 pages. While the first, longer part of the study appears as mainly based on published sources, Victor von Leyden was most fortunate to be invited by the Maharadsha of Travancore, a vassal state in the far south of the Indian continent, supposedly through family or diplomatic connections:[15]

> Um so wertvoller war mir daher die Einladung des Maharaja von Travancore, durch die im Verein mit dem liebenswürdigen Entgegenkommen des englischen Residenten Mr. Culling-Carr mir die Möglichkeit geboten wurde, einen Staat kennen zu lernen, der unter konservativen Herrschern seine uralten Verfassungs- und Regierungsformen zum grossen Teil bewahrt

---

[14] I am grateful to Lothar Weiß (2000), who examined Victor von Leyden's role in the history of the Preussische Kommunalaufsicht between 1926 and 1932, as well as to Renate Citron-Piorkowski (2017), who provided a case study of my grandfather's fate as one of the fourteen Jewish judges from the Preußische Oberverwaltungsgericht, who were persecuted by the Nazi regime. Both researchers studied the respective files in the Geheimes Preußisches Staatsarchiv.

[15] In one of her letters Marie von Leyden mentions a Maharadsha, but who exactly this was does not become clear.

hat. Da andererseits auch den modernen Anforderungen in weitem Masse entsprochen wird, so gilt die Verwaltung Travancores in ganz Indien als vorbildlich für die Vereinigung alter Traditionen mit gesundem Fortschritt. (V. Leyden 1910: 126)

All the more valuable to me, was the invitation of the Maharaja of Travancore, together with the amiable courtesy of the English resident Mr. Culling-Carr. This gave me the opportunity to become acquainted with a state which under its traditional rulers has largely preserved its age-old constitution and form of government. However, since modern requirements have also been largely met, the administration of Travancore is regarded throughout India as a model for the union of tradition with healthy progress.

Hence the second, shorter part of his report represents a piece of original research, a case study of the structure and administration of that very special 'model' state.

In my own transgenerational quest, the report stands out as the only direct source from the travellers themselves. Travancore marks one definitive dot on the assumed map of my grandparents' journey. More than anything else, however, the report manifests my grandfather's great belief in the British type of colonization:

Wenn mein Hauptinteresse sich ... Indien zuwandte, so fand es hier ein besonders geeignetes Feld, um Methode und Erfolg europäischer Kolonisation kennen zu lernen. ... Die alte z. T. hochentwickelte arische Kultur verlangt eine besonders geschickte Behandlung des Eingeborenen Elements [sic], bedeutet aber andererseits im Falle des Gelingens ungeahnte Entwicklungs-Möglichkeiten.

Den Engländern ist es gelungen! Der Erfolg an sich schon lässt die Frage nach dem Wie? berechtigt erscheinen. (V. Leyden 1910: 2)[16]

My main interest focused ... on India, as here I found a particularly suitable area for studying the methods and successes of European colonization. ... The traditional, highly developed Aryan culture requires a particularly skilful treatment of the native element, but on the other hand can lead to unimagined development possibilities when successful. The English have succeeded! Their success in itself raises the question of how they accomplished it.

In line with the majority of the German intellectual elite under Prussian rule, especially those of Jewish descent, young Leyden sympathized with the more

---

[16] Aryan here refers to the original historical definition as pertaining to 'people who were said to speak an archaic Indo-European language and who were thought to have settled in prehistoric times in ancient Iran and the northern Indian subcontinent' (*Britannica* n.d.).

liberal outlook of the British monarchs.[17] Hence in his report he admonishes his own government to follow the British example: 'Die englische Verwaltung hat in Indien ein Kulturwerk geschaffen, das in der Weltgeschichte seines Gleichen sucht' (V. Leyden 1910: 174). ['In India, the English administration has achieved a degree of cultural progress without equal in world history.']

With such views, as I have to recognize today, my grandfather unambiguously advocated British imperialism. Commending the colonial administrative system in India, with a special emphasis on the tax system, he also endorsed the blatant racism on which it was built. Forster's *A Passage to India*, published only fifteen years after my grandparents' first 'passage', foregrounds, through its plot and the character portrayals, the outright racist nature of British India. Without giving agency to those opposing the system, his novel at least lets an independent India appear on the horizon. It was left to an author of our own times, descendant of the formerly colonized, to bring the *Rising Man* (title of Abir Mukherjee's novel of 2016) on stage. Set in 1919, the novel thematizes the atrocities of the British army in the Amritsar Massacre of that year – several hundred people of a peaceful uprising were killed – and brings the protagonist, a British police officer, face to face with a leading pro-independence activist.

My grandparents' cosmopolitanism did not allow any awareness of such political undercurrents in the India they visited in 1909. It is left to me, their descendent and chronicler, to uncover the tragic, historical irony inherent in their passages to India. On *my* journey I see the unperturbed world travellers of the early century scurry forward towards the dread of the 1930s, to their own destiny of racial discrimination and persecution.

'Reichlich jüdisches Blut in den Adern'[18]

This is the clue for us to turn the spotlight around to what was happening, in full synchronicity with my grandparents' world tour, at the *Landratsamt* of Glogau, a provincial town in the far South East of the Reich. Hardly to be called a coincidence, Landrat Singelmann had been asked to write a report about his

---

[17] In her letter to Lulu of 24 November 1904, Marie mentions the yearly 'Victoria Day' celebrated by the Women's Club on 21 November, the birthday of 'Empress Vicky'. Queen Victoria's eldest daughter and her husband Frederick, who died of cancer after 99 days of rule, stood for progressive, liberal ideas of rule against the reactionary and militarist tendencies enforced by their son Wilhelm II.

[18] 'Plenty of Jewish blood in his veins.'

assistant administrator, whose worldliness contrasted starkly with the narrow-minded outlook of the province.

In my imagination, I see Singelmann, a truly Prussian civil servant, as he is looking up at the golden-framed portrait of the Kaiser, stern gaze, regalia, all gloss and glaze; twirling his own upward-pointing moustache, he is dipping his nib into the ink pot on his desk. With much glee and an important look on his face, he commits himself to his task. 'Regierungsassessor Dr. von Leyden,' he writes, in neatly curved letters,

> besitzt gute Fähigkeiten und auch gute Kenntnisse in den Verwaltungsangelegenheiten. ... Da er vorher wohl nur in größeren Städten gelebt und gearbeitet und keine Gelegenheit gehabt hatte, die Verhältnisse im Osten der Monarchie und besonders die eines vorwiegend ländlichen Kreises kennenzulernen, fiel es ihm zunächst schwer, sich in die Anschauungen und Bedürfnisse der hiesigen ländlichen Bevölkerung hineinzufinden, und diese zu verstehen, zumal er auch durch manche rasseneigentümlichen Anschauungen, wie in seinen politischen Ansichten der hiesigen ländlichen Bevölkerung fernsteht. – Leyden nennt sich selbst national-liberal; nach meinen Beobachtungen muß er wohl dem linken Flügel dieser Partei zugezählt werden. – Daß Regierungsassessor von Leyden reichlich jüdisches Blut in den Adern hat, und daß seine Gattin – eine geborene Reichenheim – der Abstammung nach Vollblutjüdin ist, dürfte bekannt sein. Gewisse Rasseneigenschaften sind in dem Auftreten beider unverkennbar.
>
> [VvL] has good skills and also a good knowledge of administrative matters. ... Since he has probably only lived and worked in larger cities, he will not have had the opportunity to get to know the conditions in the Eastern part of the monarchy with its predominantly rural districts. That is why it was at first difficult for him to get to grips with the views and needs of the rural population, and to understand them; due to the viewpoints peculiar to his race as well as to his political outlook, he is quite removed from the views of the local rural population. Leyden calls himself a national-liberal, although according to my observations he should be counted among the left wing of this party. As is generally known, government assessor von Leyden has plenty of Jewish blood in his veins, and his wife – née Reichenheim – is a thoroughbred Jew by descent. Certain racial characteristics are unmistakable in the appearance of both.

What an ironic echo this report is, written on 26 August 1909, to Marie von Leyden's letters from the same time, which are full of love for and anxiety about the well-being of the couple faring on distant shores. No wonder that their tour around the world will have aroused the jealousy of a provincial district administrator who would never have been able to afford such an outlandish trip. What a bitter historic irony too that already in the early twentieth century, social resentment mingled with such an overt expression of anti-Semitism, as Freiherr von Seherr-Thoß, Singelmann's superior and recipient of the report, remarks in a note he added.[19] What a foreboding of what would happen to my grandfather more than two decades later when he was catapulted out of his fulfilling career as a high-ranking civil servant in the Prussian government because he could not disprove his Jewish ancestry.

Das Schicksal eines 'nichtzeitgemäßen' Spitzenbeamten[20]

The demolition started with the 'Papenstreich' of 1932. All high-ranking personnel in the Prussian Ministry of Home Affairs not conforming with the government were dismissed or demoted. My grandfather, who by then was Regierungsdirektor and Head of the Prussian 'Kommunalverwaltung' (local governments), a position of much political influence (Weiß 2000: 161), was transferred to the post of Senatspräsident des Preußischen Oberverwaltungsgerichts (President of the Higher Administrative Court) in Berlin, which was a position of honour but without any political influence. In April 1933, with the introduction of the Gesetz zur Wiederherstellung des Berufsbeamtentums (Law for the Restoration of the Professional Civil Service), all Jewish personnel were screened for their ancestry. My grandfather, who could not prove that all four grandparents had been baptized straight after birth, was forced into premature retirement (Weiß 2000: 182), 'a blow from which he never quite recovered' (A. Leyden 1964: 179). In her book *Verjagt aus Amt und Würden* [Kicked Out of High Positions] (2017), Renate Citron-Piorkowski presents case studies of altogether fourteen judges of the Oberverwaltungsgericht in Berlin, who underwent the same fate as my grandfather, the 'fate of a top-ranking official "not of his time"'(Weiß 2000: 180). Dismissed from office, losing their status, income and dignity had tragic if not fatal consequences for their lives. On 26 December 1938, Citron-Piorkowski's own grandfather, who was also

---

[19] 'Wenn das Urteil des Landrats Singelmann auch aus etwas antisemitischen Herzen kommen mag, so kann ich es doch nur als durchaus zutreffend bezeichnen' (GStA PK, I. HA Rep 184, Pers.-Akten Nr 11621, Bl 114 ff). ('Though Landrat Singelmann's appraisal might come from an anti-Semitic heart, I can only fully endorse it.')
[20] 'The fate of a top-ranking official "not of his time"' (Weiß 2000: 180).

among the fourteen disgraced top-ranking legal practitioners, took his own life (Citron-Piorkowski and Marenbach 2017: 39).[21]

Retreat into the mountains

I remember the sundial with its large iron hand on the wall of my grandparents' house in Partenkirchen. Its shadow, as we children were fascinated to learn, would wander from morning to evening and point to the hour numbers painted into a garland around the bar. I remember the big-lettered 1935, the year the house was built, painted onto the waving banner. In blue and red colours, it all looked so cheerful and confident, engraved on the massive white wall of the Bavarian style house. 'Das Häuschen' – 'the little house' – it was affectionately called by all the family, who treasured it as their centre once my grandparents had had to leave Berlin. I also remember the dark brown wooden balconies and shutters, the wood carvings by my grandfather, ornaments in- and outside the house; and of course, more than anything, the spectacular panorama view of the Alps with the Alpspitze at its centre and the Zugspitze in the background. Our grandfather would tell us all the names of every single mountain peak. Photos showed my young mother or one of my uncles, sitting next to their father smoking a cigarette, as they were taking a break from their climb with him.

Trying to imagine now, so many decades later, what it meant for my grandfather, this decision to build that house; the decision to retreat into the Alps, which he loved so much, where he could acquire new skills, wood-carving and skiing, what it meant for him and his family to adapt to the situation after that blow of being dislodged, at the age of 53, so abruptly from a fulfilling professional and social life in Berlin to a life of (unwanted) leisure in a Bavarian village. How did he, my grandmother, their children – my uncles and my mother – react, how did they read the signs of the time?

In his letter from Bombay of 25 September 1933, two weeks after his father had handed in his – enforced – letter of resignation, my uncle Rudi tries to reassure his mother:

---

[21] A commemorative plaque in the building of the administrative court was mounted in 2017. It lists the names of the fourteen judges who were chased from that court by the NS in 1933 (see press release of 11 October 2017: https://www.berlin.de/gerichte/oberverwaltungsgericht/presse/pressemitteilungen/2017/pressemitteilung.638682.php; accessed 18 August 2023).

Berlin und das Heimathäuschen dort mit einem anderen in den Bergen einzutauschen, ist für uns nichts schweres, zumal es doch Pläne sind, die wir immer für Euren 'Alterssitz' gehabt haben, nur dass sie früher in die Tat umgesetzt werden.

To exchange our home in Berlin with another in the mountains does not weigh heavy on our hearts, especially since these are plans we've always had for your 'retirement home'. It's just that this will happen earlier than planned.

Rudi, anxious to quell his mother's anxiety, did not foresee that less than five years after the anti-Semitic blow of 1933, he and his brother Albrecht would have to provide a haven of escape in the most traumatic phase of my grandparents' life.

On 10 November 1938, after just three years in their new home, Luise was summoned to the town hall by NS-Kreisleiter Johann Hausböck. She was told she had to quit Garmisch-Partenkirchen, like all forty-four Jewish residents, within forty-eight hours. On leaving the town hall, she had to walk through a line-up of Nazi mob, spitting at her and assailing her with foul anti-Semitic swearwords.[22]

Hastily leaving their Bavarian home, they first went to stay with my parents, Otto und Biba Veit, in Berlin. From there they obtained monthly travel permits (December 1938 to February 1939) for Switzerland, where they were taken in by friends of the family in Les Avants (near Montreux). They also had the great luck to be granted an entry visa for India, issued on 12 December that year by the British Consulate in Berlin, as my grandfather's passport shows.

Jewish immigration into India was very restricted. Different from other countries with high numbers of Jewish refugees from the Nazis – the United States, Great Britain, France or Italy – India was still a British colony. Only about 1000 European Jews were granted immigration visa into India between 1933 and 1945 (Roy 1999: 32). Only because by then Albrecht (see LTD, A.-G. I. 1967), and Rudi were British citizens, they were able to effectuate visa for their parents (see Figure 11.4).

The second passage to India

'10. III. 1939 SS Conte Verde.' (L. Leyden 1939)

---

[22] Leyden, I. [Wolfgang von Leyden's widow] 2008, personal communication 19/20 March. See Schwarzmüller (2006). In November 2010, a memorial with forty-four steles was erected in Garmisch-Partenkirchen to commemorate the forty-four victims of Nazi terror ('Denkmal für jüdische Nazi-Opfer eingeweiht' 2010).

Figure 11.4 Immigration visa for European Jews to India.

With great difficulty I have managed to decipher the first few lines of the diary my grandmother started on the day they boarded the ship that would bring them to safety. The Conte Verde, I found out, was an Italian ocean liner which brought thousands of Jewish refugees from Venice to Shanghai, via Bombay, where my grandparents were headed. In my thoughts I follow my grandmother mounting from their first-class cabin to the panorama deck. Flags of steam are trailing behind the black-rimmed chimneys; muffled noises can be heard from the third-class decks below. With one hand clutching her wide-brimmed hat against the breeze, the other shading her eyes against the sudden brightness, she pauses and lets the salty air fill her lungs. But being my grandmother, she does not linger. 'Where do I find the writing room,' she asks one of the stewards nearby. 'Ah, la Sala di scrittura, Signora?' he replies and accompanies her to a room decorated in opulent Italian style, with chairs and desks in dark wood, ornate lamp shades, carpets and tapestry in plush brocade ('Conte Verde' n.d.). With a deep sigh of relief, she opens her notebook, which is to help her keep the harrowing memories of the past months at bay.

The blueprints of the one hundred pages duplicate notebook in which she started her diary are filled up to the very edge of each line in my grandmother's hardly legible handwriting. I had to commission a historian to transcribe it for me. Yet, different from the 1909 world tour, where I only had my great-grandmother's letters *to* the travellers, I am extremely happy to have this direct source of that second passage across the Indian Ocean and their first few months in India. What a different state of mind they were in from when they set out on their voyage thirty years earlier (see also Veit-Wild 2014).

Morning bridge and chocolate cake

Formerly colonial tourists, they now came as refugees. Yet, thanks to the social status of their sons, they were still privileged; integrated into the German/Austrian Jewish exile community which mingled with British colonial society (cf. Franz 2020).

In my grandmother's diary entries, I find exact portrayals of this, tinged with her typical mixture of empathy and gentle mockery:

> Es wurde ein bißchen talky, talky gemacht, die Nasen gepudert und erfreulicherweise holte man uns schnell zum Bridge, der ein recht heiter und unterhaltender war. (1 April)

> There was a little talky-talky and powdering of noses. Fortunately, we were taken fairly quickly to play bridge, which was quite cheerful and entertaining. (1 April)

> Zur Regel will ich diese Morgenbridge nicht werden lassen, finde sie sehr verwerflich, und geben ein Armutszeugnis. Aber einigen will ich jetzt folgen. ... Ich sehe gerne Menschen, es macht mir Spaß. Sie sind alle so unbelastet, ahnen nichts von der Welt woher ich komme, kennen kein Leid und das ist wohltuend. (18 May)

> I don't want to let this morning bridge become a habit, I find it very inappropriate, a sign of decadence. Yet I will join some for the time being. ... I like to see people; I enjoy their company. They are all so unencumbered and have no idea of the world from where I come. They know no suffering and that is soothing. (18 May)

> Zum Tee bei Frau Treibmann, typischer Spießer-Kaffeeklatsch wie er in jeder Provinzstadt zu Hause sein kann. Lange Debatten über eine mißglückte Chocoladentorte! Als ob die grade die Ursache aller Probleme der Welt sei! Die glücklichen und ahnungslosen Dämchen! (26 May)

> Tea with Mrs. Treibmann, typical bourgeois coffee gossip that can be found in any provincial town at home. Long debates about a failed chocolate cake! As if that were the cause of all the problems in the world! These lucky and clueless ladies! (26 May)

Lulu is conscious of being an outsider, but different from her husband, whose spirit seems rather resigned, she is open to the culture into which she has been placed by fate. Thanks to her son's in-depth knowledge of Indian culture, history and art, her mind moves towards a transcultural view of her surroundings:

> Sonntag frueh der Molch [Rudi] u. ich mit Auto z. den Jogeshwari cave-temples. Vater lockt es zu wenig, er bringt nicht das Interesse dafuer auf, ich bedaure es, es geht ihm viel Schoenes verloren. (8 Aug)

Fussing about getting Victor occupied, she writes: 'I am glad about every table of Bridge I can organise for him' (21 May).

Krishna temples and Malabar dances

Lulu's diary of these first five months in India – luckily, she taught herself to type, so her entries from June 1939 onwards were easily legible – draw a vivid, almost ethnographic picture of her encounters with Indian art and culture, and though she suffered tremendously from the climate, her notes convey her deep impressions with the landscape, flora, fauna and people of the unknown tropical country. On her trips with Rudi, she sucks it all in; describes, in detail, the ornaments of a Krishna temple at Old Mahabaleshwar, rich and elegant, the many versions of the cobra motif hewn in stone. Or the Vagoli temples, with their view over a small lake amidst green landscape, or a frieze chiselled in basalt with the ten incarnations of Vishnu. 'Es ist eine schöne Zeit, die ich mit Rudi dort verbringe,' she writes after one of the trips, 'er weiß so viel zu erklären und zu berichten, ich glaube eine so genußreiche Stunde hatte ich keine, seitdem ich die Heimat verließ' (7 April). ['It is such a lovely time, I am spending with Rudi, he knows so much, can explain so well and recount what lies behind. I think I have not had such an enjoyable hour since I left home.'] Inspired by the impressions from these, my grandmother immerses herself in books on Indian culture:

> Ich versuche systematisch taeglich über den Hinduismus weiter zu lesen, es fesselt mich ungemein. Gestern waren R. u. ich zu einem indischen Tanzabend im Privaten Hause. Sued indische Taenze, Kathakali, es sind die alten

> dramatischen Taenze v. Malabar. ... Der Tanz wird nur von dem Trommelschlag begleitet u. manchmal v. Floeten-toenen, die fuer unser Ohr nicht die rechte Harmonie immer haben. ... Ein suedindischer Dichter will diese Taenze neu beleben, sie drohen in Vergessenheit zu geraten, er hielt eine Einfuehrungsrede in Malabisch, was keiner, auch die vielen anwesenden Inder nicht verstanden, es wurde uebersetzt, selbst das war schwer verstaendlich. Die Sprache klang sehr sonderbar, wurde sehr breit gesprochen, die Zunge immer sichtbar, lag breit, flach im Munde. Hart wie ein Gerattel kamen die Worte aus d. Munde. (29 July)

> I try to read up systematically on Hinduism, every day, it is so fascinating. Yesterday Rudi and I were invited to a private home, for an evening with Indian dances. South Indian dances, Kathakali, the old dramatic dances from Malabar. ... This dance is accompanied by drumming only, and sometimes the sound of flutes which, for our ear, do not always have the right harmony. ... A South Indian poet wants to revive these dances, as they threaten to sink into oblivion. He gave an introduction in his own Malabarian language, which nobody understood, not even the many Indians guests. It was translated, but even that was difficult to understand. The language sounded very strange, with a broad pronunciation, the tongue always visible, square and flat in the mouth. The words, as they came out, sounded harsh and rattling.

In spite of all the inspiration and joy she found in her new surroundings, Luise remained in a state of high-strung anxiety. Throughout her animated depictions, her worries erupt like bolts of lightning, in short entries such as, on 28 April:

> Tag mit Hitlers Rede! Rudi brachte ersten Teil Abends bereits mit, Kunde ging vom Flottenvertrag mit England und von dem mit Polen! Die Zukunft scheint dieselbe zu bleiben, die Welt weiter in Spannung und Ungewißheit!

> The day with Hitler's speech! Rudi brought the first part already in the evening, there were rumours about a naval agreement with England and with Poland! The future seems to remain the same, full of tension and uncertainty.

She was right in her worries and premonitions. While she was, in Bombay, united with two of her children, she would be separated for the six years to come from the three others who had remained in Europe.

With the outbreak of the Second World War, my grandfather, like all German citizens on British territory, was interned as 'enemy alien'. He was released after six weeks with the help of the Jewish Relief Association.[23]

---

[23] I hold documents of my grandparents' correspondence during the internment and Victor's release.

Victor and Lulu remained in India up to 1948, care of their sons. They then returned to Germany and were eventually able to move back into their house in Partenkirchen. Victor was paid a state pension but in postwar Germany was not again given the chance to work in his professional field again. At the time of his return to Germany, he wrote to Konrad Adenauer regarding a possible employment in the new government. As Lord Mayor of the city of Cologne during the Weimar Republic, Adenauer had been in Leyden's charge in the Prussian Home Ministry. Adenauer only sent a short non-committal answer (Adenauer 1984: 322).

'Berlin's loss was Bombay's gain'[24] – Transculturality at last?

My grandparents' travel stories, as has been shown, are at odds with the binary patterns of postcolonial discourse. They came from a privileged class in the Kaiserreich – the German Empire – and hailed a colonial venture but attracted the scorn of their own state. They became refugees, exiled from the West, but were harboured by a colonial power. Their story also shows that exile does not always imply victimhood but may open doors to a transcultural encounter.

It was left to the next generation to walk through such doors and partake in transcultural commonalities (Welsch 2009). Victor's and Lulu's son, Rudi von Leyden, came to Bombay in 1933, 24 years of age, because he did not see the chance of a professional career in Germany. His doctorate of geology was revoked by the University in Göttingen, once they found out about his origins. He became of great influence in the Progressive Art Group (PAG) formed by young Indian artists[25] around India's Independence – a cradle of what could be termed a truly 'transcultural imagination' (Schulze-Engler 2009: xiv).

In their obituaries after Rudi von Leyden's death in 1983, former members of the PAG call themselves lucky that political circumstances brought him to 'the country that adopted you' (Khanna 1999: 188), someone who was 'straddling several worlds':

---

[24] Quote from an obituary by Kekoo Gandhy, art gallerist and one of Rudi's closest friends ('Rudi's got mail' n.d.).
[25] Among them Ara, Raza, Husain or Souza whose works later gained international fame and millions of dollars at international auctions. The PAG in general and Rudi's role in particular have been widely discussed (see Franz 2007, 2008, 2010, 2014). Two monographs about my uncle are forthcoming, by Franz and by the Indian art writer Reema Gehi Desai.

he was a European in a colonial space, but nonetheless with an ambivalent relationship to British colonial powers due to his German roots; a political émigré, part of a small but significant community of European Jews in cosmopolitan Bombay during the war; and a man deeply interested and invested in Indian culture and especially the flowering of Indian contemporary art. (Arbuthnot 2018)

Rudi, my uncle, was also my godfather. Fortunately, his weekly letters to his mother, which he started on the first day of *his* passage to India[26] and kept writing until they were able to join him and his brother in Bombay, did not vanish into thin air but, over time and space, eventually travelled into my hands.[27] Reading through the vivid chronicle of my young uncle's adventurous, creative life in Bombay of the time, I feel deeply connected to him. If not godfather in the Christian sense, he was a truly kindred spirit. Had he not suddenly died of a heart attack in 1983, he would have visited me and my family in Zimbabwe, where we had just settled and where I was walking in his footsteps.

References

Adenauer, K. (1984), 'Brief on Victor von Leyden, Wiesbaden 11 October 1948', in R. Morsey and H.-P. Schwarz (eds), *Adenauer – Rhöndorfer Ausgabe: Briefe 1947–1949*, 322, München: Siedler.

Arbuthnot, M. (2018), 'Bombay Satire: Rudolf von Leyden's Political Cartoons in India in the 1930s and 40s', *British Library Asian and African Studies Blog*. Available online: https://blogs.bl.uk/asian-and-african/2018/12/bombay-satire-rudolf-von-leydens-political-cartoons-in-india-in-the-1930s-and-40s-.html (accessed 10 August 2022).

'Benoit Oppenheim der Ältere' (n.d.), *Wikipedia*. Available online: https://de.wikipedia.org/wiki/Benoit_Oppenheim_der_Ältere (accessed 11 March 2022).

---

[26] In his letter of 22 May 1933 from Antwerpen, where he went on board, I find the sentence: 'Mamsichen, Du solltest Dich auch wirklich nur freuen, ein Jahr ist doch zu kurz, um eine grosse Trennung zu bringen.' ('Mamsi dear, you also should only be happy, one year is too short to bring about a major separation.') Rudi, 25 years of age, was planning to join his brother Albrecht in Bombay for a year in order to orient himself professionally. As we know, his mother's premonitions were right – the year extended into a very long separation. After a very fulfilling life in the sphere of the arts, Rudi only returned to Europe at the age of retirement. ('The Outsider's Gaze' is the title of a forthcoming monograph on R. von Leyden by Indian arts writer Reema Gehi – see Maddox https://www.mashindia.com/the-wanderlust-of-art-writing/)

[27] The letters from his brother Albrecht von Leyden to his parents (1927–67) are held by the British Library in London (reference: MSS Eur C 322).

Bieger, L. and N. Maruo-Schröder (eds) (2016), *Zeitschrift für Anglistik und Amerikanistik*, 64 (1): *Special Issue: Space, Place, and Narrative*. doi: 10.1515/zaa-2016-0001

Britannica, T. E. O. E. (n.d.) 'Aryan', *Encyclopedia Britannica*.

Citron-Piorkowski, R. (2017), 'Dr. Victor von Leyden', in R. Citron-Piorkowski and U. Marenbach (eds), *Verjagt aus Amt und Würden: Vom Naziregime 1933 verfolgte Richter des Preußischen Oberverwaltungsgerichts: 14 Lebensläufe*, 94–102, Berlin: Hentrich & Hentrich.

Citron-Piorkowski, R. and U. Marenbach (eds) (2017), *Verjagt aus Amt und Würden: Vom Naziregime 1933 verfolgte Richter des Preußischen Oberverwaltungsgerichts: 14 Lebensläufe*, 94–102, Berlin: Hentrich & Hentrich.

'Conte Verde, Sala di scrittura, Lloyd Sabaudo, Passagierschiff, Ansichtskarte' (n.d.), Available online: https://www.ebay.at/itm/384758215664?hash=item5995607 3f0:g:zbQAAOSw2JhiHOh8 (accessed 11 March 2022).

De Certeau, M. (1988), *Practices of Everyday Life*, Berkeley: University of California Press.

'Denkmal für jüdische Nazi-Opfer eingeweiht' (10 November 2010), *Merkur*. Available online: https://www.merkur.de/lokales/garmisch-partenkirchen/denkmal-juedis che-nazi-opfer-eingeweiht-999753.html (accessed 11 March 2022).

Ford, J. (2015), 'Introduction: Transnational Memory and Traumatic Histories', *FORUM: University of Edinburgh Postgraduate Journal of Culture and the Arts*, Special issue 4: 1–5. Available online: https://www.academia.edu/28023455/Introduction_Transnational_Memory_and_Traumatic_Histories (accessed 24 October 2022).

Franz, M. (2007), '"Passage to India": Österreichisches Exil in Britisch-Indien 1938–1945', in C. Schindler (ed.), *Dokumentationsarchivs des österreichischen Widerstands: Jahrbuch. Schwerpunkt: Namentliche Erfassung von NS-Opfern*, 196–223, Vienna: LIT.

Franz, M. (2010), 'Sanskrit to Avantgarde: Indo-osterreichische Initiativen zur Dokumentation und Förderung von Kunst und Kultur', in G. Krist and T. Bayerova (eds), *Heritage Conservation and Research in India: 60 Years of Indo-Austrian Collaboration*, 15–34, Vienna: Böhlau.

Franz, M. (2014), 'Exile Meets Avantgarde: ExilantInnen-Kunstnetzwerke in Bombay', in M. Franz and H. Halbrainer (eds), *Going East – Going South: Österreichisches Exil in Asien und Afrika*, 403–32, Graz: Clio.

Franz, M. (2020), 'From Dinner Parties to Galleries: The Langhammer-Leyden-Schlesinger Circle in Bombay – 1940s through the 1950s', in B. Dogramaci, H. Roth, L. Karp Lugo, M. Hetschold and R. Lee (eds), *Arrival Cities: Migrating Artists and New Metropolitan Topographies in the 20th Century*, Leuwen: Leuwen University Press. Available online: https://www.jstor.org/stable/j.ctv16qk3nf (accessed 18 August 2023).

Franz, M. (ed.) (2008), *Mapping Contemporary History: Zeitgeschichten im Diskurs*, Wien: Böhlau.

Hartmann, R. (2007), 'Japanische Offiziere im Deutschen Kaiserreich 1870–1914', *Japonica Humboldtiana* 11: 93–158.

Herz, L. (1936). 'N. Reichenheim und Sohn: Geschichte eines Werkes und einer Familie', unpublished.

Honda, T. (1903), 'Zur parasitären Ätiologie des Karzinoms', *Virchows Archiv für pathologische Anatomie und Physiologie und für klinische Medizin* 174: 96–130. doi: 10.1007/BF02042892

Khanna, K. (1999), 'To Rudolf von Leyden: A Letter Out of Season', in A. Bhatti and J. Voigt (eds), *Jewish Exile in India 1933–1945*, 186–9, New Delhi: Manohar.

Leyden, A. von (1964), 'Victor von Leyden: 1880–1963' [Obituary], *Alpine Journal* 69: 177–80.

Leyden, E. von (1910), *Lebenserinnerungen*, Stuttgart, Leipzig: Deutsche Verlags-Anstalt.

Leyden, L. von (1939), 'Diary 10 March to 30 August', unpublished.

Leyden, V. von (1910), 'Zwei Beispiele aus der unmittelbaren und mittelbaren englischen Verwaltung', in 'Indien: I. Die Grundsteuer in Britisch Indien. II. Der Vasallen-Staat Travancore', unpublished.

LTD, A.-G. I. (1967), 'Information for the Photographic Trade [Farewell Edition for Albrecht von Leyden]'.

Maddox, G. 'The Wanderlust of Art Writing', MASH [Online], https://www.mashindia.com/the-wanderlust-of-art-writing/ (accessed 1 February 2023).

'Memorial Ernst Viktor von Leyden (1832–1910)' (n.d.), *Engadin St. Moritz Tourismus AG*. Available online: https://www.maps.engadin.ch/en/point/monument/memorial-ernst-viktor-von-leyden-1832-1910/25151747/ (accessed 11 March 2022).

Mikkonen, K. (2007), 'The "Narrative Is Travel" Metaphor: Between Spatial Sequence and Open Consequence', *Narrative* 15: 286–305.

Mohl, O. von (1904), *Am Japanischen Hofe: Kammerherr Seiner Majestät des Kaisers und Königs. Wirklicher Geheimer Legations-Rat*, Berlin: Dietrich Reimer.

Mukherjee, A. (2016), *A Rising Man: A Novel*, Toronto: Penguin Random House Canada.

'Norddeutscher Lloyd' (n.d.), *Wikipedia*. Available online: https://de.wikipedia.org/wiki/Norddeutscher_Lloyd (accessed 11 March 2022).

'Ottmar von Mohl' (n.d.), *Wikipedia*, the Free Encyclopedia.

Prein, P. (2005), *Bürgerliches Reisen im 19. Jahrhundert: Freizeit, Kommunikation und soziale Grenzen*, Münster: LIT.

Roy, H. (1999), 'Passing Through: Jewish Exile in India 1933–1945', *Biblio: A Review of Books*, 4 (March–April): 32.

'Rudi's got mail' (n.d.). Available online: http://mobiletoi.timesofindia.com/mobile.aspx?article=yes&pageid=4&sectid=edid=&edlabel=TOIM&mydate

Hid=07-09-2009&pubname=Times%20of%20India%20-%20Mumbai&edn ame=&articleid=Ar00400&publabel=TOI (accessed 23 January 2014).

Salomon, A. (2019), 'Marie von Leyden [Obituary]', reprinted in Peter Voswinckel, *Verwässerung und Verleugnung einer Gründungsgeschichte der Onkologie. Ernst von Leyden und seine Bedeutung für Disziplinbildung und Internationalität*, Berlin: Deutsche Gesellschaft für Hämatologie und Medizinische Onkologie (2019). doi: 10.4126/FRL01-006429431

Schulze-Engler, F. (2009), 'Introduction', in F. Schulze-Engler and S. Helff (eds), *Transcultural English Studies: Theories, Fictions, Realities*, ix–xvi, Amsterdam: Rodopi.

Schwarzmüller, A. (2006), 'Garmisch-Partenkirchen und seine jüdischen Mitbürger: November 1938'. Available online: https://www.gapgeschichte.de/jude n_in_gap_ereignisse/1938_11.htm (accessed 24 October 2022).

Spode, H. (n.d.), 'Der Aufstieg des Tourismus', Deutsches Historisches Museum Blog. Available online: https://www.dhm.de/blog/2017/03/08/der-aufstieg-des-tourismus/ (accessed 8 March 2022).

'The Imperial Hotel, Tokyo' (n.d.). Available online: https://en.wikipedia.org/wiki/Imp erial_Hotel,_Tokyo (accessed 9 March 2022).

Ting, D. (2010), 'A Gem of a Hotel in Kyoto, Japan', *TravelAge West*. Available online: https://www.travelagewest.com/Travel/Hotels/A-Gem-of-a-Hotel-in-Kyot o-Japan (accessed 9 March 2022).

Veit-Wild, F. (2014), ' "Es ist kein Traum, dir auf deinen ersten richtigen Brief zu antworten …" Luise von Leyden als Chronistin jüdischen Exils in Indien', in I. Hansen-Schaberg and M. Kublitz-Kramer (eds), *Das Ende des Exils? Briefe von Frauen nach 1945*, 88–104, Munich: Text und Kritik.

Weiß, L. (2000), 'Preußische Kommunalaufsicht zwischen Reformen und Krisen: Victor von Leyden (1926–1932)', *Geschichte des Westens*, 15 (2): 157–84.

Weniger, M. (2018), 'Sammler und Konjunktur: Benoit Oppenheim und seine Skulpturensammlung', unpublished.

Welsch, W. (2009), 'On the Acquisition and Possession of Commonalities', in F. Schulze-Engler and S. Helff (eds), *Transcultural English Studies: Theories, Fictions, Realities*, 3–36, Amsterdam: Rodopi.

All unpublished sources are from the Leyden Family Archives held by Flora Veit-Wild in Berlin, Lucie Velterop von Leyden, The Hague and James von Leyden, Lewes, UK.

Afterword: 'Objects in the rear-view mirror'

Yvonne Adhiambo Owuor

Where the mind is without fear and the head is held high
Where knowledge is free
Where the world has not been broken up into fragments
By narrow domestic walls
Where words come out from the depth of truth
Where tireless striving stretches its arms towards perfection
Where the clear stream of reason has not lost its way
Into the dreary desert sand of dead habit …

Rabindranath Tagore, Gitanjali

A book of chapters serves as a stop-off point to mark one of the swansongs in a long and rare life of an academician, a German man of letters, who by fate, will or circumstances, or also a latent power of prophecy, transformed the spaces he inhabited into sites of rigorous multipolar engagements, of reorienting cartographies and generating the most dramatic sites of majority world intellectual and human encounters.

This is no hagiography. Prof. Dr. Frank Schulze-Engler, latterly of the Department of New English Literatures and Cultures at the Institute of English and American Studies of the Goethe-University (Frankfurt am Main), would spear any such attempts with acerbic wit, an ache for rigour and contempt at flattery that is without a logical argument or accurate, and global bibliographical references.

I will probably depart from the Schulze-Engler standards, not because of a desire to flatter – we share a contempt of that. You see, there are two souls who have midwifed a core aspect of my life, to whom I owe an unpayable debt of gratitude: The first is the late Binyavanga Wainaina, who hauled me kicking, screaming and scared into literary galaxies, the other is Frank Schulze-Engler, who surreptitiously nudged me centimetre by centimetre into falling into the deep academic waters I had so fiercely cursed before.

I will get to the meaning of these chapters at some point, but this is also a story thread of how an 'If I ever darken the door of another academic institution I must turn into a unicorn' Kenyan woman artist-author became a sought-after fixture in diverse academic spaces and forums.

It starts with a most innocent letter of invitation received on 20 December 2010 inviting me to the International Symposium (had to look up 'Symposium') on 'Habari ya English? East Africa as a Literary and Linguistic Contact Zone' to be held at Goethe-University Frankfurt, Germany, 23–25 February 2011. It is signed by Frank Schulze-Engler.

The symposium's title, 'Habari ya English?' was the primary seducing factor, the hope of playfulness and also the lure of visiting a Germany I had previously only read about, led me across this unknown threshold. Moreover, I was not expected to do anything more than show up with a few notes for a panel session.

Ha!
Prof. Dr. Frank Schulze-Engler is a sneak storm.

A first meeting in Frankfurt, a thrilled conversation about the theme and its sense of play, my wonder at the topics proposed, my emphatic confirmation that 'I am not an academic; I do not speak academese'.

'Yes, yes', Professor Dr. Frank Schulze-Engler answered, 'But I had a thought …' Shine in his eyes, 'I wonder … and it is no obligation … but we now learn that our intended keynote speaker has had to drop out … would you occupy that slot … ask the *marvellous* questions you pose and … we are just a few of us … Not a long keynote at all … and …' wave of hand and soft chuckle, 'speak your heart, stir the pot, it would be *wonderful* …'

Into the labyrinth.

That tentative 'yes' to a most unexpected proposition led me to working through the night preparing a 'keynote speech' (looked up 'what is a keynote speech') for an academic conference, and also cursing myself every five minutes, and blaming my fate on an overindulgence in Riesling (first ever sampling) and a sublimely served Schnitzel.

That lecture, my first academic lecture, was step one across a once-shunned threshold. What happened, and I look at the guiding notes now, was the work of a consummate teacher gently nudging one towards the pleasure of unravelling a question, of engaging contrary ideas and arguing in text, of welcoming references, footnotes, citations, not as handcuffs, but instead playmates. And that 'random' talk becomes a reviewed text, the text is published in a special journal and finds its way into the works of others who in turn use it to sustain or dispute their own arguments. And my resistance gradually dissolves. Through Frank Schulze-Engler, I learn what others probably take for granted, that there is room in academia for a wild and imaginative experimentation with ideas, that one can play with others' thoughts and experiences to re-imagine worlds; that knowledge buried or hidden in the crevices of the majority world has equal merit and power as that which had long been elevated and privileged in the modern world, that works and thoughts and a community of thinkers have the power to rehabilitate amputated literatures, histories and epistemologies, that there is room for creative lunacy and playfulness, that seriousness in delivery is also not a handcuff. It requires a particular tinge of lunacy to be able to not only create a vibrant, viable, sought-after space for a deep immersion into the literatures of the world, but to also hold firmly to a vision of a 'world … not … broken up into fragments/By narrow domestic walls …'. If there is one of many strange things modern geopolitical posturing teaches, it is the large number of people and institutions invested in dicing and slicing the earth into manageable chunks, into absolute categories and specific life-views, a selection of which are accorded odd and excess advantage over other parts. Daring to assert and prove otherwise becomes a Sisyphean undertaking of a thousand and one unseen skirmishes. To succeed in carving out a space, an oasis to which a venerable caravan of think-icons pause to replenish, reflect, think, project, lecture, speak, engage, encounter, celebrate, feast, learn, imagine, meditate, mediate, dispute, debate, wonder, imagine, play and conjure ideas, possibilities, visions, thoughts and dreams, is the stuff of legends. It is legacy-making on steroids. That is what Frank Schulze-Engler also means.

That Symposium in 2011 was before my books *Dust* (2013) and *Dragonfly Sea* (2019) got published, before I wore for myself the tag 'writer'. Among the many meaning-making, fostering hands these works fell into were Frank's. It is no small chance that the surprising and delightful experience of having my works so well-received, explored and expressed in Germany happened because of the generous heart, mind and spirit of this unusual teacher.

Much will be made about the stratospheric potency of Frank Schulze-Engler's academic work, his interventions, the tough foundry of knowledge through which he drove his numerous impressive students who shine bright in their own areas of specializations. The nature of valedictory messages incline to this. Yet the other task, that of sacred human formation capacity, of gently nurturing the stranger and drawing out light that only he could see, and doing this with seemingly unconscious ease, of pushing, suggesting, correcting until a simple thought gleams from its essence, and the thinker looks again at the emerging word in astonishment, 'Yes, exactly. This is it'.

These chapters are gestures and signposts to the many ways and influences of Frank; tributes to ideas, to the vitality and generative quality in the worlds of literatures in English that enchanted Frank and led him to his cornerstone themes. Yet, behind each is a human being whose minds, hearts, spirits and thoughts have been nurtured, for better or worse, by an encounter with a human being. This is legacy.

This book is titled, *The Many Worlds of Anglophone Literature: Transcultural Engagements, Global Frictions*. It might also have been called 'Multipolarities', in response to the unstated question of how the work would be found to be relevant today. Multipolarity as notion has acquired refreshing and meaningful currency now. In his early venturing into the multipolar and multilocal possibilities, Frank has been milking the proverbial sacred topographical cows. He was one of the ground-laying pioneers who, without too much noise, created spaces and projects to rethink, reflect on and interrogate, for example, the 'Indian' of *Indian* Ocean, prodding us to reconsider what has been left out, the history of naming, what is erased and what gets denied by a myopic geo-marking of this most cosmopolitan of worlds mediated by an ocean that is a 'cradle of globalization'.

'Afrasian', proposes Frank. 'Afrasian Ocean. Afrasian Memories. Afrasian Worlds'. Afrasian complications and cosmopolitanisms. As the neologism has crept into increasingly common use, Frank Schulze-Engler (inadvertently?) participates in an imaginative and literary rehabilitation project, a restoration of an '*"ocean of notions"* [...] *the most embayed ocean [that] yields a rich harvest for the imagination* [...] *in its poetics and politics*' (Moorthy and Jamal 2010: 4; emphasis added) to its myriad historical custodians and their linguistic and poetic fluidities.

As the metaphorical centre of the globe shifts 'eastward', and the rest of the Western world scrambles to catch up with the zeitgeist, they will find some pre-laid tracks by the Department of New English Literatures and Cultures of the Institute of English and American Studies.

As it acquires momentum and finally gets formalized and institutionalized, Frank Schulze-Engler's offerings will settle into place as if they have finally reached the home they had long anticipated for themselves.

The words, assemblages by renowned international scholars, explore aspects and elements of literatures in English(es) in their diversity, concepts, paradoxes, commonalities, stylistics and intentions. Each chapter gestures to the delightful polyphonic character of the literary 'Anglosphere' in both its nature, and in its engagement with English as a language channel.

There are themes here that show up like familiar relatives in the department's symposia: Transregionalism is one, Transculturality is another. As Magdalena Pfalzgraf and Hanna Teichler succinctly reflect in their introduction, '[t]ransculturality entered English literary studies out of the need to account for the globality of Anglophone literatures around the world and understand their multipolarities and relationality beyond the idea that the West constitutes a centre to which the literature "of the rest" would invariably look towards or write back to' (4). The fictional spaces and geographies to which the chapters allude, or refer, suggest other (rather than new) maps of a world that invites renewed reading, not in English, but in the assorted 'Englishes' generated by creators for whom the vehicle of language can be adapted to bear the weight of the distinct worlds from which these come. Whatever else is explored and revealed, the promiscuous resilience of language, in this case, English, its elemental *transregionalism* is particularly compelling.

'The experience of being in the world is one of constant navigation, of locating oneself in relation to others, of orientation in space and in time, of charting a course, of placement and displacement, and of movements though an array of geographical and historical phenomena', writes Robert Tally Jr in his 'Literary Cartography: Space, Representation, and Narrative' (2008). There are questions one has for Frank Schulze-Engler, the type of questions one might extend to a cartographer: Where did he acquire the intellectual prescience that led to the creation of and support for transcultural and transnational 'navigational' site of and for literary enquiry and engagement in a world that had dedicated itself to firm lines within the boundaries of the long-indulged 'Posts', -colonialism, -modernism? Now that time and geopolitics have caught up with Frank's 'orientations', what does he anticipate will come next, literarily speaking?

'*Where the world has not been broken up into fragments/By narrow domestic walls…*'

…this book of essays.
…Frank's many worlds.
In gratitude.
Vale.

Yvonne A. Owuor
Nairobi, Kenya

References

Moorthy, S. and A. Jamal (eds) (2010), 'Introduction: New Conjunctures in Maritime Imaginaries', *Indian Ocean Studies: Cultural, Social, and Political Perspectives*, 1–31, New York: Routledge.

Tagore, R. (2003), *Gitanjali/Rabindranath Tagore*, South Australia: Axiom Publishing Stepney.

Tally, R. T. (2008), 'Literary Cartography: Space, Representation, and Narrative'. Paper presented on 1 May 2008 at the International Society for the Study of Narrative Conference, Austin, TX.

Index

Note: Figures are indicated by page number followed by "f". Endnotes are indicated by the page number followed by "n" and the endnote number e.g., 20 n.1 refers to endnote 1 on page 20.

Abu-Lughad, J. 46
Achebe, C. 15, 55, 90, 92
Adamson, J. 169
Africa 5
  culture 218–25
  languages 88
  musics of 51
  slave and indigenous populations 70
Africanism 44
African Literature 87, 88
Afro-European Literature 94
Afropean: Notes from Black Europe (Pitts) 3, 25, 209, 218–26
Against Decolonisation: Taking African Agency Seriously (Táíwò) 93
Against World Literature: On the Politics of Untranslatability (Apter) 43
ageing, process of 141–4
ageism 23, 24, 142, 143, 145, 151
Ahmed, L. 3, 216, 217
Aidoo, A. 146
Albert, G. 200
Aldridge, A. 46
American Comparative Literature 45
Anglophone knowledge systems 151
Anglophone travel writing 25, 215–17
animal subjects life 117
animal writing 117, 118
anticolonialism 5
anti-Hegelianism 74
Anzaldúa, G. 69
Aotearoa New Zealand 26, 233–5, 239
Appiah, K. 240
Apter, E. 43
Arab Anglophone 209, 216
Aristotle 67

The Atlantic Sound (Phillips) 225, 245
Atlas on the European Novel 1800–1900 (Moretti) 47
Auerbach, E. 16
Australia 5, 100, 188, 216, 235
autobiography 121–4, 127, 138
  turn of theory 123
Awake: A Dream from Standing Rock (Dewey) 159, 170

Back-to-Africa project 222
The Bafut Beagles (Durrell) 111
Baldwin, J. 33, 35
Balibar, É. 68
Barras, A. 175, 176
Beck, U. 240
Benjamin, W. 32, 61
Benveniste, É. 62
Berlin 277–8
Beyond 'Other Cultures': Transcultural Perspectives on Teaching the New Literatures in English (Doff and Schulze-Engler) 157, 164
Bhutan, refugee migration 234
The Black Jacobins (James) 163
Black Lives Matter 3, 209
Black Mountain poets 54
Black Power 222
Bloom, A. 45
Boehmer, E. 218
Boochani, B. 159, 216, 217
A Border Passage: From Cairo to America – A Woman's Journey (Ahmed) 3, 216
Brah, A. 239
Brazil 45, 47
Brechtian anti-poetry 54
Breinig, H. 66, 68, 74

British colonialism 266–8, *see also* colonialism
Butler, J. 125

Cahier d'un Retour au Pays Natal (Césaire) 57
Canada 5, 100, 188, 245
capitalism
 corporate 110
 international 10
 vs. Marxism 14
Caribbean 3, 5
 migration 128, 131
Carroll, J. 160
Carstens, P. 199, 200
Casanova, P. 9–10
Centre for Contemporary Cultural Studies 129
The Centre for Transcultural Studies of the University of Pennsylvania 151
Chaka (Mofolo) 54
Chakrabarty, D. 15
Chakraborti, R. 236, 245–8
Chatterjee, U. 144
Cheah, P. 11–14, 137
China Daily (newspaper) 1, 2
Chinweizu, I. 94
civilization, culture of 68
Civil War 236, 238, 243
Cixous, H. 68
A Clear Dawn: New Asian Voices from Aotearoa New Zealand (Morris and Wong) 234, 250
climate change 155, 156, 166, 167, 205
Coetzee, J. M. 49–50, 55
Cohen, L. 144
Cold War 41, 168
collaborative memoirs 122
colonial cosmopolitans 262–6
colonialism 9, 72, 88, 98, 110, 151
 British colonialism 266–8
 language of 91
colonial Jamaica 129, 130
colonial power 35
colonization 147
The Comedy of Survival: Literary Ecology and a Play Ethic (Meeker) 112
Concilio, C. 144
Conrad, J. 57, 144

Conscripts of Modernity: The Tragedy of Colonial Enlightenment (Scott) 135–8
container theory 189
Contrapunteo Cubano del Tabaco y el Azucar (Ortiz) 5, 69
Cooke, S. 169
Cooppan, V. 47
cosmopolitanism 118
COVID-19 pandemic 23, 141, 155
critical gerontology, *see* ageing
Cry, the Beloved Country (Paton) 55
Cuba 5, 6, 70, 71
Cuban Counterpoint: Tobacco and Sugar, *see Contrapunteo Cubano del Tabaco y el Azucar*
Cuban culture 70
Cuban music 71
Cuban transculturation 71
cultural identity 124, 133
culture 5–7, 21, 25, 41, 42, 44, 50, 74, 88, 90, 151, 157, 176, 179, 188, 205, 235
 anthropological theories of 69
 global mobility 210–14
 migration 210–14
 pluralism 94

Dagnino, A. 213, 214
Damrosch, D. 9, 13, 20, 41–3, 45–54, 56, 57
David, J. 10, 16, 17
The Da Vinci Code (Brown) 55, 56
Davis, G. V. 4
Decolonising the Mind: The Politics of Language in African Literature (Ngũgĩ wa Thiong'o) 16, 87, 88, 90, 93–6, 100, 101
Deleuze, G. 78, 79, 82, 176
Denecke, M. 168
Denney, P. 169
Der Einfall des Lebens. Theorie als geheime Autobiographie (Thomä, Kaufmann and Schmid) 123
Desai, A. 149
Dewey, M. 159
Dharwadker, V. 47
diasporic self 128–35
Di Chiro, G. 167

Dictionary of the Khazars: A Lexicon Novel in 100,000 Words (Pavić) 52
Dignity Foundation 148
Disgrace (Coetzee) 55
displacement, processes of 131–5
Diwali festivals 234
Doff, S. 163–5
Dowd, J. E. 145
The Dragonfly Sea (Owuor) 2, 3, 27, 33, 285
The Dream of the Red Chamber, see Hung-loumeng
droughts 146
D'Souza, D. 45
Dupuis, G. 213, 214
Durrell, G. 22, 109, 110, 116
  The Bafut Beagles 111
  My Family and Other Animals 110, 111, 113–15
  The Overloaded Ark 111
  sunken garden 112

ecocritical narratology, concept of 12
ecocriticism, *see* transcultural ecocriticism
economic policy 95
Edwards, W. J. 144
Eliot, T. S. 57
English
  in African education 91
  conceptualize literature in 18
  in Indian education 15
  literary studies 4
  role of 16, 17
  as a Foreign Language (EFL) 163
entanglements 13, 26, 27, 67, 131, 240
environmental justice 156, 166
environmental theory 168
The Epic of Gilgamesh (Sandars) 51, 56
Epstein, M. 213
Erpenbeck, J. 241
Eurocentrism 37
Europe
  culture 72
  metropolitan cities 218–25
The European Tribe (Phillips) 219, 225
excentric proximity 32–3

Familiar Stranger: A Life between Two Islands (Hall) 3, 23, 121, 122, 124, 125, 128, 130–5

Fanon, F. 33–7, 67, 76
feminism 44
Fiji Indian population 235
Finlayson, C. 198, 200, 204
Fondo, B. 152
Forster, E. M. 256
Fukuyama, F. 213

Garvey, M. 222
Germany 26, 44, 118, 160, 162, 259, 277, 284, 285
Ghosh, A. 144, 159, 175, 215, 217
  The Hungry Tide 159, 168, 175, 177
  The Iman and the Indian 215
  The Shadow Lines 144
Giddens, A. 136
Gilroy, P. 222
Glissant, E. 15, 126, 176
global capitalism 16
Globalectics: Theory and the Politics of Knowing (Ngũgĩ wa Thiong'o) 88, 95–102
globalization 12, 14, 75, 100, 150
global mobility 210–14
Global North 14, 143, 225, 236, 248
The Global Soul (Iyer) 215
Global South 10–12, 14, 19, 24, 143
Gnanalingam, B. 236
Gochberg, D. 44, 45
Goethe, J. W. von 7–9, 14, 41, 42, 44, 45
Goodall, J. 22, 109, 115
Gould, S. J. 117
Go, Went, Gone (Erpenbeck) 241
Grace, P. 147, 148
Grande, S. 171
Grant, C. 220
'great civilizations' approach 45
Gremels, A. 13, 15
Grey Areas: An Anthology of Indian Fiction (Raja) 144
Guattari, F. 78, 176
Guillén, C. 44

Haitian Revolution 136
Hannerz, U. 68
Haraway, D. 108, 109, 116
Hariharan, G. 148, 149
Harlem Renaissance 54, 222
'Harry Potter' novels 55

Heart of Darkness (Conrad) 57, 144
Heidegger, M. 12, 14
Helff, S. 237, 238, 246
Helgesson, S. 137
HelpAge India 148
Hepp, A. 211, 218
Hicks, H. 248
Hindu
   Brahmin widow 149
   Dharmasastras 145
   philosophical traditions 145
   social practices 145
Hofmeyr, I. 15, 53
Hogan, J. 127
Hogan, R. 127
Hung-loumeng (Ts'ao Hsueh-ch'in) 54
The Hungry Tide (Ghosh) 159, 168, 175, 177
Huntington, S. P. 213

ideological conflicts 95
Ihimaera, W. 3, 25 *see also The Whale Rider*
Iliad (Homer) 51, 56
illegal aliens 77
Imagining Ageing: Representations of Age and Ageing in Anglophone Literatures (Concilio) 144
The Iman and the Indian (Ghosh) 215
imperial/imperialism 3, 4, 9, 12, 15, 35, 44, 88, 94, 151
India 3, 5, 6, 12, 15, 23, 24, 26, 27
   administration of Travancore 266, 267
   Bombay 277–8
   British colonial administration in 259, 266
   caste system 241
   colonial administrative system in 268
   diaspora and cultural production 234
   economic power 236
   family and community 148
   immigrants 145, 233
   Jewish immigration 272, 273f
   Krishna temples 275–7
   local cultures 142
   Malabar dances 275–7
   middle-class homes 148
   migrants 233
   territory, concept of 247

   travel writing 215
Institute for World Literature 43
intercultural approach 101
In the Shadow of Man (Goodall) 115, 116
Iovino, S. 157
I, Rigoberta Menchu: An Indian Woman in Guatemala (Menchú) 52
Iyer, P. 215, 217

Jamaica
   childhood and youth in 128
   history of 121
   language and culture 136
   migration 130
James, C. L. R. 136
Jewish refugees 272, 273
Joshi, A. K. 142

Kakar, S. 145
Kaufmann, V. 123
Kenya 91, 94, 216
Kēpa, M. 145
Khair, T. 215
kinship, concept of 22, 23, 25, 109, 114, 199, 200–2
Kiwi Indian cultural production 234
Knowles, S. 215
König, D. G. 163
Könönen, M. 142
Krishnamurthy, M. 235
Kristeva, J. 62, 78
Kuhn, H. 168
Kumar, S. 145
Kunow, R. 144
Kymlicka, W. 94

Lahiri, J. 145
Lamming, G. 132, 133
Laplanche, J. 34
La Revolution du langage poetique (Kristeva) 77–8
The Last Burden (Chatterjee) 144
Leask, B. 160
Lehmkuhl, U. 173
Leyden, E. von 258, 263
Leyden, M. von 258f
   envelopes of letters by 261f
life writing 23, 138
The Location of Culture (Bhabha) 174

Long Walk to Freedom (Mandela) 55
Looking for Transwonderland (Saro-Wiwa) 215
The Lord of the Rings (film) 55
Lösch, K. 66, 68, 74
Lüsebrink, H. 173
The Lusiads, see Os Lusiadas

Mad Max: Fury Road (Miller) 159
Makerere Conference of African Writers of English Expression 87–8, 101
manageability, propensity of 43
Mandela, N. 55
Mandela: The Authorised Portrait (Mandela) 55
The Man Who Would Not See (Chakraborti) 236, 238, 239, 240, 244–50
Māori
 culture 189, 193
 identity 187
 language 194
 sociocultural ecosystem 147
Marechera, D. 8
Marggraf, A. 72
Matigari (Ngugi wa Thiong'o) 97
McClintock, A. 114
McFalls, L. 173
McLeod, J. 108, 174
Meeker, J. 112
memoir
 diasporic self 128–31
 relationality 121–6
 theory 121–6
methodological nationalism 159
MeToo Movement 209
migrants 75–76
 experience of 77
migration 18, 22, 210–14
 Bhutan 234
 Britain 130, 131
 Caribbean 128
 India 145
 Myanmar 234
 New Zealand 26
 Sri Lanka 234
 West Indian 132
Milhouse, V. H. 210
Miller, G. 159

Mills, C. W. 124
Miyoshi, M. 46
mobility justice 156, 166
modernism/modernity 13, 14, 57, 135
 institutional processes of 137
 postcolonialism's misconception of 88
 technical and economic globality of 73
Moeke-Maxwell, T. 147
Mofolo, T. 54
Moretti, F. 10, 12, 20, 47, 48, 53
Mo, T. 174
Moving the Centre: The Struggle for Cultural Freedoms (Ngũgĩ wa Thiong'o) 88, 90, 94, 96, 100, 101
MULOSIGE Project 43
multiculturalism 6, 69
Muslims 246
Mwangi, E. M. 15, 95
Myanmar, refugee migration 234
My Family and Other Animals (Durrell) 110, 111, 113–15
myth of 'wild Africa' 116

Nation (news website) 2
nationalism
 disavowal of 8
 ethnic and cultural 7–8
 xenophobic ethnonationalism 37
nation-centric obsession 101
Nayeri, D. 216, 217
Negritude 222
neo-Marxism 44
Neumann, B. 137
New Negro Movement 222
New Zealand 3, 5, 25, 26, 187
 asylum seekers 241
 illegal refugees 241
 Pākehā and Māori in 189
 sports 243
 Sri Lankan diaspora in 240
Ngũgĩ wa Thiong'o 7, 9, 13, 14, 21, 55, 87, 88
 Decolonising the Mind: The Politics of Language in African Literature 16, 87, 88, 90, 93–6, 100, 101
 globalectical approach 90
 Globalectics: Theory and the Politics of Knowing 88, 95–102
 "Gone with the Drought" 146

Matigari 97
Moving the Centre: The Struggle for Cultural Freedoms 88, 90, 94, 96, 100, 101
The Nicomachean Ethics (Aristotle) 67
9/11 2, 36
No Aging in India: Alzheimer's, The Bad Family, and Other Modern Things (Cohen) 144
#NODAPL movement 170, 171
No Friend But the Mountains (Boochani) 159, 216

Odyssey (Homer) 51
Old Age in African Literary and Cultural Contexts (Chiangong) 144
Olson, C. 54
Ondaatje, M. 146
One Day I Will Write about This Place (Wainaina) 216
ontological consciousness 34
Oppermann, S. 157
Origin of Species (Darwin) 114
Ortiz, F. 5, 6, 47, 69–72, 210
Os Lusíadas (Camões) 54
Other Routes: 1500 Years of African and Asian Travel Writing (Khair) 215
Out of Place (Said) 132
The Overloaded Ark (Durrell) 111

Pākehā 147, 187–9, 191–6, 198, 200–3, 205, 206, 242
Palestine 217
Pan-Africanism 222
Pavić, M. 52
Pennycook, A. 212, 213
Phillips, C. 6, 94, 114, 225
  The Atlantic Sound (Phillips) 225
  The European Tribe (Phillips) 219, 225
Philosophical Investigations (Wittgenstein) 80
The Pilgrim's Progress (Bunyan) 53, 55
Pitts, J. 3, 25, 218–26
The Pleasures of Exile (Lamming) 132
Plomer, W. 53
political systems 95
politics of identity 37
Pontalis, J.-B. 34
postcolonialism 44, 212

postcoloniality
  globalectical approach 102
  vs. transculturality 24, 156
postcolonial literature 4–7, 12, 13, 24
postcolonial studies 126, 142
postcolonial theory 100, 159
postcolonial thinking 37
postmodernism 74, 211, 212
poststructuralism 212
Pratt, L. M. 151, 160–1, 168, 172, 212
Progressive Art Group (PAG) 277
Proust, M. 78–81
psychoanalytic theory 34

racism 66, 75, 220, 268
Raja, I. 144
Rajan-Rankin, S. 144
Rakow, K. 163
Rama, Á. 73
Rastafari 222
refugee camps
  in America 216
  in Manik 243
  in Sri Lankan 244
refugees 75–6
Reichardt, D. 72
Return to My Native Land, see Cahier d'un Retour au Pays Natal
Rhodes Must Fall 3
Riemenschneider, D. 234
A Rift in Time: Travels with My Ottoman Uncle (Shehadeh) 217
The River Is Me (film) 199, 204
Rohit, R. 243
Romeo and Juliet (Shakespeare) 54
Rushdie, S. 235, 239

Safran, W. 239
Sahota, S. 241
Said, E. W. 16, 70, 132, 133
Sangakkara, K. 242
Santí, E. M. 70
Sarkowky, K. 23
Saro-Wiwa, N. 215, 216, 217
The Satanic Verses (Rushdie) 235
Saussure, F. D. 66, 74
Schmid, U. 123
School of Oriental and African Studies in London 43

Scott, D. 123, 135, 136
Scott, J. 128
Selasie, T. 87, 89
self-consciousness 124, 125
settler colonialism 73
The Shadow Lines (Ghosh) 144
Shames, G. W. 211
Shehadeh, R. 217
Sheller, M. 156, 167
Simmel, G. 134
Sing, Unburied, Sing (Ward) 159
Six Yards of Silk (Krishnamurthy) 235
Slovic, S. 169
Slow Man (Coetzee) 55
Smith, Z. 69
Soble, A. 107
Sodden Downstream (Gnanalingam) 236–9, 240–5, 250
Sour Sweet (Mo) 174
South Africa 53, 55
South American Trans-Modernities 73
South Asian migrants 234, 235
sovereignty
  colonial power of 35
  nationalist patrimony 33
  patriarchy 33
Sri Lanka
  Civil War in 236, 243
  refugee camp 244
  refugee migration 234
  Sita's memories of 242, 243
  Tamil refugee 236
Standing Rock Sioux Tribe protests 170
Stein, M. 68
Stockholm symposium 43, 45, 53
Strich, F. 8
Stürmer, M. 168
sugar 70–2

Táíwò, O. 93
Tamil refugee 236, 240
Tamil Tigers 241
Taylor, D. 213
Te Awa Tupua Act 25, 192, 197, 201–5
Telles, E. 130
Things Fall Apart (Achebe) 15–16, 55
'third space,' concept of 130
Third World 33–6

Third World liberation 5, 11, 33, 34–6
Thomä, D. 123
Tiemann, U. 193, 195, 196
tobacco 70–2
Tompkin, J. 13, 137
Toward the Decolonisation of African Literature: African Fiction and Poetry and Their Critics (Chinweizu) 94
transcultural approaches 158–67
transcultural communication 215–17
transcultural ecocriticism 158, 167–77
transcultural globalectics 95–101
transculturalism 108, 114
  modern processes of 157
transculturality 101, 108, 155
  academic use of 5
  development of 4
  on English literary studies 4
  inter-textual analysis of 32
  vs. postcoloniality 4–7, 156
  and redress 189–98
  World Literature 7–15
transcultural life writing 125–8
  conscripts of modernity 135–8
transcultural modernities 116
transcultural negotiations 32
Transcultural Odysseys: The Evolving Global Consciousness (Shames) 211
transculturation 72, 73
  concept of 69, 109
transgender 68
trans-indigenous groups 171
transversal 78
  provisionality of 79
travelling theory 69, 215
Travel Writing and the Transnational Author (Knowles) 215
Treaty of Waitangi 193–5
Truth and Reconciliation Commission in South Africa 195
Turbott Wolfe (Plomer) 53
Turner, V. 172

The Ungrateful Refugee: What Immigrants Never Tell You (Nayeri) 216
United States 41, 46, 47, 55, 63, 77, 101, 171, 174, 175, 188, 216, 272
urbanization 147
US Beat poetry 54

van Dyk, S. 143
Venuti, L. 46
A Visit of Charity (Welty) 143
Vogt-Williams, C. 249

Wainaina, B. 215–16, 217
Walkowitz, R. L. 16, 17, 19, 248
Wallerstein, I. 41, 47, 48
Ward, J. 159
The Waste Land (Eliot) 57
Watt, I. 53
Welsch, W. 6, 68, 156, 157, 164, 168, 176, 177, 213, 214, 237, 255
Welty, E. 143, 144
West Africa 3
West-Pavlov, R. 10
The Whale Rider (Ihimaera) 3, 25, 187, 189–91, 199–201, 203–6
Whanganui River 187, 188, 192–4, 198–201, 205, 206
Whanganui River Claims Settlement Act of 2017 25, 192, 193, 198, 201–4
What Is World Literature? (Damrosch) 41

White, H. 127
White Teeth (Smith) 69
Wilson, E. O. 112
Wittgenstein, L. 80
Wizard of the Crow (Mwangi) 95
Wordsworth, W. 15
worlding 23, 125
    from transculturality to literature 7–15
    of transcultural life writing 135–8
World Literature 7–15, 41
    conception of 99
    recognition of 88
World Literature and Thought (Gochberg) 20, 44, 51
World Republic of Letters (Casanova) 9
world systems theory 41, 42, 48
The Wretched of the Earth (Fanon) 33, 35

The Year of the Runaways (Sahota) 241

Zheng He 1
Zuckmayer, C. 157

www.ingramcontent.com/pod-product-compliance
Lightning Source LLC
Chambersburg PA
CBHW071804300426
44116CB00009B/1199